After the Great War

Also available from Bloomsbury

*Britain and Interwar Danubian Europe: Foreign Policy and
Security Challenges, 1919–1936*, by Dragan Bakic
*The League of Nations and the Refugees from Nazi Germany: James
G. McDonald and Hitler's Victims*, by Greg Burgess
The Great War: Myth and Memory, by Dan Todman

After the Great War

Economic Warfare and the Promise of Peace in Paris 1919

Phillip A. Dehne

BLOOMSBURY ACADEMIC
LONDON • NEW YORK • OXFORD • NEW DELHI • SYDNEY

BLOOMSBURY ACADEMIC
Bloomsbury Publishing Plc
50 Bedford Square, London, WC1B 3DP, UK
1385 Broadway, New York, NY 10018, USA

BLOOMSBURY, BLOOMSBURY ACADEMIC and the Diana logo are trademarks of
Bloomsbury Publishing Plc

First published in Great Britain 2019
Paperback edition published 2021

Copyright © Phillip A. Dehne, 2019

Phillip A. Dehne has asserted his right under the Copyright, Designs and Patents Act,
1988, to be identified as Author of this work.

For legal purposes the Acknowledgments on p. ix constitute an extension
of this copyright page.

Cover image © Photo of the Supreme Economic Council, probably taken at its offices at
26 Rue de Bassano, Paris, May or June 1919 (© Courtesy of the Department of Rare Books
and Special Collections, Princeton University Library, Bernard M. Baruch Papers, Box 701)

All rights reserved. No part of this publication may be reproduced or
transmitted in any form or by any means, electronic or mechanical,
including photocopying, recording, or any information storage or retrieval
system, without prior permission in writing from the publishers.

Bloomsbury Publishing Plc does not have any control over, or responsibility for, any
third-party websites referred to or in this book. All internet addresses given in this
book were correct at the time of going to press. The author and publisher regret any
inconvenience caused if addresses have changed or sites have ceased to exist, but can
accept no responsibility for any such changes.

A catalogue record for this book is available from the British Library.

A catalog record for this book is available from the Library of Congress.

ISBN: HB: 978-1-3500-8704-0
PB: 978-1-3502-0139-2
ePDF: 978-1-3500-8757-6
eBook: 978-1-3500-8758-3

Typeset by Newgen KnowledgeWorks Pvt. Ltd., Chennai, India

To find out more about our authors and books visit www.bloomsbury.com
and sign up for our newsletters.

For my parents

Contents

List of Illustrations		viii
Acknowledgments		ix
Introduction		1
1	Bringing Baggage to Paris	13
2	Getting Down to Business: January	39
3	Fashioning the Covenant: February 1–14	61
4	Feeding Germany: Mid-February through March	77
5	Impending Catastrophe: April	107
6	Ending the Economic War: May	133
7	The Mentality of Appeasement? June	157
8	After Paris: July to December	179
Conclusion		203
Notes		217
Bibliography		273
Index		289

Illustrations

Map

Paris during the 1919 Peace Conference   xi

Figures

1.1	Postcard of the Hotel Majestic, 19 Avenue Kléber	16
1.2	Postcard of the Hotel Astoria, 133 Avenue des Champs-Élysées	18
4.1	Photo of captured German artillery, Place de la Concorde, Paris, early 1919	78
4.2	Photo of captured German warplane, Place de la Concorde, Paris, early 1919	78
4.3	Autographed photo of economics and trade advisors from the US delegation posing with Marshal Foch	84
4.4	Busts sculpted by Jo Davidson in Paris	101
6.1	Photo of Cecil after a League executive meeting on May 5, 1919	136
6.2	Portrait photo of Cecil taken in Paris during the Peace Conference, given to Baruch and signed, "Your sincere friend, Robert Cecil"	139
6.3	Photo of the Supreme Economic Council, probably taken at its offices at 26 Rue de Bassano sometime in May or June 1919	143
7.1	Program for League of Nations Union Demonstration at Albert Hall, June 13, 1919	170
8.1	Caricatures of Hugh and Robert Cecil	193

Acknowledgments

Many people helped me to create this book over the past few years. This project straddles a few historical themes, which has allowed me to field ideas from it at a topically and geographically scattered array of conferences. I appreciate suggestions big and small from (in no particular order) Samuël Kruizinga at the Legacy of World War I Conference, Silvia Conca and Dominique Barjot at the World Economic History Congress, Peder Fuglevik and Mark Wilson at the Business History Conference, Tammy Proctor at the Resistance to War Conference, Clotilde Druelle-Korn and Alex Dowdall at Les Mises en guerre de l'état colloquium, and R. J. Q. Adams, Peter Catterall, Martin Farr, Stephen Hague, George Robb, and James Sack (among others) at various enjoyable Mid Atlantic, Western, and Southern Conferences on British Studies. I have also benefited from discussions on this topic with Tolya Levshin, Peter Marsh, Michael Miller, Rory Miller, and Susan Pedersen. Certainly I am forgetting a few. If I benefited from your advice but left you out, I apologize, and I hope you let me know about it the next time we meet.

I gratefully acknowledge the permission of the Master and Fellows of Churchill College, Cambridge, to quote from the papers of Maurice Hankey and Philip Noel-Baker. I would also like to express my gratitude for the permission of the Hatfield House Archives and Library to quote from letters between Lord Robert Cecil and his wife Lady Eleanor Cecil. It was fabulous having the Hatfield archivist, Robin Harcourt-Williams, show me around the house a few years ago. As Gaynor Johnson helpfully explained in her biography of Cecil published in 2013, since the death of Professor Ann Lambton in 2008, it is unclear who inherited the copyright of the Cecil papers. Despite my sleuthing through a variety of channels, this remains unchanged. Echoing Professor Johnson, if ever presented with the opportunity, I would be tremendously pleased to ask the copyright holder for permission to quote from Cecil's papers.

I appreciate the assistance of the staff at the Mudd Manuscript Library, the Marquand Art Library, and Firestone Library of Princeton University. I acknowledge with gratitude my use of the Bernard Baruch, Gilbert Close, Ray Stannard Baker, and Raymond Fosdick papers, all cared for by the archivists at Mudd. At Firestone one can access virtually any secondary source that exists, an extraordinary privilege that I have attempted to utilize to the fullest. These libraries at Princeton are wonderful places to read and to work.

In London, I thank the archivist at the Royal Albert Hall, Suzanne Keyte, for helping me to understand the logistics of early twentieth-century mass rallies in the hall. I also thank my friends Susannah and Ricky Fancelli for their wonderful hospitality during my research trips there over the past decade.

At St. Joseph's College, New York, I appreciate the support of the Office of the Provost, the Office of the Dean in Brooklyn, and my chairs Monica Brennan and James Blakeley. St. Joseph's provided various research and conference grants and a sabbatical, enabling me to undertake this research and writing over the past decade. I especially appreciate the assistance I received from librarians Lauren Kehoe and Mayumi Miyaoka, who purchased useful books, helped me to identify resources around New York City, and gathered an array of sources through interlibrary loan.

I thank Rhodri Mogford, Beatriz Lopez, and everyone at Bloomsbury for their unflagging support for this project. I tremendously appreciated the comments of the peer reviewers, and I hope that revisions I made to the manuscript satisfactorily address most of their suggestions.

My friends Seth Armus and Eric Reed read drafts of this book and gave me excellent suggestions about things to add, and (especially) things to cut out. Among her many qualities, my wife Tanuja has long been my closest reader. If there are still too many digressions or confusions, it is my fault entirely.

I thank Jack, Maceo, Usha, Lucca, and Alex for being great kids and for periodically allowing me time to work on this book. And I'll also thank our good dog Lola, because if I left her out, the others would never forgive me.

I dedicate this book to my parents: my mother Carol, and my father John, who have always been curious about everything.

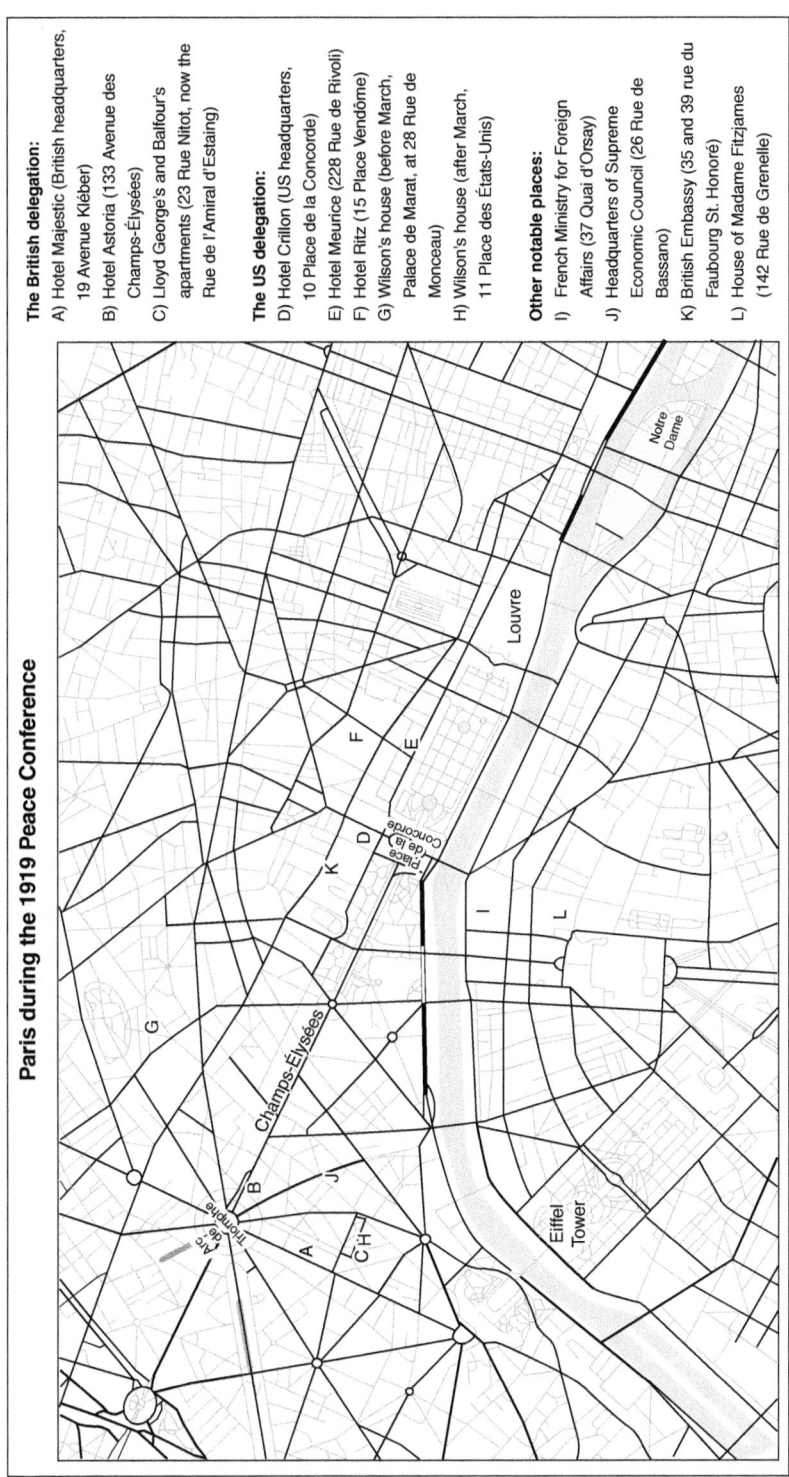

Introduction

During the first six months of 1919, after more than four years of an unprecedentedly miserable and destructive war, global statesmen traveled to Paris in the hope of creating a permanent peace. The leaders of the victorious Allies, including US president Woodrow Wilson, British prime minister David Lloyd George, and French premier Georges Clemenceau, lived in the same city for nearly six months along with the representatives of many other allied and neutral nations. They met in various forums both official and informal on a nearly daily basis. In this challenging and exciting environment, each hoped to enhance the security and prosperity of their own countries, even as they also aimed to create lasting peace in Europe.

The Paris Peace Conference is often judged as an ignominious failure for producing the Treaty of Versailles, which the Allies forced Germany to sign on June 28, 1919. As aptly summarized by the prominent diplomatic historian Zara Steiner, the Treaty of Versailles has consistently suffered "from a highly critical historical press."[1] To its most strident critics, this treaty's fundamental unfairness, particularly its territorial and monetary demands on Germany, fueled the rise of the Nazis and thus made the even worse Second World War inevitable. Wasting an unprecedented opportunity, Wilson and the other leaders in Paris failed to create "anything even coming close to a sustainable postwar order for Europe."[2] The continued dominance of caustic judgments of the Treaty of Versailles both in the popular imagination and among some academics has been remarkable and, to historians, quite frustrating.[3] Steiner is among those revisionists who argue that Versailles Treaty critics significantly overstate its harshness and also overvalue German reaction against the Treaty as the fundamental cause of the rise of the Nazis. Some have further downgraded the importance of the Treaty by noting that the Paris Peace Conference was merely the first of a series of international conferences and diplomatic agreements through the 1920s, all of which attempted to create European peace.[4] Regardless of one's stance about the fairness or flaws of the Treaty of Versailles, analyses of the Paris Conference have always focused on its connection to the ultimately failed peace with Germany.

The hegemony of this focus on "the origins of WWII" has obscured other important truths about global international relations during the interwar years, and about the Peace Conference in particular.[5] This book attempts to expose the Paris Peace Conference roots of some obscured aspects of interwar internationalism. It shows how those who labored in Paris in 1919 perceived vast problems in the European economies and politics and acted accordingly to try to solve them. While highlighting some of the Conference's successes in solving specific short-term problems, this book describes the creation of institutions that, even before the Treaty was signed, were already addressing existing needs and could plausibly cope with more significant international crises in the future. The Paris Peace Conference resulted in more than a flawed treaty.

As this book shows, a number of these successes fit, perhaps surprisingly, under the theme of "economic warfare." Economic war has occurred in a variety of forms across human history and can include any attempt to hurt a targeted economy with the aim of sapping their society's will to struggle on. During the Great War, the Allies waged a truly global economic war, one that significantly and directly impacted not just the people fighting on European battlefields but also the trade and politics of people around the world. The Allied naval "blockades" constituted the most visible part of their economic war against the Central Powers. In Britain before the war, some Admiralty planners considered warfare against Germany's economy as a strategy that could compel victory on its own.[6] Starting in late 1914, they set up a long-distance siege in the North Sea controlling naval traffic to and from Germany and confiscating cargos deemed "contraband." As the war progressed, the Allied economic war evolved with an ever-increasing focus on "interallied" cooperation and the continual development of new strategies to create economic imbalances that would force German capitulation. Allied blockade measures eventually included rationing agreements with business communities in neutral European states; efforts to funnel global shipping, food, capital, and other resources to Allied countries and away from Germany; and attempts to nurture businesses in neutral countries to replace German competitors deprived of business by the blockade.[7] Although some have argued that the ratcheting up of these economic measures proved only that might made right, the historian Isabel Hull suggests that the blockade consistently embodied British desires to reestablish the rule of law, "to bring about change multilaterally and to exercise coercion obliquely and gingerly."[8]

There is controversy about its impact on the ultimate outcome of the war, but this nuanced economic campaign became arguably "one of the greatest of the Allied weapons in World War I," undermining the German home front and thus Germany's war effort.[9]

As will be seen, many of the officials and politicians involved in these various but connected wartime Allied economic efforts then played central roles during the Paris Peace Conference. Their experiences with blockade and economic controls tremendously influenced their work in Paris. They theorized and negotiated ways to ensure peace by fashioning a future constructive role for economic warfare in the League of Nations, an unprecedented international organization crafted at the Peace Conference. At the same time, they refashioned Allied economic controls created during the war to help reverse the destruction that the Great War inflicted on Europe. These economic lessons of the Great War were then embedded in the League of Nations, with the hope that the threat of facing universal economic sanctions would lead countries to reconsider before launching a war.

These significant movements at Paris toward international economic cooperation for peace are best observed by focusing on Lord Robert Cecil. Known later in his life as Viscount Cecil of Chelwood, he remains one of the few leading men who never published an account of his long days in Paris. Many in Woodrow Wilson's coterie, including Colonel Edward House, Robert Lansing, and Herbert Hoover, produced blow-by-blow descriptions of the first six months of 1919. Similarly in Britain, David Lloyd George, John Maynard Keynes, Maurice Hankey, and Harold Nicolson, among others, published their own versions of the Conference experience, feeding a reading public in the 1920s and 1930s intrigued with the roots of their teetering world. In the case of Keynes, his book published quickly after the Peace Conference shaped the policy debates of the 1920s and 1930s, both encapsulating and fostering the mentality favoring appeasement of Germany, a frame of mind that dominated Britain's foreign policy between the wars.[10] Yet these publishing successes undoubtedly led to a general overstatement of the importance of each of these men at the Conference. None of these adequately describe the unique role of Lord Robert Cecil in crafting the peace.

Cecil himself never attempted to remedy the omission. It was *en vogue* during the Conference to keep a diary, as many of the delegates looked to posterity. But Cecil's Peace Conference diary, written at the end of most days and typed out by his secretary, was compiled for his wife and has never been published. Although Cecil eventually wrote two memoirs, both touched only minimally on this critical moment in world history.[11] Each instead focused on defending his actions during the interwar years. The 1920s and 1930s, when he became Britain's lead advocate for the League of Nations, have defined Cecil's life both for his defenders who praise his intention and effort and his critics who deride him as a crankish peacenik, not only the very embodiment of the "utopian illusion" of internationalism but also a power-hungry leader of pro-League organizations in Britain.[12] Lord Robert Cecil has often been portrayed as the leader of an influential set of passionate, foolish British idealists, "bigotedly certain" of the universal truth of their views, and certain that public opinion favoring peace would alone empower the League with a decisive "moral force."[13] His defenders see actions such as the Peace Ballot effort in 1934–5 as proof that Cecil's pro-League activism embodied "the will of the people."[14] On the other hand, according to the caustic judgment of Stephen Roskill, Cecil's support for international disarmament through the 1920s and 1930s forced Britain and its allies "to negotiate with the dictators from weakness."[15] Cecil's legacy as the paradigmatic interwar idealist was epitomized by the irony of him being awarded the 1937 Nobel Peace Prize.[16] It came at the moment when authority had obviously drained from the League of Nations, with Italy and Japan scorning the League's incomplete economic sanctions that aimed to force their retreat from conquests in Ethiopia and China. According to "realist" critiques, it should have been self-evident from the start that the League was a "covenant without swords." Yet instead, Cecil and his supporters defended the importance of the League against all who doubted it, in the process leaving Britain and the other European democracies woefully unprepared for the even worse war to come.

Cecil's story at the Peace Conference has long been synonymous with his assistance to Woodrow Wilson in creating the plan for the League, the so-called Covenant.[17] The apparent power of the United States enabled President Wilson to place the Covenant as a central pillar of the Versailles Treaty.[18] Some argue that Wilson's unwavering support of an unrealistic vision for a League was the core reason why the Paris Conference failed to craft a lasting peace. In July, the president brought back to the United States a "horrible mess" of a peace. His ensuing whistle-stop tour across the country aimed to rally popular support for the League but instead overstressed his fragile health and led to a debilitating stroke. Wilson refused to compromise with the "reservationists" who were particularly wary of the possibility that the League would control US foreign policy. As a result, the Senate twice failed to ratify the Treaty.[19] The resurgent isolationism of the United States and its abstention from the peace crippled the League at birth.

Yet saddling Wilson with the entire credit, or blame, for the fashioning of the League overlooks important contributions made by others. At the end of the Conference, Woodrow Wilson thanked Cecil in a personal letter: "the laboring oar fell to you and … it is chiefly due to you that the Covenant has come out of the confusion of debate in its original integrity."[20] According to one of the president's confidantes, Wilson claimed that Cecil "is the greatest man in Europe" and perhaps "the greatest man he has ever met."[21] David Hunter Miller, a pivotal US negotiator who helped draft the Covenant, attributed it "to the sagacity of Viscount Cecil."[22] A number of historians have agreed that Cecil's time in Paris was so focused on the League that he should be considered "the true architect of the Covenant."[23] In Gaynor Johnson's recent biography of Cecil, she sees his place in the Paris talks as a significant one, both for the League and for his own life. To Johnson, the Paris Conference culminated Cecil's wartime pivot from his pre-war political focus on domestic policy to his post-war specialization on the League and collective security.[24]

There is some debate over whether Cecil's efforts creating the League went along with, or against, the policies of the British government. George Egerton and Johnson are among those who suggest that Cecil's enthusiasm and ambition led him to create a League with powers beyond those envisioned by Lloyd George or others in the British government. Yet Peter Yearwood explains that during the war, Cecil was only one of many who came to consider that a League "guarantee of peace" could be central to British and European international relations, with the mandate for consultation before use of arms "making resort to war procedurally difficult" and thus "practically impossible."[25] According to Yearwood, in 1919 many others in Britain considered this a viable guarantee, although for most British politicians this expectation diminished as the 1920s wore on. All of this forces a recognition that many people beyond the United States hoped for much from the League. In 1919, tremendous political and intellectual forces in all the Allied countries pushed for a League.

The idea of a League that could guarantee peace might sound preposterous. Since the Second World War, it has been easy to dismiss the League of Nations as "foredoomed to failure," an idealistic fantasy created by men who were overwhelmed by their abhorrence of war.[26] Peace Conference historiography since the 1920s has suggested that virtually everyone knew that the League had no capacity to "ensure the possibility of peaceful change," beyond that easily mocked power, global "public opinion."[27] French calls during the Conference for a League army were definitively rebuffed by their Allies. In explaining this, the historian Robert Boyce argues that all the British and Americans really expected was that the League should be "a deliberative body" powerless to enforce peace.[28] In the end, according to Anthony D'Agostino, collective security under the League was really no more structured than under the Holy Alliance after 1815, with the powers continuing to act solely "according to their own national interests."[29] To the historian Hugh Cecil (Lord Robert's grandnephew), the League as conceived was "bound to be inadequate at preserving peace."[30] Critics of international governance have argued that the League's inability to defuse the threats to world peace from Germany, Italy, and Japan during the 1930s proves that when faced with the greatest crises, international organizations will always inevitably fail.[31] In the cases of the Italian invasion of Ethiopia and the Japanese occupation of Manchuria, the League proved incapable of forcing recalcitrant members to do the League's bidding and thus was fundamentally unable to enforce international law as embodied in the League Covenant. Historians have recently uncovered significant ways that the League of Nations actually did matter during the 1920s and 1930s, by creating and buttressing certain norms of behavior among and even beyond its member states, and by acting as a "force field" that usefully drew together various global internationalists and their institutions.[32] But even these histories highlight the real limits of League authority. In a fundamental sense, the League has long been judged as ultimately lacking real power, incapable of enforcing its own writ.

This book will show how at the end of the Peace Conference in 1919, the League appeared to some not just as idealistic but also as practical. It uncovers why Cecil and others considered the League well supplied with instruments of real power. Judgments of the League as powerless have largely ignored the potential capacity of a League to implement a global economic blockade against any country that broke the world's peace. The leading statesmen, including Wilson, Clemenceau, and Lloyd George, had not fully come to terms with economic forms of coercion, as during the war years, these men largely left the blockade to others. As a result, in histories of the Paris Conference that focus on these leaders, there is little appreciation of the general significance of economic warfare to the creators of the League. For example, while detailing the British and US rejection of the French proposal to create a League of Nations army, Margaret MacMillan suggests that the French alone desired to "give the League teeth."[33] This judgment exemplifies how historians and politicians have long fixated on the centrality of military capacity in judging the peacekeeping power (or lack of power) in the hands of the League and its successor, the United Nations.[34] But this ignores that in 1919 the League was perceived as having some potentially sharp teeth indeed. Many expected that the League could effectively dissuade aggressive states with the threat that they would face a devastating collective economic warfare. Those who judged the wartime Allied blockade to be a success believed in the overwhelming power envisioned in Article 16 of the League Covenant, under which an aggressive power would face:

> the severance of all trade or financial relations, the prohibition of all intercourse between their nationals and the nationals of the covenant-breaking State, and the prevention of all financial, commercial or personal intercourse between the nationals of the covenant-breaking State and the nationals of any other State, whether a Member of the League or not.[35]

League advocates recognized that the desires of the French for a League with military power had some rationale, and that in the end, the League might have to do more than blockade to break the will of a belligerent. But with planning by the League Secretariat and by individual states, "immediate and universal boycott and blockade" could be "a weapon of immense power" against any aggressive states, as it had been during the Great War.[36] Economic blockade might work not just as an adjunct to military conflict but also as a decisive coercive tool on its own.

In other words, the Peace Conference continued the wartime evolution of that ultimately modern form of coercion: the international economic sanction. Since 1919, in many cases these sanctions have been entirely economic, with no real military component, and no real expectation that they would lead to military action. Efforts to control a targeted country's trade and financial transactions by international actors such as the League of Nations, the United Nations, and the European Union have not always worked. Some have concluded that "effective sanctions mean military and naval sanctions and sooner rather than later."[37] Certainly, economic sanctions during the 1930s did not deter aggressive powers from their descent into the Second World War. But over the past century, they have become a standard way that belligerent states are dealt with by the international community. Arguably they often succeed in meeting the goals of the sanction-wielders, which are sometimes symbolic ones merely aiming to express moral disapproval but also include the goal of alleviating or avoiding military conflict.[38] Oona Hathaway and Scott Shapiro have recently shown how the idea of international economic sanctions as a tool to enforce peace spread among international lawyers in the 1920s.[39] By the end of that decade, many internationalists in the United States even believed that an avowedly neutral United States might be willing to utilize economic sanctions "to persuade countries to keep the peace."[40] This book pushes the advent of this idea a few years earlier, highlighting the centrality of the First World War and the Paris Peace Conference to the idea that economic statecraft might allow the international community to maintain peace between nations.

In a strange way, one can see economic warfare as one of the "peaceful legacies" of the Great War, with the fighting of the war leading to new possibilities for peace activism.[41] This book describes the development of a segment of peace activists animated by the belief that League-organized economic warfare might serve as the ultimate guarantee of peace.[42] The League was created not by woolly-eyed idealists, let alone by pacifists, but rather by the former Minister of Blockade Cecil and his comrades, who during the Great War had devised and operated the Allied economic offensive. For them, international economic cooperation was not just a "higher form of realism" than the isolationism that prevailed, and failed to maintain the peace, during the 1920s and early 1930s.[43] In a more specific sense, their League ideas were realist in being based not on abstract ideals but rather on specific experiences. These blockaders had learned during the war that power meant not just weaponry but also control of access to economic globalization and material prosperity. The organization of the League would make the development of sanctions regimes simpler than during the war. Rather than having to cobble together an ad hoc alliance, the League would supply a ready-made one.

Cecil has often been regarded as focused entirely on fashioning the Covenant at the Conference.[44] However, he also worked for months on a connected aspect of the Peace Conference that is often ignored or lamented as a failure: the attempt by the Allies to feed destitute central Europeans and revitalize the European economies. From early March through the signing of the Treaty at the end of June, Cecil chaired the Supreme Economic Council (SEC), a high-level interallied body tasked with relieving famine in central Europe and helping to restart European and global trade.

Doing this meant interfering with the Allied economic war. The continuation of the blockade against Germany after the armistice has been denounced by some historians as the most horrific cruelty perpetrated by the Allies during the entire war, as it corresponded with a few months of widespread starvation among German civilians. In the judgment of British historian Avner Offer, during the first six months of 1919, the "blockade became decisive" in forcing Germany to sign the unfair, dictated Treaty of Versailles.[45] To Paul Vincent, the continuation of the blockade after the armistice proved that vindictiveness and even cruelty drove the Allies who fashioned the peace in Paris.[46] On the other hand, Mary Elizabeth Cox has shown that the weights of German children recovered immediately following the war, proving that food aid was getting through.[47] Sally Marks simply dismisses the idea of an intentional "hunger blockade" as a myth.[48]

In examining the efforts of the SEC, this book shows that many delegates in Paris rejected vindictiveness and were truly concerned with what seemed a true emergency situation in central Europe. As will be seen, the SEC effort to relieve the plight of the people of defeated Germany largely succeeded and was really the opposite of a "hunger blockade." The SEC has usually been derided for its perceived failures or its powerlessness.[49] Even during the Conference, the SEC was criticized by the South African and British Empire delegate Jan Smuts, Cecil's comrade on the League Commission, as just "another talking shop which does nothing."[50] But an examination of the efforts of the SEC, its subcommittees, and its staff suggests that the interallied SEC had real successes in alleviating much German suffering during very chaotic emergency circumstances. Since 1919, any perceived successes in feeding starving Germans have been attributed entirely to the United States and in particular its food czar, Herbert Hoover, whose humanitarian efforts both contemporaries and historians have often judged as "nothing short of heroic."[51] This perception of US unilateral humanitarianism in 1919 needs significant correction. By highlighting the central place of the SEC in the alleviation of German hunger, this book shows how colleagues from a number of countries dealt with post-war European humanitarian crises in a truly multilateral, international fashion.

The SEC then took on another constructive role, attempting to make some of its activities and institutions permanent facets of the League of Nations as its earliest organization developed during the spring and summer of 1919. This book describes how the League was up and running, and dealing with practical problems, even as negotiations for the Treaty of Versailles proceeded. Working for the League became a possibility as early as May, as institutions and personnel slipped from national bureaucracies into international. The conjunction of League development and famine relief efforts sharpens our understanding of a blossoming network in Paris of men and women who subsequently led internationalist political efforts in their own countries and within the League during the 1920s and 1930s.[52] This book shows how these new internationalists embodied a broad "spectrum of internationalist thought and action."[53] They were not just motivated by pre-war internationalist trends and by their experiences of the war but also by their post-war peacemaking experiences in Paris. Not waiting for the 1920s, this book shows how "international society" developed during 1919, both in Paris and then, surprisingly, in London, where the League was headquartered through the rest of the year and into 1920.[54] The Conference atmosphere enveloped and changed many of its participants, creating new international links and new expectations for the global community. For a broad number of men in Paris, revulsion against the carnage of war opened significant "political space for the internationalist alternative," not just within the sphere of the Paris Conference but also within the domestic politics of individual allied countries.[55] Their hopes for peace and rebirth, mixed with but not diminished by anxiety and fear, set an influential tone for the interwar period.

There have been some truly great histories of the Paris talks. But since the publication of Keynes's blockbuster *The Economic Consequences of the Peace* in the last days of 1919, most have focused on the conduct of the "Big Four," the leaders of the victorious nations of Britain, France, Italy, and the United States. Margaret MacMillan's *Paris 1919* is a relatively recent epitome of this type of history of the Conference, focusing on the diplomatic meetings of Wilson, Lloyd George, Clemenceau, and Vittorio Orlando while placing these in the changing context of politics within and between the European and American states.[56] Certainly these few men made the final decisions about the shape of the Treaty, and uncovering details of their deal making and their clashes has created an extremely interesting body of history.

However, this book looks to expose the importance of less renowned individuals to the activities and results of the Conference. In Paris "the essential decisions were made by the very few," but this book shows that not all lasting decisions were made by the Big Four.[57] As will be seen, Cecil was both unique and a paradigm of a powerful yet second-tier delegate. Although he was not one of the five official British delegates, he was perceived by most within and beyond the British delegation to be among the five most powerful Britons there. He often succeeded in bringing his own specific concerns to the forefront of the Conference. Like some other second-tier delegates, at times he was the center of action, at others he was jockeying for the attention of the Big Four. Sometimes he found ways to accomplish things without the men above. As will be seen, Cecil was pushy and vocal, yet also diplomatic and consensus-building, a master at infighting and at the preparations necessary for successful committee work. A notable recent series of biographies uncovered how participation in the Paris Peace Conference transformed the careers of national leaders from countries around the world. However, few of those men made any significant impact on the Conference itself.[58] This book explains not only how the Conference changed Cecil but also how certain second-tier delegates could at times change the flow and outcome of this critical and unprecedented international event.

By following Cecil through the six months he spent in Paris and also during the Conference's immediate aftermath, this book provides a telling example of how the world of the Peace Conference proved complicated, confusing, and yet increasingly familiar to its participants. Not only is examining the day-to-day details of negotiations undoubtedly critical to understanding the resulting peace, but this book also suggests that the details of the negotiators' everyday lives also mattered.[59] According to Cecil's cousin, the witty and wise (and somewhat aged and disengaged) British Foreign Secretary Arthur Balfour, "at this Conference all important business is transacted in the intervals of other business."[60] Cecil attended a wide array of teas and dinner parties across Paris with global grandees and celebrities. He went sightseeing with family and friends. He looked at and posed for art. He played golf and tennis, and tried out his foreign language skills. In all of these forums, Cecil relaxed and socialized, but he also conducted business.

Cecil was invited to some of these events simply because he was a Cecil. After the Great War led to the wholesale destruction of the remaining power of European monarchies, the aristocratic Cecil was one of the few men at the Paris meetings who might have felt at home among the statesmen of the Congress of Vienna over a hundred years before. And yet at the same time Cecil, an expert on the economic and political globalization of his age, also exemplified the modern-style technocrats who constituted a significant segment of the Conference delegates. Cecil serves as a paradigm of both the old and the new diplomacy in Paris, of the pre-war aristocratic domination of politics and society, and also of the post-war Europe of experts, popular sovereignty, and mass politics. As will be seen, the tensions within Cecil's life were those of the peacemakers in Paris more generally, all looking to restart the prosperity and dominance of European ways, while fundamentally doubting that things could ever be the same again.

This book argues against judging the Paris Peace Conference of 1919 based on the failure of the Treaty of Versailles to create long-term peace in Europe. It exposes the place of economic warfare as a central facet of the Conference, while at the same time posing the Conference as a pivotal moment in the development of modern international economic institutions, including economic sanctions. Those in Paris who focused on issues of economic warfare did not expect (let alone crave) future harshness, poverty, and starvation but rather anticipated that they had found a way to encourage and enforce peaceful international interactions. Rather than viewing the Peace Conference in premonition of the horrors that came just two decades later, this book stresses the sense of possibility and hope felt by many in Paris 1919.[61]

1

Bringing Baggage to Paris

After more than four years of punishing combat, the fighting in Europe finally stopped with the armistice on November 11, 1918. During the Great War, Europeans bled more than during any previous war in the continent's long history, even as they drew in allies and expended resources from around the world. Facing the unprecedented carnage of industrialized warfare, soldiers and civilians from all countries had grown increasingly disgruntled and brutalized by the end of 1918. Many placed the blame for the slaughter on the fundamental failure of politics and existing leaders. Revolution threatened everywhere, and the Russian Tsar, German Kaiser, and Austro-Hungarian Emperor all fell.[1] By November 1918, much of the map of Europe had been erased through years of war between empires that no longer existed. With more than a million soldiers dying in the armies of each of the primary European combatants, and the fear of famine and starvation gripping many European peoples, unprecedented difficulties faced the leaders of western civilization. Over the course of the 1800s, the people and rulers of Britain, France, Germany, and the United States had grown accustomed to global dominance. Yet as their representatives met in Paris in early 1919 to craft a peace treaty, even the victors, some of them awash in wartime debts, faced the stark possibility of their own financial and moral bankruptcy.

And yet many who came to Paris perceived significant hope for the future. They wanted to revitalize and reconstruct political and economic institutions across the world. They looked to create new countries that embodied national identities, which were expected to satisfy national desires and move the world toward a permanent peace.[2] They felt entrusted with fulfilling the aims of many of the millions of returning soldiers of all nations, whose feelings were well summarized by the novelist Henri Barbusse's mud-soaked and exhausted French infantrymen after a night of horrific bombardment by German artillery: "There must be no more war after this one."[3]

Despite much public talk of war aims and more secret official planning for the post-war world throughout 1917 and 1918, the Paris Peace Conference opened with all of the leading nations seemingly unsure where to start. For the participants, there was a lengthy list of possible issues to cover, and an unprecedentedly broad, indeed global, array of constituencies that demanded servicing. President Woodrow Wilson's Fourteen Points, unveiled in his speech to the US Congress on January 8, 1918, included only some of his own hopes for the future shape of the relationship between the various nations of the world. However it remained uncertain throughout the Conference, both in the mind of the President and among the Allies he negotiated with in Paris, as to whether the United States Senate would go along with whatever they created. Without Senate ratification, no treaty could become law in the United States. Without the United States, could any peace actually work?

In January 1919, David Lloyd George, the British prime minister, was more securely in charge of his country's parliamentary government. His electoral mandate had just been secured by the overwhelming victory of his "coupon" candidates in the December 1918 election, although to maintain a majority for his coalition with the Conservatives in the House of Commons, he sliced what turned out to be a lethal stroke through the middle of his own Liberal Party. Lloyd George's belief in the critical importance of nurturing a peaceful Germany was tempered by the hopes of many British people (at home and across the British Empire) for a punitive, or at least a paying, peace with Germany. Both Lloyd George and Wilson came to Paris recognizing and yet straining against the need to placate the citizens of deeply wounded France, whose aging Premier, Georges Clémenceau, had earned his reputation over the previous four and a half decades as the "Tiger" of French politics. Together the three leaders faced critical and unprecedented international problems: how to support the newly forming "national" states in the tattered remnants of the empires of the Habsburgs, Romanovs, and Ottomans; how to treat the Marxist regime that had gained control of much of war-ravaged Russia; and most obviously, what to do about the defeated enemy, Germany. Finally, these three statesmen, and an unquantifiable but likely overwhelming bulk of the people in their countries, looked to address the most fundamental question posed by the very existence of such wide-ranging peace talks, namely, how to avoid a similar or even more devastating war in the future.

There were no lack of opinions and ideas about all of these issues, and each of the Allied nations and many others who wished to get a hearing sent their best and brightest, and most politically and socially connected, to the

Paris Conference. Delegations from places like Poland and Czechoslovakia, countries that had not existed before the war, were led by important men expected to create new governments in new countries.[4] Other countries sent small delegations appointed by their Foreign Ministries. For example, Brazil's Foreign Minister Domicio da Gama picked Epitácio Pessoa, an old Senator with extensive experience of living in France. In Britain, conference attendees were appointed by a variety of ministries and by the Prime Minister. The five official British delegates represented each of the main political factions in Britain, but they were complimented by a wide array of career and temporary bureaucrats, leading politicians, and anyone the Prime Minister or his staff believed capable of creating useful ideas and making wise decisions.

In this final capacity, Lloyd George asked Lord Robert Cecil on December 3 to head the League of Nations section of the British delegation.[5] Even though Cecil had resigned from Lloyd George's government less than a fortnight earlier, he could not turn down the chance to build a new world. The Prime Minister knew that Wilson wanted a League of Nations as part of the peace, and he recognized that no one understood the issue better than Cecil. Over the previous three years, Cecil had become the most important advocate in Britain for a League.

The Eclipse of the Old Diplomacy

Cecil arrived in Paris on January 6, a Monday, in better shape than most of the rest of the British delegation, although probably characteristically slouched and rumpled. The train was only an hour and a half late, which "means we were very lucky," Cecil wrote to his wife the next day.[6] The lack of fanfare for the arrival of men like Cecil to the Conference contrasted sharply with the incredible outpouring of affection from the cheering throngs and the jubilant press that followed Woodrow Wilson everywhere he went since his arrival in Europe on December 13, 1918.[7] But Cecil's arrival at Paris was noted by the British press as a sure signal that the Allied delegations were massing in Paris.[8] Cecil was expected to play a big role in the talks.

Crossing the Channel by steamer, followed by transferring to the Paris-bound trains, remained a chaotic process. Cecil had done it many times as a child traveling to his family's holiday villa, the "Châlet Cecil," along the coast near Dieppe every August and September.[9] He had also made the journey in less pleasant circumstances during the war on a number of occasions. Soon after the war began he went to France to look for his missing nephew, an officer in the British Expeditionary Force lost during the Battle of the Marne. At that time Cecil stayed for nearly five months, creating the "Wounded and Missing Enquiry Department" of the British Red Cross Society in the process.[10] Later, as an undersecretary at the Foreign Office (FO) and then as Minister of Blockade, Cecil journeyed to Paris for various interallied meetings related to the economic war against Germany. As these wartime meetings often took place in Paris, Cecil knew the city, at least slightly. Like most British men of his privileged background, he also understood its language, if somewhat clumsily.

Few in the British delegation were better prepared for both the surface opulence and the organizational chaos that awaited them in Paris. Cecil had grown up in rarified circumstances at Hatfield, the palace north of London that belonged to his family ever since it was built by his namesake Robert Cecil, the First Earl of Salisbury, in 1611. He recognized that the Hotel Majestic, where most of the British delegation was staying, was a fine establishment, even if it was buzzing and overcrowded with British officials trying to figure out what was going on (see Figure 1.1). Cecil brought with him a small entourage, including his secretary Frank Walters and the young FO hand Philip Baker, who had been a Quaker conscientious objector, ambulance corps founder, and champion British runner at 800 and 1,500 meters in the Olympics. Amid the chaos of personnel trying to figure out what was going on, a number of others detailed from the FO to the Conference quickly clustered around Lord Robert's rooms.

Figure 1.1 Postcard of the Hotel Majestic, 19 Avenue Kléber. Author's collection.

Cecil, after all, had been one of their chiefs since May 1915, when as a Conservative Member of Parliament he joined the wartime coalition government and entered the FO as its Parliamentary Undersecretary. After his arrival at the FO, Cecil quickly grasped control of Britain's economic war, eventually becoming the first Minister of Blockade in February 1916. On his first day at the Conference he ran into Eyre Crowe, who as the Assistant Undersecretary and the head of the Contraband Department during the war had been a critical subordinate to Cecil over the previous three years.[11] Looking on it years later, it might have seemed that all the advisors from the government, military, and industry, "all the best brains," were "specially summoned from England," efficiently shuttling in and out throughout the Conference.[12] But like virtually all of the best brains roaming the Majestic in early January, Crowe was unsure of what he was supposed to be doing. Many among the British delegation reveled in their superfluity during the January days before the Conference really kicked into gear, taking advantage of the opportunity to revel in the end of war, to dance and socialize through the drizzly Parisian winter evenings. But like Cecil, Crowe itched to get to work immediately. Cecil took advantage of the nebulousness of the organizational situation and put Crowe to work on writing a paper to present to the Americans rejecting mandatory arbitration of international disputes. "Of course it was quite admirable," Cecil explained to his wife.[13] Since at least November 1916, the two men had spent much time debating the possibilities of international treaties to uphold peace, and on the issue of mandatory arbitration, Cecil had long since come around to Crowe's view.

Cecil was only one of a number of leading British delegates scooping up assistants as they presented themselves in Paris, but his office came together and got to work faster than most.[14] According to James Headlam-Morley, one of the FO advisors who traveled to Paris with Crowe, at the middle of January most people were simply hanging out in the Majestic's lounge, but everyone was abuzz with the knowledge the League of Nations people were working in "a separate flat in the Majestic where Cecil, Percy, (Lionel) Curtis and Baker are evolving elaborate schemes."[15] Soon Cecil's office was the only one other than Balfour's in the first floor of the nearby Hotel Astoria that was fully furnished, many others remaining completely bare (see Figure 1.2).[16]

Crowe and Cecil were not the only ones distressed by the disarray within the British delegation in those early days of January.[17] Like many others, Cecil immediately blamed Lord Hardinge, the Permanent Undersecretary at the FO, for failing to plan sufficiently for the Conference. Hardinge "appears to have surpassed himself in incompetence." Staffers and clerks had no idea what to

Figure 1.2 Postcard of the Hotel Astoria, 133 Avenue des Champs-Élysées. Author's collection.

do, and critical papers were slow to arrive from London.[18] It took a number of days before he even procured enough wood for the fireplaces of the delegation's offices in the Astoria.[19]

Hardinge's difficulties in January provide a perfect example of the transformative nature of this Peace Conference, where precedents of the old ways of doing diplomacy were immediately overturned. Cecil had long thought little of Hardinge, the former Viceroy of India. During the war, the two men jousted over a variety of issues.[20] Cecil had been among those in the FO pushing for a wholesale reassessment of the ministry's duties, particularly aiming for it to take on permanent new duties pushing British trade. Hardinge followed a traditionalist vision of an unbridgeable division between diplomacy and commerce.[21] In the words of Cecil's biographer Gaynor Johnson, "the enmity between Cecil and Hardinge was intense, petty and sometimes personal."[22] Hardinge had resented the newcomer Cecil's control of the FO's most interesting and important wartime work, namely the organization of the economic blockade of Germany.[23]

At some point after the United States entered the war, Hardinge was tasked to plan for a possible peace conference. When proposing in October 1918 an administrative apparatus for the British delegation at a peace conference, Hardinge claimed to Lord Balfour that he had been working on these "elaborate preparations" for the previous eighteen months.[24] Some historians have agreed with Hardinge that under his guidance the FO prepared for the Peace Conference in a thorough and exemplary fashion.[25] But despite his color-coded and harmoniously balanced workflow mandalas, Hardinge's plans were actually quite nebulous and were fatally rooted in the past. He assumed that the conference proceedings would take place in French, and that as host the French government would, as in past international conferences, operate the conference secretariat that would coordinate all treaty drafting and précis-writing. This placed Hardinge laughably out of step with the prevailing focus on the monolingual Woodrow Wilson. The dominance of US power made it inevitable that much of the Conference would occur in English. Hardinge also believed that the final settlement with the enemy would be concluded before any League of Nations could be cobbled together, again failing to take into account the expressed wishes of President Wilson. His assumption that as hosts the French would run the secretariat met opposition from other British government officials, including men like the powerful Cabinet Secretary Maurice Hankey, who had learned during the war that the secretary's powers of setting agendas and writing official minutes could be instrumental in shaping policy outcomes. Hardinge was certainly off his peak form, still in grief over the wartime deaths of his eldest son and wife, and also limping from an accidental fall that broke his leg at the end of 1918.[26] Despite being a longtime FO grandee, Hardinge could be surprisingly undiplomatic. When they met for a moment after dinner on January 10, Cecil was shocked to learn that Hardinge had blithely told an American reporter that Britain had wanted to invite all the parties in Russia to attend the Peace Conference, but were rejected by the French.[27] Cecil believed that decisions on what to do regarding Russia's place at the table should be made before they could be announced, and that any announcement should be done in a way that would not unnecessarily irritate France or any of the possible governments that might arise in postrevolutionary Russia.

However unprepared Lord Hardinge was for the diplomacy of Paris, Cecil's criticism was perhaps too harsh. The French only proposed their own "preliminary" plan for the organization of peace discussions on January 10, which itself, in the words of the French diplomat Jules Cambon, was simply "une improvisation."[28] Woodrow Wilson had elevated his own lack of planning to a policy, assuming that others would appreciate the supposed open-mindedness that it would illustrate. As a result he refused to talk about his preferred agenda or any ideas for the League throughout his long cruise with his delegation aboard the USS *George Washington* from the United States to Europe in December. By all accounts the US delegation arrived at Paris feeling rudderless.[29]

Initial disorder within the British delegation was probably inevitable. Both the War Cabinet and Whitehall were surprised at the abruptness of the German collapse, having prepared for the war to last through the winter.[30] Overlapping boundaries of various officials and bureaucrats had been a significant difficulty throughout the war, as Cecil himself knew so well from his work as Minister of Blockade.[31] Unsurprisingly considering their expertise in such cross-departmental organization, it was Cecil's men who soon found themselves creating the new organizations that serviced the Peace Conference. For example, Henry Penson of the Ministry of Blockade's War Trade Intelligence Department organized the information clearing house that throughout the Conference parceled inquiries to the relevant delegates, and created lists announcing daily meetings and documents prepared by various sections and departments.[32] The administrative chaos did not end completely, however, until Maurice Hankey stepped in. Before the war Hankey organized and ran Britain's Committee of Imperial Defence, and during the war he served as the very active secretary of successive Cabinets, War Cabinets, and Supreme War Councils (SWCs). He knew how to control the flow of information between decision-makers and the ones who supplied them with knowledge and advice. On January 22, Hankey firmly took over the British delegation, and Hardinge was given the title "Organizing Ambassador" and shunted aside. The Paris Conference proved to be the low point of his career.[33]

Hardinge was just the first of many casualties in Paris from the old order of diplomacy. Although a century earlier Napoleon had aptly characterized the English as a nation of shopkeepers, for much of the world's population in the early twentieth century ruled over or otherwise affected by the expansive British Empire, Britain appeared more a nation of officials, with mandarinized hierarchies the norm within most ministries. Yet the Great War fundamentally changed this respect for authority and rank, and not just among any disillusioned Tommies fresh from the trenches. As they created a more total and global war, nebulous overlapping and ever-evolving duties had become absolutely standard for those working in various ministries, both old and new. This marked not just operations within the British government, but also official London's relationships with their Allied counterparts. Necessity meant that the constant change would likewise mark Britain's peace delegation after the war. And besides, the Prime Minister, David Lloyd George, liked it that way.

Lloyd George's Man?

As the new year began, Lloyd George was flying high as the man whose most fervent supporters believed won the war for Britain. The newly expanded electorate appeared to agree. The final vote count finished on December 28, and indicated that many of the Conservative Party and Liberal Party candidates given Lloyd George's "coupon" as supporters of his coalition government had been elected to the House of Commons. After the election, his followers controlled two-thirds of the seats, facing across the aisle a ragtag and disparate group of Labour Party MPs, Irish nationalists, and Liberal Party supporters of the former Prime Minister Herbert Asquith. Although the Conservatives could probably have ruled without a coalition led by Lloyd George, from their leader Andrew Bonar Law on down they had no stomach for going it alone. Instead Law and the other Tories sensed that they, and Britain, continued to need the leadership of the Welshman to guide the country through its recovery from the horrific war.

Lord Robert Cecil was one of those Conservatives bestowed with a Coalition coupon. He was also among many who called Lloyd George "the little man," if not to his face. For the notably lanky, 6 feet 2.5 inch Cecil, this referenced not just the Welshman's relatively short stature, but also his periodic pettiness and his reputation for slipperiness and even immorality.[34] In 1912, accusations arose that a group of leading members of Herbert Asquith's Liberal government, including the then Chancellor of the Exchequer Lloyd George, had benefited from inside information when investing in an American subsidiary of the Marconi company. Cecil helped to lead a parliamentary committee that examined the charges, and over the next months proved himself one of Lloyd George's most vociferous critics both inside and outside the House of Commons. The two also sparred that year over the proposed disestablishment and disendowment of the Welsh Church, with Cecil attacking the nonconformist Lloyd George's desire to destroy the Church of England in Wales. Lloyd George responded by playing the class card—only families like Cecil's benefited from the church establishment, their hands "dripping with the fat of sacrilege."[35] Before the war it would have seemed highly unlikely that the radical Welshman and the landed English conservative could possibly become allies.

Yet for Cecil, by 1919 "the little man" was almost a term of affection for Lloyd George, a man whose company Cecil found unfailingly entertaining and whose infectious dynamism and drive Cecil believed had been critical to the British victory in the war. On the second morning after Lloyd George arrived in Paris on January 12, Cecil had the first of a number of private breakfasts with the ever-energetic Prime Minister. The breakfast table was one of the Prime Minister's favorite places to conduct business, often in the presence of his teenage daughter Megan, who lived with him in Paris. True to form, Lloyd George skimmed through some draft resolutions that Cecil brought pertaining to the League of Nations, giving his full if somewhat superficial support. Then the two set into gossiping about the Conference in general. Lloyd George had just met with Wilson and Clemenceau together for the first time the previous day; Cecil agreed that the French and Americans seemed to have difficulties getting along. Lloyd George expressed his irritation with the insolence and solemnity of the US Secretary of State Robert Lansing; Cecil suggested that Lansing "was merely rather stupid." Both agreed that the Polish situation was an enigma, and that Britain had probably supported the National Party there too quickly. Both laughed at the excitement of George Curzon, left at least temporarily in charge back at the FO in London, with both the aged Foreign Minister Arthur Balfour and Cecil, his potential replacement, away in Paris. When Lloyd George told the departing Cecil "to come to see him at breakfast frequently, and tell him anything I heard," the Prime Minister appeared completely sincere and friendly to Cecil, who thereafter took him up on the offer on at least twelve other mornings before the end of June.[36]

In a typical description of the relationship between these two men, Peter Yearwood wrote that Cecil "regarded Lloyd George with distaste and patrician contempt."[37] But this breakfast, and many other meetings in early 1919, suggest this was at least not always the case. Over the years of war, throughout frequent meetings and conversation over a wide range of issues, the connection between Cecil and Lloyd George had become a friendly and even gossipy one. However much he criticized Lloyd George as a member of the opposition before the war, and however much he would later disparage Lloyd George's coalition government during the early 1920s, particularly for its foreign policy decisions and its lackluster support for the League of Nations, in January 1919 Cecil was to a surprising degree Lloyd George's man. The Conservative Cecil's career had prospered to an unprecedented degree under this Liberal Prime Minister. In an article just days after the armistice, the *Manchester Guardian* singled out Cecil as one of the great success stories of the Lloyd George government. During the war Cecil had built upon his reputation and was "now unquestionably one of the greater luminaries in the political firmament."[38] Cecil had been a real oddity in a coalition administration odd in every way. His Conservative and Unionist bona fides were untouchable, as the son of the venerable former Prime Minister

Lord Salisbury and as a devout and dogged supporter of the perquisites of the established church. Yet Cecil advocated causes, particularly a staunch free trade stance and an advocacy of women's rights, that had put him somewhat on the fringe of the Unionists even before the war. Lloyd George undoubtedly considered Cecil useful. Cecil was one of only a handful of ministers who retained their portfolios when Lloyd George overthrew Asquith as Prime Minister on December 6, 1916. As the leader of an administration devoted to mastering the technicalities of the new total global warfare of the twentieth century, Lloyd George respected Cecil's abilities and actions as Blockade Minister. Indeed, on November 28, even before his closest advisors had drawn up the plan that catapulted him to the premiership, Lloyd George ran past Cecil the idea of pushing aside Asquith to create a new government whose goal would be to intensify the war effort, and was pleased to find that Cecil was "very full of the same sort of thing."[39] Lord Beaverbrook claimed that when asked to serve in the Lloyd George coalition, Cecil "crawled in with infinite reluctance," but this seems untrue.[40] Getting Cecil on board was obviously of no small importance to Lloyd George when he decided to stage his parliamentary coup. Cecil had long since lost any faith in Herbert Asquith, but as late as December 2, he remained wary of Lloyd George, suggesting to Conservative leader Bonar Law that Lloyd George's terms for the coalition would mean "that George is practically dictator!"[41]

But by the start of the Peace Conference two years later, Cecil harbored no doubts that when it came to prosecuting a war to the end, Lloyd George had succeeded far better than Asquith ever could have.[42] Cecil felt uncertain about Lloyd George's post-war aims or the depth of his support for the League of Nations, but he admired the Little Man's energy and intelligence and his overall strengths as a wartime leader. Cecil attributed Lloyd George's success largely to his support for radical transformation in the British government, with the expectation that roles and duties must continue evolving as circumstance demanded. Throughout the first three years of the war, Asquith followed the accepted practices of the British form of Parliamentary government. He held regular meetings of the entire Cabinet, enabling all members to have their say. However during the war, when everyone was weighed under a deluge of work related to their own ministries and new responsibilities on interdepartmental committees, attendance at these meetings was often seen as a waste of time. Cecil, for one, saw Asquith's Cabinet meetings as opportunities to catch up on his private correspondence or even on his sleep.[43] Lloyd George's use of a smaller executive committee, the so-called War Cabinet, and even more privately his so-called "Garden Suburb" of advisors headquartered in makeshift offices in the back garden of 10 Downing Street, streamlined decision-making while also, rather surprisingly, making decisions more open to real debate among advisors representing a variety of viewpoints.[44] Despite not falling within the tiny core of Lloyd George's primary advisors, like Philip Kerr and Maurice Hankey, throughout the last two years of the war Cecil acted as a close second-tier advisor and was often invited to the War Cabinet meetings. As a member of the House of Commons known for his blunt willingness to speak his mind on any of a variety of subjects, Cecil prospered within this wartime ad hoc-ism, as new ministries popped into existence, and others were transformed.[45]

Even before Lloyd George took power, Cecil utilized his early perch in the FO to simultaneously create and command the new Ministry of Blockade, in the process becoming the predominant authority in the government on its relationship with the world's neutral countries. Under Lloyd George, Cecil in 1917 and 1918 joined and led a variety of interdepartmental committees where ministers, politicians, and unofficial advisors wrote reports and memos that helped to shape the Coalition government's policy toward its allies and toward various nonbelligerent nations' countries around the world. Lloyd George relied on him extensively especially in foreign affairs, allowing Cecil to "substantially" write his pivotal January 5, 1918 war aims speech to the Trades Union Congress, an address that preempted Wilson's Fourteen Points speech a few days later.[46] As a result of his accumulated expertise within Britain, Cecil immediately dominated the meetings of international authorities, such as the Interallied Maritime Transport Council and in early 1918 integrations of the Allied blockades. At times Cecil found the lack of simple hierarchy a stumbling block for effective decision-making; he complained to Lloyd George in October 1918 that as the relevant FO undersecretary on the situation in Turkey, he should have been invited to a recent War Cabinet discussion on the subject.[47] Yet Cecil also recognized the need for new administrative organization, and during the war advocated further expanding government activities on a permanent basis, calling, for example, for the creation of an "Economic Minister" who could become part of the War Cabinet to answer all economic questions that arose in that body's discussions.[48]

Tellingly, Cecil suggested that Austen Chamberlain, the son of the man whose calls for imperial preference ripped apart his father's Conservative Party in the first decade of the century, should be appointed to this post of Economic Minister. Cecil had advanced into the upper echelons of British governing circles by the end of 1918, and Lloyd George himself believed that Cecil "has greatly improved his position during the war," suggesting the existence of an ambition and hunger for power unsurprising for a man from his family.[49] The historian Peter Yearwood argues that in 1918, Cecil craved Lloyd George's job, and that the Prime Minister actually considered Cecil a political threat.[50] Yet even as he proved a star in a government filled with excited and ambitious men looking both to win a war and to prove themselves, Cecil showed often, in both words and actions, surprisingly little personal ambition. Cecil's resignation from Lloyd George's government just days after the armistice, the result of an argument with Lloyd George over Welsh Church diseendowment, is ordinarily seen as the ultimate example of Cecil's conservatism. Most of his contemporaries considered completely anachronistic and arcane his staunch support for what he considered "our National Church," even those with whom he led the failed cause against disestablishment between 1912 and 1914.[51] The bill to take away the endowments that had been given to the Church of Wales over the previous centuries had passed through Parliament only days before the war began. Although its enactment had been postponed for the duration of the war, everyone knew this was merely temporary. The decision of the Nonconformist Lloyd George to enact the law in the days after the armistice led Cecil to resign, in what would become the ultimate example of his notorious penchant for principles guiding his politics. "Really silly of him," his friend, the Liberal MP H. A. L. Fisher, wrote to his wife. "Bonar Law (the leader of Cecil's Conservative Party) thought that Bob Cecil has shown a strange lack of proportion and so do I."[52]

Yet Cecil's resignation from the government was probably not simply the act of a pious high churchman, but was also quite political. Peter Yearwood suggests that Cecil's resignation was a highly calculated political move that embodied his "deviousness" and "ambition," done under the misguided hope that it would trigger more resignations and the collapse of Lloyd George's coalition government.[53] But there is no indication that in November 1918 he expected anyone else to resign. He was not naïve about the marginality of the Welsh Church issue to British politics. Rather, his resignation was a characteristic act of self-immolation, another manifestation of his unresolved struggle between personal reticence and aggressive activism, between lack of ambition and belief in his ideas and capabilities.

Cecil had threatened to resign at least nine times, for a variety of reasons, between October 1916 and June 1918.[54] Lord Edward Grey, his old Oxford friend and boss at the FO, talked him down on a number of occasions during 1915 and 1916. In May 1918 he explained to his cousin, the former Prime Minister and present Foreign Secretary Arthur Balfour, why he would soon have to resign over the government's support for Home Rule in Ireland.[55] The next month he sent a stridently worded letter of resignation to Lloyd George over government policy toward Russia, where he favored forceful intervention in Siberia against the Bolshevik "enemy."[56] Lloyd George replied with a long letter pleading that the Cabinet agreed with him and that a Russian intervention would be pressed upon the other Allies in the Supreme Command at Versailles as soon as conditions on the western front relented. Didn't Cecil recognize the crisis atmosphere created by the German offensive, or see the logistical and diplomatic barriers to a unified policy toward Russia, with the Japanese and US mistrusting one another? After mulling it over for a fortnight, Cecil wrote again that his resignation was final. Only cajoling from cousin Arthur brought Cecil back into the fold two days later.[57] But when the war ended in November, Cecil no longer felt "in duty bound" to continue to serve as he had during the summer, and thus after some discussions over the course of the preceding two weeks with Lloyd George, Balfour, and Conservative Party leader Andrew Bonar Law, Cecil issued his resignation on November 21.[58] News of Cecil's split from the government made the front page of the *New York Times*, and full-length copies of his letter of resignation letter were printed in newspapers across Britain including the *Times*, the *Manchester Guardian*, the *Scotsman,* and the *Irish Times*.[59]

One might suggest that there was something Machiavellian about how Lloyd George treated Cecil, using his skills when wartime circumstance compelled Cecil to serve, all while knowing that he would resurrect the Welsh Church issue whenever he saw fit to rid himself of Cecil. Cecil may have hoped through the middle of November 1918 that Lloyd George might change his mind. Despite his periodic rhetoric on the topic, Lloyd George had never focused much attention on disestablishment, and his attention had only decreased over the decade before the war.[60] And in April 1915 Lloyd George gave a strident speech favoring a Postponement Bill for disestablishment, in opposition to the demands of his fellow Welsh Liberals. After Lloyd George, "shaking with excitement" until he "almost collapsed with exhaustion," left the Commons, Cecil congratulated him for "the most courageous speech that had ever been made in the House of Commons."[61] But in reality disestablishment had been only one of a number of issues that had been decided upon right before the start of the war, with implementation to be suspended until the conclusion of the war. Lloyd George could not plausibly put it off further; although the issue may have been marginal in Britain as a whole, disestablishment had been central to the Liberal Party's platform in Wales since the 1890s.[62] In November 1918, Cecil was virtually the only man in the United Kingdom who put a fuss up about the Welsh Church; his friends and even his avowedly loyal and influential brothers Hugh Cecil and Lord Salisbury deserted him on the issue. Resigning from the government seemed incredibly rash; one newspaper lamenting his loss as "a high-minded and universally respected Minister" suggested that his reasons for resigning were "irrelevant... futile, and show a lack of sense of proportion."[63] Cecil was known for taking principled stands, but Lloyd George does not seem to have taken the threat of Cecil resigning any more seriously than the previous times he threatened to leave the government. In December 1918, Lloyd George was shocked and completely unprepared for Cecil's resignation. It took him weeks to figure out how to replace Cecil at the FO despite constant prodding from Balfour.

In the eyes of Lloyd George, and indeed of everyone who pondered what Cecil was doing, Cecil had resigned at the moment when his power was still ascending rapidly. From the middle of 1918 Cecil had obtained the unique and unprecedented position of Assistant Secretary of State at the FO, and was considered by many as Balfour's near equal in power within the ministry and in governing circles. Cecil could have expected much if he remained in the folds of the governing coalition after the war. Everyone knew that the aging Balfour wanted to retire from office as soon as possible, likely at the conclusion of the Peace Conference, and according to Lloyd George himself, the Foreign Secretaryship-in-waiting position had been Cecil's for the taking after the election planned for December 14. In Lloyd George's words, Cecil's resignation "had made one man perfectly happy, and that was Lord George Curzon, who beamed all over at being in charge of the Foreign Office!"[64] And to what end? As Cecil noted to Lloyd George at the end of his resignation letter on November 21, "except on this one point (of Welsh disestablishment) I remain a convinced supporter of the Coalition."[65] Bizarrely enough, Cecil continued to "carry on" his work at the FO on a daily basis until the eve of the Peace Conference, acting as the de facto Foreign Secretary while Balfour was away at Cannes, and actively participating in Imperial War Cabinet (IWC) meetings through the last day of December. On January 3, he found himself in the truly weird situation of conveying to George Curzon an invitation from Lloyd George for the former Viceroy of India to become the Deputy Foreign Secretary while Balfour was at the upcoming Peace Conference in Paris.[66] In effect, Cecil had been tasked by his former boss with appointing his own replacement. Cecil himself recognized the situation as ridiculous. In the bemused words of General Sir Henry Wilson, who met with Cecil at the FO on January 2, "Cecil is not even a Minister, and has no power, and ought not to be in the Foreign Office at all, and says so."[67]

Both Cecil's sense of principled purpose, and his apparent lack of personal ambition, did not fit in as well with the grasping culture of early-twentieth-century British politics as it might have in earlier eras. In the eyes of the conservative writer Harold Begbie, it was Cecil's "sense of humour, an engaging sense of diffidence, a continual deviation towards a mild and gentle cynicism ... which keeps him from leadership."[68] Cecil believed his value was obvious but did not expect much from it, a man for whom *noblesse oblige* meant a focus on the *oblige*, eschewing self-promotion to focus instead on results. Many aspects of Lord Robert Cecil's background fed into his mentality going into the Versailles conference. Despite successive Reform Acts that expanded the electorate during the nineteenth and early twentieth centuries, he still lived in a society that generally believed that his nobility gave him capacities to rule. Deference to title and rank remained strong, and name and family mattered tremendously in ruling circles and in society as a whole.[69]

He had really never seemed that interested in taking up the family business of politics. A successful if not notable barrister, Cecil displayed no apparent political activism during the 1880s and 1890s, despite the fact that his father, the Third Marquess of Salisbury, then served as the Conservative Prime Minister. Sibling rivalry seemed to play little part in his thinking. Even when his younger brother Hugh entered Parliament in 1895 at the age of twenty-five, Lord Robert remained on the sidelines. His appeared a classic upper class family, one son, Edward, in the military and colonial administration, another, William, as the Bishop of Exeter, two others in politics. All had silly nicknames within their tight knit family—Linky, Jem, Bobbety. Bob might be judged as an outlier in this family, relatively unambitious in his chosen career (although law was considered a proper profession for a younger son of a peer).[70] Robert Cecil was no rebel, living a life divided between rural estates and London society, regularly attending services, and marrying well within his class in 1888 to Eleanor Lambton, the daughter of the Earl of Durham.

Lord Robert Cecil's candidacy in the general election in January 1906 came almost on a whim. When the East Marylebone seat became vacant due to a retirement, Cecil was asked to stand for election by the local Conservative party of which he had been honorary president for the previous few years.[71] His political career appeared completely unplanned, but not exactly fortuitous—his name mattered to the outside world, and upholding his family legacy mattered to himself. At age forty-one, he was the last of his generation to enter the House of Commons, ten years after his younger brother Hugh and thirty-one years after his eldest brother, James ("Jem"), who on the death of their father in 1903 ascended from the Commons to the Lords.

Cecil's father had been a powerful figure in British politics, perhaps less legendary than his Conservative predecessor and sometimes mentor Benjamin Disraeli or his Liberal rival William Gladstone, yet a renowned and commanding leader of both party and nation. Cecil would often claim that his own ideas regarding the immorality of tariff reform and the necessity of world peace came directly from his father. Being a Cecil meant a great deal to his politics before the war began. Upon entering the House of Commons, he supported his brother Hugh's unsuccessful efforts to push tariff reformers out of the Conservative Party, the issue that had roiled the party since Joseph Chamberlain raised the issue in 1903. The Cecils' identification with and decades-long domination of the party made Chamberlain's challenge to its Free Trade dogma a very personal struggle.[72] The Cecils lamented what they saw as a more crass politics, centered around business interests and the unjust "ethics" of profit.[73] Lord Robert in particular showed a principled unwillingness to back down, even if it risked splitting the Conservatives. He spoke often in Parliament, never afraid to tell his fellow MPs what he thought, and quickly gained a reputation among his peers and the press as a significant debater.

Hoping to retain his general support in the House of Commons despite his resignation from the government, the coalition endorsed his candidacy in the December 1918 election. However Cecil by no means considered himself beholden to the policies of Lloyd George's administration, and appeared eager to become a free agent, a rogue Conservative Member of Parliament willing to stand up for his principles. Supporting the creation of a League was only one of many points in Cecil's campaign manifesto, the bulk of which focused on domestic issues, particularly on his worries about the deteriorating relationship between the working and capitalist classes.[74] It came as a shock to Cecil when just a few days later, Lloyd George asked him to lead the British delegation to negotiate the creation of a League of Nations.[75]

Yet Cecil was the logical choice to head the League of Nations section. Lloyd George knew what he was getting when he appointed Cecil to this post. Cecil was a master of navigating the conflicting desires of various British government departments and allied and neutral governments during the war. Tellingly, the US legates in wartime Europe, particularly Woodrow Wilson's confidante Colonel House, hoped that Cecil would be named to head the British negotiation team on the League. Lloyd George could pitch the appointment as a "gesture" to President Wilson.[76] The Prime Minister was impressed by Cecil's experience with the subject of the League, even if he was somewhat wary of Cecil's most bold positions. Cecil had been working on a League scheme longer than anyone else in the government, and throughout 1918 advocated for a League vociferously along Whitehall and in Westminster. According to George Barnes, who became the British Labour delegate in Paris, at the time of the armistice, among all parties and the British public at large, Cecil stood as "the recognized leading exponent of the League."[77]

Cecil's Idea of a League of Nations

Despite his rift with Lloyd George over the Welsh church, by the time he arrived in Paris Cecil was certainly ready to move on. For him, the main thing that mattered in January 1919 was the possibility, and even the likelihood, that he could play a central role in creating an international agreement that would enable the world to avoid future wars. He had become convinced by mid-1916 that some sort of League of Peace would have to be established, and he acted throughout the rest of the war in the government as the primary vocal advocate for such a league. And at the start of 1919 it seemed like his ideas might become a reality, as they appeared to correlate with those of President Wilson, the most powerful man in the world.

During the 1920s and 1930s Cecil would prove a famous and lifelong proponent of the League of Nations, both within Britain and around the world. A number of explanations have developed for why he became so focused on the League. His grandnephew, the historian Hugh Cecil, suggests that family history, namely the influence of his father Lord Salisbury, fed Cecil's hopes that the great powers might band together for peace.[78] He also highlights the influence of Cecil's conversations with Sir Edward Grey, the Liberal Foreign Secretary who Cecil served under from the spring of 1915 until the fall of the Asquith government.[79] Grey believed that the war could have been avoided if some sort of conference diplomacy had been mandated among the great powers. Grey began to speak in favor of a League, and discussed such a League with Woodrow Wilson's close advisor Colonel Edward House, perhaps as early as late 1914.[80] Mark Mazower recently argued that Cecil's primary influence was Leonard Woolf, who along with his wife Virginia were friends of Cecil and his wife, and who in 1916 wrote an influential book, *International Government*.[81] Other historians believe that Cecil was drawn to the League due to his deep conservatism. According to Maurice Cowling, Cecil expected that the League of Nations would help to preserve Christian civilization in the face of the threats of destructive global warfare and international socialism.[82] Still another explanation for the humanitarianizing of Cecil was his short and depressing stint working on behalf of the British Red Cross in France during the last months of 1914.[83] His anti-militarist "pacificist" credentials were cemented in the late 1920s when he led (failed) efforts to push for universal disarmament.[84] With an extremely different explanation, the US Secretary of State Robert Lansing claimed that Cecil favored the League simply to continuation of the wartime alliance, a "Quintuple Alliance," "a powerful international oligarchy possessed of dictatorial powers" that would have "the power to compel obedience" over the weaker nations of the globe.[85]

Yet the acceptance of such emotion-driven rationales for his abhorrence of militarism, some cited later in life by Cecil himself, has led to a failure to really examine what he was actually doing when he formed his ideas about the League of Nations in 1915 and 1916. During these months, he developed the Cabinet-level post of Minister of Blockade. His entire attention was focused on creating and implementing Britain's unprecedented global economic war against Germany.

The Ministry of Blockade was supposedly not a posting of Cecil's choosing, one that spoke toward his sense of duty rather than to any of his own predilections.[86] Yet through 1915 and 1916, Lord Robert Cecil was far from passive as leader of the British blockade. He was an instigator and an innovator with tremendous power over Britain's economic war. In October 1916, Lord Grey (recently ennobled that July) pled with Cecil to stay on as Blockade minister with a panegyric to Cecil's efforts: "For me to have to work in this office with another Blockade Minister than you would be the last straw. And there is no one else who could run the Blockade without the risk of confusion!"[87] Only Cecil, to Grey's mind, could maintain the confidence of the permanent career officials in the FO, particularly Eyre Crowe, while also successfully navigating the divisions with other ministries, and also smoothing out the friction with neutral countries that came as part of the blockade. His diplomacy with European neutrals was constant, public, and assiduously thoughtful in maintaining Britain's right to interfere with their oceanic trade. Britain's blockade effectively rationed the imports of certain goods into European neutral states and controlled their access to British controlled merchant shipping, with Cecil arguing all the while that these measures were the necessary and legal offshoot of Britain's economic war against their German neighbor. He rammed new weapons of war like the Statutory List, a blacklist of Germans in the neutral Americas, past the Board of Trade and other resistant ministries. Cecil was a master of the diplomatic and bureaucratic wars that characterized Britain's completely novel economic war.[88] He was an active participant at many top-level meetings both under Asquith and Lloyd George, where his successes as blockader gave him a voice in much broader issues of imperial policy. The blockade, in short, made Cecil a conspicuous success during the war.

Like many in Britain by 1915, Cecil fully believed that maximizing the economic blockade was a necessary adjunct to any total war on the battlefields, grinding down the ability and willingness of the German war machine to fight on. Cecil recognized and worried that the economic conflict caused hardship for ordinary people.[89] By cutting off Germany's foreign trade, there would be less food and higher prices, which might even lead to hunger for many Germans. But hopefully this would lead the Germans to stop fighting. Defeating Germany was necessary, but perhaps it could be done while minimizing the immense bloodshed and destruction of combat.

Focusing on the blockade led Cecil to develop an understanding of the interconnectedness of the global economy of the early twentieth century and the ways it limited the autonomy of even a great power. Although he would not have put it in such terms, it was Cecil's understanding of the process of globalization that led him to believe that a League of Nations could actually succeed. He believed that the adherence of the Allies to the initially British economic war increased over the course of the war and that this made the economic war tremendously effective by the time of the armistice. Although he undoubtedly witnessed as Blockade Minister a number of ways that Britain's "enemies" got around his economic war, he (and most others in the British government) believed that the blockade by 1918 had successfully crippled the German war effort. He thought that it could have worked even better if it had been made universal, if all countries joined Britain's fight against the German economy.[90] His experiences as Blockade Minister led him to believe that such a universal economic war was possible to construct and operate, and that a real league of all the nations could use the economic weapon to target any future lawbreaking country.[91] Running the Blockade fundamentally shaped Cecil's vision for the League.

This comes through clearly in his earliest pronouncements on the creation of a League. Among British efforts to build the League of Nations, Cecil's memorandum of September 1916 to the Cabinet is often pointed to as a critical early salvo.[92] In one of his memoirs, Cecil claimed that this memo was the "earliest British germ of the Covenant."[93] These "Proposals for Maintenance of Future Peace" suggested avoiding future bloody wars by forcing countries to engage in a conference of "High Contracting Powers," before they started to shoot. During this cooling-off period, diplomacy would substitute for warfare. Cecil's goal was certainly to avoid incredibly destructive military combat. To his mind in 1916, civilized peoples must always resist militarism. The recognized problem was that there had never been a sanction that could force a military power to submit before the fight even began. Cecil offered a truly new mechanism of compelling countries to enter a conference, namely the "blockade as developed in this war." "No doubt for its full effect an overwhelming naval power is requisite," Cecil explained. "But much could be done even by overwhelming financial power, and with the two combined no modern State could ultimately resist its pressure." Even countries that would not join a shooting war, he speculated, might be persuaded to "join in organized economic action to preserve peace." In Cecil's plan, "each of the High Contracting Powers shall thereupon cut off all commercial and financial intercourse with the wrongdoing Power, and as far as possible shall prevent such Power from having any commercial or financial intercourse with any other Power, whether a party to this treaty or not."[94] In short, Cecil's memorandum was far less a structure for a League of Nations than a proposal for global economic war against any recalcitrant country. There is no vision for any bureaucracy or any permanent organization, merely a treaty obligation.

It is notable that Cecil himself later attributed his memo to his own thoughts. Cecil claimed no knowledge of Grey's earlier nebulous discussions with Colonel House about such international cooperation. "My first connection with the League idea was in September 1916 when I wrote an FO paper on the subject," Cecil later explained simply to Grey's biographer, G. M. Trevelyan.[95] Cecil was certain that his ideas were his own, that they developed from his experiences. The blockade had taught him that "in the modern world, military force is not every thing," he wrote in an August 31, 1917 memo on "the Economic Policy of the Allies." The power of the blockade left him "full of hope," as "it may be ... that a League of Nations, properly furnished with machinery to enforce the financial, commercial, and economic isolation of a nation determined to force its will upon the world by mere violence, would be a real safeguard for the peace of the world."[96] Fighting economic war led Cecil to create the idea for a League specifically tailored to fight economic wars for peace.

Cecil maintained this emphasis on universal blockade throughout his wartime advocacy within the government for a League of Nations. Among leading Leaguers, he was the only one in high office, with tremendous access to the highest corridors of power both under Asquith and under Lloyd George. His efforts led in early 1918 to the appointment of the Phillimore Committee to investigate ideas for a League. The resulting report, one eventually shared with Colonel House and Woodrow Wilson, called for a League with the capacity to wage economic wars.[97]

His unique power was magnified by his strangeness as a Conservative politician who favored the League. In a mostly Conservative Cabinet, Cecil worried that the skepticism of those like Leo Amery and the ever-present Cabinet Secretary Maurice Hankey might prevail over the hopefulness of internationalists like himself and the South African Premier Jan Smuts. Cecil at times suggested that he felt like a radical, lamenting humorously to his wife that "without the hope that this war was to establish a better international system I should be a pacifist."[98] But his professed desire to intensify all aspects of the British war effort in 1916 makes clear that Cecil was no supporter of anti-war stances. He accepted the need to comprehensively defeat German armies, and thereafter always recognized the possible need for military force if economic sanctions did not bring belligerent parties to the negotiating table. On the advice of Eyre Crowe, he excised from his September 1916 League memorandum a call for general arms limitations. When Woodrow Wilson's advisor Colonel House told Cecil during a private meeting on January 8 that he wanted a League to "lay it down that in no circumstances should war take place in the future," Cecil rejected this, knowing it would be a non-starter with either Lloyd George or Clemenceau. Cecil was pleased when Greek Prime Minister Eleftherios Venizelos, a respected and influential Leaguer, supported British proposals that rejected compulsory disarmament, "moderate plans which he ascribed to me, not unjustly."[99] Cecil was sure his scheme as it stood, with its focus on economic sanctions, could truly work to persuade most countries to toe the line of international law. In 1919, he saw disarmament as not just unrealistic, but unimportant compared to the establishment of his universal blockade system. Only later, in the mid-1920s, did disarmament become one of Cecil's signature causes, and indeed the one for which he was most ridiculed during the international rise of fascisms in the 1930s.

As Blockade Minister, Cecil found that he was in effect cobbling together a universal blockade against Germany throughout the war. Integrating Britain's blockade with the French was tough enough, and the entry of the United States into the war in April 1917 only enhanced the difficulties of interallied coordination. Through painstaking diplomacy and compromises, the economic noose had tightened around Germany. Cecil proved an adept negotiator, persuading the United States to create an Allied financial blockade in June 1918.[100] By supporting the creation of new techniques, like the Statutory Lists of German-tainted companies in the Americas, Cecil continually ratcheted up the economic war until the signing of the armistice. In late 1918 he was far from alone in believing that economic collaboration between the Allies had succeeded in bringing Germany to its knees.

Cecil's unique vision of a League of economic warfare was exemplified by his speech at the Birmingham Town Hall of November 12, 1918. It was pure happenstance that this long-scheduled inaugural address as the new Chancellor of the University of Birmingham occurred on the day after the armistice was suddenly concluded. It would seem an ideal time to discuss the structure of the post-bellum peace, yet the impact of Cecil's speech was undoubtedly overshadowed by the euphoria of the end of the war. It received some interesting commentary in the Edinburgh daily the *Scotsman*, but otherwise received little press.[101] Cecil considered it the crucial outline of his League of Nations position, and he believed it would eventually become the government's official proposal. He had circulated a lengthy synopsis to the War Cabinet a month before he gave it. He spent a long time crafting this speech, especially for a man who once told his wife that his best speeches were given extemporaneously, without no notes beyond a brief outline of his main points.

Cecil's Birmingham address stands as the most clearly reasoned description of his beliefs about the League. A League must ward off future wars by mandating an international conference before any power resorted to arms. This League would be supported by all who recognize the horrors of war, and would be based upon the economic interdependence and "inter-allied economic organizations" that had developed during the war. In Cecil's view, internationalism was increasingly in vogue, seen in the universal outpouring of revulsion to warfare, in the growth of international labor organizations and the growth of Bolshevism, and also (most tellingly) in the growing recognition "that all civilized states are parts of one economic whole." All League members must be ready to "secure submission of the dispute to such a conference" by using economic and military force, but in reality "economic coercion is in this connection especially important." Disarmament might be ideal, but it could only come about after such international cooperation had first proven successful.[102] It is unlikely that national governments would create an international army to enforce the peace, but in any case, Cecil was sure that such an army was unnecessary. "I attach very great weight to the use in this connection of the economic weapon," Cecil explained to the Birmingham audience. "The events of this war have shown that an international boycott would be extraordinarily effective." Even though Britain's economic war against Germany had been hampered by its "novelty" and the early unhappiness of neutrals, "we have still been able to do a good deal by our blockade and kindred operations. If all restrictions on the use of this weapon by the League were swept away and it were put in force ... by the whole or almost the whole of the countries of the world against one offender, it would mean certain and irretrievable ruin for that country. It may be hoped that such a menace would cool the ardour even of a German professor." Cecil assured the audience that such a universal blockade could work—"as far as technical questions go there are good grounds for asserting that they present no serious and certainly no insuperable difficulty"—as long as a League was created to organize it.[103]

From his experiences as the head of the British blockade, Cecil recognized that a League whose members controlled the sinews of global trade, such as shipping, banking, and communications, could create a blockade of a belligerent power that would be adhered to not only by League members, but also by countries outside the League. As he explained in a draft League of Nations Convention that he circulated in December 1918, if the League prohibited trade and financial relations between its members and any "covenant-breaking State," they should be able to likewise prevent trade between non-League states and the covenant-breaking belligerent.[104] For Cecil, there was no reason to explain how this could be done—he had done so during the war. In setting up his rationing agreements with European neutral states that restricted their trade to Germany, and by extending the British economic war overseas through increased controls on British shipping, coal supplies, financial institutions, and telegraph services, he forced companies in neutral countries to stop their interactions with blacklisted German companies for fear of losing their access to British facilities critical for foreign trade. The British, largely on their own although increasingly with the assistance of their Allies, had been experimenting throughout the war with controls on both belligerent and "neutral" countries. With the assistance of everyone in a post-war League of Nations, comprised at the least of all the wartime Allies and Associated powers (i.e., Britain, France, the United States, Italy, and Japan), economic war could be the decisive and bloodless weapon to maintain peace and international law after the war. Such a blockade could be a "new panacea," a "peace weapon," and will be seen as "the sheathed sword of the successful duelist: no weaker swordsman will desire to see it drawn from its scabbard."[105]

Cecil was far ahead of most of his British contemporaries in his understanding of the global marketplace and its implications for future warfare. By 1918, both Conservative and Liberal politicians of all stripes were more impressed by the need to maximize national power than the need to shape future internationalism.

In planning for the post-war, British businessmen and politicians either favored a complete lifting of all economic controls and a reassertion of laissez-faire, or the maintenance of economic warfare and blockades indefinitely against Germany, a country that many expected to have continued animosity against for the indefinite future. The armed services were quite impressed by the power of the blockade. In a War Office memo on the subject, Brigadier General Cockerill in late 1917 doubted that blockade could be used by a League of Nations to prevent war, as there would be too many financial incentives for neutrals to continue trade with a blockaded power. Yet at the same time, rather inconsistently, Cockerill recognized that a League with such power to impose an economic war could in effect force neutrals to break their neutrality.[106] This was Cecil's point entirely. Neutral countries would have to respect a blockade for fear of being blockaded themselves if they did not comply. A League holding the capacity to threaten economic warfare could enforce the peace.

*

As a result of his wartime work, both on the blockade and elsewhere, his connections with politicians and people in Britain from all ends of the spectrum, from Lloyd George to Asquithian Liberals to his family's old Conservative party, his powerful leadership in advocating within the government for a League of Nations between 1916 and 1918, and at the same time his outsider status as having resigned from the government when the top levels seemed so clearly within his grasp, Lord Robert Cecil came to Paris in January 1919 seen by both his fellow British delegates and those from other countries as a highly respected yet enigmatic statesman. In the largely unplanned circumstances of Paris in January 1919, a path remained open for Cecil to carve out his influence in the offices of the Parisian hotels and ministry buildings, where the Allied leaders hoped to shape a more peaceful system of global international relations.

2

Getting Down to Business: January

As the Peace Conference sputtered into action, the legacy of the Allied economic war was immediately apparent. Within just hours of his arrival at the Hotel Majestic, leftover blockade questions demanded Cecil's attention. The American food controller Herbert Hoover cornered Cecil the morning after he arrived, dreading the possibility of mass famine in Central Europe. Hoover had become globally famous and revered for his work to feed Belgians who lived under German occupation during the war. Hoover begged Cecil to help create an Inter-Allied Council on Food Supplies. Cecil agreed that aside from the obvious humanitarian reasons, relieving the onset of famine in former enemy lands was critical to restoring political stability across a central Europe threatened by Bolshevism. As the former chairman of the Allied Maritime Transport Council (AMTC), Cecil understood and sympathized with the difficulties of arranging shipping space that so vexed Hoover. Cecil reminded Hoover that the AMTC had worked admirably in parceling out shipping and directing food supplies among the Allies during the last year of the war. He did not have to point out the irony; Hoover himself had persuaded President Wilson on the signing of the armistice to withdraw the United States from joint allied control of shipping and food purchasing.[1] Hoover, a doctrinaire free trader, had persuaded Wilson that the British, French and Italian governments wanted to maintain interallied controls so they could force lower prices upon US farmers while cruelly squeezing the German people as punishment for the war.[2] And yet now here was Hoover frantically attempting to reestablish an interallied economic council. Cecil could not help but doubt Hoover's intentions. In the wake of the British and French decision on December 31 to cancel food orders coming from the United States, Hoover's alarmism appeared more concerned with maintaining US pork exports than any humanitarian desire to feed the starving Germans.[3] Indeed, Hoover fretted to President Wilson the next day that the British goal was "to break the American (pork) market."[4] The Iowan was undoubtedly learning well how to stand up for American farmers, showing a political astuteness that would contribute to his election as president in 1928.

Cecil said he could not join Hoover's new committee, but would cable the FO to urge the quick appointment of a British representative. His refusal to get more engaged may have had significant consequences; Arthur Salter judged the ineffectiveness of Hoover's Council of Supply and Relief over the next month to be at least in part due to the lack of the "personal authority of Lord Robert Cecil."[5]

But from the moment he arrived in Paris, Cecil was determined to focus his immediate attentions on the League of Nations. Since mid-November he had been laying the public relations groundwork in Britain for the primacy of the League over all other goals of the Conference.[6] In small meetings in the Hotels Majestic and Crillon, and around various Parisian dinner tables, the League was crafted before the League of Nations Commission began meeting on February 3. Cecil campaigned tirelessly to develop generalized support for a League, while also working with a handful of British and American insiders to draft a Covenant that embodied the specific principles he found most critical. As will be seen, the extent of Cecil's successes in setting the agenda and writing the document fundamentally belies the notion that the League was Woodrow Wilson's creation. Wilson may have named it, but the Covenant was also Cecil's.

Between the Tiger and the President

Although the Peace Conference delegates met periodically in large plenary sessions where the official representatives of all the Allied and Associated Powers attended, historians have followed contemporaries in recognizing that the real decisions took place during the intimate sessions of the representatives of the greatest powers—France, Britain, the United States, with Italy and Japan as periodically important participants. Perhaps it was inevitable that in three-pronged negotiation, many decisions would be made two against one. The connections that immediately developed in Paris that January between the League of Nations teams of the US and British delegations have often been portrayed as an attempt by the Anglo-American world to stitch up a League without any input from France, a continuation of tenuous but real contacts built up during the war by a British government eager to create a "pax Anglo-Americana."[7]

However, Cecil's January belies any notion that British and American negotiators ignored, let alone spurned, the French. Cecil himself met with leading

Frenchmen from his first day at the Conference, when he ran into Clemenceau outside of Colonel House's office in the Hotel Crillon. Clemenceau greeted Cecil "with much affection, and asked me whether I had become an American. I said 'Certainly, I was ready to be a Frenchman but you would not have me!' This he indignantly denied."[8] Such joking suggests the high spirits and hopes of both men at the start of the Conference. The next day, Cecil was surprised, overwhelmed, and even giddy when Ferdinand Foch, Marshal of France and the victorious Supreme Commander of the Allied Armies, dropped into his office in the Majestic along with his advisor, General Maxime Weygand. Foch was lobbying on behalf of his desire for France to gain permanent control of the Rhineland, a proposal which Cecil noted would entail "very great difficulties."[9] In response, Foch expressed his own doubts about the practicality of a League. However, Cecil believed that Weygand was supportive and hoped that the junior officer might persuade Foch of the importance of international cooperation.[10] A few days later, Cecil had a gossipy lunch at Larue's, one of the most elegant restaurants in Paris, with Etienne Clémentel, the French Minister in charge of a variety of commerce-related departments since 1915. They had worked together on wartime shipping issues.[11] On January 9, Cecil met with the man he and everyone else expected to be the French point man on the League, Léon Bourgeois. Bourgeois was known for his championing of the Permanent Court of Arbitration in The Hague during the years before the war, and during the war had headed a commission that in July 1918 created a French plan for an armed League. Newspapers in early January ran stories describing the expectations that the League issue would be sewn up even before the plenipotentiaries gathered in Paris, not simply through Anglo-American alliance on this issue, but also because of Bourgeois's assumedly pro-League stance. Cecil himself went out of his way in an interview with *Le Matin* on January 11 to praise the thoroughness and thoughtfulness of the French plans for the League compiled during 1918, an interview that was quoted extensively in newspapers around the world.[12] But on meeting Bourgeois, Cecil was disappointed by what he saw, an "old gentleman (who) is rather feeble physically, and cannot see anything much, so that he has to ring for what he calls his 'collaboratrice' whenever he wants a paper."[13] Throughout early January, the chief British delegate on the League assiduously attended to his French counterparts. Unfortunately, Cecil worried, the French had not settled their own ideas about the League, and were slow to officially appoint their own staff to deal with the issue.

At the first Plenary Session of the Peace Conference, on January 25, the League became the official initial goal of the Conference. Balfour and Cecil, sitting next to each other, passed notes like aged schoolboys. During the long-winded speech by Bourgeois, whose "tears streamed" down his face as he recalled his pre-war attempts to safeguard peace at the Hague and at other conferences, Cecil jotted a note to his cousin that "if this old humguffin" kept on at such length in the League Commission meetings that were coming up, he would "destroy the whole show."[14] Balfour passed the note on to Lloyd George, who replied "that is no doubt why Clemenceau put him on!"[15]

To Cecil, the League seemed bound up by French prejudices. In particular the sense of anti-Americanism among the French delegation, and among the various French people he dined with, was shamelessly apparent. Cecil was by no means a lover of all things American; he thought their manners overbearing, their speeches full of platitudes.[16] Yet the Frenchmen and women he spoke to complained incessantly about rude behavior by American GIs in Paris, including stories of drunken fistfights with French soldiers. He also found himself put off by what he saw as unrealistic French expectations. After a dinner party with many Americans and Frenchmen, Cecil wrote that none of the French who were present believed in a League "except so far as it was a cloak for a perpetuation of the alliances between France and England to dominate the world."[17] Cecil faced such cynicism during his many mealtime social engagements across the city in January, and he worried about the "Paris atmosphere."[18]

Cecil quickly assumed the mantle among the English-language press as the primary conduit of League information for the media. He supported the general US plans in an interview to the Associate Press on January 9 that closely followed Wilson's position that the creation of a League was the "indispensable" first step to creating a lasting peace.[19] Throughout his time as Minister of Blockade, Cecil had given press briefings every Friday to American correspondents and fully understood the power inherent in being the dispenser of news to newspapermen.[20] On January 14 he presented to American journalists what the Associated Press called "the most comprehensive statement yet undertaken by any of the delegates to the peace conference," in which he specifically tamped down suggestions that the League would have armed forces at its disposal.[21] His statement to reporters on January 20 that Germany would not be admitted to a League until its new government proved itself stable and trustworthy garnered front page headlines the next day in Atlanta, Boston, Chicago, and New York. A similar press conference with British reporters two days later gave him the opportunity to describe the critical necessity of a League that might head off war through mandatory conferences. Reporters remarked the apparent sincerity of Cecil's attitude, "and his anxiety to be of service to the public."[22]

Yet despite his desire to align with the United States in the League negotiations, Cecil through early January was unable to pin down whether Wilson actually had a League plan. In his memoirs, written decades later, Cecil lavished praise on Wilson for keeping the drum beating for the League. But when he finally got Wilson's initial scheme for the League on January 21, the plan seemed to Cecil an unimpressive plagiarism of the ideas of Jan Smuts and the Phillimore Committee, and was "a very bad document, badly expressed, badly arranged, and very incomplete."[23] Cecil knew, from early on, that steering and persuading Wilson must be his goal if he was to succeed in creating the type of League that he desired.

Over the war years, Cecil had developed an easy rapport with Lloyd George and Clemenceau, and with House and some others in the American delegation, a rapport that would continue with most of them throughout the Conference. Informality would never, however, mark Cecil's meetings with Woodrow Wilson. The president lived in the Palace Murat, a private residence blocks away from the rest of the US delegation, with "policemen watching his street and soldiers watching his door, and an army of private secretaries waiting for you in the hall." Dealing with Wilson in person was difficult. During their early meetings, Cecil treated Wilson with "the utmost deference" and got little for it, then began to press him and found that worked better. "He is, if one may say so, a trifle of a bully, and must be dealt with firmly, though with the utmost courtesy and respect—not a very easy combination to hit off. He is also evidently a vain man, and still with an eye all the time on the American elections." Cecil quickly surmised that Wilson's prime desire was that the final product should be "nominally at any rate, his scheme," even if it was produced by others.[24] Wilson appeared to Cecil as rather autocratic and unwilling to negotiate in a normal, give and take fashion.[25] "I do not personally like him," wrote Cecil in his diary. "I do not know what it is that repels me: a certain hardness, coupled with vanity and an eye for effect."[26] Yet Cecil, ever realistic, knew that successful plans for any League would have to appeal to Wilson.[27] Cecil decided on January 22 that regardless of its faults, which he thought myriad, the British League committee should use Wilson's draft as the template upon which amendments should be prepared. This would appeal to Wilson's desire for control, even while incorporating into the Covenant all the attributes Cecil and his League Section felt necessary.[28]

The American who immediately received Cecil's closest attention was Colonel Edward House. House held no official position in the US government; he was not even really a Colonel. Yet by the end of the war, House had emerged as President Woodrow Wilson's closest advisor, the only man who Wilson trusted as his primary envoy to the European powers. Secretary of State Robert Lansing attended a number of Cecil's meetings with House in the first weeks of January, and would later claim that his draft plan of January 31 was important, but Cecil was not alone in dismissing Lansing's authority, and no one had any doubts that it was House whose opinions mattered most to President Wilson.[29] By the end of the month, Cecil and House appeared in total accord on the Covenant.[30]

It had also become apparent to Cecil that among House's advisors, the one he would like to work with most was David Hunter Miller, and thankfully House obliged Cecil by making Miller the prime and on some days the sole US negotiator drafting the League Covenant.[31] Cecil recognized Miller, a lawyer and an advisor to House, as a practical lawyer uninterested in rhetoric or platitudes, but understanding the critical importance of negotiating minutiae.[32] With the FO legal advisor Cecil Hurst they comprised a trio of lawyers drawing up a craftily worded contract, burning the midnight oil to satisfy their clients, the governments of Britain and the United States. Miller claimed before their first meeting on January 19 that he "had no instructions at all," so from the start they worked from Cecil's draft.[33] According to both men, their "talk was very frank" through all their meetings.[34] Miller helped clue in Cecil to the real political limits imposed by the US Constitution, particularly when it came to creating a treaty obligation that might commit the United States to war. Cecil accepted that they should keep to the structure of the president's draft so that Wilson might more readily accept whatever amendments they created.[35] In such things, following Wilson's lead seemed pragmatic and jibed well with his and Lloyd George's predilections to focus his primary attentions on negotiations with the United States, rather than with France.

Dealing with the Difficult Dominions

Aside from his absolute certainty that a League must be created, and that its operations should be rooted in his wartime experiences operating Britain's economic war, Cecil remained largely flexible about the form of the permanent organization of the League.[36] In a memo to the War Cabinet on December 17, he suggested meetings at least annually, and also as needed, between the leaders of the Great Powers, with unanimity necessary in making binding decisions. Perhaps following the Olympic spirit of his League of Nations aide, the champion runner Philip Baker, all member states would meet every four years. A permanent secretariat, ideally led by someone not from one of the

Great Powers and based in neutral Geneva, Switzerland, would administer any existing and new interstate bodies and function as a conduit of information and diplomacy between League members.[37]

But Cecil knew that there were many ideas about the structure of the League. In Paris, Cecil ran the "League of Nations Section" of the British delegation. Meeting in his rooms with these men and discussing various ideas for the League structure became a standard part of his everyday schedule throughout January and early February. Unsurprisingly it was largely compromised of men he worked with on the blockade, including Eyre Crowe and Cecil Hurst, the international law advisor to the FO who had emerged as a critical defender of the legality of the British blockade during the war.[38] Others involved in these daily meetings included the Round Table imperialist intellectual Lionel Curtis, Lord Eustace Percy from the FO, and others from the Ministry of Labour, the Colonial Office, and eventually from the Admiralty.[39] Early the group leaned toward a League plan drawn up by Baker, but despite significant input by various members of the British League Section, the drafts and plans that emerged from these meetings (of which no minutes survive) show the tenacious fingerprints of Cecil, who dominated the proceedings and outcomes.

Interestingly, the British League Section did not have representation from Australia, New Zealand, Canada, South Africa, or India. The position of these British "Dominions" compared to other countries represented at the Peace Conference was highly unusual. Each considered itself a separate and sovereign state, yet each had long been part of the British Empire. Each had sent to Europe many thousands of soldiers to fight tenaciously for the Allied cause, and in the Imperial War Cabinet they wielded influence on Lloyd George and the British government. In the United States, many suggested that if the Dominions sat at the League table, the British Empire would have five more representatives than any other state. In Paris, the prime ministers of Australia and Canada made it clear that they followed no imperial edicts in making their policies. Yet exemplifying their "double status," they regularly caucused together in Paris as the British Empire Delegation (BED).[40]

The sovereign yet empire-bound status of the Dominions only seemed odd to people outside the Empire. The general sentiment of most people both in London and in the antipodes was that what was good for one was good for the rest. In a private meeting at the FO on New Year's Day with Jan Smuts of South Africa, Billy Hughes of Australia, Charles Doherty of Canada, Baron Sinha of India (the recently ennobled first Indian member of Britain's House of Lords), and William Lloyd, the prime minister of the sparsely populated Dominion of

Newfoundland, Cecil argued that his plans for a League, with annual meetings between the leaders of the Great Powers and quadrennial meetings of all the League members, could work well for the Dominions, which would continue in other ways to sway British Imperial policy for the annual meetings.[41]

Cecil was sure his plans served both Britain and the Empire. However, as his wartime efforts with the blockade put him in contact with many leaders of the world's neutral nations as well as those of the Allies, he had a unique international network of foreign leaders and opinion makers. In Peace Conference forums, Cecil's wartime experiences gave him clout and connections different from those of other British delegates. Serving as Britain's Minister of Blockade taught him the value of internationalism and of acknowledging global commitments. His negotiations in Paris throughout early 1919 led many foreign leaders to recognize that his passion for a League of Nations was genuinely intended to help not just British security, but global security.

The prime ministers of the British Dominions had learned somewhat different lessons from their experiences in the world war. The institutions they cut their international teeth on were not interallied economic and diplomatic forums but rather the Imperial Conferences and meetings of the IWC in 1917 and 1918. Participation in IWC debates was heady stuff for "Farmer Bill" Massey, the prime minister of New Zealand. To him, attendance at the IWC validated the decision of the New Zealand government to declare war in August 1914. Membership in the IWC proved that he and New Zealand more broadly were pivotal members of a truly imperial government looking out for all its members, and fed Massey's conviction that the British Empire was the true embodiment of God's providential plan for mankind.[42] For him, the war was a necessary event with positive results.

Billy Hughes, prime minister of Australia, likewise proclaimed a semireligious love of the British Empire and a tremendous skepticism of any non-British League of Nations. A decade after the Conference he wrote a book about the British "Commonwealth," explaining how this empire of "free and equal nations" is "the great outstanding feature of the world to-day."[43] He and Cecil sparred in the War Cabinet during the months before the armistice. When Hughes claimed that Australia and New Zealand had been kept out of the loop about Britain's secret treaty with Japan, Cecil reminded him that both governments had been informed of these Japanese claims in March 1915, and that both British Dominions had acquiesced to Japan's control of certain islands.[44] When Cecil suggested that the British government should publicize the Phillimore committee's suggested plans for a post-war League of Nations, Hughes was adamant that the IWC should decide League policies first, an idea intended to obstruct any agreement.[45] Far from seeing the war as a brutal bloodbath, martial spirit defined Hughes, set in his belief that the soldiers of Australia had engaged in "glorious deeds of valour" that must never be forgotten by Australians.[46] As a member of the Conference's Reparations Commission, Hughes proudly demanded more money from Germany than anyone else.[47] And he was constantly outspoken and forceful in the semiregular meetings of the BED, from which Lloyd George took some cues. For Hughes, the Conference was a time to obtain rewards for Australia and himself, rewards more important than mere peace itself.

A more brilliant and heroic figure, South African General Jan Smuts became in 1917 part of Lloyd George's inner War Cabinet, a minister without portfolio who Lloyd George assigned to a variety of war-related tasks. His extraordinary story, as the leader of anti-British guerrillas during the Boer War who a decade later became a significant pro-British statesman, gave the charismatic Smuts widespread popularity in Britain. Smuts became involved in thinking about a League soon after his arrival in Britain in early 1917, and in December 1918 he presented to the War Cabinet, and then published, his "program" for how to create a League at the Peace Conference. This has often been seen as a critical document in the evolution of what eventually became the Covenant of the League of Nations, as it definitely influenced Wilson. As a result, Smuts was named as Cecil's codelegate representing the British Empire on the League of Nations Commission.

Yet Smuts, like Massey and Hughes, arrived in Paris under the assumption that his country deserved to permanently annex the German colonies his armies had conquered in the early days of the war. By the start of the Paris Conference, Massey, Hughes, and Smuts believed firmly that as actors in the British imperial cause, they should work to expand that Empire—imperialism was in their history, in their nature, in their blood—and that taking permanent control of nearby German colonies in the South Pacific and South West Africa was the inevitable and just result of the victory of the British Empire in the Great War, a victory after all bought by the sacrifice on the battlefields of Europe and Asia of so many volunteer soldiers from their distant Dominions. They were quick to take offense against any Briton who suggested anything other than annexation.[48]

Cecil's primary goals were entirely different than this. He wanted a peace that would safeguard the global interests of Britain, including its Empire. But he definitely did not envision the peace as an opportunity for territorial aggrandizement. In the earliest days of January 1919, Cecil warily hoped for some compromise through the use of "mandates." The mandates concept was based on ideas of Smuts, and might allow acceptable levels of Dominion control over Germany's overseas empire. But he hoped that each mandate might be considered as ruled in the name of the League. After a group of delegates from the United States described some of their thoughts about the League of Nations, Cecil wrote that there was "a good deal to be said" for their suggestion that in mandatory states the League of Nations flag should be flown with that of the national flag of the mandatory nation.[49]

Smuts opened Cecil's eyes to the Dominions' very different ideas on the day of the Conference's first plenary session, where the delegations approved the creation of a commission to craft the League of Nations. In conversation afterward, Smuts assured Cecil that all of the Dominions were against any language that would "tie their hands" in their mandates. Cecil concluded with surprise that "they are out for annexation pure and simple." Referring to the Wilsonian moment that dominated the Conference in its early January days, Cecil simply couldn't imagine that Smuts's position could win the debate "in the open, in the present state of feeling."[50] But over the next few days Cecil grew more pessimistic, as Lloyd George laughed at breakfast at how "the Colonials" like Massey and "even Smuts" had rattled the Americans with their strident annexationism. By January 25 Cecil announced to his League section that he was "very much afraid of the imperialism of the Dominions."[51]

Cecil recognized that on the League Commission he represented the entire British Empire, and had no choice but to stick up for the Dominions in all his dealings with Colonel House, who wanted any Mandates to be ruled strictly under the auspices of the League.[52] But within the British delegation he pushed back against Hughes. Over the next few days he sent Lionel Curtis, J. H. Thomas, and the journalist Wickham Steed to "bring Hughes to reason."[53] On January 26 Cecil contacted both Lloyd George and Balfour to focus their attention on Hughes and "the South Africans" who were fighting against mandates. "Hughes is of course in this matter a pure and unadulterated reactionary. But it is evident that if they succeed in securing annexation for themselves we cannot resist it effectively in other cases, and we are practically again in the atmosphere of the Congress of Vienna." If the Dominions were allowed to gain territory, how could the British resist territorial grabs by the French and Italians?[54] At breakfast on January 28, Cecil reacted "with some vehemence" when Lloyd George appeared reluctant to put pressure on the Dominions.

At the BED later that day, Hughes and Massey opposed the basic idea of mandates as too limiting on their powers over captured German territories.[55] Massey asked petulantly if anything would happen if Australia, for example, controlled Samoa but did not fulfill its mandatory pledge to send an annual report to the League. Cecil responded that he was sure this would never happen, or at least could only occur "in the case of gross misgovernment by Australia."[56] Hughes responded with his fears that any League control would allow Germans or Japanese to freely migrate to New Guinea. But Lloyd George, supported by Cecil, stood his ground in supporting League mandates.[57] After the meeting, Hughes invited Cecil to his room to look for a solution. Cecil left believing that Hughes might accept the three class mandate system that was being floated as a compromise between the desires of the United States and the Dominions, with different levels of control for different mandate situations.[58] Once the Council of Ten approved the principle of mandates on January 30, Cecil believed that the great powers had agreed to ignore any further entreaties from Britain's Dominions, who would simply have to live with mandates.

Certainly personality differences only enhanced the likelihood of disagreements between Cecil and the Dominion leaders. Cecil and his friends from the FO laughed at dinner one evening as Paton described "the extreme unreasonableness of the more distinguished persons he had to cater for, especially the Dominions prime ministers."[59] No one saw Hughes's demeanor as anything other than pushy and irritating. Even his own aides disliked him.[60] But it was Cecil's relationship with Smuts that was particularly surprising. "Will you enjoy working with Smuts?" Nelly asked him in a letter at the end of January.[61] The two men would have seemed to share many of the same preoccupations, including a desire to placate the United States while creating a League that could guarantee postbellum international peace. From Smuts's later appointment of Cecil as South Africa's lead delegate to the League of Nations Assembly in 1920, a country Cecil had visited only once in his life, one might have assumed that they developed a true friendship during the Peace Conference. But Lady Cecil undoubtedly knew that her husband did not feel close to the South African. Cecil notably did not succumb to the cult of Smuts that influenced so many other members of the British and imperial delegations, not to mention many historians since.[62] The two men disagreed over how to handle the League Commission, with Cecil flatly opposing Smuts's suggestion that they simply give into Wilson on all issues other than the annexation of former German colonies.[63] And by the end of January, Cecil had come to see Smuts's commitment to the League as largely rhetorical or symbolic, rather than practical. In many histories of the birth of the League, Smuts is portrayed as a leading creator, with Cecil as more "a prophet than a planner."[64] If anything the opposite was true. Smuts's soaring rhetoric undoubtedly helped to spread the idea that for the good of humanity, a League was needed and must be part of a post-war world, but when it came to crafting a workable agreement, Smuts was nowhere to be found. Many of the early January drafts of the Covenant, crafted by Cecil's League of Nations Committee, passed through Lloyd George even before they were seen by Smuts.[65]

In the eyes of Cecil and many others, Smuts's earnest idealism appeared pretentious and made him rather a windbag. Cecil mischievously described how Lionel Curtis "indulged in Homeric laughter" when told about Smuts's long dinnertime speech to Cecil "on the advantages of complete straightforwardness and honesty, and the importance of merely doing your duty and not caring about the result."[66] When paired with his demands for permanent control of former German colonies, Smuts's pretentions appeared baldly hypocritical. The imperialism of these now-independent pieces of Britain's empire could throw a significant wrench into the possible settlement. Cecil grew increasingly vexed at the inability of Smuts to figure out a way to get Hughes and Massey to hold their tongues.[67]

By the end of January it had already become quite apparent to Cecil that many of his fellow British delegates held less faith than him in the possibility of the League solving all of their myriad problems. Over the years since 1916 when he first adopted his League ideas, Cecil had continually confronted skepticism and even some antipathy among many British officials and politicians. Even among his League staff in Paris there was some skittishness. Lord Eustace Percy complained privately to him that the war was due to "German idolatry of organization and material power, and the League of Nations was merely an exaggeration of the German specific." Cecil scoffed that the League would not bring universal organization, but was simply a practical way to head off military conflict. Cecil knew Percy's family well; like the Cecils, the sons of the Duke of Northumberland were prominent in Conservative circles. To Cecil, Lord Eustace's complaints exhibited his "Percy-like frame of mind" rather than adding up to a reasonable criticism of the League idea.[68]

More trenchant and important criticism came from those who advocated a League of the wartime Allies. Maurice Hankey, the influential secretary of the British Cabinet in its various wartime permutations, argued that the ideal League would simply extend into peacetime the interallied machinery of military consultation that developed in Versailles during the latter stages of the war.[69] Although he definitely hoped to gain Hankey's support for whatever League resulted from the negotiations during the Peace Conference, Cecil wanted nothing to do with a League of the Allies. From the start of the drafting process, Cecil and his advisors recognized that the greatest difficulty would be to legitimize the League in the eyes of the world. How, he wondered, could we "provide for a working body of the League which would be small enough to be efficient and yet would not expose us to the charge that the League was merely a device for putting the whole international power into the hands of the present Allies"?[70] Somehow, a real League of Nations must appear less like a League of victors and more a League for all.

Yet in Lloyd George's inner circle, both Hankey and Philip Kerr favored a League that continued the SWC. Their skepticism about Wilson's nebulous idealism influenced the prime minister, who through January showed respect for but no deep interest in the League. During one private breakfast on January 20, Lloyd George bent Cecil's ear on whether the various Russian factions should be allowed to send emissaries to the Conference or whether the Conference should send a mission to Russia.[71] Cecil warned that even a peaceful diplomatic mission could be murdered by the mysterious and violently unpredictable Bolsheviks, and that if this happened, Britain would be completely unprepared for the war that it would be honor-bound to launch against Lenin.[72] The prime minister valued Cecil's experience with the Russian question gained over his previous years at the FO, War Cabinet, and in various ad hoc committees on Russia.[73] Russian policy was important to Cecil, who had tendered his resignation from the government in June 1918 over their refusal to intensify Allied intervention in Siberia against the Bolsheviks (on that occasion, Lloyd George coaxed Cecil back into the fold).[74]

But this attention to other issues, albeit important ones, meant that the two men only reached the issue of the League as the breakfast dishes were being taken away. And then the prime minister spoke directly from a memo written by Philip Kerr that sketched out his long-held line on turning the Supreme War Council into the League.[75] Since Lloyd George had become prime minister, Kerr served as his main foreign policy advisor. Before the war, as editor of the Round Table, Kerr had called for imperial federation. During the war Kerr began considering the possibility of broader international government, but in January 1919 his proposal resisted Wilson's insistence that League membership must entail obligations to go to war in certain circumstances.[76] But was this really what Lloyd George thought about the League? Cecil remained unsure. In his reading of Kerr's scheme, Lloyd George seemed less than definitive that it was the path forward. If he was raising such options as a ploy to delay the creation of a League until after the peace with Germany was settled, it seemed odd—Lloyd George knew of Wilson's insistence on creating a League first. By the end of the meeting, Cecil "did not commit myself" to Kerr's limited League, and Lloyd

George did not order him to follow Kerr's plan when negotiating with other powers in the League Commission.[77] Cecil knew well that he must take into account that any plans he negotiated would eventually have to be put before the Cabinet for approval.[78] But he left the meeting doubtful that Lloyd George had solid commitment to any particular League ideas, and felt sure that the prime minister was persuadable.[79] Undoubtedly the Little Man believed that some sort of League must be created. Cecil felt empowered to negotiate as he had been doing, and expected that if he did so in a reasonable fashion, he could eventually carry the British government with him on whatever League resulted.

Negotiating the Movable Feast of Paris

Even as the daily grind of work on the League developed, with Cecil running between the British residences and the offices of the US and French delegations, Cecil's wartime expertise called him to other duties that he simply could not escape. Lord Reading, the former British Ambassador to the United States, had been sent to France in response to Cecil's earlier telegram of January 7 that relayed Hoover's message about Europe's desperate food needs. Yet soon after his arrival in Paris on January 11, Reading begged Cecil to take the reins instead. Cecil was reluctant, and would only ever consider it "on the distinct understanding that I did not thereby become a member of the Government."[80] After dinner on January 16, the American food experts Alonso Taylor and Herbert Hoover cornered him in the hall of the Majestic, urging some quick action to alleviate starvation in Vienna. Cecil said he had no knowledge of the subject, and did not know what difficulties were in the way of supplying the Austrians, but he would speak to Reading.[81] Over the next few weeks Cecil continued to push the food issue away.

Cecil had found himself consulted and drafted into service on a wide variety of issues. After a breakfast meeting on January 15, Lloyd George encouraged Cecil to return soon to talk about the Middle East.[82] When Edvard Benes, the Foreign Minister of the nascent state of Czechoslovakia, popped by Cecil's office, Cecil listened attentively as Benes outlined his schemes for new boundaries and blocs to secure the new eastern European states. He pressed Benes on the critical issue of Poland, the pivot state between Germany and Russia, before finally turning the Czech out of his room so he could get his more pressing League work done.[83] He liked Benes and the Czechs, "the most organized of the minor Slavonic peoples," especially when compared to the Poles.[84]

Obviously the line he tried to hold, between working for the League and his supposed unwillingness to work for Lloyd George's government, blurred both in his mind and in the minds of others. He could not help but care about the FO, about diplomacy, and about finishing the missions that he had begun during the war. And in the Parisian winter, there were many who believed him capable of helping to fix a tremendous variety of global problems.

Undoubtedly not all of the respect paid to him was due to his abilities and accomplishments. In Paris, Cecil's aristocratic status as the scion of an ancient landed family proved an integral part of his everyday life, giving him entrée into a wide variety of dinner parties and other soirées. On his second night in Paris, Cecil dined at the British Embassy with Lord Derby ("Eddy") and his wife. Both families had long lineages leading the Conservative cause in Britain, and Cecil regarded a meal with Derby as a time to gossip about London society rather than to deal with substantial issues. Aside from stirring up a fuss at the start of the Peace Conference when insisting that he remained, throughout the Conference, the sole official British ambassador to France, Derby played virtually no role in crafting the peace.[85] Cecil was at home in the world of European nobles and royalty, with whom he mixed regularly at luncheons and dinners across the city. He always dined with others, sometimes in the Majestic but often in private homes, at times accompanied by members of his extended family who kept arriving in Paris, eager to not miss out on this unprecedented social events surrounding the Peace Conference. Cecil and the people he dined with often talked pointedly about League or other peace treaty issues, but there were also much more free-flowing discussions. Most were not strictly regarded as working dinners, yet in the rather chaotic and unstructured atmosphere of the various Allied delegations in January, virtually any situation was an opportunity for lobbying. The line between acquaintance, friend, and advocate was never clear, as each delegate, both official and ad hoc, pushed for his or her causes in any way possible.

This incessant lobbying led to some very notable dinner parties. For example, Cecil spent a few long January evenings with "Arabian Lawrence." They had become friendly acquaintances during Cecil's work in the Eastern Committee, the Cabinet body that throughout 1918 planned British policy toward the disintegrating empires of Russia and Turkey. Both men seem to have been quite comfortable with each other, and both enjoyed wide ranging and blunt discussions.[86] T. E. Lawrence considered Cecil a real decision-maker and put a significant amount of time in with Cecil as part of his campaign to get Prince Faisal, his Arab ally, recognized by the Peace Conference as the representative of a true Associated Power due a seat at the bargaining table. Cecil had met with Faisal at the end of December in London and sympathized with Lawrence's broader aims of repudiating the wartime Sykes-Picot agreement, which ignored the wishes of Arab leaders like Faisal by promising a significant swath of Syria and Palestine to the French.[87] Although he generally favored Lawrence's efforts on behalf of Arab independence (which he also realized favored British rather than French interests), at dinner one evening Cecil offended Lawrence by suggesting that his stance regarding the future of the Middle East was too uncompromisingly anti-French.[88] A few nights later Lawrence got back at Cecil, claiming at a dinner with both Balfour and Cecil that Lord Curzon was the only one on the Eastern Committee who had been of any use during the war.[89] Lawrence used the latter dinner as an opportunity to lobby Balfour on behalf of Feisul. Balfour said he would get to work on it the next morning; characteristically, he did not. It was in such unofficial settings that important business often got done.

Among those with whom Cecil socialized, the issue of Syria would not die. One of his press contacts, M. Philippe Millet of *Le Temps*, warned him about the worries of many Frenchmen regarding the future of Syria, and urged Cecil to find a way to avoid potential disagreements between Britain and France on the issue.[90] On the other side, Cecil heard many who favored repudiation of wartime agreements with France. The British Zionist leaders Herbert Samuel and Chaim Weizmann suggested that Britain should be put in control of Palestine, and claimed that they had signed an agreement with Faisal to support Jewish plans if he received the Arab lands he desired.[91] During a breakfast meeting on February 4 with Smuts and Lloyd George, Cecil vocalized his fears that caving in to Clemenceau over French control of Syria would inevitably cause strife between the Arabs and France. Perhaps France should be "given Constantinople to look after" instead. Smuts cornered Cecil after the meeting, lecturing Cecil as to the "great influence" that Cecil had on Lloyd George and urging him to write a memo on the critical importance of this Syria issue to the creation of a real peace. Cecil did not have "the slightest hope that it will produce any effect," yet wrote to Lloyd George a forthright plea on behalf of Faisal's claims to independence in Damascus. "Though I have no kind of right to interfere in the matter I should like to be allowed to express my views on the Middle East," explained Cecil.[92] He was surprised when he heard the next day from Balfour that Lloyd George in the Council of Ten advocated exactly the position laid out in Cecil's memo.[93]

It was not the last time Cecil found himself dogged by the Middle East during the Peace Conference. When Gertrude Bell came to Paris in March, she talked his ear off on behalf of a Middle East settlement that limited French claims.

Cecil had known Bell, the British expert on Mesopotamia, since the months before he joined the government in the spring of 1915, when she served on his staff at the Wounded and Missing Enquiry Department of the Red Cross.[94] Their mutual respect and friendship meant they were often together. Even while he was intently focused on the League, he could not help but become involved in other pressing matters.

He claimed that eating meals at the Majestic, where the talk was "ceaseless shop" and the food was horrid, could become miserable, but that going elsewhere to dine was too time consuming.[95] Yet often he did leave, dipping into the uniquely fashionable season of the post-war Parisian winter. For Cecil the best times to socialize were around the dinner table. Many of his letters to his wife regale with tales of people he met, such as at a small dinner attended by Princess Marie Murat, and at another tea with her sister Princess Lucien Murat, the author and artist.[96] He escorted the socialite Margot Asquith (wife of the former prime minister) and her daughter Elizabeth to lunch at the Rothschild home just hours before attending the second League Commission meeting that afternoon.[97] Cecil always had time for events with such women. At times his diary, written for his wife, is incredibly preoccupied with describing the clothing and relative attractiveness of the women he met. When Nelly Cecil relayed to her family news about her husband's social engagements, her brother D'Arcy joked "he'd better start a League of Ladies instead of a League of Nations."[98] Cecil truly enjoyed opportunities for frivolity and fun in his social life.

And he indulged in a few of the other entertainments available to delegates. Cecil spent a handful of afternoons golfing, usually with his secretary Frank Walters. Conditions on the links during the French winter were poor; Walters tore a ligament when he slipped on a course on January 18. Being in Paris also brought out Cecil's inner *flâneur*; after lunch at the Majestic one day with his niece and some of her young friends, "we sat in the hall and admired the celebrities."[99] Like many others, he spent much time walking around from meetings to meals, engaging in conversation. Cecil did not appreciate all of the Parisian culture, however. One evening he went to "a kind of music hall entertainment," a tedious production filled with unintelligible slang. He and Walters rode the Métro home, "a cold, dull and long means of progression."[100]

Unsurprisingly, he also spent time with his family. The seven children of Lord Salisbury were notoriously clannish in preferring each other's company over other people, and this life-long tendency was quite clear in Cecil's relations with the children of his siblings.[101] With his twenty-four year old niece Mima (Lady Beatrice Edith Mildred) and her husband Billy Ormsby-Gore (the future

Lord Harlech), and Mima's slightly older sister Moucher (the Lady Mary Alice Gascoyne-Cecil, the future Duchess of Devonshire) he spent one Sunday afternoon traipsing through the very dark Cathedral of Notre-Dame. They stopped across the road to view the famous stained-glass at the medieval church of Sainte-Chapelle, but the glass had been removed during the war to protect it from air raids, and there was little to see.[102] Throughout the months in Paris, Cecil spent a lot of time, especially at dinners and on Sundays, with his nieces, who well typify the hangers-on attracted to Paris in early 1919. He took tea in the temporary flats of young British aristocrats like Sir Sidney Peel and his wife Lady Delia Peel, the daughter of the Earl of Spencer. Paris was the place to be that season. Some of these twenty-something children of privilege attempted to help the British delegation, and their lack of skills contributed to a sense among many delegates that the quality of the clerical assistance available to them in Paris was not up to normal standards. Other young aristocrats spent their days looking to be cultured, at concerts and lectures, or at least looking for entertainment.[103] Cecil's nieces were among many who regularly danced late into the night, sometimes in the basement hall of the Majestic that the British delegation commandeered for that purpose.[104] After years of war, they wanted fun.

What was perhaps most surprising to Cecil was what a celebrity he had become. He was asked to give a variety of speeches.[105] His reputation preceded him wherever he went in Paris, in the salons and in the offices of the various delegates. "Americans & French are always throwing bouquets to me," he warned his wife. "There is some danger of my head being turned."[106] Bernard Baruch, the wealthy Wall Street financier and close economic advisor to Woodrow Wilson, had imbibed the image of Cecil's sagacity to a more intense degree than most others; he professed shock when he met Cecil for the first time at one of these nightly dinner parties, explaining that he had always expected Cecil to look like "an old man with a long white beard."[107] Cecil was less impressed, dismissing Baruch as a self-centered bore. It would take a few more months in Paris for Cecil to arrive at a more positive opinion of the Wall Street financier.

Despite his love of dinner conversation on topics other than work, Cecil often found himself discussing the League. His dinner companions, a somewhat random assortment of transnational grandees, could drive Cecil mad with their interested yet uneducated talk about the League of Nations. After one dinner, he wrote that would have to invent an excuse to avoid a future lunch with Lady Antoinette Johnstone, the American wife of the British diplomat Sir Alan Johnstone. She was "a tiresome female" who throughout dinner had professed "a great desire to be instructed" on the League.[108] Yet his own personal predilections for a sociable life made him ever-available for such bores. One imagines that he could easily have dined alone, or with his staff, as did many of the others in the various delegations. Virtually every day in David Hunter Miller's diary ended with "Dined at home." Herbert Hoover later wrote with pride of how during his eleven months in Paris he rarely went out, saw no one but officials, and never went to the theater, museums, or even shops.[109] Even Woodrow Wilson, who during his first five years as president had been an inveterate Washington socialite, hunkered down in his Paris home rather than indulging in his passions for golf, the theater, and other outings.[110] In contrast, Cecil kept an active and varied social calendar. He liked to meet people and converse and in Paris he found ample opportunity to do so.[111]

Cecil's celebrity and authority was exemplified in his appeal to the unprecedented international press corps that poured into Paris in January. Hand in hand with the expansion of American power across the world, US newspapers sent out escalating numbers of foreign correspondents since the start of the century.[112] In an admittedly exceptional case, the *Chicago Daily News* routinely had over thirty full-time correspondents stationed at various foreign locations.[113] For both the United States and Britain, the expansion of news services like the Associated Press and Reuters in the early twentieth century fed a clearly growing public appetite for foreign news.[114]

But the Paris Conference brought an entirely new level of foreign affairs coverage. Not only the wire services and the big newspapers sent reporters, but also many smaller papers from across the United States, and from across the world. In what was likely a slight overstatement, the *Times of India* suggested that one thousand journalists were attending the Conference, "of whom five hundred are Americans."[115] In reality at least 150 came from the United States, as American reporters wrangled for excuses to be sent to cover what promised to be a grand event in the grandest city in the world.[116] The American corps developed a real group spirit traveling together to the Conference on the USS *Orizaba* and USS *George Washington*. On these ships they talked, lectured, and drank together (one historian labels it as the first real "convention" of journalists). By the end of the voyage, the US journalists on the *Orizaba* had organized themselves into a professional organization, the "United States Press Delegation."[117] In Paris many lived together in the Hôtel de Vouillemont, across from the Crillon. Throughout the Conference the US press tended to travel in packs.

Not a few of the American writers completely lacked foreign policy experience or knowledge of international issues. The Progressive politician and writer for the McClure newspaper syndicate William Allen White claimed that journeying across the ocean with Norman Angell (who himself was traveling to Paris to write for some British newspapers) was "my introduction to international politics … I was abysmally ignorant."[118] Despite such ignorance, it was expected by many of the journalists and the Conference delegates that the American correspondents could guide public opinion at home. In the end, American journalists were from the most powerful country in the world.

American journalists, influenced heavily by Wilson's rhetoric, bought into the Conference the idea that its processes would embody "open diplomacy." Whether they would get into actual conference meetings was an open question, but they expected that at least Wilson himself would be available to the press on a daily basis.[119] Instead, the US journalists quickly registered their disappointment at their lack of access to both the individual delegates and the conference events. The president was surrounded by privacy. Clemenceau and Lloyd George persuaded Wilson that the Allied leaders would address the press only through official communiqués.[120] "The press are raging at the lack of facilities given them and wish to attend all meetings," wrote Harold Nicolson in his diary on January 17. "They have gone to great expense in sending their best people here, and they are given no information."[121]

Cecil attempted to fill this information vacuum. He immediately began regular meetings and interviews with journalists from an array of countries, both taking part in public interviews with groups of foreign and British press correspondents, and meeting with editors and writers individually. Cecil particularly focused his attention on journalists from the United States; in one mass interview on January 14 he met with "great numbers of them, 30 or 40."[122] He hoped to bolster support in the United States for the League, making a point to rebut those journalists "from opposition papers" who claimed that a League would invalidate the Monroe Doctrine. But with the same intent, Cecil often demanded anonymity during these meetings. He wanted to get his news spin out, while avoiding the charge that he was meddling in the political life of another country.[123]

From the first day of the Conference, and throughout their near-daily meetings with Cecil over the next months, House and Lansing argued that Wilson would be able to persuade the American people to support the creation of a League of Nations.[124] Cecil recognized from the very start that the most critical feature of any League of Nations would be whether it could gain political support in the United States. The balance over the next months would be to figure out how to slip as many of his own desiderata into the final League plan, while making it a politically plausible success from the perspective of a US electorate historically wary of entanglements in Europe.

*

At the end of January, Cecil found himself at the center of perhaps the most multifaceted diplomatic negotiation in the history of the world, one carried on in offices, restaurants, and salons across the French capital. The League Commission was about to begin meeting, and Cecil worried a bit that he did not yet know how the Commission would work, or how he would deal with the overwhelming presence of President Wilson as its chairman. But he was certain, as he noted repeatedly in his diary, that "my plan" would be utilized as the critical template during the upcoming negotiations in the League Commission. Cecil believed that what his team had come up with by the end of January balanced well the interests of Britain and its Empire with those of France, the United States, and the many other nations represented both formally and informally at the Conference. It could create a viable and lasting League that could use the power of public opinion and the threat of economic warfare to enforce a general peace in Europe and perhaps across the entire world. It was a tall order, but after three weeks of this strange social gathering in Paris, interacting with politicians, socialites, and the global press, he remained optimistic that it could work.

3

Fashioning the Covenant: February 1–14

Other than the expectation that Germany would face punishment for losing the war, perhaps the most basic assumption in Paris in 1919 was that a League of Nations of some sort would be created. Not only Woodrow Wilson demanded it. In the words of David Hunter Miller, among the global public there was "almost universal sentiment in favor of *some* Association of Nations for international peace."[1] This desire was apparent not only across the political spectrum in Britain and France, but also among the increasingly globally aware leaders of anti-colonial movements across the British and French empires.[2] Lloyd George had no passion for a League, but came to Paris certain it must be created. Far from hoping to sink the League by appointing Léon Bourgeois as France's League negotiator, Clemenceau at the start of February considered it possible that a League might provide some protection against any resurgence of German militarism.[3] No one yet knew exactly what a League would look like, but everyone knew what war looked like, and if there was a chance that a League could curtail future warfare, it must be tried.

So Leaguers had the benefit of a significant tailwind as January ended. Cecil optimistically believed that very little difference existed between the Anglo-American plan he had brokered in January and the ideas coming from the French.[4] He would have preferred to stitch up the entire Covenant in private talks between the great powers, in a continuation of what had occurred in hotel suite meetings and late night drafting sessions during January. But by February, Cecil succumbed to the inevitability of a broader committee, which would bring smaller countries into the negotiating process.

He quickly began a series of private meetings with the likely representatives to exchange pleasantries and to give them copies of the Anglo-American plan. Cecil wished to size up what opposition might exist, and clearly hoped to predetermine the outcome of the League Commission. Some delegations appeared pliable. The Portuguese, hopeful of large British loans, made no secret of their desire to follow the British line completely. Cecil also judged that the Chinese representatives, including the impressive young diplomat Wellington Koo, appeared amenable to his ideas.[5] Cecil's wartime experiences negotiating blockading and rationing with the Dutch made him wary when talking with John Loudon, the Dutch Minister of Foreign Affairs. But Loudon could be avoided, as Holland and other neutrals did not have seats on the Commission.[6] Cecil did not know what to make of the desires of countries like the Netherlands to join a League crafted by the wartime allies. How could neutrals be included in a peace treaty? In opposition to the Dutch claims on a place in the post-war League, Belgian Foreign Minister Paul Hymans repeatedly turned up at Cecil's office to press the rights of his particularly aggrieved nation and of the smaller Allied powers in general. Creating further difficulties, Cecil was uncertain of support from the rest of the British delegation. As word of the importance of his daily meetings spread, Cecil's British League committee had grown out of hand, as Australian and Canadian representatives showed up along with more members of the armed services, wrecking the possibility of "useful conversation" among his closest aides and advisors.[7]

Finally, Woodrow Wilson was again proving unpredictable, suggesting just hours before the first Commission meeting to both his American and British advisors that the Hurst-Miller draft Covenant, drawn up in nonstop negotiations over the previous days and nights, should be shelved for a return to his own initial plan. Wilson was only persuaded to return to the negotiated document by a very stern Cecil, who upon hearing of Wilson's change of heart rushed to see the president and brusquely defended the efforts of himself, Hurst, and Miller. For Cecil, Wilson's vacillation was just another incident "exceedingly characteristic of ... (Wilson's) incapacity for cooperation resulting from a prolonged period of autocratic power."[8] "He is a little inclined to think that he is President not only of the U.S. but of the world as well."[9]

Balancing all of these interests and egos would be exceedingly difficult. And yet when he left the first meeting of the League Commission that evening, Cecil felt hopeful and satisfied. He had cowed the US president in private, then worked to alleviate Wilson's resulting nervousness during the Commission meeting.[10] Despite their argument minutes before the meeting began, Cecil and Wilson ambled into the meeting side by side, and throughout the afternoon's discussions, Cecil supported Wilson to the fullest. "There really is very little to say in the committee, since we are, except on a few points, all agreed—at least I hope so."[11] Orlando and Bourgeois complained that they had not seen the draft Covenant until the meeting and were not provided with a French translation, but Wilson and Cecil shrugged off their suggestions that the Commission should start with a discussion of principles before even considering any concrete proposals. Noting that "the whole world is watching," Cecil urged fast action to capitalize on public attention.[12] The Commission agreed to base their discussions on the Anglo-American draft, and that evening, Cecil confided in his diary that he expected that building consensus in the League Committee would be relatively easy.[13]

Through the League Commission meetings over the next two weeks, culminating with the presentation of the Covenant by Wilson to a plenary session of the full Peace Conference on February 14, Cecil remained assured that the planned League met his desires. At the League Commission meetings, Cecil established himself as pushy and authoritative, an expert on the subject and an important politician on both the British and global stages. He spent much time playing the role of conciliator between the French and the United States. He did not win all the arguments over the shape of the Covenant or the League itself, but far from being bowled over or outplayed by the stubbornness of Bourgeois or the global clout of Wilson, Cecil found things going his way.

The League Commission at Work

The League Commission meetings provide a microcosm of the way that interactions between the Americans, British, and French often dropped into clichéd patterns throughout the Conference. At least on the face of it, the Commission had far more than three voices. By the third meeting, fourteen countries were represented at its daily meetings. But as in the Council of Ten and later in the Council of Four, Italy's prime minister Orlando consistently felt ignored by his supposed Allied peers. The Italian contingent to the League Commission played no significant role. The League meetings, like the Peace Conference in general, centered wholly upon the need to create agreement among the French, British, and Americans.

The nineteen delegates (the United States, Britain, France, Italy, and Japan sent two apiece) congregated in the huge office of Colonel House, on the third floor of the Hotel Crillon. They sat around a large circular table, covered in red felt, with their advisors and translators in scattered seats behind. Wilson sat as chairman, but his preference for free-flowing conversation and informality meant there was "constant talking and translating," with delegates who did not know French or English listening to whispers from their more knowledgable advisors explaining points made in the other language. There were no podium presentations, and no one rose to speak.[14] Wilson and Cecil did the vast bulk of the talking in the League Commission meetings.

Wilson and Colonel House sat side by side with Cecil and Smuts, and Anglo-American whispering, particularly between House and Cecil, sometimes was less than *sotto voce* and provoked the other delegates to silence.[15] But each of these delegations was a lopsided partnership, as House and Smuts remained virtually mute over the thirty hours of meetings held during the ensuing week and a half.[16] By the first League Commission meetings in early February, it had already become obvious to Cecil that Smuts "apparently wishes to leave the great bulk of the negotiations on the League of Nations in my hands." The South African had refused to attend most of the negotiation and diplomatic sessions that dominated Cecil's schedule leading up to the Commission meetings.[17] His ensuing silence in the Commission would become proverbial even among men who did not attend its meetings.[18] Perhaps Smuts kept quiet intentionally, as his biographers Lentin and Hancock argue, allowing Woodrow Wilson to feel in charge of the process.[19] But in practice, it reflected the reality that the backroom negotiating and round table diplomacy on behalf of British imperial interests fell upon Cecil's shoulders. Smuts' rhetorical gifts and charisma went unused during League negotiations. By the time the Covenant was presented to the broader conference Plenary Session on February 14, it was an open secret that Cecil towered above Smuts in leading the British League effort.[20]

Many who participated in the ten meetings between February 3 and February 13 noted Cecil's demeanor. He was a tall man, but a notable sloucher. His sister-in-law Violet described him two decades earlier as "the strangest-looking creature ... with a head like Savonarola on a body almost deformed by a round back," and his posture had certainly not improved over the intervening years.[21] Yet despite his rather unimpressive physical presence, he commanded respect in these meetings. According to Miller, Cecil's views "were obviously those of a statesman of long experience," and he acted with patience and a "willingness to listen to argument" that gave many of his pronouncements a judge-like finality.[22]

Cecil was also unique among the representatives of the Great Powers in utilizing and understanding both French and English. Wilson knew only English, while both the Frenchmen, Bourgeois and Larnaude, spoke only French. Orlando never even attempted to make the case for Italian as one of the conference's working languages. He spoke exclusively in French, and relied heavily on an ad-hoc group of translators to understand his Anglo-Saxon counterparts. Cecil ordinarily spoke in English, but understood French well, and at times spoke "in a rather halting French which he himself described as a jargon."²³ Yet his knowledge of both languages only enhanced his role as the intermediary between the United States and France.

Starting in the second meeting, the Commission tackled the various Articles of the Hurst-Miller draft Covenant one by one, with discussions leading either to redrafting sessions or to a vote to approve. During these meetings, most of which lasted around three hours, a number of the final Covenant's twenty-six Articles were approved without any discussion at all. Most redrafting was done outside the Commission in meetings by ad hoc subcommittees. Cecil served on all of these. All of this drafting and redrafting was done in English.

One significant early challenge was over what Cecil termed the "Executive Council" of the League. Cecil wanted this to be a core group of the great powers, with no others present. He believed this would create "a much more workable instrument of administration than one to which minor Powers were admitted on some arbitrary system."²⁴ He also believed that a great power council, initially a sort of continuation of the wartime alliance until Germany and Russia were considered fit to join, simply reflected the reality of global power, with small nations not truly on the same playing field as powers like Britain and the United States. The Belgian delegate, Paul Hymans, opined that Cecil's proposal "is a revival of the Holy Alliance of unhallowed memory."²⁵ "Distrust of the Great Powers did not come very well from Belgium," Cecil retorted pointedly; he did not have to mention that a primary rationale behind British entry into the war was to protect Belgian sovereignty against the invading Germans.²⁶ Yet Cecil was not blindsided by Hymans' request; indeed his British League committee had been grappling with exactly this conundrum of the position of the smaller states.²⁷ Wilson himself had once supported the idea of minor countries gaining seats on the Executive Council, where it was assumed that all members would have a veto.²⁸ By the end of January, Cecil believed that negotiations had persuaded the president that minor countries would be invited to the executive whenever their interests were being discussed, and in certain cases would have the right to demand that their concerns be transferred from the executive committee to the full League Conference.²⁹

But when the French and Italian delegates supported representation of the small powers, Cecil reluctantly gave into their demands for a few Council seats to be rotated among the small powers, with the Great Powers maintaining permanent representation. Cecil found ridiculous this idea that their sovereignty made all nations deserving of a voice in the League, even though the tangible economic and military power of some nations vastly outweighed that of others.³⁰ A Council including smaller states diverged sharply from the ideas for the

League favored by influential members of the British delegation, particularly Maurice Hankey and Philip Kerr. They preferred a continuation of the SWC, run by the United States, Britain, and France. Hankey chastised Cecil in one late night conversation that giving in to the small nations over the place of the great powers in the League would not be acceptable.[31] However for Cecil, the makeup of the Council was not the most critical issue facing the Commission, and he did not accept that the SWC could work in conditions of peacetime, as it would not "have the compelling power of fighting an enemy to keep it together."[32]

Another big question was who should lead the League. There seems to have been general acceptance within the League Commission that Cecil would choose and recruit the new League executive, or at least there was no objection raised to his near complete control of the process.[33] His preferred choice since December 1918, the Greek leader Eleftherios Venizelos, pulled himself out of the running early in February. This was perhaps for the best, as he soon proved not the best of peacemakers. Venizelos's efforts in Paris aimed to get the most for Greece out of the remnants of the Ottoman Empire, which soon led Greece into conflict with Italy.[34]

Cecil next alighted on Maurice Hankey, who had expressed significant interest in the League in various War Cabinet meetings and reports during 1918, and who at the end of the year expressed much satisfaction with Britain's League plans.[35] Hankey was British, which Cecil had thought a downside; ideally the League would be led by someone outside the great powers. Some historians have suggested that Cecil's ideas for a "Chancellor" suggested that the League's leader should have significant power to set its agenda and to utilize League resources against specific Covenant-breaking states.[36] But this interpretation really overstates Cecil's adhesion to a strong-Chancellor plan, and underestimates both his flexibility and his pragmatism. He would have liked a visionary, but he knew that more than anything, the League needed an organizer. To Cecil, Hankey appeared in many ways a superior candidate to Venizelos, less inspirational and charismatic but more practical minded and highly skilled in administration. Hankey's connections with the leaders of the British government in all political parties could only help to improve the prospects of that government taking the League seriously. He had authored many of Britain's pre-war plans in the Committee of Imperial Defence.[37] During the war Hankey created and headed the Cabinet Office, the War Cabinet, and the IWC. Hankey was supremely confident of his own abilities to create a working mechanism of the League, and even doubted that anyone else could really do the job. And he was looking for a new challenge.[38] Cecil assumed that much of the League organization would be fashioned on the fly by the people who ran it, something for which Hankey appeared uniquely qualified.

In some ways the choice between Venizelos and Hankey mirrored the fight in the League Commission between those who aimed for a Covenant that would satisfy the most extraordinary hopes for a new world order, and those who hoped for a realistic and relatively limited plan that could be fully implemented from the start. One early maximalist argument pressed initially by both Wilson and some of the small states on the Commission centered on whether to include a guarantee of territorial integrity in the Covenant. Under this, all members of the League would pledge to respect the present borders of all their fellow member states. This idea vexed Cecil tremendously, both because he was sure the British government and the Dominions would not go for it, and even more so because all those who supported the guarantee did so while "almost openly expressing the view that it would not be kept, as a kind of demonstration."[39] It was ridiculous, he thought, that any country should pledge their willingness to fight to maintain the borders of states in Eastern Europe that were not even states yet. If the Covenant was to be a constitution for a League, then it should include only things that could be carried out "literally and in all respects."[40] He refrained from stating openly that it was exactly this clause that could foster criticism or even rejection in the US Senate; Cecil knew well that Wilson was notoriously touchy on the subject of the political viability of the Treaty in the legislature back home, and resented any "advice" on the subject even from his own advisors, let alone from foreigners.

As Wilson desired, a territorial guarantee entered the League Covenant as Article 10, but Cecil was satisfied that it was left vague. Rather than mandating a specific response, the Article left it up to the Council "to advise" what to do upon the invasion of a member state. Furthermore, the British League committee helped to devise a possible way around the problem by crafting articles that allowed the League Assembly the possibility of revising treaties and other "international engagements" that no longer made sense. This idea, the root of the eventual Article 19, suggested that the League could create and recognize changes when expediency, logic, or circumstance demanded.

The issue of obligatory arbitration of disputes, another of Wilson's desires, proved amenable to a similar compromise. Most agreed that a modified International Court could pick up on the project of the Permanent Court of Arbitration, created in The Hague during the decade before the war. However Cecil knew that making arbitration mandatory and binding in all circumstances would be broadly opposed on both sides of the Atlantic. If the war had proven anything to the victorious powers, it was that their hands must not be tied, but rather they "must be free to fight for the right as we see it." Despite hoping for "the realization of a dream, a world without war," Cecil believed that "if other more civilized methods fail, we must have the right to seek the arbitrament of arms."[41]

It was well put, the Anglo-French position in a nutshell. Yet the US representatives must be placated, and Wilson must be satisfied. Cecil believed he could square the circle by paying close attention to the exact drafting of the relevant Article, pushing for ambiguity over exactly which disputes might be decided by an international court and over who would decide if arbitration should be utilized.[42] The drafting process, and his attention to detail paid by Cecil, Miller, and House, effectively took the edge out of the arbitration Article of the Covenant, Article 13, which talks only vaguely about international disagreements that might be "generally suitable for submission to arbitration or judicial settlement." One might argue that they created a meaningless article, but at least it would lower one stumbling block to the negotiations.

A similar aspiration arose in discussions on whether to ban the private manufacture of weapons. Many people throughout the world believed in 1919 that the war had been extended, and perhaps even initiated, by arms manufacturers looking to profiteer from the killing. In his emotive and influential December 1918 League plan, Smuts argued that making money from the weapons trade must be one of the permanent casualties of the Great War. In the mid-1920s Cecil became known for his advocacy of such controls, but in 1919 he was no arms control absolutist. Most practically, he considered it an issue that would wreck the Covenant's chances of meeting with approval from the governments of any of the Great Powers. Yet Wilson reintroduced it to the Commission table. After an awkward discussion, Cecil was happy that the delegates were persuaded to finesse this issue by crafting Article 8, which simply directed the future executive council of the League to consider ways to curtail arms trafficking.[43]

Another idealistic cause that entered the Commission debates suggested that the League should safeguard the rights of religious and ethnic minorities in League member states. As a man claiming to follow Christian ethics, Woodrow Wilson pushed briefly for the idea of an article in the Covenant that would guarantee the rights of religious freedom to all people in every member state. As another notably religious man, Cecil thought Wilson's proposed religious freedom article likely to lead to calls for League intervention in the internal affairs of member states. Even just talking about such interventions suggested League overreach, and would hurt support for the League. Cecil alerted the Commission to the fact that religious inequality was a fundamental part of British law, surprising his colleagues "by informing them that in England the Catholics, who are fairly treated as things are, could not possibly be set on a footing of perfect equality with their Protestant fellow-citizens ... no Catholic can ascend the throne as monarch, nor sit on the woolsack as Lord Chancellor in the Upper House."[44] Cecil initially felt a sense of relief when the Japanese delegate Baron Makino lumped his own article for racial equality in with Wilson's on religious equality. The issues were quite comparable, but the racial amendment was toxic.

The Japanese amendment called for all member states "to accord as soon as possible to all alien nationals of states, members of the League, equal and just treatment in every respect making no distinction, either in law or in fact, on account of their race or nationality." The BED opposed the Japanese proposal under the leadership of Hughes, whose racism was at the core of his political appeal. The "White Australia" policy (rejecting Asian immigrants on the basis of race) was, according to one historian, "the one policy which almost all Australians accepted," "the corner stone of the national edifice" in the words of Hughes.[45] Hughes's opposition also had a strategic angle, resting on his wariness about Japanese intentions in the Pacific, and his unhappiness about the British government's acquiescence to the secret terms of its treaty that allowed Japanese control of all German territories north of the equator.[46]

Similar wariness of all things Japanese ran high in the western United States.[47] And the Japanese amendment seemed tailored to attract international attention to segregation in the Jim Crow South, something few US politicians would have supported in 1919. As the president of a racially divided country and himself a known racist, Woodrow Wilson would never accept Makino's amendment. Both amendments were shelved in the Commission's final meeting on February 13. Cecil spoke during that meeting about his admiration for the sentiments of Makino's proposal, but acknowledged that the delegates from the British Dominions disliked it, and he hoped that the Commission might postpone debating it. House then withdrew the religious amendment that Wilson had been pushing.[48]

Bigotry undoubtedly had much to do with the rejection of these amendments. But Cecil supported the underlying goals of both the religious and racial amendments. His rejection of the racial and religious freedom amendments reflected simply what he perceived as their impracticality in the context of Paris in 1919. Putting such words into the Covenant could sink the whole League, providing ammunition for those who derided a strong League as unrealistic or fanciful. To Cecil's mind, such equality amendments were aspirational rather than functional, and as such had no place in the League's charter. Cecil blamed Wilson for the fact that such sentimental and impractical gestures even rose to the attention of the Commission. The man was too focused on "vanity and an eye for effect," supporting "idealistic causes without being in the least an idealist himself."[49] He worried most when these ideas gained the rhetorical support of the French and Italians. Ironically Cecil, oft chastised by historians and contemporaries for his principled stances on issues like free trade and the Welsh church, spent much time in February criticizing others for being too focused on principle rather than practicality.

However, the most irksome matter of principle that Cecil had to face came from the French. Looking for security guarantees against any future German resurgence, Leon Bourgeois repeatedly raised the idea that the League should have an international army, or at least an international general staff, so it could quickly punish any treaty-breaking country. Foch and others in the French high command envisioned the League solely as a group of the Allies, perched to unleash aggression against Germany. But this would mean that real peace with Germany was permanently out of the question.[50]

This argument had already become exhausting to listen to a week earlier. According to House's assistant Stephen Bonsal, in a drafting committee meeting during one of Bourgeois's soliloquies, "Cecil raised his arm on high and seemed to be overcome by an utter weariness which he could find no words sufficiently eloquent to express. At last, catching breath, he said, 'Oh, M. Bourgeois! Do not begin that all over again. We have heard you so often and so patiently. Your plan will lead nowhere,'" except perhaps to an alliance between the United States and Britain, with France left out because "of incompatibility of temper."[51] The very idea of a League "was practically a present to France" from the United States and Britain, both of which could stand apart from European affairs if they desired.[52] Cecil judged Bourgeois as well-meaning but well past his prime, prone to rambling and off the mark speeches.[53] The promotion of a League army was "a perfectly fatuous proposal," Cecil complained, utterly impractical. Bourgeois knew that neither Britain nor the United States would support it, nor would those among the rest of the world fearful that a League could simply be an extension of the wartime alliance into post-war domination.[54] Both United States and British leaders had often voiced their expectations that all countries would eventually be allowed to enter a League, even present enemies like Germany. Bourgeois would have to back down.[55]

Cecil was certainly personally irked at Bourgeois and Ferdinand Larnaude, the second French League delegate, for pressing the League army issue in very longwinded speeches throughout the meetings of the Commission, but he was not the only one who felt that the Frenchmen were unnecessarily belaboring the Commission's debates.[56] Why, he wondered, were the French so insistent on destroying Allied unity? He repeatedly explained "very clearly the risks that the French were running by their perversity."[57] Were the French introducing the subject in an attempt to sabotage the League project entirely? He lamented that French negotiators "seem to be elaborately and laboriously engaged in destroying the last remnants of sympathy felt for them by the Americans, and doing so without getting any real tangible advantage in return."[58] The "irritating pin pricks" of French diplomacy willingly sacrificed important interests for no real gains.[59] Other than the issue of an army, there were really no substantive differences between the three powers on the issue of the League, at least as far as Cecil could see.

Perhaps French actions were not driven by a particular anti-Americanism, but rather were symptomatic of a specific French style in their relations with everyone. Like other Britons throughout the centuries, Cecil believed that whatever their individual qualities, it was hard to trust the French. One day he ran into Etienne Clémentel, the French Minister of Commerce, who asked Cecil for advice. Despite his trepidation, should he preside over one of the committees created by the Peace Conference? Cecil sympathized with his friend and comrade who had helped since their first meetings in August 1917 to create interallied committees controlling shipping and some raw materials.[60] But he could not help but think what a surprising circumstance he was in; "I cannot imagine (an Englishman) confiding his grievance to a Frenchman, nor enlisting his help in such a matter."[61] Cecil was only coming to understand the uniqueness of his own international network.

When describing this flurry of February meetings, it is tempting and easy to focus on the drama of disputes within the Commission. Conflict can make for a more lively story. But in Cecil's eyes, the meetings were cordial and for the most part, decisions were made without serious difficulties. On the issue of military commissions, Cecil explained, "I understand the view of my French colleagues but my thought is, if we try to do too much, we shall accomplish nothing. I have gone as far in this matter as the public opinion of my country will support me." Larnaude responded that despite their disagreement, "we pay homage to Sir Robert in full appreciation of the spirit of conciliation which he has always shown."[62]

Most of the Articles of the draft Covenant that Cecil presented at the first meeting were simply accepted by the Commission with no debate. Cecil gained complete support for all the Articles of the Covenant most dear to his heart. For example, Article 12 called for countries to submit disputes to arbitrators or to the League Council, with admonition to not resort to war for at least three months after the arbitrators announced their decision. This "cooling-off period," the dream of Lord Grey when the war broke out in August 1914, had been a critical piece of Cecil's initial 1916 plan. Now in 1919 it flew through the fourth Commission meeting with virtually no discussion, and no opposition at all.

The next day, Cecil's economic sanctions plans passed unanimously, becoming Article 16 of the final Covenant. The Article stated that any country would face universal sanctions if they ignored their commitments to engage in dispute resolution and a cooling off period before going to war. Any belligerent power that broke its agreements had "committed an act of war against all other members of the League" and thus deserved a group response. All signatories to the League Covenant would be committed to joining this League-declared economic and financial war. In practice, Cecil explained, states next to an aggressor would on their own initiative install blockades, and the "Executive Council will by its decisions dispose of the hesitations of the other States."[63] Sanctions could evolve according to circumstances, in a process akin to that of the Allied wartime blockade.

Despite the intensity of his focus on Commission business, Cecil's diary of these days includes little about the Commission meetings. Episodes that turned the heads (and found significant space in the diaries of) his fellow Commission members were left unaccounted in Cecil's diary. The best example of this was the full-day subcommittee meeting of February 12, where Cecil led others including Venizelos, Larnaude, and the Serbian diplomat Milenko Vesnitch in a critical redrafting of the entire Covenant. Vesnitch's brief obituary two years later in the *New York Times* specifically mentioned his attendance at this meeting, which aimed to "settle some of the difficulties which had threatened to be insurmountable" at a "critical phase" of the League negotiation.[64] It was in other words a vital moment, but Cecil wrote in his diary that "not much of interest" occurred. Most of his diary entry focused on describing the comically extreme nearsightedness of the Portuguese delegate.[65] Considering that he was writing the diary for his wife, underplaying or omitting dramatic moments and significant meetings appears startling. Cecil was not quiet about the meetings because he was worried about breaking confidences. He bluntly recorded his personal thoughts about the men and ideas circulating around Paris elsewhere throughout the diary. If his letters and diary are any indication of his wife's taste, Lady Cecil enjoyed gossip, and she wholeheartedly supported her husband's interest in creating a League of Nations. Instead, the lack of his writing on the Commission indicates that he did not view the meetings as episodes of unbridgeable conflict, but rather as moments where consensus was being created. Much of it he could literally slouch through. At the final meeting on February 13, Cecil as Chairman, "sitting low in his chair and holding the lapels of his coat, read the 26th Article," which was accepted without discussion."[66] And thus the League Commission's meetings appeared to be at an end. Cecil had little to report to his wife because things were going well.

And the feeling of well-being regarding the League went beyond his meetings with the other Commissioners. Before the tenth meeting of the Commission, in which Cecil sat as chairman and the Covenant draft was approved, Cecil lunched with Maurice Hankey. The secretary of the British delegation had been following the proceedings, having insisted ten days earlier that Cecil provide him with a précis of the Commission's daily efforts. Cecil had expected some skepticism from the Cabinet secretary, but found that during their lunch Hankey "was quite civil about the League of Nations, observing that without being a Cabinet Minister I appeared to have 'bounced' the League of Nations Commission very successfully!"[67] Cecil launched into his recruitment drive. Recognizing that the League needed an organizational expert to get it off and running, he asked Hankey to become the first "chancellor" of the League. Hankey agreed to consider the offer carefully, and according to his diary and letters he spent the next weeks asking advice from his friends and pondering the possibility of building this new organization of potentially tremendous global importance from its very beginning. By mid-February, Cecil believed that the League process was concluding successfully.

At the Supreme War Council

Starting on February 8, Cecil became embroiled in a significant new duty. That morning he breakfasted with Lloyd George, and as always their discussion lacked focus on the ostensible reason for their meeting, as they gossiped and joked about the relationship between the Archbishop of Canterbury and King George V, and the liberalism and outspokenness of the Bishop of Durham. It was only when the prime minister was halfway out the door on his way to catch a train London-bound that he stopped and remembered that he meant to ask Cecil to take charge of Britain delegation to the proposed Supreme Economic Council (SEC).

Cecil had heard a "chorus" of rumors over the previous week declaring that he was to be placed in charge of relief and supply in Europe.[68] He was wary of taking the post, feeling that someone in the Cabinet should be responsible for it so that they could answer on behalf of the government in the Commons.[69] Yet he also recognized that the new Council might be exactly what he had wanted a few months earlier, a true continuation of interallied unity on the economic front, like the disbanded AMTC. There had been some wasted weeks due to the destruction of the AMTC by Hoover and the Americans, but maybe, Cecil thought, the new SEC could take charge of Allied assets anew and use them to rejuvenate the European economy.

As a result, Cecil found himself suddenly engaged in meetings of the SWC. He was called to attend the afternoon after the sixth League Commission meeting because blockade issues were to be addressed. Cecil noticed the rather haphazard layout of the men in Foreign Secretary Pichon's office at the Quai d'Orsay, with Clemenceau at a writing desk, Foch lounging on a sofa, others in straight-backed armchairs under the windows. Cecil was exhausted, and after listening to a few tedious speeches he actually fell asleep for a few minutes. He did not miss what he was there for, however. At the very end of the meeting, Wilson proposed that a "Supreme Economic Council" should be appointed to supervise all the various Allied economic bodies, and this was accepted without any discussion.[70] Clemenceau agreed that the SEC should be put in charge of all blockade-related questions, including everything related to the issue of supplying food and raw materials to Germany.[71]

Amusingly enough, Cecil fell asleep at the SWC again two days later, probably due to the lingering effects of a cold. Like many others during the Peace Conference plagued by illness, Cecil succumbed to sickness at what might appear to be the worst moment on February 6, in the middle of the League Commission meetings. Luckily it was not the Spanish influenza, which plagued many in Paris and around the world that winter. Cecil blamed his sore throat and slight chill on smoking too much and on the greasy food and lack of exercise. Most of all he blamed it on the uncomfortable conditions in the League Commission rooms, with the Americans insisting on "vile heat" in overcrowded rooms.[72] He took no time off, still conducting regular press conferences and the daily League Commission meetings.

Wilson chided him about his slumber when they saw each other at the League Commission the next day. But he had not slept through the whole SWC meeting, instead finding himself drafted into another committee, divided between groups of military and economic experts working under Foch to figure out how to get the Germans to keep to their armistice terms.[73] In the ensuing meetings of this economic committee, with Cecil and John Maynard Keynes of the Treasury as the two British representatives, it became clear that the primary economic pressure that could be placed upon Germany would be to continue to refuse to send food. When they met with Foch, they found the general had already drawn up a report and simply wanted Cecil's signature. Cecil refused, instead agreeing with the British Director of Military Intelligence, General William Thwaites, that the Allies should immediately send final naval and military terms to the Germans rather than simply renewing a temporary armistice. Foch's unwillingness to have a real discussion spurred an outpouring of vitriol from Cecil, who was then frustrated that not all of what he said reached the Field Marshal because his interpreter "did not venture to repeat what I said."[74] It was the first of many intense and polarized debates over how to deal with the limitations of an armistice that was signed by the Germans in the desperate days of early November 1918, an agreement that now seemed to hinder the creation of a longer-term peace deal.

*

At the presentation of the League of Nations Covenant to the Plenary Session of the Peace Conference on February 14, Wilson read out the text of the Covenant verbatim, then followed with some comments. Cecil contributed a short speech, then Orlando spoke briefly with what Cecil judged as "an Italian excess of gesture which was almost comic," followed by the inevitably "dismal oration" of Bourgeois.[75] The Frenchman's prattling on in public about the amendments he had raised, and failed to pass through, the League Commission was highly irritating, but Cecil was satisfied that all recognized the Bourgeois proposals as a nonstarter. Rather than paying attention to that speech (or to the translation which outlasted the speech by a few minutes), Cecil penned a quick letter to his wife.[76] In the "great room very full—very 'stuffy' & very much gilded," Cecil sat between Joseph Ward of New Zealand and Robert Borden of Canada, and enjoyed himself. With "Woodrow on his right and AJB on his left," Clemenceau was "quite amusing to watch," gossiping and joking, pretending to sleep, "cursing the secretary." Cecil averted his eyes from men across the horseshoe table from him, the "hideous and inscrutable" Siamese and the "very dirty!" Romanians next to them. He pondered his "husky voice," explaining that he should probably "give up the vice" of smoking.[77] Cecil was obviously satisfied and in his own amused and self-mocking way wanted to share the moment with Nelly. He was one of many who found it comical when William Hughes demanded the opportunity to discuss the League plan in the Plenary. When Hughes stood up, Balfour supposedly muttered "que je lui déteste" to Clemenceau.[78] Rather than allowing a discussion as Hughes wanted, Clemenceau simply declared the sitting of the Plenary Session to be over. It was a signal success for Wilson and Cecil, perhaps the high point of the Conference for both of them. All of the world's most important leaders, from France, Britain, and the United States, had coalesced around their plan for a League.[79]

The League Commission meetings in February 1919 appear as a unique moment of interaction between the Great Powers and the rest during the Peace Conference. It was very unlike the SWC or the Council of Ten, the groups of Allied leaders that served through February as the Conference's executive bodies. It was also different from the various sub-committees concerned with territorial questions, reparations, and other war-ending issues, all dominated by bureaucrats and advisors of the Great Powers. These powers dominated in the League Commission, as Cecil and Wilson both emerged satisfied with the Covenant approved by the Plenary Session on February 14. However by including representatives from minor countries like Greece, Belgium, and Serbia, in even the most delicate and significant discussions, and in allowing them to speak on behalf of issues of racial and national equality, the Commission set precedent for the League that it created, one in which all member voices would be heard, whether convenient for the great powers or not.

How should Cecil's work during the first weeks of February 1919 be judged? Of course some considered the entire League idea ridiculous. Field-Marshal Sir Henry Wilson wrote in his diary after the Plenary Session that "one delegate after another talked nauseating nonsense about peace."[80] But such cynicism was in the minority. Clearly Cecil should be exonerated from any charges that he simply followed the US president in creating a Wilsonian League. Although Wilson got his way on many things he wanted, so did Cecil. Had Cecil gone rogue in the League Commission meetings, ignoring Lloyd George and creating a League that the prime minister could not fully support?[81] This judgment is too critical. Cecil did not keep anything from his largely uninterested prime minister.[82] Cecil recognized flaws existed, but the Covenant looked like a basic, solid, and broadly supported foundation upon which the League could evolve and succeed. At a basic level he felt satisfied the League would exist. Wasn't this why he had come to the Peace Conference in the first place?

And yet success did not bring an end to his duties, as Cecil stayed in Paris for most of the next four months. During that time, he worked even harder than he had through the middle of February, in the process finding new ways that the issue of economic warfare lingered into the peacemaking.

4

Feeding Germany: Mid-February through March

A month into the Conference, what surprised many of the delegates was that in some ways, the war was still being fought. The peacemakers in Paris understood that the Germans had laid down their arms. On a daily basis, they strolled past hundreds of surrendered German artillery pieces packing the vast Place de la Concorde, directly in front of the US delegation headquarters (see Figures 4.1 and 4.2). These guns littered Paris; according to Balfour's secretary Ian Malcolm, on two occasions during the Conference, Balfour went out for a stroll on dark evenings and "fell over enemy guns which were decorating the streets in unexpected places."[1] With this display of their surrendered, mute weaponry, all could palpably recognize that Germany lacked fundamental war resources and no longer remained capable of restarting the war on the battlefields. With only a little hyperbole, Herbert Hoover speculated that the remaining German army could not stop even two Allied divisions.[2]

Yet the end of shooting had certainly not brought peace to Europeans, many of whom continued fighting in national wars of imperial dismemberment into the 1920s.[3] And in fact the armistice had not even really meant the end of the Allied war against the Germans. The economic war, or "blockade," still operated. Allied proscriptions against German trade intensified the difficulties faced by the German people. At its peak in November 1918, the Allies' economic war rarely used force, other than the threat of Royal Navy action against contraband shipments. By the end of 1918, Allied economic controls choked German supply chains of food and fuel. They dominated world shipping through requisitioning and leases, and enforced negotiated rationing agreements with businessmen in the European neutral countries. It was a confusing yet multilayered and largely effective net that deprived German industries of export opportunities, ended German access to international finance, and even undermined the prospects of German businessmen operating in neutral countries around the world.

Figure 4.1 Photo of captured German artillery, Place de la Concorde, Paris, early 1919. Courtesy of the Department of Special Collections and Archives, Eastern Kentucky University, Walter J. Binder Papers.

Figure 4.2 Photo of captured German warplane, Place de la Concorde, Paris, early 1919. Courtesy of the Department of Special Collections and Archives, Eastern Kentucky University, Walter J. Binder Papers.

This global economic war succeeded in curtailing imports into Germany of all types of supplies including food, while funneling needed supplies to the Allied people and armies. Some contemporaries, and some historians since, considered the blockade "the most potent weapon in the Allied arsenal."[4] Although this economic war had a distinctly interallied character by 1918, the economic war had been almost entirely created by the British, in a process directed since 1915 by Lord Robert Cecil.[5]

Ending the economic war would mean allowing people in Germany to trade freely with anyone outside Germany. It would also mean dropping blacklist restrictions on those targeted as enemy traders in countries around the world. Many opposed both of these possibilities. Some aimed to maximize German resources available for any future reparations payments, and worried that open trade would cause German assets to flow abroad before the Allies could get their hands on them. Lloyd George and Clemenceau also fretted that a flood of cheap German exports might swamp their countries' own post-war industrial recoveries. In early 1919 neither the British nor the French were ready to withdraw wartime economic controls on their own citizens and businessmen. Why would they allow the German exporters to reenter trade-hungry global markets when their own businesses could not? Assuring the continued flow of vital supplies to their war-rationed citizens and bolstering the employment prospects of returning soldiers were top priorities for these Allied leaders.[6] The war had not bit as hard for most people in the United States, and perhaps unsurprisingly its delegates in Paris could more easily follow their ideological preference in calling for reinstatement of business as usual for European commerce.[7]

Finally, there was an angle on the blockade debate related directly to the prime aim of the Conference itself. Would giving up the blockade mean giving up the Allies ability to coerce Germany into accepting their peace terms? Other than a handful of French *revanchistes*, few had the stomach for a military occupation. As a result, economic controls were considered the primary way of ensuring that Germany would sign whatever treaty was presented to them. Cecil recognized that despite his own rejection of Foch's desired harsh peace, the Generalissimo was probably right that the continued economic war could ensure that the Allies got what they demanded from the Germans.

Yet the blockade had one signal thing against it, both then and since. It was blamed for the intensified starvation of central Europeans during the early months of 1919.[8] In 1918 few questioned the morality of tightening the blockade during the war, and even of stopping the flow of food to the German civilians including women and children. It was a total war and it needed to be won by any means available. Reports of bare store shelves and tightened rations in Germany always provoked gleeful triumphalism among Allied blockaders, and probably contributed to the overblown sense of British leaders like Hankey and Cecil that economic war-related social stresses in Germany proved pivotal to the ultimate Allied victory.[9] As a tactic that particularly targeted women, children, and other civilians, some had argued against the wartime blockade on humanitarian grounds. Herbert Hoover despised the Allied blockade when negotiating the passage of food shipments to occupied Belgium. But after the United States entered the war in April 1917, even Hoover argued that the United States must work with their Allies to reinforce the blockade.[10]

However, it was one thing to use control of food as a weapon during war, and something far different to use it when the battlefields were quiet. Not only did it seem more cruel during peace, but the political ramifications might be earthshattering. Rumors of revolution in Berlin percolated through the press accounts in Paris. Would starvation lead to capitulation, or would it drive the German people into the hands of the Bolsheviks?

Charged with ending the starvation of the people of Central Europe, the new Supreme Economic Council (SEC) first met on February 17. Excited to be among its members, Cecil energetically took up the difficult task of dismantling the Allied economic controls that he had so industriously crafted over the previous four years.

In the Supreme Economic Council

Immediately after the Plenary Session approved the League Covenant on February 14, Woodrow Wilson jumped on a train to Brest, then clambered aboard the waiting USS *George Washington* and steamed off to the United States. Since January he had planned to make this journey back to lobby Congress before their session ended and also to give speeches selling the public on the League. The most optimistic hoped that Wilson would persuade the US public to support an unadulterated version of the Covenant, and then the Conference could move forward. With the president away from Paris, the League Commission had to await news from across the Atlantic.

Cecil had no particular desire to stay in France and was clearly sick of being away from home. He missed his wife and his seat in Parliament, and was only slightly able to alleviate his pining for both with a brief trip back to England from February 18 to 24. At this point it seemed unlikely to Cecil that he would only return to Britain on two brief occasions between February and June.

He immediately made his return apparent in the House of Commons, where the House gave him a "cordial welcome" on Wednesday February 19.[11] In his characteristic fashion, he immediately dove into an arcane debate over revising Commons procedures for Standing Committees and Parliamentary oversight of government ministries. Quibbles that Cecil made over the wording of the proposal were accepted by Andrew Bonar Law, the leader of the Conservative Party, with the House of Commons then agreeing to the amended proposal.

He also read the newspapers. British people were not merely reveling in their victory over the Germans. The misery of war had led many people, from all classes, to gain a new (or renewed) sense of grievance about their own society. Coal miner union leader Robert Smillie threatened to utilize his leverage over the country's primary energy source to demand potentially transformative concessions from pit owners. He wanted not simply better pay, but rather a new management model to give the miners some input into the "commercial side of the thing."

Cecil responded in a lengthy letter printed in the *Times* on February 24, comparing this desire of workers to gain some responsibility for the overall state of their industries to their desire to be consulted (through elections) about the state of their governments. Wage earners needed their industries to succeed even more than the owners or managers, Cecil explained, and thus working men deserved "some share in the management of those matters which are of even greater importance to labour than to capital."[12] This call for "copartnership" had been one of the central, yet characteristically quixotic, platforms of Cecil's parliamentary campaign in December, when he claimed it was the "remedy" to stave off class warfare. The idea had been bandied about mostly within Labour Party circles since before the war, and the Board of Trade issued official reports on copartnership both before and after the war. It was a vague term best identified with profit-sharing, where employees would gain bonuses somehow commensurate to their contribution to the success of the business. It could include the "Whitley Councils" idea developed by a 1916 Commons select committee to create employer-worker committees at the factory, company, and industry levels. According to the Board of Trade, companies employing nearly a quarter-million workers had developed some type of copartnership by 1919, mostly annual cash bonus schemes. In February 1919, the Labour Co-partnership Association demanded that workers gain some control over businesses either as shareholders or as members of management committees. According to the Board of Trade, municipal gas companies had long run copartnership committees that succeeded in "smoothing away friction which may arise between individual workmen and the management," while also administering employee insurance schemes. In some cases employees were even elected to boards of directors.[13] This British movement was part of a post-war European-wide drive toward such corporatist structures.[14] In February, Cecil's calls for copartnership were reinforced by his weeks in Paris where the alternative to such concessions to the workers seemed obvious, namely the revolution and apparent disintegration of society in Russia and central Europe.

While in London, Cecil also took to the British press to advocate for the League. With a Reuters interviewer on February 22, he aggressively repudiated claims that the League of Nations was "academic" rather than "practical." Although it "would be quite foolish to suggest that the mere signing of a League of Nations Covenant will then and there produce a millennium, it may, and, if given a fair chance, certainly will, produce a better international atmosphere." According to Cecil, it provided a new way to settle international disputes, and it would be far from toothless: its decisions "will be enforced by the whole economic and military power of each of the nations of the League. Economic sanctions will be put into force automatically if any nation attempts sudden war." Cecil concluded that the critics lacked a plan of their own. "Are they content to go on with the pre-war system? What safeguards against future war do they suggest? Or are they content to run the risk of a renewal of a world war under still more terrible conditions than those we know, involving beyond question the destruction of the whole fabric of European civilization?"[15] Although Reuters was a British news service, stories based on this interview ran in important US papers such as the *Baltimore Sun*.[16]

One wonders whether it felt odd to Cecil to engage in such definitively domestic political issues on this quick return to Britain. His activity was noticed by Lloyd George, who in conversation with Lord Riddell noted how Cecil's position had risen during the war, and suggested that like all Cecils, Lord Robert was ambitious for power.[17] For Cecil the trip was only an interlude. Excited about his appointment to the SEC, Cecil quickly returned to Paris for the second SEC meeting on February 25.

Some have gone so far as to suggest that the SEC was make-work that aimed to shunt potential critics like Cecil and Keynes into subservient roles.[18] However, Cecil could not resist the call for his service in the SEC because he, and many others in Paris, saw it as a forum of potentially great power. "My new work looks as if it will be a very big thing," he opined excitedly to his wife; "It is all about commerce of which I know little and finance of which I know nothing."[19]

Sarcasm marked many of Cecil's letters to his wife (as did her responses to him). He knew that many members of each of the Allied delegations respected his wartime experiences in coordinating Allied transportation, finance, and food. Cecil was appointed to the SEC not to sideline him, but rather because he understood Europe's war economy.

Cecil had been a critical creator of much interallied cooperation in the blockade, most of which was seen as conspicuously successful. He had chaired the War Trade Advisory Committee in late 1915 and 1916, and the Allied (or Inter-Allied) Maritime Transport Council since its creation in the spring of 1918. He knew how to run a meeting, how to propel a committee through his agenda, and how to get decisions implemented. And he knew how to build a working organization on the fly. In creating and developing the Ministry of Blockade during the war, Cecil rallied a skilled staff to support his goals. The Ministry of Blockade took command of a disparate group of committees and departments that themselves had been created mostly on an ad hoc basis during the first years of the war.[20] It was exactly this type of organization that the disorganized Allies, mired in "pure administrative muddle," needed in February 1919.[21]

In an extremely broad remit, the SEC was tasked with looking into all "transitory" economic issues during the period of reconstruction, including everything that was needed to economically restore countries (allied, neutral, and enemy) that suffered during the war. At the first meeting on February 17, the SEC took under its wing a variety of existing groups, including the AMTC, the Inter-Allied Food Council, the Supreme Council of Supply and Relief, and the Superior Blockade Council. In its meeting of February 25, all of the Council's work was subdivided among Finance, Blockade, Raw Materials, Shipping, Food, and Transport "sections."

Although Belgium and the British Dominions asked for representation on the SEC, the Council successfully resisted these entreaties, and thus mirrored the increasing focus of the higher SWC upon the representatives of the Big Four: Britain, France, the United States, and Italy. Each of these allies had their own desires, and prioritizing between these differing goals was a juggling act. The Italian delegates, for instance, began to talk at the second meeting about the tremendous problems their country was having in feeding itself and in obtaining enough coal. Silvio Crespi, the Italian food minister, explained how food supplies arriving from abroad were insufficient to meet demands, both due to lack of funds and lack of shipping. With such shortages for their own population, how could Italy be expected to act as a conduit of food into the undoubtedly starving cities of the former Austrian empire?[22] The Italian need for shipping, food, and

84 *After the Great War*

coal became a staple agenda item in SEC meetings throughout the spring. The French delegation piggybacked on Italian complaints by describing the similar (if lesser) problems faced by France. Cecil's unhappiness about the French League of Nations delegation undoubtedly carried over into his unhappiness with the stance that France took in the SEC, which he considered often petty and vindictive toward Germany.

US policymaking also appeared inconsistent and amateurish. The US delegates were far from united in their views, and at times argued openly with one another (see Figure 4.3). Cecil found he could benefit from this organizational weakness of the US delegation. All five US delegates "are apparently of equal authority, and rather jealous of one another."[23] Hoover was pushy and brusque, and clearly had pretentions of being in charge. Seeing it as the logical extension of his wartime

Figure 4.3 Autographed photo of economics and trade advisors from the US delegation posing with Marshal Foch. Seated from left are Herbert Hoover, General Tasker Bliss, Foch, Bernard Baruch, and Henry M. Robinson. In back row, Thomas W. Lamont, Whitney Shepardson Norman Davis, Colonel Edward House, Gordon Auchincloss, Vance McCormick. Notably, Hoover is sitting to the side with his arms crossed. Courtesy of the Department of Rare Books and Special Collections, Princeton University Library, Bernard M. Baruch Papers, Box 699.

focus on humanitarian relief for Belgium, Hoover kept beating the drum for the need to send food to central and eastern Europe. As the head of American Relief Administration (ARA), he had requisitioned a staff of Army officers who since December 1918 had begun setting up relief offices across Europe.[24] As a result of the high public profile these efforts gave him, one biographer has suggested that Hoover was the third most important US delegate in Paris, after only House and Wilson himself.[25] House was among many who thought that Hoover might be preparing to run for president on the Democratic ticket in the next election. Before and throughout the Conference, Hoover fixated on the need to maintain American control of the relief effort. To Hoover, the United States was supplying all the relief and thus deserved all the credit, but also he believed the United States should dominate because it was "the most disinterested nation" and thus likely to devise the fairest way of reconstructing Europe.[26]

However Hoover's wartime efforts had not won him subservience from his American colleagues. Vance McCormick for one disliked Hoover's pretentions of being in command.[27] McCormick, in charge of the War Trade Board since 1917, had been a leader of the US economic warfare effort. He and Cecil got on well with one another, having first met when McCormick came to London in November 1917 along with Colonel House to coordinate Allied warfare. Cecil had McCormick over to his home for Sunday lunch, and by McCormick's second week in London the two were trading confidences about their governments' desires for how shipping tonnage could be allocated in different ways.[28]

Bernard Baruch also questioned Hoover's control. Baruch had led the War Industries Board in the United States over the final year of the war, and became US representative on the Raw Materials Section of the SEC. Along with Norman Davis, Baruch and McCormick also served on the Reparations Commission, which began meeting in early February. In both roles, an understanding of the financial and commercial state of all European states would be pivotal.

Compared to the fractious Americans, the British in the SEC operated in lock step behind their chief, Lord Robert Cecil. Cecil missed only one of the twenty-two meetings of the SEC that took place through June 16, and was acknowledged by members of the British Cabinet as the chief of the British team at the SEC.[29] At many meetings, Britain was represented by Cecil and only one or two other men, often Mitchell-Thomson or Keynes. Cecil had mixed feelings about his fellow British delegates. He thought highly of Keynes, but had always disliked working with the obstructionist Llewellyn Smith of the Board of Trade, a doctrinaire laissez-faire advocate who had been a thorn in Cecil's side when he was Minister of Blockade. But whoever turned up for the British had no doubt that they were

Cecil's underlings, and this authority structure was recognized by the rest of the British government as well. When the Treasury sent a letter nominating Keynes as their representative on the SEC, they addressed it to Cecil.[30]

In a reprise of problems he faced when creating the League, Cecil's work in the SEC triggered fresh disputes with the leaders of the British Dominions, all of whom Cecil looked down upon and a few of whom Cecil despised. Again the Dominions wanted representation, but their urge to expand the size of the SEC went against Cecil's sense that the best way to get things done in any situation was through small committees of committed and capable individuals, rather than large committees where too many constituencies were represented. The SEC, like the Conference as a whole, worked best as a meeting of the Big Four powers, and no one else. Their demands for seats on the SEC riled up Cecil, who in his diary exploded with frustration against the idea "that on to every body of importance one or more of these very second-rate individuals is to be put, but I do not know that I should feel so bitterly about it if it was not for the ineffable Hughes."[31] Just a month into the Conference, Cecil truly despised "that shrimp" Hughes.[32] He was not alone; Woodrow Wilson considered him a "pestiferous varmint."[33] Yet on this issue Cecil got his way, persuading the BED meeting on February 27 that he should be the chair (with his wartime collaborator Salter the secretary) of the "British Empire Economic Committee," which would advise the British delegates at the SEC.[34] In effect, Cecil was charged by the BED with advising himself, and the Dominions accepted that the SEC would remain a preserve solely of the Big Four.

Crafting Compromises

In the months between the signing of the armistice and the creation of the SEC, questions of what to do about the Allied economic war plagued the Peace Conference. The end of war meant the end of unity bought by shared sacrifice in blood and treasure. Some of the mechanisms and organizations that had united the Allied economies had been consciously dismantled in a rush at the end of the war. US authorities claimed to want to restart normal trade, but Wilson and Hoover also wanted the United States to control any organizations aiming to rehabilitate and feed Europe. Some Americans like Hoover felt certain that they could best do such work, as they lacked the long term animosities that plagued the European states. Hoover also wanted the United States to receive what he saw as proper credit for its beneficence.[35] Immediately upon reaching Europe in December 1918, Woodrow Wilson demanded that Hoover be named as the Director of Relief and Rehabilitation. With breathtaking arrogance, Hoover voiced doubts that his new appointment really mattered, suggesting that his continuing position as United States Food Administrator constituted the most effective aspect of his power.[36] To Hoover, the US role as the primary food supplier empowered him to run the European relief effort. US leaders swaggered with full knowledge of their country's financial and industrial dominance.

This ignored other types of power and influence held by the Allies. The continued blockading operations of British cruisers in the North Sea and administrators in London, and French railwaymen and soldiers who controlled the frontiers, gave the European states, not America, control of access to German territory. Unified British and French control of the bulk of the world's shipping space, both under their own flags and through leases of neutral ships, gave them tremendous power over supplying Europe throughout 1918, and this coordination proved critical to the Allied victory in the war.[37] US finance loomed large, but France and Britain also held assets critical to the resumption of European trade, and none had effective leverage to force the other two into any specific blockade policy during the first few months of the Conference.

Herbert Hoover, Vance McCormick, and other US delegates continually claimed that they were the most humanitarian-minded of the Allies, looking solely to feed starving people throughout Europe. They saw this as proven in their call for the Allies to immediately drop their blockade on Germany. This would allow Germany to spend its gold reserves on food imports.[38] These demands faced significant opposition from the British, French, and other Allies who looked to preserve German gold for eventual reparations.

Hoover was one of many who claimed that ending the blockade and restarting free trade was the cure for European economic woes. Germany should be allowed to spend its resources to feed itself. Yet his claims of ideological purity rang false to others. Starting in December 1918, British, French, and Italian food administrators all proclaimed their unhappiness about Hoover's insistence on upholding fixed-price contracts negotiated early in 1918 for purchases of grain, pork, and dairy products from the United States. Commodity prices were plummeting in southern hemisphere markets like Argentina and Australia; shouldn't the Allies be allowed to purchase this cheaper food instead? Hoover remained an Iowan at heart, and refused to countenance the repudiation of contracts, worried for the American farmers who had increased their production based on those prices. If someone must feel financial pain, Hoover would make certain that it was not American farmers or packers.[39] According to the very cynical Keynes, "when Mr. Hoover sleeps at night visions of pigs float across his bedclothes and he frankly admits that all hazards the nightmare must be dissipated."[40] Even Hoover realized that his own intransigence favoring free trade created a "shrill note (that) ran through all of our negotiations over organization and removal of the blockade."[41]

Other allies argued that the greater problem was transport. In the eyes of the French, the Germans had pledged to hand over their entire merchant marine, with a total carrying capacity of slightly over two million tons, at the Agreement of Trier on January 17, 1919.[42] All the Allies had coveted German ships throughout the war as replacements for their own ships sunk by U-boats. Both France and Italy particularly lusted after these ships, seeing them both as the solution to their dilemmas of how to carry food supplies into their own countries and also as initial, tangible pieces of the spoils of victory.

The German government, however, faced a revolutionary situation at home and needed to both prove itself and feed its people.[43] They could point to the negotiations leading up to the November 11 armistice signing, when German negotiator Matthias Erzberger extracted a last-minute promise that the Entente would supply Germany with food until the creation of a real treaty.[44] Despite the earlier agreements, the fact that many of their merchant ships still floated in German harbors meant that the future of these ships remained negotiable. With the Allies severely restricting the flow of money and goods in and out of Germany, these docked and ready ships were all the leverage Germany held to ensure that the Allies would follow through on the terms of the armistice to supply needed food to the war-deprived German people.

In a memorandum for the BED on March 2, Cecil outlined both the fundamental economic problems facing Europe and his proposed solutions. Cecil recognized that the political results of this humanitarian crisis could be terrible. Like many others, Cecil had worried much about the possible spread of mysterious, nefarious Bolshevism from Russia westward. He felt certain that it was the economic calamities of wartime Russia had created a perfect revolutionary situation in 1917. "Of such material are revolutions made, and if further revolutions take place anarchy and complete economic destruction must almost inevitably ensue. If such a catastrophe took place in Central Europe it is at least doubtful whether the political institutions of any of the European countries would be strong enough to resist this new strain put upon them."[45] Failure of the Allies to help would turn the idle and suffering Germans into riotous mobs. He suggested that the natural flows of the European economy would be partially solved by the United States offering credits to Italy and France, whose resulting purchases of Central European goods could get things moving again. In return, the French would allow the raising of the blockade. Cecil now suggested a new variable, that ending the blockade would be accompanied by a threat to reinstate it if needed. This threat alone should force the reeling Germans' compliance with any eventual peace terms, enabling the Allies to influence German policy as completely, yet less painfully, than if they maintained the blockade. This power of threatening collective economic warfare was also baked into the League's draft Covenant, so reshaping the wartime blockade might even help to get the League off the ground.

The armistice signed on November 11, 1918, included the caveat that it was would need to be renewed regularly until the signature of a peace agreement. Renewal negotiations had occurred a few times since, and were coming again in early March. Reports issued from the Blockade, Food, Finance, and Shipping sections of the SEC on March 1 to brief the Allied delegation that traveled to meet the Germans at Spa, where the Germans had their headquarters in 1918 and where the initial armistice had been signed.

Surely there was some bargain that could be arrived at, as each side wanted what the other had. Yet the armistice renewal talks, beginning the evening of March 3, broke down within twenty-four hours. On the train back to Paris, Keynes wrote a lengthy report describing the impasse. The German government felt unable to give up its ships, fearing an outcry from the German people unless the Allies promised far more food than the mere 270,000 tons of food already agreed to. The Allied negotiators insisted, however, that Germany had already signed an agreement that the ships would be handed over, and that without this happening first, not even the 270,000 promised tons of food would be sent.[46] Both sides pointed to the failure of the other to follow through on stipulations in the initial armistice; the allies that they would provision Germany, the Germans that they would hand over their merchant shipping.

Like Keynes, Cecil felt despondent about the failure at Spa. On March 6 he wrote to his wife that he was "a good deal frightened at the conditions in Europe— or should be frightened except that the war has left me without any power of feeling emotion."[47] The next day he was "quite in a fuss! I've been blowing up my secretaries—& indeed everyone else—probably the effect of fatigue & the annoyance of seeing the whole of Europe drifting to Revolution for want of food while the folly & perversity of war prevents one from supplying."[48] Cecil called together a special meeting of the SEC on March 7, and led the discussion about three competing resolutions aiming to supply Germany with food until the next harvest.[49]

Hoover's plan noted that Germany needed about 300,000 tons of food per month, the transport of which (considering turnaround times in harbor and return journeys to grain suppliers across the Atlantic) would require the use of perhaps 800,000 tons of German shipping, about 1/3 of their total tonnage in harbor. Germany would be assured that if they handed over all their ships, at least a third would be assigned to the transport of food until the fall harvest. The US plan further suggested that Germany would be encouraged to trade commodities and set up credits with neutral countries to pay for this food. In contrast, the blunt French resolution presented by Étienne Clémentel demanded more from the Germans than it promised. If Germany complied with the November 11 armistice terms and handed over all of its ships, the Allies would guarantee the shipment of only the 270,000 tons of food they already agreed to send (much of which was warehoused in Rotterdam, ready for shipment to Germany). France would give no assurances of future supplies. Likewise the French plan did not mention any possibility of lifting the blockade and allowing the restart of free trade.

Cecil's plan fell between these two extremes. He had been involved in negotiations with neutral states to gain control of interned German ships throughout the war, and as the leader of the AMTC during the war he led the Allied efforts to rationally apportion increasingly limited cargo space and commodity flows between the Allies and the rest of the world. Certainly the continued lack of shipping was widely acknowledged; Vance McCormick felt the shortage of shipping made it feel like "we are at war again," and Bernard Baruch wrote exasperatedly in his diary that "it appears to me that the whole world is mad on the subject of shipping."[50] Cecil recognized more than most the extreme difficulties and complexities of shipping control. But he also believed for economic, political, and humanitarian reasons in the absolute necessity of feeding Germany. Holding access to food over the heads of the desperate German people, starving and humiliating the enemy, would not make for a stable peace. Following on the tentative suggestions of Friedrich von Braun, the chief German negotiator at Spa, Cecil envisioned a series of good-will gestures from both sides. If Germany simply sent twenty ships to the Allies, the Allies would dispatch all the food they were holding in storage in Rotterdam when the ships left German harbors. They would send the remainder of the 270,000 tons as soon as the Germans delivered 100 ships. As long as all the German ships left German harbors within a month, the British plan further pledged a very generous 400,000 tons of food per month until the autumn harvest, and would put the issue of payment off for future negotiations.

At the ensuing, tempestuous meeting of the SWC, the intransigent French stance was immediately undermined by Lloyd George's dramatic reading of distressing reports about the starvation of German children. According to Lloyd George, the commander of British soldiers occupying the Rhineland had sent a telegram stating that his soldiers, appalled by the suffering of the German children, were giving their own food rations to the children.[51] Although the SEC had decided the day before that all three proposals to feed Germany would be presented, Cecil just pitched his own.[52] He straightforwardly insisted that measures to reopen food trade with Germany must be reciprocal and immediate: "The Germans must promise to deliver the ships. The Allies must promise to start delivering the food as soon as Germany started releasing the ships. The Germans must be allowed to pay in gold. The blockade must be lifted to the extent of allowing them to start exporting some goods and buying food from neutrals."[53] The fear of getting hit by a renewed blockade would be even greater for an already revictualing Germany than for a starving and hopeless one.

Clémentel responded that the Germans were not in as desperate straits as the British thought, and that they should give the Germans no more than what was pledged in the November 11 armistice.[54] But Lloyd George spent much of the rest of the meeting criticizing the French stance and restating fears that starving Germans would become Bolshevik. At his most caustic, Lloyd George suggested that France's finance minister Louis-Lucien Klotz was particularly greedy for heavy reparations because he was Jewish.[55]

Lloyd George's strident and offensive line (which in Cecil's words "was very entertaining, but not I think very judicious") enabled Cecil to play the conciliator.[56] The Allies agreed that Germany should first pay for food imports with any funds they received from hiring out their ships over the next few months, with any money they made exporting commodities, and by utilizing credits they might find from neutral sources abroad. The issue of the use of German gold was elided by Cecil's rewording of the SEC proposal to state that gold reserves in Germany could be utilized as collateral for loans to purchase food, rather than shipped in outright exchange for food. Clemenceau and Loucheur gave way and agreed that this would adequately safeguard the Allies claims on German bullion. Against Hoover and the United States, Cecil parried away the request that Germany be allowed to continue to hold one-third of its merchant ships so the new republic could restart ordinary trade.[57] The SWC concluded the day by approving instructions to the Allied armistice negotiators scheduled to resume talks in Brussels with the Germans, now led by the banker and lawyer Carl Melchior. As soon as Germany handed over to unified Allied control its merchant fleet, whose cargo space was necessary "to assure the provisioning of Germany and the rest of Europe," the Allies would be willing "on grounds of humanity" to immediately release the 270,000 tons of food stockpiled in Rotterdam, with pledges for another 300,000 tons of grains and 70,000 tons of fats each month until the start of September.

The terms seemed likely to meet quick German approval, as indeed they were after Keynes presented them in Brussels on March 13–14.[58] Cecil was sure they were needed, reasonable and just. He did not want to bend too far to German demands, and had some worries that the British negotiators (the First Sea Lord Admiral Wemyss, the Shipping Contoller Sir Joseph Maclay, and Keynes), pitied the starving Germans too much and might agree to give them food before they truly committed to send their ships to the Allies.[59] Cecil recognized the justice in French demands for real capitulation from the Germans.[60] The agreement reached at Brussels was far from an Anglo-American plan forced upon the French, let alone an unalloyed victory for Hoover, but rather a compromise between competing US and French plans.[61] Cecil's mediation of this dispute over supplying Germany with food illustrates well his moderation in the peace talks, spanning the gap between appeasement and revanchism.

It had been a hard week. Interallied work was always slow, Cecil wrote to his wife, but "the machinery seems to be moving a little."[62] Perhaps Germany would be rescued from the brink, giving its people some confidence in their government and persuading businessmen to put people back to work. Immediately after the Brussels agreement on March 14, the Germans released their merchant ships, were given food in return, accepted the Allies valuation of that food, and agreed to attempt to boost their coal production for export.[63] Significant supplies immediately began to flow from Rotterdam up the Rhine. The starvation of Central Europe was significantly alleviated by this agreement. The SEC had proven its worth by capturing the attention of Wilson, Clemenceau, and Lloyd George, and creating a scheme that presented destitute Germany with critical supplies.

Starting to Dismantle the Economic War

In the SEC, negotiations over lifting the blockade were beset by an extraordinary array of competing economic interests, of inter-Allied power plays, of overextended egos and personal vendettas. Americans wanted to bring down the blockade, but British leaders were uncertain, and the French were completely opposed. Because the blockade overlapped with the primary question troubling inter-Allied relations, namely the question of financial flows, loans and gold moving both between the Allies and from the Germans, an agreement to end the blockade remained impossible throughout March.

The meetings of the SEC could be brutal. One on March 10 consisted of a three hour argument between Cecil and Clémentel, who disagreed over how to ensure supplies for Italy and France and how to implement the SWC instructions to get 370,000 tons of food monthly to Germany. But as March progressed, there was significant progress on both feeding Germany and alleviating the blockade. After a flurry of reports issued from its Finance, Blockade, Food and Shipping sections, the SEC on March 24 finally persuaded the French delegates to lift many blockade restrictions, and Clémentel agreed to a list of commodities that Germany could export to pay for food.[64] At the same meeting, Cecil demanded that Italy drop its blockade restrictions on trade in the Adriatic to comply with the SWC resolution passed a few weeks earlier. Four days later, Cecil announced that Italy had now lifted its blockade in the Adriatic, and the Council of Foreign Ministers responded by supporting SEC requests to completely lift the blockades of Austria, Estonia, and Poland.[65]

Cecil found himself frustrated with the extremity of opinions among both those who wanted to lift the blockade and those who wanted to keep it. In an SEC meeting, Cecil sharply derided Mitchell-Thomson's concerns that the relaxation of the blockade on Poland and Estonia was premature.[66] But like other British delegates, Cecil was more irritated with his US colleagues who wanted to drop all blockades immediately. Hoover and McCormick consistently pushed for an end of interallied controls on European trade during the meetings of the Blockade Committee of the SEC. They believed that restarting free trade would prove the goodwill of the Allies toward their former foes, and thus solve both economic and political problems besetting the new central European states. Cecil lamented the reports of German suffering, but believed that feeding the Germans was not synonymous with ending the blockade. The Brussels agreements meant the Germans would be fed, in a discrete and specific trade agreement accomplished without "lifting the blockade" or dismantling interallied controls. Cecil respected the rights of the Allies to demand concessions from Germany in return for the final termination of the economic war. "The blockade cannot be completely raised until Germany has been disarmed."[67] The French and British, not the United States, had faced the brunt of the destructive power of the war, and they deserved some recompense for destruction and suffering.

Cecil fit into that broad swath of conference delegates from a variety of countries who agreed that the fundamental problem of the Conference was disagreement between the United States and France. It was not just French obstreperousness but also the myopia of the Americans that contributed to the divide. During one private dinner, he doubted Hoover's claim that the French were obstructing relief supplies from flowing across their borders to Germany and Austria simply "to put pressure upon the Americans to make them pay a larger share of the war."[68] He resented Hoover's claim that the continued blockade simply followed through on the 1916 Paris Resolutions, when Britain and France had suggested continuing the economic war even after the war ended.[69] Obviously, to Cecil, the French were far more motivated in their reluctance to breach the blockade by their hatred of the Germans than by any desire to somehow stick it to the United States. And furthermore, Cecil believed that everyone, not just the French, recognized the importance of US money for any European revival. It was the US delegates who must push themselves, and their nation, to understand and accept the critical role of New York bankers and Washington politicians in the future of Europe. For the global economy to succeed, communication and consensus building between the Allies would have to be maintained not just politically but also economically. To feed Europe and to restart the continent's normal economy, they must use the available German ships wisely, and must prioritize food purchases over any other uses of available German funds and credits, including saving money to pay reparations or indemnities to the Allies. Coal must be moved to regions in Italy that desperately needed it, using British ships and captured German rolling stock. These were all both political and economic issues, not simply solvable by a technical committee, as Pichon seemed to hope for, but rather with the support of political authorities in the Council of Ten.

From all he was learning in the SEC about the continuing difficulties of allocating ships, finding food, and getting finance even for absolutely necessary food supplies, Cecil felt certain of the need to continue for at least a few more months the war-style interallied central controls of shipping, blockade and trade restrictions, and finance. Limiting and guiding access to commodities and money went fundamentally against the free trade principles that Cecil held dear, and unlike Clémentel he did not believe that the allied joint controls should be made permanent, but he knew they were necessary in the crisis atmosphere of the post-war world.[70] Cecil was anything but an instinctive centralizer, but he was sure that the circumstances warranted it. For him the economy of Europe was the most important thing that had to be settled. Old rules no longer applied, as he explained to the BED: "owing to the necessities of war we had told our Allies and the Neutrals that we would not be bound by 'most-favoured-nation' Treaties." The present economic chaos must be addressed. There needed to be some set of rules to make up for what had been destroyed. "Most of the territorial questions were relatively unimportant, but these economic matters were vital. Ruin was impending on the whole world, and we must avert it." The economic questions "were vital to the peace of the world."[71]

Restarting free trade was not just popular among economic ideologues from the United States, but also among some of his British comrades. The British Shipping Controller J. A. Salter suggested that the rapid dropping of shipping controls might shock the European economy back into working order. Cecil was doubtful. "It might be right, on general principles," Cecil thought, "but I am afraid it will get us into rather a hole in providing for the necessary European services during the next few months."[72]

For Cecil, a man notorious for his supposed penchant for unrealistic idealism, favoring interallied economic controls exemplified how in 1919, necessity trumped ideology. Centralizing the various tools of blockade and economic control made more sense than destroying them. At the end of March, he created a Shipping Section for the SEC simply by reconvening the AMTC. He then held subcommittee meetings with Jean Monnet, Bernardo Attolico, and Henry Robinson (of the United States) to ensure that there would be enough tonnage for relief shipments from the United States in April. Cecil and his colleagues were finding the SEC useful in coordinating various committees and interallied organizations behind an effort to feed Europe. Similar to his work directing the evolving organs of the British economic war in 1916 as the new Minister of Blockade, Cecil found himself at the helm of the SEC in March 1919 pulling together disparate ad hoc organizations. But now these aimed to enhance German economic recovery and stabilize German society, rather than to destroy German wealth and destabilize order in the Reich.

Continuing Work on the League

Cecil's heavy work on famine relief and the blockade did not mean ignoring the League. In a variety of meetings between late February and late March, he helped to craft the new organization. On February 16, the United States agreed to having the League in Switzerland and to naming Maurice Hankey as its Secretary General. Hankey himself, however, hedged when Cecil asked him about his interest in the job, backing away on the morning of February 27 only to consider it again during a meeting with Cecil that evening. Throughout March, Cecil remained hopeful that Hankey, Britain's great wartime organizer, would not be able to resist the siren song of piecing together and leading what might become a vital global organization.

Over the month that Wilson was away from Paris, the president's absence fed the perception that Cecil was the one man remaining whose attention remained steadfastly on the interests of the League. He was constantly drawn into Allied discussions and negotiations related to the League. In a speech on the League at the Cercle Volney, he extolled the importance of continued alliances and internationalism even as he voiced his admiration for Clemenceau and for the historical importance of France.[73] When Marshal Foch pushed for a draft treaty stating that the League would supervise its military clauses, Cecil immediately assailed this suggestion as envisioning a League that would only welcome the wartime allies as members.[74] His memo to the chief British negotiator, the Director of Military Intelligence General William Thwaites, led to the rejection of the Foch plan. On March 10 the Japanese minister complained to Cecil that the League Covenant was too extreme. Cecil argued that it balanced perfectly between those in the United States who would not allow for more integration, and those in smaller countries who wished for more.[75] He also focused on the League in various dealings with the representatives of neutral powers. The *Times* described his discussions with various Swiss officials in late February to define their neutrality in a way that would allow Switzerland to join in League-led economic boycotts.[76] Cecil then on March 21 and 22 gathered a broader group representing the world's wartime neutral countries, assuring them that they would have significant roles in the League.[77] The League must develop in a way that it was open not only to the neutrals, but also eventually to Germany. A "League of Victors" must be avoided.

Throughout the weeks that Wilson was away, Cecil was left in a quandary. Should his behind the scenes efforts simply support the Covenant text passed by the Plenary Conference on February 14? It was common knowledge that Republican members of the Senate worried about the League's impact on the Monroe Doctrine, the core US policy toward Latin America over the previous century. Others questioned whether the US Constitution would allow the United States to adhere to a League Covenant. Should he press his fellow Commission members to accept that the political forces in their most critical member meant the draft Covenant must be slightly revised? Henry Cabot Lodge, the longtime Republican leader in the Senate, dramatically exposed this rift in American politics during a midnight session of the Senate bridging March 3–4. There he issued a resolution that demanded changes to the Covenant which was signed by enough supporters that the Treaty's eventual passage seemed unlikely.[78] When news of this "Round Robin" resolution reached Paris, Wilson's failure to manage the US political scene abruptly became apparent. A man with years of experience working in the British Embassy in Washington, Eustace Percy advised Cecil to publically declare that he would support any recommendations desired by Lodge.[79] On the other hand, William Wiseman, a great friend of Colonel House and leader of wartime British intelligence services in New York, suggested that Wilson should be left to manage US public opinion without Cecil's intervention.[80] Cecil was left without the advice of his fellow British delegate on the League Commission. General Smuts was laid up in London due to a serious bout of influenza and did not return to Paris until March 23.[81] But Cecil was already accustomed to deciding League business without input from the South African.

Cecil initially decided to support a no-revision stance. He explained to Percy that politicians on both the Left and Right on both sides of the Atlantic were dissatisfied with parts of the Treaty, and that this probably meant that "no American Senate, however cantankerous, will venture to reject" the Covenant.[82] A few days later, he told the US and British press corps that the League Covenant had flaws, but that more deliberation could lead to "any great improvement," and that the United States must understand that no nation would be forced to do anything against its will by the League. Each permanent member of the League Executive (including the United States) would have veto power over League actions.[83]

But when news came back from the United States about the depth of opposition to Wilson's plan, Cecil quickly recognized that the Covenant must be revised. When Wilson returned to Paris in mid-March, he returned with a snippy edge. The president believed that Colonel House had acted behind his back in working with Balfour to speed up the negotiations while he was away. Wilson never regained trust in this advisor who for years had been his most important diplomatic intermediary with the Allies.[84] He was also unhappy because his trip home appeared a failure. When they met for dinner on his return to Paris, Cecil was startled by Wilson's caustic rejection of any compromise with Senator Lodge's "reservations" to the Covenant. But while driving back to the Majestic, Colonel House privately assured Cecil that Wilson, in the end, would accept some concessions to the Republicans.[85] Angrily, Wilson even bandied about the idea that an eventual treaty would not actually need Senate approval, before succumbing to reality and reluctantly reopening negotiations in the League Commission.

This unfortunately rare occasion of Wilson bending toward a compromise with his US critics was fostered in part by the diligent support and guidance of Cecil within the League Commission. Wilson had accepted the need to create a new article for the Covenant that would guarantee the League's respect for "regional understandings like the Monroe doctrine." Everyone on the League Commission knew Wilson needed this amendment desperately to assure the Senate's support, making him vulnerable to the desires of other Allied and neutral leaders for some sort of quid pro quo.

Cecil was wary of the vagueness of a Monroe Doctrine amendment.[86] But in the League Commission, the British delegation, and Cecil in particular, clicked into gear to support Wilson's meandering lead, even while focusing on ways that revisions could benefit British interests. If anything, Cecil found himself more important to Wilson than before. Wilson asked Cecil rather than House to repudiate the arguments of Pichon and the French who called for the Covenant to be separated from the Peace Treaty itself.[87] As always, Cecil recognized the importance of intricate, hands-on involvement in the back room drafting process to ensure that his desires were met. After dinner, he and the president met with House and Miller determining the fate of specific revisions of Articles 8, 10, 11, and 14.[88]

There were other threats to the Covenant. Cecil knew that Hughes had a variety of criticisms about the draft Covenant, but hoped he might bring Hughes along by engaging him on negotiations with the Japanese delegates over the racial clause.[89] There was also a possibility that the French might scuttle the drive for Covenant revisions. Cecil could not believe the shortsightedness of the French in all aspects of the Conference. He complained to Clémentel that France was acting with "extraordinary stupidity" in arguing with Wilson over the League of Nations, even as they were "absolutely dependent upon the Americans, and to a lesser degree upon us."[90] He lost his composure when dealing with Bourgeois in a contentious March 22 League Commission meeting, insultingly deriding as "absurd" his proposed amendment calling for the creation of a permanent general staff to coordinate League military preparedness. "Apparently," Cecil wrote in his diary, being called absurd "is regarded in French as very offensive."[91] Yet Bourgeois's relentless harping on the military aspects of a League truly seemed crazy to Cecil. Just days earlier, Clemenceau had told Cecil that his government "cared nothing about" the issue of a general staff any longer, and yet Bourgeois banged on supporting it.[92] Exactly what was the French stance? Why was Clemenceau allowing such an old and overmatched blowhard to act as the French point man on the League issue?

Yet Cecil could not complain too much. He got most of what he wanted out of that meeting, including the integration of some needed legalese in the preamble of the Covenant declaring that on the signing of the Peace Treaty, Germany would agree to the Covenant without immediately becoming a member of the League. He later bragged to his wife that it was "my doing!!" that ensured women were eligible for all League bodies.[93] Everyone was sick of Bourgeois's ideas about a League army. When the Frenchman brought it up again during a commission meeting that lasted past midnight on March 26, there erupted an uproar "in which the protesting voices of Orlando, Cecil, Venizelos, and even Vesnitch could be distinguished."[94] At the end of the meeting, Hurst, Miller, and Cecil were among those appointed to redraft the Covenant.[95] In his practical minded, lawyerly way, Cecil continued to believe that satisfactory wording could bridge the gap.[96] As always, Cecil continued to feel that he was getting his way on the League.

The Personal and the Political

Particularly over the last ten days of March, Cecil found himself barraged by incessant meetings. Considering the wide variety of issues under his belt, maintaining order in his life proved increasingly difficult for Cecil and his secretaries. On March 24 alone he chaired a morning meeting of the SEC that successfully plodded through its agenda, then had lunch with Smuts to tell the South African about progress in recent negotiations on the League. This was followed by a series of meetings in the afternoon with Arthur Salter, the Secretary of the League of Nations Union (LNU), the Swiss foreign minister Rappard, General Clive, the Dutch foreign minister Loudon, the Norwegian delegation, and a subcommittee on organizing government in the Allied occupied Rhineland. Along the way there were "several other people who came in for unarranged interviews."[97] The day culminated in a League Commission meeting that lasted until 11:00 p.m. Little wonder that he fell asleep during down time in the Council of Ten. And little wonder that the stress levels of Cecil, and of his many fellow delegates subject to similar overwork and uncertainty, climbed throughout that unsteady March.

Fundamentally, Cecil found himself unable to control his tongue. A willingness to talk and opine had been a significant aspect of his personality at least since he entered politics a decade before the war, and one finds in his March 1919 work tendencies both toward effective leadership and periodic petulance. "I am glad your friends think you *feroce*," wrote his wife. "Did not your own mother say you had the jaw of a wild beast!"[98] He regularly broke in on others, cutting off an annoyed Hoover in an important meeting of the SWC. During one dinner with Balfour and Winston Churchill, he and Churchill sparred over whether to invade Bolshevik Russia and about the future of the League of Nations until Cecil, in his own words, "bit [Churchill's] nose off, and we got on better!"[99]

On another occasion he challenged Balfour and Pichon in the Council of Foreign Ministers on their belief that finance was the key problem in supplying Bavaria.[100] Cecil argued the greater problems were railway transportation through France and Switzerland, and the political question of whether supplying Bavaria should be seen as part of the German food quota, and if so whether this meant the Allies were ignoring the Brussels agreement. He agreed in the need to avoid a Bolshevik revolution in Bavaria, but Cecil fumed that Balfour and Pichon showed a fundamental lack of understanding of the Brussels agreement, which created a quota of how much food Germany as a whole would purchase from the allies, but said nothing about sending a specific amount to any particular German province. To push for food just for southern Germany could easily lead the Germans to demand a full renegotiation of the terms, and would create an uncomfortable precedent of Allied interference in Germany's internal affairs. Although he had long loved and admired his cousin, Cecil was not the only one at the Conference to suggest that Balfour, the seventy-year-old former prime minister, was off his peak form and was growing averse to making any decisions at all.

Cecil spent his Sunday mornings in March as he normally did, at church. But he also went on two Sunday afternoons to sit for an American artist on Montparnasse, Jo Davidson. The artist looked to sculpt busts, usually in just two to three hours, of many of the statesmen in Paris including Foch, Wilson, Clemenceau, House, and others (see Figure 4.4).[101] An American critic at the resulting show in Paris that June suggested that Cecil's made him look exactly like John D. Rockefeller.[102] "I'm *very glad* the sculptor is making your face long & narrow," wrote Nelly upon hearing her husband's verdict on the bust. "It serves you right for staying away so long without your wife!"[103] These sittings ate into his already very limited free time available for golf—he played only one round this month. But March definitely saw an increase in Cecil's sociability among people outside the British delegation, and indeed outside the Conference altogether.

Figure 4.4 Busts sculpted by Jo Davidson in Paris; Cecil's is at bottom right. *Art and Architecture*, vol. 9 (1920), 288.

Some of these connections came through his young nieces and nephews, Bobbety, Moucher, and Mina, who spent much time in Paris with him, and who brought others from their social set along with. After vacillating for weeks at the offer by the FO to send him to Paris to assist his uncle, Bobbety (who as the eldest son of Viscount Salisbury had the title Lord Cranborne) joined Cecil's staff on February 28 as the assistant to Cecil's assistant Frank Walters.[104] By April Cranborne's wife Betty likewise had joined the staff to assist Miss Dudgeon. "What she does I don't know," Cecil told his wife, "but she looks very decorative."[105] Betty Cranborne was one of many young aristocratic British women desirous of attending to the goings on in Paris, "most of them young and easy to look at" according to Billy Hughes, but incompetent regarding typing and other critical office jobs.[106] A month of that must have been trying; Cecil was far from the only one to blow up at his unprofessional staff for a job poorly done. He sometimes lunched or dined with his young relatives. But after dinner with the young set, they inevitably went their own ways; Cecil to his rooms alone or with other older men for coffee and cigars, leaving the youth to their Parisian fun.

But it was not all smoky backrooms among his British peers for Lord Robert Cecil. He had made some very different and interesting acquaintances over the first few months of the Conference, and these were paying off in March with an increasingly international and exotic social life. He began to eat more meals outside the confines of the Hotel Majestic, taking at least seven (and probably more) of his March dinners in either restaurants, clubs, or the homes of local luminaries. He loved getting out; he lamented in his diary on March 26 that the press of work meant that he "had to throw over a French dinner party with great regret."[107] He loved talking about things other than the Conference. And he was undoubtedly charmed by the ladies that he met at such gatherings. One might suggest that his growing flirtatiousness probably indicated his desires to get away from the Conference mentality altogether. In letters home to his wife he lamented frequently about how unattractive all the French women were who he saw in the street or in a rare walk through the Bois de Boulogne. After one, he claimed that among all the crowds, he saw not one "really pretty woman," only a few decent looking ones "and the rest positively ugly—many of them repulsive." Just the kind of thing that a man writes to reassure his wife! But he also described the allure of some of the exotic women he met, such as the dark and mysterious jewess Germaine Alice de Rothschild, and Marie, the British-born Queen of Romania, who described to him how one dress shown to her by her couturier was "nothing but a pink chemise."[108]

In one letter he wrote to his wife, which he titled "Moeurs Contemporains," he described a dinner he attended at the Ritz with his American friend on the SEC, Vance MacCormick, where he met an American woman, the Marquise de Polignac, recently married to a champagne heir and champion runner. Polignac, in Cecil's words, performed a sort of flirty Franco-American kabuki during the dinner: she first opened "a charming little box and mirror and ostentatiously powdered her nose" and then "called my attention to the lowness of the back of her dress which she regretted having worn as too low for a public place. It quite literally came down below her waist and ended in a kind of sash. I could not help wondering how she kept her clothes on as she evidently had no stays."[109] Lady Cecil responded with corresponding good humor: "you needn't be so proud of it. I could see a man naked from the waist up any afternoon in Endell St."[110] Even during his dinner with Wilson and House and their families on 18 March, a dinner with tremendous importance in the negotiating of a reasonable League, Cecil pushed the conversation to more general topics, as he and the president talked about Lord Grey's love of fishing and birds, and Balfour's love of music and golf. Cecil got even the straightlaced Wilson to open up, as they laughed about the high notes reached by the soprano diva when Wilson attended the Paris Opera a few weeks before.[111]

Those who wanted to could wall themselves off from the allures of Paris in 1919. Herbert Hoover would later brag that he saw almost no one but other officials, arguing that this cloistered life enabled him to escape the infection of European ideas.[112] Hankey claimed that between March and June he was so overworked with organizing the Big Four meetings that he usually arrived back at his rented flat at 9:30 for dinner with his wife, and then to bed every night at 11:00.[113] But Cecil's social calendar in Paris was vivid and varied. His bustling socializing underscored his openmindedness, his desire to meet new people, his enjoyment of frivolity and flirtation, and his overall good humor even when facing many difficulties. Cecil did not ordinarily keep a diary so it would be impossible to compare his social life in Paris to that when he was home. Although in pre-war life he often claimed to find society "wearisome," it is reasonable to assume that he spent many evenings out when in London before, during, and after the war.[114] But the clubby London of 1919 was not the multicultural London of a century later. Paris in 1919, on the other hand, was more international and diverse than it had ever been. The Peace Conference opened up to Cecil and his colleagues more worldly possibilities not just for politics, but also for friendship and social life.

*

By the end of March 1919 the SEC successfully solved how to supply food to a number of European peoples, including their former enemies. In just a few weeks, the SEC had already proven far more useful than its many critics have suggested. Hoover, Baruch, Smuts, and later historians claimed that the SEC meetings were full of "many words and reports that had no practical effect in action" and were only of use simply as a place "for letting off steam."[115] Hoover and his admirers would later argue that all the relief work for Europe done by his ARA was done despite, rather than as part of, the SEC.[116] He claimed that the United States bore no responsibility for the continuation of the blockade through March, and that the United States had consistently demanded for it to be lifted, reasserting free trade with Germany in all things including food.[117] American accusations about the self-serving, malevolent, or vindictive nature of the continuation of the Allied blockade during the first months of January vastly understated the complexity of the problems facing the Allies during those months and suggested a solution that had little chance of succeeding. The insinuation was that if everyone had simply followed the United States on economic issues, Germany would have been resupplied and there would have been no starvation during the armistice period.

One might suggest instead that it was the intransigence of Hoover, slow to accept compromise, that caused the blockade to remain for so long. During March, Cecil constructed working compromises between the United States and France. Cecil had played a similar conciliating role in the League Commission weeks before, and even before the armistice when he dominated wartime interallied blockade organizations. To Cecil, the SEC fundamentally spoke to questions of the blockade and his desire to finish what he had begun years earlier during the war. He believed that a controlled diminution of trade restrictions would help to reinvigorate the European economy. Cecil also hoped that success in transitioning the continent to a successful post-war economy would provide an example of the internationalist spirit of the League of Nations, a spirit he hoped would become enshrined as the basis of international relations in the post-war world.

The SEC proved again that Cecil was a unique master of the intricacies of interallied decision making. During their first meeting, the SEC members determined that the chairmanship would rotate between representatives of each of the Big Four powers.[118] Cecil was undoubtedly outranked by his US and

French counterparts, as he ran no ministry and was avowedly outside Lloyd George's government, while Hoover was the US Food Controller and Clémentel was the French Minister of Commerce. However from March 24, Cecil chaired every SEC meeting he attended, as his colleagues accepted Cecil as the SEC's permanent chair and de facto voice. He controlled the SEC agenda, advocated vociferously and mostly effectively in favor of policies he favored, and became the Council's public face both in the eyes of both the Big Four and the press. He was perhaps the inevitable leader of the SEC, as an experienced man respected by the Big Four. Even Herbert Hoover, extremely wary of what he saw as the historical bloody-mindedness of all Europeans including the British, considered Cecil a particularly "sensible man."[119] "Lord Robert big as usual" was the succinct verdict from Vance McCormick after one of their meetings; "How easy it would be if they were only all like him."[120]

In March, the SEC under Cecil's command was doing something important. In his diary on March 28, he wrote that the Council of Foreign Ministers had "given to me" the right to lift the blockades in the former Austrian empire.[121] They had also agreed to drop the blockades on Estonia and Poland.[122] It was true that Cecil and the other members of the SEC had not yet persuaded Lloyd George or Clemenceau to fully revoke the blockade of Germany. But there had been some movement, and some successes at alleviating it, and more importantly food was getting through to needy people living in enemy countries. The intentions and the actions of the SEC in March suggest that tales of the Allies vindictiveness and cruelty during that spring have been overstated.[123]

5

Impending Catastrophe: April

An entertaining evening out would seem to be exactly what Cecil needed. He always appreciated conversations unrelated to the pressing concerns of the day, and the occasion on April 2 was a promising one, a small party at the home of the Duchess de Fitzjames on Rue de Grenelle, near the Invalides. Not far from the Majestic, but *la rive gauche*. Since he met her at a British Embassy function in late January, Cecil's relationship with Fitzjames had grown into something nearing friendship. Over the course of the spring they had at least eight lunches and dinners together, many at her home, with a wide variety of guests. Fitzjames held what was well known as the last of the old style Faubourg Saint-Germain salons, replete with aristocrats and well-known artists and writers.[1] Her gatherings may have lost some of their importance even before the war, but Fitzjames herself remained one of a kind. In May, Cecil introduced her to his cousin Arthur, who thereafter found every opportunity to see her over the next few months (According to Cynthia Asquith, Balfour would "dine with almost anyone who asked him"; Ian Malcolm, Balfour's assistant, wrote that Balfour was "an inveterate diner out."[2]). Fitzjames introduced Cecil to a variety of people he had not yet met, such as Sergey Sazonov, the former Russian Foreign Minister and self-proclaimed voice of the Russian "White" anti-Bolshevik forces, and the famous novelist Paul Bourget (it is not certain whether he met the great friend of both Fitzjames and Bourget, Edith Wharton). Yet the party was less of a release than Cecil probably hoped. There was a tension in all the conversations at the Duchess's house that night, betraying a generalized sense that the world faced "impending catastrophe" and that the peacemakers would have to work hard to avoid it.[3]

The start of April proved an emotional turning point for many participants in the Peace Conference, particularly for those already overwhelmed with concern about the economic catastrophe facing post-war Europe. Jan Smuts shamed himself when, under pressure from Lloyd George, he wrote a memo to Woodrow Wilson that supported the demands of Hughes and Sumner for maximal reparations demands on the Germans. Following his own predilection for penitence, Smuts then went on an early April mission to Hungary. Appalled by the starvation of the people of Budapest, Smuts thereafter complained incessantly about the inhumanity of the Allies and the impossibility of the poverty-stricken masses of central Europe ever paying any reparations.[4]

Similarly, after his series of meetings throughout March with the German financial delegates at Spa, Brussels, and Versailles, John Maynard Keynes constantly pressured Chancellor of the Exchequer Austen Chamberlain and David Lloyd George to support an interallied debt cancellation scheme. Exemplifying his increasing stridency, Keynes labeled the payment of war loans to creditor nations as "tribute."[5] Press correspondents claimed that torpor and fear hindered decision making in Paris and blamed the peacemakers for allowing the starvation of the masses of the former central and eastern European empires. If only Cecil were Foreign Minister rather than Balfour, lamented the *Manchester Guardian,* "some policy would be applied within a week, for it is not the plans that are wanting, it is a Minister who will decide and act."[6]

Despite successes steering significant food shipments to Germany in March, Cecil likewise felt unease about the European economy. He recognized that Europe's overwhelming economic problems went far beyond those caused by the steadily-diminishing economic war. It was "the general economic position" of Europe that plagued his thoughts. The lack of available credit has "locked the wheels of industry," Cecil believed, and "we could not afford to play with the situation any longer."[7] This concern animated his discussions with a multinational array of delegates like Keynes, Philip Baker, the banker and onetime Ministry of Munitions official Robert Brand, American financial experts Bernard Baruch and Thomas Lamont, and the Frenchman Jean Monnet. His diagnosis of the problems facing economic recovery borrowed much from the contours of critiques he had been developing for weeks in league with these advisors. But could they solve the economic problem in a politically palatable fashion?

How to Revive European Trade

As Cecil saw it, the basic economic problem was a crisis in confidence within credit markets. Would-be lenders or purchasers were uncertain of what restrictions or freedoms would make global trade over the relatively short term. Ideally, all outstanding economic issues with Germany, particularly reparations, would be dealt with immediately in the Peace Treaty itself. As Cecil explained to Lloyd George, punitive demands for payments might hurt the Germans, but the greater problem was that the final reparations amount looked likely to be punted down the line to a post-treaty "reparations commission," leaving the exact amount demanded to the unforeseeable future.[8] How, in such circumstances, could any foreign government or any banker lend money that Germany needed immediately to grease the wheels of trade and transport, if there was no sense of whether, when, or how the German government would ever be able to afford to pay other debts of unknowable size? Without a final settlement and an exact dollar amount demanded from Germany, the reparations issue would remain "a heavy cloud on all financial transactions."[9]

But solving the crisis would take more than the signing of such a peace. As Cecil knew well, the economies of the major powers had become chained together during the war, as interallied economic bodies gave the Allies unprecedented types of control over certain aspects of global trade. Before the war, Cecil's politics had been avowedly Free Trade. In 1916, he had opposed institutionalizing permanent collaboration between the Allies over control of global resources, an idea that was proposed by Étienne Clémentel and some others in the French government, and approved by French and British leaders at the Paris Economic Conference that summer.[10] Cecil agreed with the general opinion in Britain that this was a sort of false promise intended to scare German businessmen, who would then nudge their government toward peace negotiations.[11]

Yet his experiences over the last years of war had led him to doubt doctrinal Free Trade, and in the emergency situation of 1919, Cecil believed that hard-to-create interallied efforts should not be thrown away.[12] In the SEC, the Allies were discussing and collaborating on such things as the adequate distribution of shipping and coal supplies. By the end of March, revived and reempowered joint Allied shipping, fuel, and food organizations were up and running under the SEC, as a significant bureaucracy quickly congregated in its headquarters at 26 Rue de Bassano, a building located near the Majestic.[13]

Cecil agreed with the French delegates that at least temporarily, the Allies should take joint measures to regulate German exports by giving the Allies the right of "pre-emptive" purchase of certain goods, instead of allowing them to be sold freely to whoever wanted them. Similarly he argued in favor of allied cooperation in finance. Cecil believed available financial credits should be distributed on the basis of the needs of the allies as a whole. In other words, the United States had to more effectively coordinate its loan efforts. "The great want of the future is money," Cecil explained, "and the only one of the Associated

Governments that has money at its command is the United States."[14] Lloyd George agreed and hoped that Cecil would work his charms, on March 26 giving him "full authority to go on and do whatever I could to induce the Americans to have a full discussion on the subject."[15]

But it was hard to see whether the Americans could create a coherent position on this question, or if they even discussed the subject among themselves. Cecil lamented "the Byzantine system of the government of the United States," with jealousy and intrigue dividing the economic experts.[16] He met with each of the Americans individually. During one dinner, Baruch explained his own financial schemes and seemed receptive to Cecil's call for US government support for some sort of broad Europe-wide loan program.[17] Robert Brand, two days later, agreed with Cecil that some sort of expert Anglo-American committee "if possible with French members also" should get together to discuss what to do.

Then, at the morning meeting of the Raw Materials section of the SEC on April 4, Cecil and Baruch sparred.[18] Looking back on that meeting later a few years later, Étienne Clémentel judged that Baruch's actions at that meeting permanently ruptured Allied "solidarité économique."[19] The minutes of the meeting suggest only that the United States refused to cooperate with Allied attempts to sell off their war stocks to Germany. As Baruch stated, the United States had no stockpiles in Europe to sell and thus could stay out of it. These official minutes (and the recollections of Jean Monnet) suggest that Cecil argued not with Baruch but rather against Clémentel and Loucheur, who favored restricting a handful of specific post-war German exports to ensure that German exporters did not unfairly benefit from their declining exchange rate.[20]

But a more verbatim set of minutes expose the real argument between Cecil and Baruch, over the possibility of setting prices for these German purchases. Loucheur and Clémentel argued that the prices received by the Allies for these goods must be at or near the very high levels they paid during the last year of the war, even for things like copper which could now be bought in world markets more cheaply.[21] Baruch was sure that such prices amounted to gouging the Germans, and in effect was a backhand way of milking reparations, even though it might impede the German recovery necessary for them to afford reparations payments. In Baruch's opinion, "it is a mistake to think that you can get more juice out of a lemon by squeezing it at both ends."[22] Cecil responded: "Your principle is sound and I have nothing to say against it as a matter of principle. I am a free-trader and do not believe in the Government's interference in matters of prices." But the war had brought "abnormal things," and the world could not simply "resume things normally." The United States needed to recognize that it must continue to fully engage in Europe. Baruch was annoyed: "It is pretty near time to adjoin and we have not come to any conclusion." When Clémentel reiterated the need for coal in France and Italy and the insufficient supply of shipping, Baruch exploded: "I have told you so many times, and told everybody else that the United States cannot control the price or distribution of anything. We could not even do it during the period of the war and we certainly cannot do it now."

Cecil immediately went to see House to try to get some help, but with Wilson ill from influenza, the Colonel said that nothing would be done until Wilson recovered. Cecil then stopped into McCormick's office, but McCormick remained fixated on the blockade, and on his perception that selfishness was behind the British reluctance to dismantle rationing agreements with European neutrals.[23] There were rumors, rebutted by the British censorship authorities in the War Trade Intelligence Department, that cables sent by American businesses ended up in the hands of their London competitors.[24] It was proving difficult to handle the Americans.

Cecil then decided to open discussions in the SEC. On April 7 he presented a lengthy and passionate memorandum on the "General Economic Position" as the first item on the SEC weekly agenda.[25] Despite his inside knowledge of the other difficult issues faced by the peacemakers, such as what to do about Russia and how to set up borders between the new states of eastern Europe, Cecil argued bluntly that "by far the most important task before the Allied Governments is to get production and internal and external 'exchange economy' working again on something like normal lines." His memo painted a bleak picture of 400 million Europeans living on the economic brink, unable to recover from the shock of war because they faced a huge variety of problems including the destruction of fixed plant and transportation infrastructure, lack of raw materials, lack of exports, "chaos of currency systems," price inflation, and agricultural collapse. In the place where difficulties were the greatest, Russia, the political and economic systems had collapsed altogether, and brutal Bolshevism reigned to solve Russia's economic problems by forcing urban workers to work the land as laborers and by allowing mass starvation of the rest. The threat that economic collapse would allow Bolshevism to spread westward appeared real. "It is obvious that there is no one remedy for existing evils," as the problems far exceeded piecemeal solutions such as shipping in food and other relief supplies. Especially in central and eastern Europe, significant problems threatened to destroy the meager existing private enterprises. Dropping the blockade would help, and at this meeting British and French representatives agreed to recommend suspension of all blacklisting measures. But Cecil listed the blockade as number ten in his list of the dozen main obstacles to European recovery. "By far the greatest difficulty is the financial one." The Allies needed to coalesce around a "comprehensive policy covering the conditions of each country," one that particularly aimed to solve the "unparalleled" financial difficulties of Europe. They needed some system to supply commercial credits, not just for the short terms of three months to which global traders had been accustomed before the war, but rather for "at least eighteen months or two years." In short, Cecil urged the Allied governments to issue joint loan guarantees for investment and trade.

Following Cecil's wish, the SEC sent a resolution immediately to the Peace Conference leaders, who were now meeting in a daily executive session known as the Council of Four, or the "Big Four." The SEC "regards the present economic position of Europe as one of the utmost gravity" and wanted the Four to recognize "the extreme urgency of the situation."[26] None on the SEC argued against the resolution. But it remained hard to tell what the Americans thought. In the next SEC meeting two days later, Cecil arrived to find the US delegates all "in a very bad temper" but he was unsure why. At the meeting, they all said "nothing new, and consequently nothing cheerful."[27]

To push the Big Four to act, Cecil went to the press. Although he believed that real negotiations could not take place in public, Cecil was always quite cognizant that favorable public opinion was pivotal to any eventual success. As the Peace Conference progressed, press conferences became increasingly standardized, with semiofficial spokesmen giving regular statements and often answering questions. Exactly what these briefings were like is not exactly clear. There were no photographs, and most were off-the-record affairs, with no direct quotes allowed, and no "official statements."[28] As the Conference wore on and it became obvious that very little of its activities would be done in public, the number of correspondents on hand steadily declined, as did the number of articles.[29]

For some, like US Secretary of State Robert Lansing, these press conferences were about influencing public opinion at home. The main result of Lansing's briefings may have been to publically expose his lack of knowledge about what his own president was doing at the Conference. Lansing's briefings late each morning were "rather dismal affairs," according to the American journalist William White. Lansing was always "visibly frightened in the presence of newspapermen and did not relax. Certainly he never unbent, and certainly he never gave us the slightest bit of news."[30] Stephen Pichon, the French Foreign Minister, played a similar role for his delegation.

But the US correspondents paid attention to the regular conferences given by the British delegation, which since at least late March and probably earlier were usually conducted by Cecil. According to Chester Wright in the *New York Tribune*, "there seems to be no American in Paris who can or will talk with the authority and freedom of Lord Robert Cecil, for instance, speaking for the British."[31] Cecil was a gawky, lanky man, "who mouthed and mumbled his words in that one-legged non-rhythm which high-class Britishers use when speaking formally. But he did know what was going on, and he did tell us. It generally checked with the truth. Certainly he never tried to deceive us. The American press respected him."[32] He had found that he could push stories to writers in ways that might help spur the Big Four to action on specific things he believed critical. Although he believed that real negotiations could not take place in public, Cecil knew by then that molding favorable public opinion mattered. Articles on the Conference rarely mentioned Cecil by name. Yet with the off-the-record nature of these briefings, it was entirely possible, even likely, that Cecil's words and ideas about the Peace Conference were entering the global news stream at an increasing rate. Cecil's successes in shaping the press narrative during the Peace Conference, following on his successes in similarly shaping the press coverage of the Blockade during the war, may have enhanced his faith in the power of public opinion, which he and his allies would often claim was the most critical foundation of the future success of the League.

Cecil took these public relations lessons to the SEC, which by early April had begun to send out communiqués (usually printed in full by important papers like the *Times*) describing the SEC functions and some of its debates and decisions. These press releases particularly focused on actions to alleviate the blockade and attempts to expedite commerce and relief throughout Europe. Such publicity, he hoped, might enhance business confidence. It also might augment the stature of the SEC and force the Big Four to attend to its demands.

Sparring within the British Delegation over the League

To Cecil, events at the start of April led him to question the months of his general equanimity and partnership with David Lloyd George. In particular, he was infuriated by the cynicism he perceived in the Welshman's handling of Woodrow Wilson. Cecil was not among Lloyd George's small inner circle who met at the Palace of Fontainebleau on the weekend of March 23, when the prime minister decided to take a more conciliatory tone toward Germany and a more confrontational one toward the United States. Particularly due to his fear of Bolshevism rising to power in Germany, Cecil favored salving German complaints by offering concessions on reparations and perhaps even territory.[33] But during a private lunch with Lloyd George on March 26, Cecil listened in horror to his prime minister's threat to oppose any American draft of the Covenant that included a phrase respecting the validity of the Monroe Doctrine as an existing regional institution that since the early nineteenth century had banned any expansion of European imperialism in the Americas. Seeing the League of Nations as a large bargaining chip to use in Britain's global relationship with the United States, rather than as a pivotal end goal of the peace talks, Lloyd George let Cecil know that he would support a Monroe Doctrine article only in return for a US pledge to limit their naval building program over the next few years.[34] The issue of a global American fleet was potentially explosive in domestic British politics, speaking directly to Britain's security fears. To maintain Britain's place both in Europe and as a far-flung Empire, a policy of global naval dominance had been sacrosanct for British leaders for centuries. Cecil was told by Lloyd George to let Wilson know the British position before that evening's League Commission meeting. Left in the role of uncomfortable messenger, Cecil grit his teeth and relayed the message to Wilson.

He then attended what he considered a very successful League Commission meeting. Cecil gained quick approval of his proposals that all League bodies "may comprise women as well as men," and of Article 19 allowing amendment of the Covenant in the future.[35] No one, he hoped, should consider the decisions of the Paris peacemakers as the final word in the new international relations regime that would develop after the war. In particular, the League that resulted from the Peace Conference must be allowed to evolve as circumstances dictated. Just as importantly from a procedural standpoint, that evening's League meeting left in the hands of a new drafting committee the rewording of each article. Invariably, Cecil established himself on this with Larnaude, Venizelos, and House. In Miller's words, the committee did more than draft but rather was "a Committee on Revision," empowered to decide on much that had been left up in the air.[36] Cecil certainly believed the re-drafters should "interpret their duties liberally, as much had to be recast and changed."[37]

Lacking any further communications from Lloyd George over the next few days, Cecil worked in this League drafting committee under the assumption that "sooner or later an accommodation will be made" by Lloyd George on the League issue.[38] Over long meetings at the Astoria on April 1–2, they hashed out a final document.[39] It did not include any mention of the Monroe Doctrine, but all knew that Wilson was planning to introduce a new article at the next League Commission meeting, and Cecil assumed that Wilson and Lloyd George must be in the midst of hashing out the naval issue during their own incessant meetings.

Cecil was thus infuriated when on April 3 he heard rumors "in the Majestic" that Lloyd George would reject any article on the Monroe Doctrine "unless America agreed never to build a fleet as large as the English." The next day, Cecil confronted Lloyd George, asking if the prime minister was no longer in favor of a League of any sort.[40] Addressing the future military balance of power between Britain and the United States lent an unnecessary divisiveness to the overall peace negotiations, Cecil believed. The balance of naval power between Britain and the United States did not have to be dealt with yet. "America is in a far stronger position than we are," he explained to cousin Arthur. "She wants nothing out of this peace, neither territory nor privileges." If Lloyd George's argument was made public, Cecil was sure the British people would not support the prime minister, as "the conception that the American navy may be a danger to us would be regarded as fantastic." In the United States it would drive opinion against the British, who desperately needed US financial cooperation.[41] Hopeful that the League might actually help to guarantee the Empire's future security, Cecil lamented that Lloyd George undervalued its potential to address and solve real security problems.

As was his way, Cecil inevitably considered resigning. As he explained to Balfour, he had accepted the leadership of Britain's League of Nations effort only because he was assured that the government would make it a cornerstone of British foreign policy. If the government's policy has changed, Cecil wanted to know. Balfour chastised him: "you can't resign on such a case!"[42] But he was not alone. Just a few days later, Wilson himself threatened to pick up and leave Paris due to his unhappiness about the state of the peace negotiations, in part due to this spat over naval construction.

However, the politically wily Lloyd George knew when he had leverage in his relations with his fellow potentates, and Wilson's need to amend the Covenant to include the Monroe Doctrine amendment could be held against him. For a few days Lloyd George did not respond to Cecil's letters, leaving Cecil surprised when an SEC request to allow German financial delegates to come to Paris was suddenly approved by the Big Four.[43] But Cecil knew he was not the only one who Lloyd George ignored those days.[44] Eventually the prime minister reached out and during a private breakfast on April 8, Lloyd George "worked very hard to fascinate me, or perhaps I should say to soothe my temper." Recognizing that the naval negotiations with the United States, entrusted to Walter Long, had stalemated, Lloyd George suggested that Cecil and House might be tasked to find a solution.[45] The prime minister entangled Cecil in the difficult web of negotiations, both in the hope that Cecil could break the impasse and also in the hope that Cecil would be less likely to resign. The prime minister knew that Cecil, overwhelmingly concerned with the issue of Anglo-American relations and confident of his own diplomatic abilities, would be compelled to take up the offer, even though it meant that he must begin with a defense of Lloyd George's own policy. Cecil immediately went to see William Wiseman, and that afternoon he exchanged notes with House.

In his letter to House, Cecil tapped into his own wartime background in supply issues and blockade to explain why the British Admiralty was rightly concerned about rumors of a planned US naval buildup. British sentiment, Cecil explained bluntly, demanded strong sea power, but economic necessity also demanded it, as Britain imported "four-fifths of our cereal, two-thirds of our meat, the whole of our cotton and almost the whole of our wool. If we were blockaded for a month or less we should have to surrender at discretion. This is not true of any other country in the world," and was certainly not true of the almost entirely self-sufficient United States. More importantly, Cecil argued, the US naval buildup showed an attitude "wholly inconsistent with the conception of the League of Nations" as a forum that could breed disarmament among its members.[46] Sewing his support for the navy together with the League of Nations, Cecil crafted a rather ingenious argument, one that Wilson might find compelling, and one which if accepted by Wilson would further compel Lloyd George to accept a powerful League.

In their ensuing meeting, House and Cecil compared and discussed the present and projected navy lists of both countries. According to House, the United States simply wished to build a fleet two-thirds the size of the British. Cecil was warily convinced by the presentation, and asked Lloyd George later that day if it was possible that the British government's own naval advisors had been overstating the significance of a post-war US naval buildup. Lloyd George was initially dissatisfied with the numbers that House provided, and "the little man was obdurate." "What will be the upshot of it I don't know," Cecil wondered, "but it is very harassing and provoking."[47] But soon enough Cecil's efforts succeeded.[48] On April 10, Lloyd George felt assured enough by Wilson's pledge that the United States had no desire to enter into a naval competition with Britain, and allowed things to move ahead on a revised Covenant.[49] The "naval battle of Paris" was over.

Yet tensions lingered into the League Commission meeting that evening when Wilson introduced his Monroe Doctrine Article with an impassioned speech denouncing any who might oppose it. Eventually becoming Article 21, it stated that "Nothing in this Covenant shall be deemed to affect the validity of international engagements, such as treaties of arbitration or regional understandings like the Monroe doctrine, for securing the maintenance of peace." According to reporters, "the British attitude had been in doubt until the last, but Lord Robert Cecil turned the scales by announcing that he saw no objection to the amendment in the form presented by the President."[50] In reality, the meeting was more touchy. When Bourgeois droned on against the Monroe amendment, "Lord Robert Cecil said that perhaps M. Bourgeois would permit him to explain again what he thought had been made quite clear."[51] The next day, Larnaude and the Chinese voiced objections, but Cecil argued that the Monroe Doctrine did not mean that the League would never operate in the Americas. After all, the League could only take action against a peacebreaking country with the unanimous support of the League Council, on which the United States would be a member.[52]

As he worked on behalf of the prime minister, Cecil hoped that Lloyd George might in return do more to support him within the British delegation. Yet the "Little Man" failed to counter continuing criticism about the League from the Dominion leaders, particularly Billy Hughes. The irascible and irrepressible Australian again proved a huge thorn in Cecil's side at the end of March, when he attacked the draft League Covenant on a variety of grounds. Hughes wrote to the League Commission about his worries that the League might develop into a sort of superstate.[53] He argued in a number of BED meetings that any Japanese "Racial Equality" clause for the League Covenant would be a dealbreaker, as he believed that it would mandate unchecked immigration into his own country. If the Japanese even mentioned their proposal during the upcoming Plenary Session, Hughes threatened a very public squabble that might spike the passage of the Covenant altogether.

Arguing with Hughes was never easy. George Barnes, the British Labour delegate, had persuaded Cecil to attend the meeting of the BED on April 8 to help counter Hughes's opposition to the International Labour Convention, which was to become Part XIII of the Treaty of Versailles (and which thus created the International Labour Organization). Lloyd George let the delegation know that Clemenceau saw the Labour Convention's quick passage as critical in the overall effort to shield Europe against the spread of Bolshevism, but Hughes led the other Dominion leaders to press for safeguards against dumping. Cecil argued that the Labour Convention, rather than bringing excessive regulations to the employment policies of League member states, would indicate to the workers of the world that the League of Nations would look out for their interests better than the leaders of international communism.[54] Balfour as the chairman persuaded the BED to declare that its "majority" believed the Labour Convention should be knitted together with the League Covenant. Barnes and Cecil had succeeded, but Cecil lamented that "the Dominion Prime Ministers did not distinguish themselves, particularly Hughes, who seems to be merely out to prevent things being done."[55]

Cecil was not simply having trouble with the ministers from the antipodes, but also with his mercurial ally Jan Smuts. At the end of March, the South African again proved his worthlessness in the League of Nations negotiations when he failed to mediate between the Japanese and Australians.[56] On the eve of the South African's trip to Budapest, where he was sent by the Council of Four to inquire about the Bolshevik revolution there, Cecil told Smuts that he would support any promises that Smuts made to the Hungarians regarding the lifting of blockade measures. "Incidentally (his absence) means that I shall have to take over such work as he was doing on the League of Nations," Cecil wrote in his diary, "but that won't mean too much."[57]

But it did mean something nearly two weeks later, after Smuts had returned to Paris. In the League Commission meeting on April 11, Baron Makino of the Japanese delegation officially put forward their "equality of nations" amendment in what many found a very persuasive speech.[58] During the Japanese statement, Cecil found that "Smuts, without giving me any adequate warning, had fled, and as I did not realise he was not going to be there I had got no one else to take his place, and had to grapple with the Japanese as best I could, which was not very well."[59] Cecil explained to his fellow commissioners that he "regretted that he was not in a position to vote for this amendment" but must follow the instructions of his government in rejecting the Japanese proposal. Transparently, Cecil was following the demands of the BED, particularly of Hughes. It was a "pathetic speech," with Cecil clearly doing a "difficult and disagreeable duty" that embarrassed him.[60] According to David Hunter Miller, Cecil was "obviously moved," and "after making his statement Cecil sat with his eyes fixed on the table, and took no part in the subsequent debate."[61]

Although only Cecil and the Polish delegate Roman Dmowski voted against the Japanese clause, Woodrow Wilson declared rather disingenuously that it could not be included in the Covenant because it had not passed unanimously; such a need for unanimity had never been spelled out or adhered to in previous

Commission meetings. Jay Winter suggests that Wilson was open-minded and even supportive of the Japanese proposal, but it seems more likely that the president truly welcomed the opportunity presented by the British of not having to reject it himself.[62] Hughes had threatened to House the previous day that if the Japanese amendment passed, he would send a cable to every US newspaperman on the west coast with a paean to the threat of Japanese domination.[63] Heaping this political rationale upon his own tendencies toward bigotry, Wilson was happy to lay blame on the British instead.[64]

But Cecil undoubtedly felt left in the lurch by Smuts, whose absence forced him to support a Dominion-led British policy that he did not agree with, and about which Smuts supposedly had expertise and knowledge. It was an embarrassing situation, and Cecil remained unhappy, but unsurprised, when over the next two weeks further attempts by Smuts to mediate between the Dominions and the Japanese fell flat.[65] The vote on the racial equality amendment turned out to be at the conclusion of the final meeting of the full League Commission, an inauspicious way for Cecil to end a set of proceedings that up until that point had gone almost entirely according to his desires.

Drama in the House of Commons

Cecil had been talking for weeks of getting home to England. On March 30, he wrote to his wife that he would hopefully get back to England for "a few days as soon as the L. of N. is re-drafted."[66] Or maybe for longer. As the pace of work quickened, he could not be every place at every time. He had become irritable and cross with his secretaries, whose every incompetence drove him crazy: "I must be odious to serve," he confessed to his wife. When Herbert Asquith, the former prime minister, came through Paris for a day and asked Cecil if they could meet for either lunch or dinner, the overscheduled Cecil reluctantly had to decline.[67]

In frustration over the League and SEC, Cecil vented to House and Lloyd George that he was "much discouraged and thought of returning to England for good."[68] According to McCormick, Lord Robert was planning to go home to inform the government that he would resign "unless he has more authority."[69] Going home would also fill a personal need. After the hard work, successes, and disappointments, Cecil wanted to see his wife. Taking a drive with his young nephew Bobbety and his wife Betty around the outskirts of Paris one morning, he came up with the idea of renting a home there for Nelly that he could visit on the weekends.[70] Maybe he could return to England for a few days to bring her back to France? Lots of others, including Lord and Lady Cranborne themselves, had taken up apartments in a Paris spring more clogged than usual with foreigners.

But Cecil's journey to London, where he arrived the evening of April 12, was also critical politically. Although he had not attended any session at Westminster except for during his brief trip home in February, Cecil treasured the fact that since his November resignation he was no longer officially part of the government and thus would be fully free to speak his mind in the House of Commons. He had been wrestling with whether he should go home to make a speech describing the problem to his fellow MPs. It could backfire, he worried; public knowledge of the economic difficulties facing Europe might simply cause even further decline in business confidence, and bankers everywhere might become even more restrictive on the few loans they were extending. If he spent too much time in his speech talking about his perception that other Allied countries were obstructing an economic settlement, Cecil worried that he might irritate the French, Italians, and Americans rather than meeting his desired goal of building a climate where consensus could be possible.[71] In the end, he decided to make a speech to the House of Commons that would "open the eyes" of his fellow MPs to "the real economic situation as I see it."[72]

Cecil went home for a week between April 12 and 19. Immediately on his return to England, Cecil set the groundwork for this speech by giving a number of interviews, which were published in a variety of British and global newspapers over the next few days. The *Times* wrote extensively about his views of the French proposals for League inspections of arms factories and for a general staff for the League. The *Wall Street Journal* explained that Cecil saw the economic situation of "the whole eastern hemisphere" as "extremely grave."[73] The *Manchester Guardian* explained Cecil's belief that the most recent League draft was far superior to the one of mid-February because of the "useful criticism" from the press and the public. Cecil defended the Monroe Doctrine Article as merely stating what all agreed was true, and explained that it would significantly improve the likelihood that the US Congress would approve the Covenant.[74]

On the afternoon of April 16, Cecil went to the House of Commons to attend the last session before its two-week Easter adjournment. He was prepared to speak about the crisis of the European economy. But just minutes before the session began, he and Lloyd George squabbled in a "rather childish controversy" over who would get to speak first.[75] Over the previous few days, Lloyd George vacillated over whether he wanted to make a speech or instead simply respond to questions from the House. Cecil had hoped to get in first, but that morning he was not calling the shots. Giving in, Cecil sat and listened to Lloyd George's description of what was going on in Paris.

A speech like this by the prime minister had been long desired by MPs of all parties, and by the British public at large. Many felt that the goings on in Paris were too secretive, breeding rumors and worries. According to the *Times*, "the truth is, of course, that the House of Commons is completely in the dark about the transactions of which the Prime Minister is to speak. To Westminster, Paris is synonymous with secrecy."[76] Fearing that Lloyd George had become too lenient toward the Germans, 233 Unionist backbenchers had sent him a telegram demanding a stern line.[77] Lloyd George needed to come home to ensure his supporters of his goals.

However, it is not an exaggeration to suggest that many were also highly anticipating Cecil's planned speech. The *Manchester Guardian* correspondent on April 14 suggested that Cecil deserved the "chief credit" for the quick work of the League Commission and was renowned among Frenchmen and Americans for "his courage, his sincerity, and the power with which he leads and guides the deliberations of the Supreme Economic Council." "In all the quiet, unostentatious, constructive work of this Conference he has been one of the master minds. Englishmen here are proud of the reputation he has won, and their pride is mingled with hope for the future."[78]

In the House, the Strangers' Gallery was packed, and Edward, the young Prince of Wales, listened to the debate from the Peers' Gallery, sitting next to the US ambassador. MPs overflowed from the benches into the side galleries. Throughout his speech, Lloyd George defended the conduct of the Peace Conference, reassured members that he would keep all of the promises he had made to them regarding indemnities and the fate of the Kaiser, and condemned the British press (in particular the *Times*, but more broadly all the Northcliffe papers) for spreading false rumors about the talks. Most of Lloyd George's speech dealt with the issue of Russia. His advocacy of staying the course and continuing aid to the anti-Bolshevik "Whites" fit him between the maximalist notion of Winston Churchill calling for military intervention, and the Labour Party's call for an end of all assistance to the anti-Bolshevik forces and official recognition of the Bolsheviks as the government of Russia.

But Lloyd George began his speech with an encomium to the necessity and desirability of a League of Nations. He claimed that creation of a League would determine whether the Conference was seen as successful or not. And the prime minister ended by explaining that it was not simply Bolshevism in Russia that was a problem, but rather that the general wreckage of the European powers and economies created revolutionary conditions everywhere. "The gaunt spectre of hunger is stalking throughout the land. The Central Powers and Russia have overtaxed their strength in the conflict. They are lying prostrate, broken," ready for revolutionary change. And yet, according to Lloyd George, the peacemakers at Paris all recognized that public opinion and war experience was giving them a real "opportunity of organizing the world on the basis of peace."[79]

Lloyd George's brilliance as an orator was exemplified in this ninety-minute speech.[80] Various correspondents described it as "the greatest triumph of the Prime Minister's whole parliamentary career," leaving his audience "not merely satisfied but delighted, after having been told practically nothing that it did not know before."[81] Upon returning to Paris the next day, Lloyd George gloated to his mistress that he had "gained complete mastery of the House, while telling them absolutely nothing about the peace conference."[82] No strong rebuttal emerged from the floor. The Scottish MP William Adamson, an old coal miner and since 1917 leader of the Labour Party, responded to the prime minister with a speech that by his own admonition he cut short, as he was satisfied with the way that Lloyd George had addressed the issues of Russia, the League of Nations, and particularly the Labour Convention which his party found so significant. Clement Edwards, the founder of the short-lived National Democratic Party, an anti-Labour, "patriotic" working class party favoring empire and tariff protections, then spoke briefly in favor of Lloyd George's decision to continue supplying the anti-Bolsheviks and proclaimed, optimistically and incorrectly, that the Whites were on the verge of recapturing St. Petersburg.

And then Cecil spoke, in a long speech interrupted a handful of times by interjected comments, to an audience much diminished in number since Lloyd George finished.[83] He made clear that he had been in Paris the past three months at the invitation of and not as part of Lloyd George's government. His comments were thus not those of the Government, although he opined that its members probably would not disagree with him. He started out by answering a few questions about the League of Nations Commission that had been posed by Adamson, explaining the consensus among all representatives on the Commission in support of the general structure and principles of the League, and in favor of the idea that it should not simply be a League of the Allies, but rather a League of all the world's countries. The correspondent from the *Times* noted that Cecil's description of the positive influence of the League Commission's publicity comprised an "unconscious" but "ironical commentary" on Lloyd George's claims about the need for secrecy in the negotiations.[84]

Cecil proclaimed that there must be an immediate settlement of the war not just territorially, but also economically. Citing graphic examples of starvation on the streets of Czechoslovakia, Austria, Bavaria, and Poland, he blamed the problem not simply on the lack of food, but the overall lack of any functioning economy at all. Half the able-bodied men of Central Europe, Cecil estimated, were "doing nothing." There were no raw materials to restart factories, no markets to sell to, no exports of any kind that might enable countries to gain funds to pay for supplies. Simply dropping the blockade would not solve these problems. "Supposing you make all the (English) Channel as free as possible, you will not do everything; you will not do very much. You may make it possible to trade. But you would not only have to put your machinery into something like good order, you would have to supply the motive power to get it going." More than simply hard work among the British, it would take a united effort among "all those countries which were associated in the war … I venture to appeal, not only to my own countrymen, but to all the Anglo-Saxon race throughout the world." They needed to figure out how to supply coal, ships, and credits to the stalled economies of Europe, and most importantly to end the uncertainty of the situation by settling the issue of indemnities and the overall Peace Treaty immediately. Without such quick actions and continued Allied cooperation, Europe could collapse, with calamitous possibilities. "The whole fabric of our civilization is in danger. Unless we can really get the conditions of Europe back to normal, unless we can succeed in getting Europe at work again, and commerce and social intercourse once more established, it is impossible to exaggerate the danger that may be before us."[85]

It was hard for Cecil to concentrate the attentions of the members before him on this broad question, He spoke with passion but offered no magic potion to solve the economic problem; an editorial in the *Manchester Guardian* lauded his speech but wished that he had suggested a definitive plan to provide the financial credits needed by European business.[86] His "manifest sincerity and seriousness … held the attenuated House in solemn and even gloomy interest." "It was a profound speech, which made a profound impression upon the House."[87] Cecil's speech was followed by a lengthy argument between Labourites and arch-Conservatives (Samuel Hoare) over Russia. The Labour leader J. R. Clynes, Minister of Food in Lloyd George's wartime government, threw his entire weight behind the government raising the blockade immediately, as it was no longer military necessary and would be a prerequisite for free flow of food and goods between countries. However the impact of Clynes's speech was blunted by an interruption, the House being summoned by the Lords Commissioners and the

Speaker announcing the traditional pre-recess Royal Assent to thirteen Acts of Parliament passed that session. When he returned to his speech, Clynes was speaking to an assembly itching to get away; the entire government front bench had already emptied out.[88] Compared to the rest of the speeches, according to the *Christian Science Monitor*, the one "in a category of its own was that of Lord Robert Cecil." However, in the final judgment, "no debate worthy of the name matured yesterday in the House of Commons."[89]

The prime minister's speech had notably addressed most of Cecil's concerns, suggesting that a primary goal of his speech was to preempt any criticism coming from Cecil's bench. Not for the first time, Cecil felt that the prime minister had given an important speech directly inspired by him. Large pieces of Lloyd George's critical war aims speech of January 5, 1918, to the Trades Union Congress came directly from Cecil's memo on the importance of creating an international organization to settle post-war disputes.[90] Now Lloyd George again publicly pegged himself to a very Cecilian foreign policy.[91] Had Lloyd George spoken in this way because he believed Cecil's line that the League was the long-term solution to global problems, or because he believed that it was what MPs and the British public wanted to hear, or because he wanted to preempt criticism from Cecil in particular? Cecil couldn't be sure. He believed that his own speech would have been more effective, and more jarring, if it had come before Lloyd George's, but what could he have done differently? Cecil had wanted to reassert his independence in Commons, and yet from the outside his line appeared little different from Lloyd George's. Despite his unhappiness over Lloyd George's use of the League as a negotiating piece in the naval talks with the United States, as the consummate British foreign ministry operative Cecil would never leak the details of confidential negotiations to the public at large. Any breach between the two men remained private. Rather than putting pressure on Lloyd George, Cecil's speech to the House of Commons strengthened the perception that the prime minister was working assiduously on the problems at hand, and that he had the support of the well-known independent-minded Cecil. At least no one at the Peace Conference or at home among the British public could doubt the importance that Cecil put on the immediate revivification of global trade as the lynchpin to concluding a successful peace. On Cecil's return to Paris, House congratulated Cecil for the speech in the House of Commons, and wished that Wilson would say something similar.[92] Lloyd George's triumph in Westminster was the talk of Paris.[93]

Returning to Paris

On April 19, Cecil took the day-long trip back to Paris, returning this time with his wife. He undoubtedly had missed her during the first three months of the Conference. Their casual intimacy percolates through their correspondence and his diary, where he constantly desired to share stories about the people he saw, both those she knew and those she did not. The array of upper crust British youth littered about Paris always made for some good gossip. Cecil let his wife know immediately when he discovered the engagement of Victoria Primrose (the young war-widowed daughter of Lord Derby) to a wounded Guardsman working at the British Embassy in Paris.[94] Cecil recognized that such things were banal and unimportant trifles compared to the work he was immersed in crafting the peace, yet he loved the gossip all the same. The day after Nelly arrived in Paris, the Cecils got together with Bobbety and Betty and went to see the new cathedral of Sacré Coeur, and the panoramic view of Paris beneath it.[95] Two days later Cecil and his wife had a private dinner in the Cranborne's flat. With his wife in town, Cecil's private life became somewhat more private as he retreated into family.

Yet he remained immersed in the greatest issues of the Peace Conference, and struggled with the same fundamental problems as before. How exactly could the United States be compelled to aid in the "economic reconstruction of Europe"?[96] Preoccupied with other issues, the Council of Four had made no decision on the SEC resolution of April 7.[97] The young Henry Morgenthau Jr., who later became Franklin Roosevelt's Treasury Secretary, discouraged Cecil by suggesting that US business opinion favored complete economic withdrawal from Europe.[98] Hoover was calling on Wilson to pull the United States out of the meetings of all the Peace Conference commissions, saying that caving into punitive measures like reparations would limit US independence and taint the US position as the world's moral leader.[99] When Cecil went to see House to talk over what to do next, House conveyed his tremendous pessimism about the possibility of any US action, but he agreed to forward to Wilson a scheme, drawn up by Keynes and supported by Cecil, for a German indemnity fund guaranteed by the allied powers "on which money could be raised and allotted to the various nations according to their claims of reparation."[100] Lloyd George likewise wrote to Wilson in support of this proposal.[101] An earlier proposal by Keynes for general cancellation of intergovernmental debts had been rejected by US representatives fearful of the domestic political consequences, as had been his idea of a German bond sale backed by Allied guarantees that repaying these bonds would have priority over all other obligations.[102] US negotiators favored instead encouraging business activity in Germany by fully ending the blockade while massively lowering reparations demands. But Cecil hoped that Keynes's new plan might be pitched as a compromise between France and the United States. It was a lack of liquidity, of money sloshing through the system from customers to suppliers to employees, which Cecil and Keynes found the greatest problem. Simply cancelling proposed reparations or ending all blockade restrictions would not immediately make European business more liquid, but extending new loans to "countries whose individual credit is temporarily destroyed" would. Such loans could go to both wartime allies and enemies, who could "trade on their prospects of reparation from the enemy states or capitalize their future prospects of production."[103] Once European trade restarted, the web of loans could be serviced and repaid. However, Wilson fundamentally opposed this idea, and made sure his Committee of Economic Advisors agreed with him.[104] The president was no longer listening much to Colonel House, who had clearly lost much of his standing within the US delegation since Wilson had returned from the United States in March.

Cecil also confronted challenges on the League. Maurice Hankey finally decided that he did not want to be the Secretary General of the new League, and a letter to that effect awaited Cecil when he returned to Paris. Hankey had become the full-time secretary of the Council of Four since the end of March. He had thought long and hard about the League post for months, enlisting the advice of friends like his mentor Lord Esher, who was unequivocally opposed, preferring that Hankey use his skills to improve the organization of an Imperial Cabinet. Hankey had even worked out for himself some plans for how he might run the League.[105] The "Sketch Plan of Organization," printed and circulated on March 31, shows how closely he had considered the offer. Pulled together by his staff, the plan described at length the new departments that would have to be created, the types of duties that various officials would do on a daily basis, and even addressed the issue of remuneration and pensions for employees at the League's Secretariat.[106] As late as April 12, Hankey still appeared to be seriously considering the job, writing wistfully to his wife that he had just met a Swiss woman who talked up the natural beauties of the League's prospective site in Geneva, "with perfect bathing, and mountains quite near."[107] However Hankey clearly relished his role with the Council of Four during the Conference and did not want to give it up. And he had a hard time envisioning himself ever leaving the Cabinet Office that he had created, which had given him the closest access to the prime minister and a leadership position within the British government. His diary suggests that it was a long discussion with Lloyd George on the way back to Paris from London on April 14 that led him to the conclusion that "the British Empire is worth a thousand Leagues of Nations," and that he would stay in London where he could do "more for the peace of the world ... than in Geneva."[108] Hankey later claimed this decision showed his foresight in understanding that Wilson would not carry support for a League in the United States, and thus that it could never succeed.[109] Cecil Hurst had confided to Hankey that his American friend, David Hunter Miller, doubted that any Treaty with a League could ever pass through the US Senate.[110] In any case, House and Cecil quickly moved on to their next choice for Secretary General, the longtime British Foreign Office mandarin Eric Drummond. Drummond accepted the job, but the failure to get Hankey to climb aboard the new project was troubling and reflected the serious reservations about the League held by many British delegates.

In a pair of April 21 meetings with the BED, Cecil presented the revised League draft treaty. Hughes derided Article 1 which focused on League membership, asking how could it be decided by the League whether any country had "fulfilled their obligations" to be deemed eligible for entry into the League. Robert Borden, the Canadian prime minister, complained that the guarantees of the territorial integrity of all members embodied in Article 10 went much too far. Cecil had suggested the same to Wilson earlier, suggesting that it was pointless to include an article that no one (including Wilson) really believed was true for all circumstances.[111] But to the Dominion leaders, Cecil countered that Article 19 allowed for the revision of all treaties and territorial positions, and that Article 10 was "merely one of the safeguards" that embodied the spirit of the Covenant, showing that all countries were "interested in the preservation of peace" and opposed to all forms of "aggression." In response to further questions and criticism, Cecil gave spirited defenses of Articles 8, 9, 11, 15, 16, 18, 20, 21, 23, 25, and 26.[112] It was an exhausting meeting. At the end, he decided that he had to make a handful of minor changes, all of which were then agreed to by Wilson and put into the final Covenant.[113]

Yet Cecil felt that in the end he had carried the BED with him in the meeting, and that they acquiesced to the League. He was likely wrong; despite his best efforts, it seems that Hughes, Borden, and the others in the BED never accepted the League as an instrument that could help ensure British, Imperial, and global security.[114] As Clement Jones, the secretary of the BED, would later write in his perceptive and humorous portrait of the Australian prime minister, Hughes from the start "objected to the spirit no less than the letter of the Covenant of the League."[115] But characteristically Cecil remained optimistic that when they were eventually confronted with what he believed would be overwhelming public support for a League, the political leaders of the Dominions would come on board.

Cecil also believed, fundamentally, that the Dominions' opinions were not the ones that mattered. He reported specifically and solely to Lloyd George, the man who had appointed him to his various positions at the Peace Conference. And he remained certain that the prime minister had voiced no opposition to his work leading the League Commission and the Supreme Economic Council. After the BED meetings of April 21, Cecil explained to McCormick that his government had "given him full authority on Supreme Council matters" and that a "drastic relaxation of blockade" would have "easier sailing from now on."[116] Their speeches in Parliament indicated that Lloyd George and Cecil were firmly on the same page. In a lunch meeting on April 23, the two worried about blockade-related obstructionism not from Hughes or anyone else in the British delegation, but from Clemenceau and the French. They finally decided that a reasonable way to spur the Council of Four to act on withdrawing the blockade, thus forcing the issue on Clemenceau, would be for Cecil to get the SEC to pass a resolution calling for a complete end of blockade restrictions. This resolution would then put the issue on the agenda for the Four. At the same time Lloyd George would pass Cecil's paper along to Wilson and Clemenceau "as the British proposition."[117]

When the SEC met that afternoon, Cecil led off the meeting urging the council "in the economic interest of the European nations as a whole" to end all restrictions on trade with Germany, other than the exports of gold, silver, securities and weapons, with the threat that the Allies would reinstate all trade restrictions if Germany's actions demanded it.[118] Clémentel, the French delegate, stuck to the line that no end of trade restrictions should occur until the peace was signed. Hoover and Clémentel then argued again about whether it was blockade restrictions or the failure of the United States to supply adequate credit facilities that lay at the heart of Germany's dead economy. In his heart Cecil believed that neither side was wrong, but it was only the blockade that was at present under the purview of the SEC, and thus it was the blockade that he could aim to reshape. Cecil's resolution got as much from the US delegates as he thought possible. Hoover had told him bluntly on a number of occasions that the United States would never reimpose the blockade after it had been lifted. But the US and Italian delegations ended up declaring their full support for Cecil's motion, and over French objections, the three other Allies decided to send the resolution to the Big Four.

The flurry of SEC-related work was diffuse and unabating. He responded to Mitchell-Thompson's protest from London against the diminution of the blockade that had already occurred.[119] He wrote a proposal to Balfour and Lloyd George suggesting that it was time to remove censorship on cables and wireless, something that since the withdrawal of the blacklists had no blockade value.[120] On April 28 he presided over a "desultory meeting" of the SEC where he thought little was accomplished, although the SEC did resolve that because Germany was never going to find a way to fully import the 370,000 tons of food monthly authorized by the Brussels agreement, they would immediately suspend the requirement that shipments of food from the European neutrals to Germany must be preapproved by the Allies.[121] He met with Henry Wilson the next day, trying to figure out how the Danube could be used for distributing food from Romania.[122] The Big Four had not responded to their request on lifting the blockade of Germany.[123] Yet Cecil and the SEC kept working to feed central Europe.

And at the same time he continued to work on League issues. Cecil led an Organizing Committee that met repeatedly in late April and early May to figure out how to pull together a first League meeting. He met repeatedly with Eric Drummond on how to start up the League. Cecil was unsure whether the FO official and former private secretary to Asquith, Grey, and Balfour, would be up to the task, or whether "he will feel himself rather lost without official superiors and machinery to support him."[124] Drummond was "oppressed by his new duties."[125] But Cecil believed he was capable of organizing a small bureaucracy and the regular diplomatic meetings that Cecil assumed would be the primary mission of the League secretary, perhaps not as adroitly as Hankey could have done but sufficiently well nonetheless. He had his surrogate Frank Walters support Drummond's qualifications and capabilities to US delegates wary of appointing a mere "secretary."[126] And he also tried to help Drummond by utilizing his British League staff. By mid-April, Philip Baker had begun answering inquiries from a variety of international organizations eager to align with the League.[127] Already the role of the League was expanding beyond that specifically outlined in the Covenant, even thought the Covenant itself had not yet even been approved by the Peace Conference.

Cecil admitted to uncharacteristic nervousness before the April 28 meeting of the Plenary Session of the Peace Conference when the final League Covenant would be presented. Always attuned to gossip, he heard rumors that "there was going to be every kind of row, and that Hughes the Australian was going to oppose the League tooth and nail, etc., etc. I did not believe any of them and said so, but of course there was always the possibility that they might be true!" And yet the meeting went entirely according to plan, its only defect being "its excessive dullness" and some embarrassing squabbling within the French delegation, with Pichon berating Bourgeois for bringing up amendments that had long been rejected by the League Commission, followed with Clemenceau ridiculing Pichon's proposal to make the microstate of Monaco a member of the League.[128]

As he often did during such large-group meetings, Cecil kept himself occupied by writing a letter to his wife, who he had deposited just the previous day at a small hotel overlooking the Seine called "La Tete Noire," a remnant of the old chateau of Madame Pompadour in Bellevue.[129] Nelly's hat box flew off the roof of their car on the way, but luckily it was found by a passerby the next day and brought to her. He doubted that the "strange countrified little inn" along the Seine would be comfortable enough for her, and worried that the entire "Paris experiment" of having her in France was not working out well.[130] Other wives lived with their husbands during the Conference. David Hunter Miller and his wife passed the months in the luxury of the Hotel Meurice, with Mrs. Miller socializing and traveling with the wives of Colonel House and Auchincloss.[131] But Lady Cecil had not enjoyed the atmosphere of Paris and of the Majestic in particular.[132] Even with her closest old friends, her hearing problems augmented her natural shyness to isolate her in many social situations.[133] Undoubtedly she found out quickly during her first few days in Paris that she would not see as much of her busy husband as they had anticipated.

Rebuilding Europe's economy remained uncertain, but at least the League was coming out fine. He received personal congratulations from Venizelos for his "decisive" efforts on behalf of the League, and from Woodrow Wilson, who noted "that the laboring oar fell to you and that it is chiefly due to you that the Covenant has come out of the confusions of debate in its original integrity. May I not express my own personal admiration of the work you did and my own sense of obligation?"[134] The press in Britain generally favored the Covenant, or at least did not express opposition.[135] Plans were circulating for the first meeting of the League to take place in the East Room of the White House in October, before its move to permanent headquarters in Geneva.[136] Despite some stumbles along the way, a Covenant that looked basically acceptable to all had been approved by all the Allied powers. It looked plausible that the League might mark, as Cecil hoped, a fundamental transformation in the nature of diplomacy.

*

Throughout April, Cecil worried about the future of interallied unity and how it was needed to nurse the revival of the European economy. Despite some real successes in alleviating Europe's post-war economic catastrophe, over the course of April Cecil and the others calling for collaborative measures did not yet persuade the Big Four to undertake any of their plans for engineering a true European economic recovery. He worried about the starvation and social dislocation that he saw in Central Europe, not out of a humanitarian impulse, but due to his fears that it would destabilize any peace. Likewise efforts to finalize the League Covenant had proven more aggravating than Cecil had anticipated a few months earlier. Cecil's relationships at the Conference were changing throughout April, most notably his relationship with David Lloyd George. By the end of the month, he was tense. So was everyone else in Paris.

6

Ending the Economic War: May

The rain-swept streets of Paris were quiet but uneasy throughout most of May Day. The traditional day of international socialist solidarity, May 1 had actually never ranked as a notable day on the calendar for the Parisian workers. They embodied a century and a half of the French revolutionary spirit, but the descendants of the *sans-culottes* had long marched to their own drum. However, during the early months of 1919, the perspective and influences of these workers had become globalized. The peacemakers living and working in their city made Parisians conscious of the breadth of global political instability, and also sensitive to the possibility that tremendous, fateful, worldwide transformations were underway.[1] The most radical French trade unionists hoped that the planned May Day demonstrations might trigger a true revolution.[2] The threat of unrest led the French government to ban the planned protests and to bring in soldiers and horses to reinforce the police. Throughout the day, the city appeared empty, with buses still, the Metro shuttered, and with strikes of restaurant workers making it hard for Parisians to get a meal.

In the late afternoon, tens of thousands of demonstrators ignored the protest ban and attempted to congregate at the Place de République, and ended up fighting "pitched battles" against the soldiers and police. Hardened by the years of brutal warfare, and emboldened by their fears of Bolshevik provocation, the Parisian police acted "un peu dur" when facing off against the rioters, but they succeeded in driving the workers out of the city center.[3] Over 700 police and protesters were injured, with two demonstrators shot dead.

The angry confrontations around Opera and République mirrored the mood of those meeting in the Crillon and the Majestic, where leaders made momentous decisions to accept conflict rather than consensus. As with the police response on the streets of Paris, the threat that Bolshevism might spread throughout Europe provided the impetus to internationalist policies and institutions. During May the Allies worked to relieve the economic collapse in central Europe. This humanitarian process went hand in hand with the evolution of the economic war and the development of the earliest League institutions.

Feeding Europe while Transforming the Blockade

Clemenceau, Wilson, and Lloyd George met almost continuously throughout May with various experts and advisors pulled into their private meetings as needed. Over the previous four months, they had broken repeated informal deadlines, and the delegates remained uncertain how to finalize the peace. Immediate concerns constantly got in the way. Perhaps he was influenced by the tension brought by soldiers milling outside his window in the Place de la Concorde, planning to face off against the workers emerged and angered by the economic dislocation of France, but during the May Day meeting of the Four, Woodrow Wilson argued that if the blockade did not end immediately, "Germany would go to pieces." Lloyd George, suspecting that the real motivation behind the president's anti-blockade stance was his desire to submit businesses and farmers in Britain and Europe to an onslaught of US competition, responded that Germany's real need was for credit from the United States. When Wilson responded that US finance experts had rejected the British scheme on the table for just such credits, Lloyd George retorted that something needed to be done, that the Allies needed to come up with some sort of comprehensive financial solution that could be presented to, and accepted by, the Germans.[4]

Their meeting adjourned without any decisions on any of these issues. This was not surprising, considering how the discussion on blockade bled into other points of crisis and stalemate that overwhelmed the Four at this time. But the paired solutions for the economic malaise—ending the Allied economic war while making US credit available to Europe—were continually pressed over the next week by Cecil, both to assist his prime minister in his efforts to obtain financial guarantees from the United States, but also to prod Lloyd George into rapid action on ending the blockade.

Why would Lloyd George oppose raising the blockade? In early March he had notably chastised Clemenceau and the French for allowing German children to starve. Yet by early May, in his "enigma variations" Lloyd George had come to see things differently.[5] The blockade was the one aspect of fighting the war where the British undoubtedly dominated the Allied partnership. The British Admiralty controlled the seas, stopping or permitting overseas trade with Germany as the British Ministry of Blockade recommended. Similarly, the blockade forbade

Germans from accessing the British banks that still dominated global merchant banking. British authorities had led the Allied economic war committees that had pieced together an increasingly unified war by the end of 1918. As a result, proposed changes to the blockade were for the British an obvious chip to use in negotiations with the United States. Moreover, maintaining the blockade remained a political winner in Britain. The lust for vengeance, rued Cecil, led even good men like Lord Sumner to support "the most extreme proposals" for sucking all assets out of stricken Germany.[6] Giving it up might limit Britain's ability to ensure that the Treaty sufficiently penalized Germany.

Finally, by the start of May the Brussels agreement looked like it was working, and that food was actually getting to the Germans. The United States claim that a full end of the blockade was the only move that could alleviate European suffering appeared simply false. The SEC's Superior Blockade Committee memo for the SWC on "The Present Position with Regard to the Blockade of Germany" noted that "in effect Germany is now free to import all the food for which she can pay."[7]

After the May Day meeting, Lloyd George told Cecil that the Big Four had found it impossible to suspend the blockade as requested by the SEC, for fear that doing so would mean giving up the economic lash compelling the Germans to sign the Treaty. In response, Cecil pushed through the SEC on May 5 a resolution for its Blockade Section to coordinate with military authorities in creating contingency plans to restart a lifted blockade (see Figure 6.1). It was an idea he had been considering and pushing the previous two weeks. To those who saw blockade as "the principal lever for securing peace," ensuring that the Germans would sign whatever treaty was presented to them, Cecil now argued that a superior lever for gaining German acquiescence would be to lift the blockade, with the open threat to reimpose it if the Germans acted badly. "If you have starved a man for some months and you then begin to feed him with the threat that if he does not do as you wish you will starve him again, it is more likely that he will be impressed than if you continue the former régime unchanged."[8] This was questionable logic, for certain, yet it took into account the misery of Central Europeans and the threat of revolution.

The SEC also decided to find out exactly what primary resources German businesses needed to restart their production, and ordered the Raw Materials Section (led by Cecil) to meet with the German finance delegates now headquartered in Versailles. Finally, the SEC also supported (over Hoover's objection) sending a plea from the Raw Materials Section to the Council of Four describing "the extreme urgency of supplying raw materials to Europe"

Figure 6.1 Photo of Cecil after a League executive meeting on May 5, 1919. Courtesy of the Department of Rare Books and Special Collections, Princeton University Library, Gilbert F. Close Papers MC 202, Series 4: Paris Peace Conference Photographs, Box 2.

without which peace would not occur.[9] While the US delegates still rejected any sort of joint financial backing by all the Allies, Cecil remained hopeful that the ensuing debate was "of considerable advantage in loosening the position" of the US representatives, who "are now beginning to realise that they must do something."[10] Maybe he could find a way to open up US coffers for at least some of the European states that needed it.

As had become his way, Cecil publicized his positions to rally support for his policy. A communiqué went out from the SEC to the press, highlighting the ways that they had mitigated the blockade restrictions on German trade, in particular by allowing German funds and credit in neutral countries to be utilized by Germans for purchasing imports with any proceeds from German exports available to pay for imports. Finally it also included a statement that the SEC's Blockade Section was drawing up plans for blockade restrictions that could be immediately put into effect if Germany refused to sign the Treaty.[11] This statement was published broadly in newspapers around the world, even before it was approved by the Four. Responding to these SEC resolutions, Lloyd George pointed out to Clemenceau and Wilson once again that the United States needed to support a credit scheme to help restart the European economy.

The Big Four invited the SEC delegates from each country to attend the meeting of the Four the next day. True to form, all of the five leaderless American delegates to the SEC showed up. As House explained it privately to Cecil the day before, "they were all as jealous of one another as prima donnas and it would be quite impossible to send any one of them to represent any of the others." "Truly," Cecil opined in his diary, US "ideas of organization are extraordinarily primitive."[12] Cecil brought along just John Maynard Keynes.

Cecil led off the meeting of the Four with a long speech explaining in plain terms the economic problem that threatened the possibility of ever making peace. People needed more than food—they needed to get back to work, not just in Germany but across Europe. The blockade must be relaxed at least for its psychological effect, mitigating the sense of mistrust that existed. But according to Cecil, simply raising the blockade was insufficient to address Europe's deep economic problems. Even if the economic war ended immediately and all Allied restrictions on trade were revoked, not much trade would occur, as companies and businessmen lacked the credit with which to buy raw materials from abroad. As an example, Cecil described a textile factories in Lodz, Poland, that could not restart its operations and get its employees working again until its owners procured raw cotton and wool from abroad. But they had no money to buy these materials or exports to trade for them.[13] Germany found itself out of funds to pay for food shipments that were already in transit; they presently owed nearly £30 million out of their total of around £70 million in purchases. But who would loan Germany money to pay its bills, when there was still no sense of whether Germany would ever be in a position to pay them back? He urged support for Keynes's proposal for US loans to the Allies, with the promise of future reparations payments from Germany as the collateral. Keynes believed this would heal the credit crunch that continued to cripple European business, although some of his fellow British Treasury officials feared they could increase British government indebtedness.[14] Herbert Hoover considered it a reasonable scheme, but US Treasury advisors were fundamentally opposed to extending such significant loans, seeing them as virtually unsecured.[15]

The Four approved a few of Cecil's proposals. They called for making "semi-public communications" with border neutrals about how a dropped blockade could be restarted and reinforced more strongly than ever if Germany failed to meet Allied demands. When Cecil brought up difficulties with trade along the

Danube river, with the French and British each controlling different parts of the river, Clemenceau and the others supported his call for a commission led by British Admiral Troubridge to coordinate the two authorities. But on the finance issue, the Four remained undecided.

Inevitably, yet another committee was created, the "European Economic Committee," on May 9. It was created at Cecil's suggestion; according to Baruch, Cecil had been pushing the possibility since at least April 21 and had then taken it up with House, aiming to create a committee of two men from each country, "quite private," to investigate the European situation and to suggest a plan that would enable Germany to get credits for purchase of raw materials.[16] It has been suggested that this committee was make-work for Cecil and Keynes, "two of the strongest critics of the treaty" who were thereby "kept out of circulation for a month," with its eventual reports ignored.[17] But Cecil rightfully saw it as was another potential back-room opportunity to finally pin the US advisors to a solution. In a peace conference where control and power were never clear, a new committee might actually make a significant difference. Cecil saw Norman Davis, "the American financial man," as the pivotal player, and went to see him just a few hours after the Council of Four approved the new committee.

The other US delegate was Bernard Baruch, who explained to Cecil privately that there had been much controversy over whether he or Hoover should get the post. Cecil periodically found the Wall Street financier embarrassing. Cecil joked that despite his sense that Baruch was an honest man, Baruch spent so much time talking about his own honesty that Cecil could not help worrying that the American might be a liar.[18] The two argued in the SEC, but Baruch had developed a tremendous respect for Cecil. Baruch collected signed photos of various luminaries at the Conference, but his letter asking Cecil for a photo came earlier, on May 7, and was more gushing than any other he wrote: "The opportunity of meeting you and the friendship which I know will result constitute one of the brightest spots in a most interesting five months."[19] During the first week of May, they had a number of private discussions and dinners, where Cecil's suggestions seem to have shaped the evolving ideas of the Wall Street financier.[20] On the same day he wrote asking Cecil for a photo, Baruch dictated an unprecedented lengthy letter to Woodrow Wilson calling for new "special commercial credit advances" from the US Treasury to the struggling nations of eastern Europe, including Italy, with the intention to help merchants in these countries buy imports. "Whatever the amount may be, it is an obligation that we cannot escape," Baruch wrote to Wilson. Relieving "prostrate" Europe was the "fitting climax to the part that America has played in the war" and was the greatest possible way of utilizing the unique resources of the United States.[21] Baruch appeared newly amenable to the type of plan on offer from Britain.

Cecil's own second on this new committee was of course John Maynard Keynes, a man whom Cecil had been spending a lot of time with over the previous month, and who was likewise hopeful that the new committee could finally reshape the economic decisions of the Big Four.[22] Throughout the early months of the Conference, Keynes's remit had been to advise the British delegates to the Reparations Commission. The British were utterly and consistently divided between those who wanted to demand only small reparations to allow Germany to recover and build a successful republic, and those who wanted high reparations to punish the Germans and to appeal to jingoist and anti-German electorates at home.[23] In the inevitably blunt words of Billy Hughes, everyone on the Reparations Commission saw it as offering "cash prizes to all," with all delegates following the aim of "scooping the pool of as many millions as possible."[24] By mid-May, Keynes was reaching the heights of his

Figure 6.2 Portrait photo of Cecil taken in Paris during the Peace Conference, given to Baruch and signed, "Your sincere friend, Robert Cecil." Courtesy of the Department of Rare Books and Special Collections, Princeton University Library, Bernard M. Baruch Papers, Box 713.

frustration regarding the Conference. He was influenced by the grim tidings of Melchior and the other German financial experts he had met with periodically since mid-January. Keynes was also irritated by the intransigence of the French and especially of the British "twins" Sumner and Cunliffe for their heavy yet nebulous reparations demands. He was frustrated with Woodrow Wilson, who had not supported Keynes's loan program or other constructive solutions for Europe's financial problems.[25] Perhaps, Keynes suggested, Wilson was far from the humanitarian that others perceived him to be.[26]

To help bolster their cause, Cecil found new sources of information about the state of the Central European economies. At Cecil's instigation, the Treasury had sent Francis Oppenheimer to Paris with the intention that he would lead an exploratory financial mission to Vienna. Cecil had been looking for a way to get Oppenheimer to Paris since the start of the Peace Conference.[27] During the war Oppenheimer had served as the Commercial Secretary in the Hague and was instrumental in crafting and operating the Netherlands Overseas Trust, an organization pivotal to the rationing of neutral trade with Germany and thus central to the British blockade.[28] In 1916, Oppenheimer had come under significant criticism from Britain's jingoist press for his family's roots (some considered him doubly suspect as both German and Jewish). At that time, he had come to rely on Cecil as his most staunch supporter in the FO and in the House of Commons.[29] Although he was nominally the Treasury's appointee, Oppenheimer met with Cecil immediately after his arrival at the Majestic, and his old FO boss gave him his new orders. "I knew nothing about Austria and had had no Treasury training," Oppenheimer told Cecil. "I was a genuine dilettante in finance. Lord Robert insisted. He wanted an independent opinion."[30] Cecil charged Oppenheimer with finding out what securities or other assets would be available in Vienna as collateral for loans to finance immediate purchases of food. For the longer term, Oppenheimer could uncover how likely the new Austria was to have a post-war economic recovery. Over the course of the rest of May, Oppenheimer sent constant telegrams advising Cecil of what he was learning in Vienna, providing a critical new supply of real information about what was going on in the shattered former capital of the Habsburg Empire.

Initially, the European Economic Committee proved less pliant than Cecil had hoped. Keynes had come up with what Cecil recognized as "an extremely ingenious scheme for providing large sums of money for everybody by a kind of joint guarantee of German indemnity bonds." But when Cecil and Keynes pushed this plan, they were frustrated by Davis's reticence to take a stance. Davis "always coming rather near to making a definite proposal, and always drawing back at the last moment, much like a little boy bathing in the sea for the first time."[31] Baruch, the other US delegate to this committee, could never understand Davis's position and didn't really trust his compatriot; as he wrote in his diary, "I am always impressed with the fact that Davis is very secretive about what he is doing, and have in mind that he is doing something with which he does not keep me conversant."[32] But Baruch was likewise skeptical that the US government should take on financial liabilities secured only by potential German reparation payments, and weakly claimed that these financing issues went beyond his authority, or that of any existing committee, to decide. Keynes then showed what Cecil perceived as intemperance when he refused to even consider negotiating an alternate plan. Cecil recognized the art of the deal was everything, and lamented that Keynes was too "intolerant of fools."[33] The excited and petulant Keynes had nearly reached the end, moping to his mother the next day that he was preparing to resign from the Treasury.[34] After Chancellor of the Exchequer Austin Chamberlain's pled with him to stay, Keynes remained in Paris, but spent the next few weeks blasting away at the injustice of the high reparations demands proposed by the British negotiators Sumner and Cunliffe.[35]

However Cecil saw positive signs. For him the European Economic Committee's meeting of May 24 appeared a turning point. Davis announced that he had spoken to President Wilson, and would recommend on his return to the United States that the War Trade Corporation should advance money to help European trade resume. He would also recommend that the Treasury ask Congress to defer interest payments on Allied war debts for three years. Davis asked the committee members to keep this pledge "a profound secret."[36] Soon Baruch told Keynes that likewise he would accept Keynes's plan if it was edited to indicate that "private credits and individual effort" were preferable to public credit.[37] These indications of a change in the attitudes of the US policymakers suggested to Cecil that a scheme to reboot Europe's financial system might be coming together.

Likewise on the blockade, compromise appeared possible. At the meeting of the Four on May 14, Cecil alleviated the disparate concerns of Lloyd George and Wilson, who then both supported all three measures he put before the Council. The first measure called for publicity for the Supreme Blockade Council's memo on the many ways that the blockade had already been shorn down, including the full lifting of blacklists in neutral countries, and the significant opening of borders for most German exports and for those on a free list of articles that could be imported into Germany. This also included the Allied pledge to lift all blockade measures completely as soon as the Germans signed the peace (in other words, well before it was ratified by any national parliament.[38] Cecil saw this as proof to the world of the "approaching removal" of the entire economic war.[39]

Cecil's second measure called for publicizing the Allies' ability to reimpose the blockade at will, if Germany refused to sign the Treaty.[40] Advised by Hoover's deep suspicion of the Allied blockade, President Wilson initially suggested that restarting any lifted blockade would only cause a humanitarian crisis and would be "a much more terrible punishment than a simple military occupation." But Clemenceau argued that economic sanctions were preferable to having "our soldiers killed," and Lloyd George hewed very closely to the line that Cecil had been pushing for the previous month, that the simple threat of a future "general stoppage of trade" was a "severe penalty" and would lead the Germans to demand of their government "Sign! Sign! Sign!"[41] Wilson gave in, and that evening Cecil issued the official statement, stating that the SEC approved plans enabling a quick reimposition of the blockade on Germany, if it was ever deemed necessary.[42] The threat was issued.

To Cecil, this was the international community putting into practice his ideas about utilizing economic power to cow recalcitrant nations. For him economic war, or more accurately the threat of economic war, was the primary weapon in the arsenal of the League of Nations. And now he intriguingly pushed, in another measure before the Big Four, for the first real attempt to use this new power of the League. Into Paris over the previous weeks trickled reports of warfare among the new states of Eastern Europe, with Polish forces invading the Ukraine, and the Serbs refusal to send along relief supplies to the Banat region (an area contested between Romania, Serbia, and the new state of Hungary). The peacemakers faced incredible difficulties trying to figure out how to force a cease-fire between the Poles and the competing Ukrainian and Bolshevik factions in Galicia.[43] Cecil argued that both Poland and Serbia could be pressured to follow the will of the Allies. What needed to occur, he argued, was "to issue a ukase from the Great Four saying that no one who went on fighting should get the slightest assistance financial or economic from any of the Associated Governments, irrespective of whether they were right or wrong."[44] The Four should give the SEC the power to apply economic pressure on the two Eastern European countries, withholding needed coal from Serbia and food from Poland.[45] After little debate, the Big Four agreed that "the Supreme Economic Council should be free to take such action as seemed to them desirable in such cases."[46] In effect, Cecil's SEC was given the opportunity to test Article 16 of the League Covenant. As a result, the SEC told Serbia that as soon as it shipped food to the Banat, they would authorize Serbia to receive coal.[47] Likewise the Supreme Council issued a telegram to the

Polish leader General Pilsudski on May 27, saying he must end operations in east Galicia or lose his supplies coming from the Allies. A month later the Peace Conference leaders changed their minds, acknowledging Polish occupation of the region, but it is notable that the threat of losing supplies apparently caused the Poles to temporarily halt their operations.[48] Eventually Poland took the land, holding onto it until the Nazi and Soviet invasion in 1939.[49] Despite the ultimate result, in Serbia and Poland, the SEC in May 1919 provided an early example of the forceful anti-war economic sanctions regime that, many expected, would soon be wielded by the League of Nations. Even before the end of the Conference, the SEC was already operating a new, powerful internationalist diplomacy (see Figure 6.3).

The SEC could do such things because of its overall success and general usefulness. On the fundamental issue of feeding Germany, the SEC had proven

Figure 6.3 Photo of the Supreme Economic Council, probably taken at its offices at 26 Rue de Bassano sometime in May or June 1919. Seated are Vittorio Orlando (Prime Minister of Italy), Etienne Clémentel (French Minister of Commerce), Lord Robert Cecil, Silvio Crespi (Italian Minister of Supply and Food) and Herbert Hoover (Director General of Relief and head of the American Relief Administration). The photo includes a number of the SEC members and staffers, including Bernard Baruch, Norman Davis, Thomas Lamont, and J. Arthur Salter. Courtesy of the Department of Rare Books and Special Collections, Princeton University Library, Bernard M. Baruch Papers, Box 701.

its worth since March, when it led the rebuilt Allied Maritime Transport Executive to divide German merchant ships, parcel out cargos from the various Allied food executives, and loaded and send loads from overseas ports to central Europe. The Enemy Tonnage Sub-Committee of the SEC reported on the significant shipments of food aboard German ships in the United States, with the US Food Administrator allocating 327,080 tons of various foodstuffs to thirty-eight German ships since April, along with 127,225 tons on twenty-six ships from the Rio de la Plata region of Argentina and Uruguay.[50] Despite later claims that Hoover's ARA controlled relief efforts during these months, Hoover found himself at the same time unable to gain control even of the US flagged ships promised to him by Wilson.[51] Instead it was the SEC's power to prioritize cargos on both the German-flagged ships and on those of the Allies, particularly Britain, that enabled the Relief Administration to feed the starving Germans. At any given moment in May, according to Hoover, there was "nearly one hundred million dollars of food in motion towards Germany."[52] In working to feed Austria, Hoover's power to requisition railway stock came from the SEC.[53] The SEC also enabled the Allies to help each other. Along with the food, in May and June these ships took some coal cargos to fuel-starved Italy, a goal Hoover lamented as a waste of money, but one that the SEC pushed through nonetheless, following its mandate to restore the European economy.[54]

Hoover was concerned that publicizing the possible reinstitution of blockade measures on Germany might hurt German finance and make it hard for Germany to pay for this food already on route, but the SEC alleviated this problem by hatching an agreement that all the Allied governments would consider any losses on these shipments a charge to their Allied expenses on the war.[55] There remained unresolved questions about how Germany might pay for all of the food they were receiving—most was getting paid for with gold and securities, but not all—but at least it was getting there, thanks much to the operation of the SEC. There might still be undernourishment, the Director General of Relief's mid-May report on the European food situation the previous month stated, but other than in off-limits Bolshevik Russia, "there was no acute starvation."[56]

Throughout the spring of 1919, a lot of criticism circulated about the slowness of the Allies to alleviate the humanitarian disaster. Historians have often agreed that the vindictive British and French held back the United States from implementing a policy that could have fed Germany faster.[57] To Hoover, the United States eventually succeeded on its own; the ARA embodied "a generosity unparalleled in the history of mankind," as the United States "saved hundreds of millions of lives in Europe from famine, pestilence, and revolutionary chaos."[58]

Woodrow Wilson's secretary Gilbert Close described an ARA map showing the flow of relief supplies into Europe as indicating "at a glance how magnificently and unselfishly America has risen to the supreme mission she is now performing. With more than four hundred merchant ships—the greatest fleet ever assembled for one purpose in the world's history—the American soldiers and sailors have taken up the challenge of the millions of discontented and starving peoples of Europe, and by giving them food, clothing and shelter are gradually bringing order out of chaos."[59] The US delegation was certain of its own greatness.

Undoubtedly the food coming from across the Atlantic was pivotal to feeding Europeans, and US intervention in the market was necessary to ensure that the food flowed. Hoover's ARA copied his wartime Belgian relief organization and was highly successful in setting up operations on the ground across Europe, taking advantage in particular of the skills and volunteerist ethos of some demobilizing American soldiers. But it should be noted that this food was not given away, but rather was sold to the European states that received it. Over a billion gold marks and sheaves of securities were extracted from Germany to pay for the food that came their way during this period, tangible assets that could otherwise have been used for reparations payments or to purchase other goods. The ARA was not a charity. While relieving German consumers, the ARA also relieved Germany of much of its gold. During the period between the signing of the armistice and the signing of the Treaty, the ARA actually made a slight profit.[60] And it disproportionately benefited American agriculture. As even Hoover admitted, the relief effort helped American farmers, giving them sales during a season when they significantly overproduced food.[61]

In May 1919, the centrality of morality to this US humanitarianism was thus questionable. Similarly, their proposed solution seemed unlikely to succeed. By mid-May even the Americans on the SEC had come to accept that it was not the lingering existence of parts of the wartime blockade that made central European recovery so tenuous, but rather the deep financial pit that the Germans found themselves in. According to the Blockade Committee report written under the direction of Vance McCormick, "the principal difficulty with regard to the import of raw materials (into Germany) is the financial one."[62] Without a solution from the top on the approval of needed credits, the SEC's Raw Materials Section stopped meeting in mid-May for lack of things to do.[63] The lack of available shipping meant that piles of hundreds of thousands of tons of coal desperately needed by Italy and France accumulated at British ports.[64] Some doubted American claims that they had no available ships—a US representative on the SEC's Coal Committee admitted that to favor US coal producers, their ships were prohibited from shipping non-US coal—but everyone recognized that financial assistance was entirely in the hands of the Americans.[65] Even the Americans now understood that eliminating the blockade would not be a panacea for Europe's economic woes.

In Hoover's assessment just two years later, "America bore the major burden in negotiating these arrangements, and … her disinterestedness, her sense of service, carried Europe through this—the most terrible period of its history."[66] Linked together with the tendency to overstate the virtuousness of the US relief effort has been derision of the SEC as a talking shop where nothing happened, one easily dominated by Hoover and other US experts who, after all, were the ones supplying the food.[67] Since the end of the Peace Conference, this criticism has been heavy and consistent. Bernard Baruch was among many who later claimed that the SEC moved far too slowly in ending the blockade.[68] Other critics have noted the council's inherent weaknesses. For example, the quasi-official history of the Conference edited by the Cambridge don Harold Temperley noted that the SEC lacked its own funds or executive powers, and merely allowed Allied controls on trade to disintegrate throughout the first half of 1919.[69] Recent historians of post-war humanitarianism have simply ignored the SEC altogether.[70]

A more fair assessment of the SEC would suggest that it operated during an extremely difficult few months with surprising efficiency, linking together the financial, shipping, and supply experts of the various Allies to mount an unprecedented operation to feed their enemies and create an opening for their economic recovery. Although many Germans and eastern Europeans more broadly suffered greatly during 1919, in the end the SEC largely succeeded in its primary goal of feeding Germans and the other peoples of Europe. Idealists, both then and since, who lament the lack of a fuller post-war European economic rebirth have judged the SEC's work harshly, but partial success should be judged as far superior to complete failure.

The League Gets Underway

Along with many articles anticipating the day's street protests, May Day newspapers carried a wave of reports about a private luncheon that Cecil, Drummond, Wiseman, David Hunter Miller, and a few others had in House's office the previous day. The *New York Times* and other US newspapers reported that the meeting had sewn up a firm timeline for starting up the League, with preliminary details to be worked out at a temporary headquarters in London, then an October meeting in Washington to formally launch the League, followed by the establishment of a permanent League headquarters in Geneva in the winter. The preparatory details would be in the hands of a committee of nine, including House and Cecil. House had already begun moving his large staff to London. The newspaper cited unnamed sources suggesting that the French would soon name someone other than Bourgeois as their delegate, as he did not speak English, whereas the rest of the organizing committee expected to operate in that language.[71]

It is likely that Cecil leaked the suggestion about Bourgeois. He had the press connections. To a group of British correspondents on the evening of April 30, Cecil defended the new League draft that had passed the plenary two days earlier. He claimed the Monroe Doctrine clause did not alter the effectiveness of the rest of the Covenant, and that the rejected Japanese racial equality amendment was meaningless compared to the real equality to be accorded to Japan as a great power on the proposed League Council.[72] Reaching out to the Dominion leaders and the imperial-minded members of the British public concerned that the mandates system entailed too much League supervision, Cecil noted that there was no provision in the Covenant for the League to change a mandate without the mandate power's consent. He also suggested, off the record, that Germany would likely be admitted to the League after a year or so on "probation."[73] In a private interview a few days later with the *Scotsman*, Cecil took the opportunity to blatantly pander by extolling his appreciation "of the manner in which Scotland from the first had given an intelligent support to this far-reaching organisation."[74] But it was not to be just a creation of the Anglophone world. When the League Organization Committee started to meet on Monday, May 5, they wisely announced Stephen Pichon, the French Foreign Minister, as their chair, while asking Drummond to start his duties as Secretary General immediately.[75]

In similar ways, Cecil set in motion League operations throughout May, well before the finalization of the Peace Treaty that formally brought the League into existence. During May 1919, the authority of the League became a reality. International organizations were persuaded to accept the League as the new focus of global efforts on a wide variety of topics. Through George Newman of the Board of Education, Cecil and his assistant Philip Baker were put on to the possibility of using the Office International d'Hygiène, created by international convention in Rome in 1907, as the basis of a League office on international health issues.[76] Likewise Cecil responded to a letter from H. A. L. Fisher by setting Baker on the path of creating an Education Commission for the League.[77] Cecil attended to the concerns of James Headlam-Morley and Lucien Wolf of the Anglo-Jewish Association about guaranteeing minority rights in Poland. After some discussion, they backed a scheme where members of the League could appeal to the Permanent Court of International Justice in The Hague, with its rulings then enforced as the League Council saw fit.[78] Likewise Cecil and Baker anticipated that this court might appoint arbitrators to deal with disagreements between the new states of the former Habsburg Empire over less important matters, "which, though of minor importance, are extremely contentious."[79] In general, it would be worthwhile to expand to as many treaties as possible things for which "recourse to the court is obligatory."[80] In these suggestions and decisions, many already existing international organizations were being drawn under the League umbrella. In an early emanation of functionalist theory predicting the inexorable expansion of the League, Baker suggested in a memo to Cecil that the simple existence of a League organization in Geneva with permanent commissions and full-time officials should itself encourage international cooperation.[81]

Philip Baker had become Cecil's most important assistant, delegated with many duties including replying to the deluge of correspondence from various individuals and organizations in Britain and elsewhere attempting to influence the activities of the League. Throughout May, if not earlier, Cecil's assistants Baker, Frank Walters, and Florence Dudgeon were already in effect working on the League, and unsurprisingly slid into formal League jobs after May under the newly appointed League Secretary General Eric Drummond.

For years after May 1919, Drummond found himself relying on the League machinery and personnel that Cecil had nurtured over the previous year. His plans for organizing what was beginning to be called the "Secretariat" envisioned an organization quite similar to the British FO, with the secretary-general assisted by a deputy and under-secretary, and then sections or commissions on any of a variety of topics (various plans called for somewhere between four and ten), all supplemented by a significant staff of translators and registry officials.[82] Throughout May and early June, Drummond succeeded not without a little difficulty in prying money from the "parsimonious" British Treasury to start up League operations.[83] By the middle of May, Drummond and the Organizing Committee had made appointments to League offices, with Paul Mantoux accepting the job as director of League's Political Intelligence branch. Recognizing the need to keep it a truly international organization, Assistant Secretary Generals were soon appointed from France (Monnet) and the United

States (Fosdick). Frank Walters mentioned to Cecil that they needed "a good Italian" to be appointed to a top job in the League.[84] By June 9, the League had a very cheap lease of £100 per month on Sunderland House in Curzon Street, a sweetheart deal from the Duchess of Marlborough. Monnet, Fosdick, Mantoux, Salter, Colban, Van Hamel, and other men from across western civilization all began to serve on the staff of the Secretariat in London, with many more hires in the works.[85]

Cecil worked to augment the prospects of the League by becoming a nitpicky reader of the reports that had begun emanating from various Peace Conference commissions and committees. When he discovered that there was no reference to the League in the Inter-Allied Aerial Commission's new "convention on air regulations," he pressed British delegate General Seely to get the Commission to adopt changes that would make it part of the League, and then asked Wilson to support this in the Council of Four.[86] Cecil advised General Sackville-West how to support the metamorphosis of the Versailles Council into the "Military Commission" of the League mentioned in Article 9 of the Covenant.[87]

Another group of meetings that Cecil became involved in mid-May were ones to draw up a reply to the German response to the League of Nations. After being presented with the Allied Peace Terms on May 7, just after they were drawn together from the wide variety of committees meeting in Paris, the German delegates ensconced in rooms in Versailles deliberated and then decided to call for wholesale changes to much of the Treaty. Over the last half of May, the Big Four spent a lot of time discussing and disagreeing about whether to take into account German suggestions before finalizing the Treaty. Their significant concerns were about borders, the Rhineland, and most painfully the question of accepting war guilt and reparations. In comparison, German complaints about the League plans were few. After meeting with some of the members of the League Commission, Cecil drafted a response to the Germans. It was highly conciliatory; the Commission was glad that the German Government favored the general idea of a League for peace, and pledged to consider German proposals for institutions like the Permanent Court of International Justice as soon as the League started operating. German ideas for making Covenant-breaking states pay for any resulting damages did not have to be put in the Covenant itself, as the Commission was "confident that this measure would in fact be adopted by the League in the unfortunate case of a breach of the Covenant." In brief, Cecil's draft assured the Germans that all their worries would be alleviated once the League began its operations. The Council of Four approved it, without discussion, and then sent it to the Germans.[88] Cecil remained far from alone in reasoning that the

League of Nations might be the long term answer to some of the most criticized aspects of the peace. Such assiduous efforts through May institutionalized the League and bolstered the legitimacy and power of its organizations by ensuring that they were comprehensively knitted into the fabric of the Peace Treaty.

Russia and the Rhineland

Continuing his escalating involvement in a variety of aspects of the Peace Conference over the previous months, on the issues of policy toward Russia and the final foundation of Germany's pivotal western border with France, Cecil evolved from his earlier efforts as a sort of gadfly within the British delegation to significant work creating what would become the fixed Allied policies. Not surprisingly in both cases he evoked and bolstered the case for the League of Nations.

Russia policy had continually perplexed the Allied leaders since the Bolshevik revolution in the final months of 1917. Most of the Allied leaders continued to view the Bolsheviks through an ideological prism. Since the October Revolution, Cecil's program toward Russia had evolved beyond initial ideologically-driven critiques of the Bolsheviks as untrustworthy socialist revolutionaries, to a more pragmatic stance suggesting accommodation with the realities of the civil war that had subsequently ravaged Russia. As a result his advice was increasingly valued by the Council of Four. In early April, the Norwegian polar explorer and amateur internationalist diplomat Fridtjof Nansen pitched his idea of a group of neutrals reaching out to the Bolsheviks to help feed starving civilians in places like St. Petersburg.[89] Many disagreed still with any acknowledgment of, let alone compromise with, Bolshevism. In the eyes of the *Times* editorialists, Bolshevism "exterminates every human product of civilization in Russia, (and) sends its missionaries of anarchy to permeate the world."[90] On May 13 the Bolsheviks themselves rejected Nansen's offer, saying that a cessation of their increasingly successful military operations was too great a price for access to Nansen's promised food.

During all of this, Cecil was appointed by the Big Four, along with Clémentel, Hoover, and Attolico, to form a small committee to examine the Russia issue again. Cecil had worked with all of them before either in the League Commission or the SEC. True to form, Cecil ran these meetings and wrote this committee's recommendations to the Big Four. Cecil explained that the Associated Governments had two options. One was to "smash the Bolshevists" militarily, yet Cecil doubted that the Big Four had the stomach for this policy. Alternatively, they could set up an economic embargo on all warring parties in Russia. Any who refused to lay down arms would be deprived of all food supplies, while the League council would be empowered to "immediately take into consideration the whole Russian problem," and eventually supervising elections by free and universal suffrage" for a Russian government. "This policy is in accordance with the general principle underlying the Covenant of the League of Nations" that the force of arms must not be resorted to, that "peace is to the interest of all concerned."[91] This would certainly be a change from the present Allied policy of supplying the White forces of Denikin and Kolchak, and would put an end to the policy of ousting the Bolsheviks through force. The subsequent Big Four debate indicated that most of them, following Clemenceau, did not believe that Lenin could be trusted even if he gave the guarantee that Cecil proposed. But they did decide to demand from Denikin and Kolchak the creation of a constituent assembly before sending any further aid.

With this, Cecil had at least half won. He opened up for discussion the possibility that the Bolsheviks might be amenable to a truce, and also nudged the Allied leaders further toward accepting the reality that the Bolsheviks might survive the supposed onslaught from the White armies. Only a month later, Lloyd George first candidly stated that he expected that the Bolsheviks would survive.[92] Cecil's committee helped lay the groundwork for this pragmatic and realistic assessment. Even more importantly, from Cecil's point of view, was the acceptance of the suggestion that the League of Nations would be able to deal with such problems as the Russian civil war in the future, with the authority to force both sides to cool off and find a negotiated settlement.

Cecil also intruded decisively into the highly contentious issue of the Rhineland. It was an issue that he had worked on briefly in a subcommittee in late March, but two months later he was troubled by the way that the Convention laying out the terms of Allied occupation was being drawn up solely by the Allied military representatives at Versailles, and in particular by the French representative Foch, who intransigently still aimed for the creation of an "independent" Rhineland under implied French domination. In late May, Cecil wrote to Lloyd George asking that the SEC's views on the future of Europe's economies should be taken account of as well, and the prime minister told him to sit down with General Thwaites, the British representative at the Supreme Command in Versailles. According to Lloyd George the two envisioned a real change in the way the Allies viewed the Rhineland. At the Big Four meeting on May 29, President Wilson supported the Cecil and Thwaites plan for a full

Allied commission to rewrite the Rhineland Convention, and Clemenceau caved in, agreeing that a commission of one civilian and one military man from each of the Big Four should get together to set up a new occupation convention, determining how martial law would be lifted and how the Rhinelanders could establish local self-government.[93]

Cecil and Henry Wilson were the British pair on this committee, facing the French team of Loucheur and Foch. Marshal Foch still hoped for either French annexation of the Rhineland or the creation of a breakaway Rhinish state separate from Germany, but by May he had worn out his message. At its first meeting on May 31, Cecil followed his long-successful practice of bringing a draft of his preferred outcome to the meeting and getting the committee to revise from that, and over the inevitable objections of Foch, Cecil's plan became the basis for the group's discussion. It envisioned quickly putting power into the hands of a civilian administration led by local Germans, with their national status left to the future. With some alterations over the course of at least five meetings over the next week, Cecil's plans were largely accepted by his fellow committee members, and thus "for the first time in the history of occupations" they created for the Rhineland a civil rather than military occupation.[94] Despite his private doubts that the civilian government would ever be able to stop a French takeover if the French military got their way, Cecil hoped the compromise might make the occupation of the Rhineland a less intrusive and more humane operation, and would set up the region's ultimate return to Germany.

A Brief Trip to London

With all of this work to do, what should be made of Cecil's unprecedented social calendar in May? Cecil was more sociable than ever throughout May, hosting and attending a variety of interesting lunches and dinners with an array of international luminaries. For instance, on May 5, sandwiched between meetings of the SEC and the League Organization Committee, Cecil hosted a "rather fun" luncheon with "Arabian Lawrence" and the socialite Ettie Desborough, one of the original members of the "Souls" along with his cousin Arthur Balfour. After they had dinner together again the next day, Cecil went along when Desborough "shamelessly requisitioned a motor belonging to a private individual to take her home. It was an extremely successful operation."[95] One can easily imagine their laughter. "I cannot tell you how divine it is here, or what fun & interest we are having," wrote Desborough to her husband afterward.[96] The next day,

Cecil brought his cousin Arthur to meet Madame de Fitzjames, with whom they had a very entertaining lunch, and that evening before dinner he stopped by Desborough's flat. A few days later he lunched with Violet Cecil, her daughter Helen, and "her singularly tactless sister, Olive." Violet was the widow of his brother Edward, and the future wife of Lord Milner; Olive, her beautiful, spinster sister, was at one time in the 1890s a model for Burne-Jones.[97] Violet had always annoyed Bob Cecil beyond belief, yet in his circle, she was unavoidable.[98] Throughout May he spent a variety of lunches and dinners with another niece who came over (a daughter of his eldest brother, the fourth Lord Salisbury), Mary Alice (known as Alice) Salisbury, along with Bobbety and his wife Betty.

Clearly, despite the difficulties of the Conference, Cecil's personal life remained quite entertaining. The opportunity to socialize with mostly British people in the Hotel Majestic had been fine in the early days of the Conference, but as the spring wore on so did the crowds at its dining room, not to mention the poor quality of the food. Earlier in the Conference he had worried that going out to dine was too time consuming or simply frivolous, a sign of lack of focus on the task at hand. When his nephew Lord Cranborne came over to be one of his secretaries, Cecil worried that he would "get absorbed in dinners and other Parisian gaieties," as indeed he did.[99] But as the Conference wore on, Cecil increasingly looked for ways to spend his evenings somewhere other than the Majestic. Over the course of the 134 dinners he had in Paris between January 7 and June 10, he ate at least a third of these meals outside the Majestic, with the frequency increasing each month. In luncheons and dinner parties he ordinarily hoped more "general conversation," a break from focusing on the issues, and on the men, he faced at the Conference.

Yet despite all of this effort to get out the Conference atmosphere, Cecil did not find himself spending much time with his wife during the weeks she lived in the inn at Bellevue. On May 6 and May 8, he drove down for lunch, but both times came back to the city immediately after for a variety of meetings. He stayed overnight on Saturday, May 11, and throughout the next day, and also went down the next Sunday, but only saw Nelly once for lunch during that week. She used his official car to travel with nephew Bobbety to engage in battlefield tourism: "I enjoyed Soissons I am ashamed to say, though it was worse than I had imagined, or rather, unless you see a nice old house in bits you can't imagine properly what a pity it is."[100] But from the start Cecil felt guilty, knowing that he could not give her much attention. "I am rather afraid this Paris experiment is turning out badly," he wrote to her.[101] Together, they agreed she should return to England on May 20.

Cecil accompanied his wife back to Britain but barely saw her there. His schedule was packed with meetings, meals, and speeches over the two quick days he spent in London. Cecil focused on a number of the issues that marked his political life over the previous five years, such as Welsh Church disestablishment. Earlier in May Cecil had found time to write a letter to the Archbishop of Canterbury, which the Archbishop read at the annual Church Defence Committee meeting at Westminster on May 15, urging them to do "their utmost" to stop funds dedicated to Church in Wales from being diverted elsewhere.[102]

Not surprisingly he also had League work. On the first morning in London he met with Colonel Fisher of the League of Nations Union, who extended an invitation for Cecil to be the chief speaker at a Union meeting at Royal Albert Hall the next month.[103] That evening he gave a highly anticipated speech to the League of Nations Committee of the Society of Friends.[104] He focused on the necessity of having the League as part of the Peace Treaty, and the need to have Germany join it as soon as possible.[105] Cecil compared the League to "a healthy infant" that needed the support of public opinion to grow and thrive.[106] The next evening Cecil went to Lambeth Palace to meet with the Archbishop of Canterbury and the Archbishop of York, both of whom he knew on a first-name basis. They wanted his advice on speeches they were planning to make about the League of Nations and the prospects of long-term peace.[107]

The next evening, Cecil presided at the annual meeting of the Labour Co-partnership Association. Declaring that the unsteadiness of the present economic situation mandated a big change in industry, "I prophesied an industrial revolution."[108] Copartnership and real profit sharing promised to create an entirely new productive relationship in industry, but nationalization, he warned, would simply mean management "by that vastly unpopular female 'DORA' (the Defense of the Realm Act)." The audience laughed.[109] Yet copartnership schemes did suggest continuing wartime government involvement in the domestic economy. For Cecil, so much of his efforts in Paris were motivated by the fear of Bolshevism spreading across Europe. He saw copartnership as entirely conservative in motivation, creating new incentives for workers that would encourage them to think like capitalists.[110] Perhaps his country could create a more fair capitalism both respectful of private property and of workers.

Despite the apparent impressiveness of Lloyd George's coalition majority, in reality British politics was in disarray in early 1919. Not only had the electorate expanded significantly before the December 1918 general election, the makeup of the British party system itself was in flux. Liberals were bitterly divided between Lloyd George and Asquith. Uncertain Tories were unwilling to rule on their own. Labour had a new patriotic National Democratic Party competing for working class votes. The historian Maurice Cowling has described (and derided) Cecil's political machinations in 1921–2 that looked to create a new centrist party, one both anti-Socialist and anti-Lloyd George, but also not Conservative.[111] One might see the earliest manifestations of this uncertain and eventually failed route forward in the few days Cecil spent in London in May 1919. Even as the Peace Conference continued, Cecil spent significant effort reconsidering his position within the uncertain firmament of British politics.

*

There were many successes at the Paris Conference during May 1919. The SEC proved critical in organizing the successful feeding of central Europe including enemy Germany, a goal accepted by the Peace Conference leaders not just a humanitarian necessity but also a primary prerequisite of any possible lasting peace. Throughout the month, Cecil and others worked diligently on nurturing the League, no longer just fashioning the concept but now bringing it to life, both in experimenting with new practices of economic warfare and in crafting and operating real League institutions. Not everything was going his way, but Cecil during May 1919 exemplified how delegates below the Big Four were critical in crafting not only the Treaty of Versailles, but also the international institutions and mentalities that might become the basis of real lasting peace.

7

The Mentality of Appeasement? June

On May 31, a number of Cabinet ministers left London and traveled to Paris to meet with the prime minister. The group that evening gathered at Lloyd George's flat at 23 Rue Nitot included Balfour, Austen Chamberlain, Winston Churchill, Philip Kerr, Sir Henry Wilson, H. A. L. Fisher, Smuts, and Cecil. After dinner, Lloyd George asked everyone for criticisms of the Treaty. Smuts led off the discussion with a bitter attack, and then the rest piled on, condemning the Treaty and demanding modifications. The complaint session lasted until midnight and then continued into BED meetings the next day.[1]

Less than a month before the signing of the Treaty, fundamental disagreements over the draft divided the Conference delegates. Both contemporaries and historians since have portrayed it as a two-sided debate. Many believed the Treaty could not bring a secure peace because it was far too harsh toward the Germans. In the words of James Headlam-Morley, "what ought to be a general agreement under the League of Nations is imposed by force upon Germany."[2] The draft presented to the Germans on May 7 caused despair not just among the Germans gathered near Versailles but within the delegations of the victorious powers. British critics, reading the entire document for the first time, worried that the burden placed on the Germans was unprecedented and onerous, that many individual clauses might be justified but that the whole was far worse than the sum of its parts. General Smuts was the loudest of those who complained throughout May that the Allied terms failed to channel the spirit of Woodrow Wilson's Fourteen Points, which many Germans cited as the basis of the armistice of November 11. There were suggestions that the different commissions planning European borders had not sufficiently considered each other when making their decisions, thus failing Wilson's charge to look out for the rights of all nationalities. Some thought hitching the League of Nations to the Treaty was likely to make the Treaty harder to ratify in their countries. Others were concerned that the Treaty, a victor's peace, would hamper the ability of a League of supposedly equal nations to operate successfully. Some judged the reparations and indemnity clauses as terribly flawed, either because they punted decisions about the size of reparations to a future commission, or because they had created such a broad definition of reparation-worthy damages that the ultimate bill would cripple German recovery.

It has long been customary to see this deluge of criticism as a sign that the Treaty was doomed from its start, and that not even those who drew it up liked it.[3] A few in the British delegation followed Smuts in "furious revolt," demanding immediate fundamental revision of the Treaty even before it was signed, and prophesying failure if this call for revision went unheeded.[4] Historians have seen in these critics of the Treaty the first manifestations of interwar appeasement, based on the sense of some of the victors that they were being too cruel to Germany.[5] Increasing numbers of British leaders fell into this category throughout the 1920s and 1930s, men whose guilt about the Treaty of Versailles encouraged them to see the justice in granting concessions to Germany, even when that meant giving in to Hitler.

However in 1919 Paris, appeasement was not predominant among British or Allied delegates, let along among their constituencies back home. Those satisfied with the justice of the Treaty included Billy Hughes, Clemenceau, and even Lloyd George himself. Some triumphalists openly scoffed at the proto-appeasers, arguing that the Treaty treated the Germans fairly and gave the victors deserved awards, or at least recompense for German-caused destruction. The most recent biographer of the irascible Australian, Billy Hughes, suggests that Paris was "his finest hour" as prime minister, as "he defied the odds to secure vital concessions for his country and Empire."[6] In particular, Hughes gained for Australia control of New Guinea, the rejection of Japanese "racial equality" articles from the Covenant, and promises for Australia of significant reparation cash—all exactly what he wanted, and with no feelings of guilt attached. "If this peace be unjust," Hughes proclaimed to the crowds in Melbourne when he returned home in September, "it is not unjust to Germany."[7] Lord Cunliffe, the governor of the Bank of England and Lloyd George's lead delegate on the Reparations Commission, would have preferred to put in the Treaty a specific and significant amount of money but expected that huge payouts by Germany would result from the Big Four's decision to call together another commission to determine the final bill. Cunliffe's success in persuading Lloyd George of the merits of nebulous but significant reparations demands was perhaps the final cause of Keynes quitting the Peace Conference.[8] But Cunliffe's desire for blood simply embodied the anger that still animated many Britons who believed in the justice of the Treaty terms. This discourse of aggrievement was reinforced when the Germans scuttled their naval fleet interned at Scapa Flow on June 21. The cynical Chief of the Imperial General Staff, Field-Marshal Sir Henry Wilson, strongly favored "not budging an inch ... because Boche understands no other argument."[9] For Philip Kerr, who drafted the Allied response to the German complaints about the initial treaty draft, the need for a "moral verdict against Germany and some form of retribution" was embodied in the very reasonable and just terms of the Treaty.[10]

And then there was David Lloyd George, the prime minister himself. As after the Fontainebleau conference in March, he again appeared to waver in the face of the Smuts onslaught and the general unanimity favoring amendments on May 31. Yet Lloyd George was disinclined to change anything in the Treaty.[11] His appeasement was of a very limited variety, and by the middle of June the British prime minister became the great embodiment of the "no revisions" stance. To Lloyd George, the political realities and public demand in Britain made a punishing treaty, particularly when it came to reparations, inevitable and necessary.[12]

What has been little acknowledged since is a third point of view, recognizing that the peace treaty draft had flaws, yet expecting that with diligent effort and the existence of new international institutions, a real long-term peace satisfactory to both the Germans and the Allies could develop and evolve. Lord Cecil's ideas and efforts throughout the last month of the Conference exemplify this verdict on the Treaty, one held by many of his fellow delegates in Paris. Up to the moments before the famous signing ceremony in the Hall of Mirrors on June 28, Cecil and like-minded internationalists ground the Treaty into what they considered an acceptable and hopefully successful form, one open to improvement over the years to come.

This portrayal of Cecil's attitude to the peace as cautiously optimistic might seem somewhat surprising. Both the apologists and the alarmists in the debate over the Treaty liked to claim Cecil as one of theirs. Lloyd George explicitly quoted Cecil when he stated that "the broad lines of the Treaty are right."[13] But more often, Cecil has been seen as a Smuts-style revisionist. He was particularly wary that the reparations clauses were too harsh and provocative.[14] Cecil believed in setting a price immediately, rather than pushing the ultimate sum to a longer-term commission, and making it a reasonable and not outrageous sum. On May 26, during one of his many lunches with cousin Balfour, Cecil "told him I was very unhappy about the Treaty," and later that day he wrote a memo about possible revisions.[15] He argued that the harshness of the Treaty might animate critics in the United States wary that it would entangle them in European affairs. Most painfully, the Treaty might lead global public opinion to believe that the British were simply unjust, and thus it threatened "our national reputation" and "moral prestige" so vital in bringing Britain many allies during the war. "It will indeed be a disastrous consequence of the Conference if the moral leadership of the nations passes from us to the United States."[16]

However Smuts's opposition to the Treaty of Versailles in the late May and early June meetings of the BED struck Cecil as overwrought and immoderate, too pro-German and anti-French. Cecil attended the BED on May 30, when Lloyd George quoted Cecil's memo on possible revisions to the Treaty, but he "took very little part, being indeed a little dissatisfied at finding myself there." On May 31, Lloyd George persuaded Cecil to attend an impromptu Cabinet meeting in the morning when Cecil spoke in favor of amending certain terms of the Treaty. And yet Cecil pointedly refused to attend the meetings of the BED later that day, saying he would only attend if they asked him to appear "as an expert."[17]

Cecil knew the BED was not a friendly venue for his ideas. He found it personally unpleasant to be there. He openly disliked Hughes, his British Empire project, and his maximalist demands on the Germans. A decade later he dismissed the Hughes of 1919 as "a little bounder much cried up by the Morning Post etc. but of no real importance."[18] And from the other side of the debate, Cecil preferred to avoid listening to Smuts's unreasonable moralizing in favor of an unobtainable ideal, even as the South African demanded high reparations and compensation from the Germans.[19] Cecil could be thin-skinned, and certainly grew irritated with many of the people he interacted with in Paris during those months of 1919, including Woodrow Wilson (who he trusted but did not like), Lloyd George (who he liked but did not trust), and virtually the entire French delegation other than Clemenceau. But the members of the BED truly rankled him.

Before the dinner at Lloyd George's, Cecil had already been considering the anomaly of his place in the British political firmament. The British ministers coming over from London "look rather askance at me—naturally enough."[20] For Cecil, Paris was developing an increasingly odd atmosphere. When Francis Oppenheimer returned from Austria earlier that day, he went directly to Cecil's office. Cecil's "welcome was encouraging. Then he took his seat, adopting his characteristic posture: leaning back in a swivel cane chair, his elbows resting on its arms, his hands folded mid-air, his feet crossed on the desk. He was ready to listen—and listen he did. I must have talked for hours." Oppenheimer discoursed about the difficulties faced by the Austrians, pinned between Italian demands and the possibility of takeover by Germany. After a time, Cecil replied: "I only represent the Government on the Committee of the League of Nations. Of course you realize that as such I have no power—*but now I regret it*."[21] Yet despite this supposed lack of power, Cecil assured Oppenheimer that his report would help with the revisions of the draft treaty with Austria, promised that he would get Oppenheimer in to talk to Lloyd George, and directed him to see Crowe and Smuts right away. Cecil also suggested sending Oppenheimer on a similar mission to Czechoslovakia. As a result of Cecil's subsequent prodding, the Big Four decided to hold off on presenting the Austrians with financial and economic terms of peace, instead sending on June 2 only the military terms. Cecil may have begun ruing the decision he made in November 1918 to resign from the Cabinet and to enter a nebulous political hinterland, but his actions and results through June 1919 show that he clearly retained significant influence in British decision-making.

And at the same time, he also dominated the highest reaches of the expanding ranks of the world's new internationalists. A speech Cecil gave on the evening of May 30 has often cited both by his contemporaries (like Harold Nicolson, who had rarely interacted with Cecil during the Conference but who attended that Anglo-American gathering) and by historians (Antony Lentin, for example) as proving Cecil's adherence to the pessimistic critiques of Keynes and Smuts.[22] He gave this speech at the meeting that founded the transatlantic pairing of the Institute of International Affairs in Britain and the Council on Foreign Relations in the United States. In addressing the gathering of foreign policy wonks from the US and British delegations, Cecil stated with his classic straightforwardness that no one was satisfied with the terms of the Treaty. Some both then and since have perceived Cecil as the master of ceremonies of this meeting, having engaged in many of the informal discussions that led to it, and then giving the keynote address creating the new Institute.[23] Some even expected he was planning to direct the Institute in Britain.[24] Through meetings over the next month to organize the Institute, Cecil's supposed support for it was cited both by those who favored its creation, like Curtis, and those like Eyre Crowe wary of its encroachment on government leadership of foreign policy.[25]

But according to Cecil, this dinner was actually the first time he had heard about the proposed organization. In his diary he described the event simply as a dinner "at the Majestic with Curtis and a number of other experts in foreign affairs, both English and American." As Lionel Curtis explained to Cecil at the dinner, the experts gathered in Paris had decided to create a transatlantic institute that would bring them together more permanently. Curtis conceived it with his *Round Table* correspondent George Louis Beer, both men struck by the possibilities that Paris exposed for a permanent transatlantic think tank.[26] Cecil thought the idea was in theory a good one, but at the same time wondered exactly what it would do and whether the plans for "a year book" and branches in London and the United States would accomplish anything. "If it merely talked it would soon disappear, and the difficulty is to find it some definite job."[27] This dinner came at the end of a long day for Cecil. He had sat through the hysteria of Smuts and the intransigence of Hughes in the BED meeting all afternoon. His comments at the dinner were brief and off the cuff. For Cecil to state that no one was satisfied with the Treaty did not underscore the necessity of appeasement but rather acknowledged that both the appeasers and the triumphalists had wanted more from the Treaty. He was bound between the uncertainty and ambiguity of the attitude of his own British delegation, his hopes that the future world could be shaped by the United States and the British together, and his sense that future revisions could blunt any unfair or unworkable aspects of the Treaty. It was flawed, but with continued cooperative efforts even the flawed peace could succeed.

For Cecil, but not for Smuts, hopes that the League could transform the international situation outweighed any problems with the Treaty. The League would hopefully end up creating "a way out for the worst parts of the Treaty."[28] A clause would be included in the Covenant (the eventual Article 19) giving power to the League of Nations to make revisions as deemed necessary.[29] The League would improve as it operated, in the same way his Ministry of Blockade had done during the war, where changes bred by necessity and opportunity had continually intensified the Allied attack on the German economy. Cecil did not flee Paris in despair, "sick of life" like Smuts, Keynes and the others who demanded wholesale changes to the Treaty.[30] At his core, Cecil believed that the complaints about the Treaty could be fixed over the years ahead as the League functioned and evolved.

Institutionalizing the Supreme Economic Council

At a press conference on May 30, Cecil claimed that everyone had the same goals and that he had experienced no difficulty working with the French and US delegations in either the League Commission or the SEC. Quoted at length in a number of US and British newspapers, he proclaimed his admiration of the United States for its initial war declaration that it aimed for no profit or territory from the war. Cecil expected that the final Treaty would embody this selflessness.[31] But he also implored the United States to realize that its sacrifices "in men and material" were less than those of its allies. He recognized that the League might entail some "sacrifice of national sovereignty," but this "inevitable result of cooperation" was a sacrifice worth making to prevent wars in the future. As Europe teetered on the edge of famine, a fundamental change in international relations "is essential to humanity and civilization."[32]

As he had shown on a number of occasions during his months in Paris, Cecil did not fully understand US politics. His American friend David Hunter Miller had successfully tutored Cecil on hurdles the US Constitution placed in the way of acceptance of the League, but this simply enhanced his biases against what he saw as the inherent limitations of the American political process. Colonel House had increasingly expressed his worries about the Republican-led opposition in the Senate, where any Treaty would have to be ratified, and Cecil worried that Wilson might be overconfident in his ability to push through a Treaty saddled with the League. In the United States, one of "irreconcilable" opponents of Wilson's machinations, Idaho's Republican Senator William Borah, read out Cecil's statement as exemplifying British hypocrisy. The British were not themselves willing to be self-sacrificing with their refusal to include the freedom of the seas in the Covenant. British attempts to meddle in US politics should be scorned, Borah demanded, especially attempts by aristocrats like Cecil.[33] In London, the *Times* noted that too much British advocacy of the Treaty and the League might only drive Republican Senators more staunchly against the League.[34] This sentiment did not die down. Even a year later, Colonel House wrote to Cecil urging him to forgo a US speaking tour he was considering for the next year, explaining that "much has been said about the League being of British origin and your visit would lend color to this statement."[35] Cecil believed in the power of public opinion to create peace, but he never figured out how to sway it in the United States.

Cecil poured himself into making sure that the SEC would continue operating during the "period of transition from war to peace conditions," a transition period he argued must last beyond the signing of the peace. Supported by the Italian, French, and Belgian delegations, Cecil argued that SEC headquarters should move to London "as soon as possible and not later than the signature of Peace with Germany." Once in London, the SEC would focus on "establishing as soon and as completely as possible the economic life and energy of Europe." In opposition, the US delegates argued that the SEC should not continue, as "most of those problems, such as those dealing with blockade, relief, and foodstuffs until the next harvest, had already been solved." Furthermore, they noted meekly, they were merely wartime appointees who were not authorized to tie their post-war successors to any specific policy.[36]

This was particularly true when it related to the SEC's policies toward Russia. Everyone realized that there would be no official restrictions on trade with either side in Russia after the Allies dropped their blockade measures against Germany and Hungary. French delegates began pressing for imposition of specific economic measures to hurt the Bolsheviks, including refusing to send food through to starving civilians in Bolshevik territory, under the assumption that feeding them would mean that civilians would exert less pressure against their Bolshevik lords. For the US delegation, Vance McCormick noted simply that there was no need to impose any blockade on any part of Russia, as the logistical and financial challenges faced by the Bolsheviks meant they would be unlikely to be capable of importing anything.[37] But the SEC decided to have its sections consider what they would do if there was a decision to include Russia in their "sphere of operations," following a British memo that displayed Cecil's increasingly apocalyptic rhetoric on the European economy: "If we do not succeed in averting complete collapse in Central and Eastern Europe we will suffer immeasurable loss or utter disaster. Millions of people who are only supported by an intensive industrial system will die, and it will take many years and millions of money to restore even moderate conditions of prosperity in Europe. It is generally agreed that we should try and straighten out the situation."[38] This could be done, he suggested, by helping to relieve the border states and the Russian territories controlled by Britain's allies, the anti-Bolsheviks. Hopefully, he suggested, creating economic stability would provoke "a desire for similar conditions in adjoining Bolshevik territory." "The money could not be spent more effectively," but to start they would need funding.

Hoover responded that the United States doubted that the Allies would continue military assistance to Kolchak or that they would decide to enter into a "definite economic offensive" against Bolshevik Russia.[39] The US delegates opposed the reports drawn up by the Food, Communication, and Finance Sections of the SEC, all of which described the humanitarian need to extend the SEC operations into Russia, and how the Allied governments must act together if they were to succeed.[40] The Food Section suggested that it could help Russia import 100,000 tons of food per month at the cost of about $150 million over the course of a year.[41] The Communication Section suggested how the Russian railroads might be revived, with sufficient funding and with a British-led group of foreign experts in charge.[42] Still undecided on what to do about Russia, the Big Four held off on installing any blockade on the Bolsheviks.[43]

Even just creating such plans for the future went against the US goals for the SEC. Anxious to reimpose free trade, most US delegates throughout the

SEC sections aimed to wind down their operations, rather than wind them up. In the SEC meeting on June 23, the US representatives again repudiated a call from the other Allies, led by the British, to ask the Council of Four for a speedy decision on whether the SEC would continue to operate after the signing of the peace, scheduled for just five days later. The British recognized that it would be too much to call for a clause in the Peace Treaty specifically giving the League authority to continue the SEC mission to coordinate food relief and cooperation on reconstruction and economic policy in Europe, but this authority might be given in a less formal fashion.[44] The lengthy British memorandum listed a number of SEC duties that needed to be continued even after the ratification of the Treaty, including providing promised foodstuffs to Germany, ensuring needed supplies of food and raw materials to European Allies, continuing international consultation on financing international trade, continuing and coordinating the necessary relief work being done by the ARA and by Britain's Food and Relief Sections, supervision of the Rhineland Commission, and coordinating Russian relief and reorganization efforts. "There is a general expectation and desire that the economic side of the League of Nations should develop out of the Supreme Economic Council," concluded the British report, and thus the Big Four should authorize "the Supreme Council to continue to function as an international body, and that as soon as convenient it should be brought under the direction of the Council of the League of Nations."[45]

This British push for a continuation of the SEC was supported by the French delegates, who contributed a detailed memo describing the history of the SEC's accumulation of powers over the previous months, and noting that for all the remaining many questions related to the reconstitution of the European economy, "the Supreme Economic Council remains qualified to handle it." Any post-war organization should continue the many activities of the SEC, at least until the League "reached a degree of organization sufficient to permit the assumption" of its residual duties.[46] The Belgians and Italians likewise agreed that the SEC should continue its operations and move to London. On this issue, all the Europeans were in complete agreement.

Slipping Away from a Nightmare?

Although the Treaty of Versailles was signed on June 28, the exodus of the delegates, journalists, and hangers-on had begun weeks earlier. The Canadian prime minister Robert Borden, for example, left for home on May 14 after working in Paris on a variety of issues related to the League Covenant.[47] T. E. Lawrence, stymied in his attempts to get his patron Emir Faisal into the negotiations on breaking up the Ottoman Empire, accepted a fellowship at All Souls College and retreated back to Oxford in April, before Lowell Thomas's film screenings in New York and London later that summer made "Lawrence of Arabia" world famous.[48]

In a characteristically dramatic fashion John Maynard Keynes, after weeks of threatening to resign, fled from Paris on June 7. He had been working with Jan Smuts over the previous week to craft a reparations scheme in opposition to the harsh terms supported by Sumner and Cunliffe. During those early June days, Lloyd George appeared willing to put a fixed reparation term into the Treaty, summoning an ill and bedridden Keynes to prepare for him a memo on alternative reparations proposals. But when the prime minister failed to adopt it immediately, Keynes wrote a dramatic letter of resignation to Lloyd George: "On Saturday I am slipping away from this scene of nightmare. I can do no more good here. I've gone on hoping even through these last dreadful weeks that you'd find some way to make of the treaty a just and expedient document. But now it's apparently too late. The battle is lost."[49]

As has been seen, Cecil was certainly not satisfied with what was taking place in Paris. He was frustrated like Keynes at what he perceived as the poor leadership of his prime minister and at the obstructionism of the US delegates. He was not fully satisfied with the outcome of Germany's League membership, which was left ambiguous rather than giving a specific date as he had hoped. On the day before Keynes left, the Big Four tabled an SEC report calling for a credit scheme to restart the economies of Europe, claiming that their need to focus on formulating their overall reply to the Germans meant the SEC scheme could not yet receive adequate consideration.[50] This inattention greatly perplexed Cecil, whose few letters and diary entries during these days have a melancholy feel to them. For instance, when asked to sign an autograph book he penned a brief epigram:

> While statesmen talk and diplomats debate
> Nearer and nearer marches unrelenting fate.[51]

This rather dreary verse encapsulated his concern about the slowness and "irresponsible delays" of the Conference.[52] His Peace Conference diary ends on a seemingly grim note that has undoubtedly affected those who have viewed him as firmly in the Smuts camp. When Lloyd George failed to support the plan that Cecil had hatched with House for allowing Germany into the League quickly,

Cecil lamented "it is very disappointing and makes me more glad than ever that I am going away."[53]

But there were a few weeks left before the Treaty would be signed, and to Cecil, things were not unambiguously grim. On June 4, the *Daily Mail* and a number of provincial newspapers reported (and lamented) rumors that the "keen intellects" of Cecil and Milner had succumbed to claims that the peace was "unworkable" and now accepted German calls for reopening the peace talks.[54] Cecil certainly did see some simple ways of making the Treaty better. He had been suggesting for months that Germany should be allowed into the League quickly. This could be seen as appeasement, but for Cecil inclusion of Germany in the League was a matter of tremendous practical significance. The sooner the League became an organization of all the great powers, the sooner it could operate to create real world peace. When in early June the German response to the Treaty expressed their desire to join the League, Cecil jumped into action. Between June 7 and 8, he and House ground out an agreement that Germany would be allowed into the League "after a brief period of probation."[55] The French accepted this in the League Commission. Although in the Big Four Clemenceau rejected the idea that Germany should be allowed quick entry into the League, reports circulated suggesting that Clemenceau had helped Cecil and House to frame the agreement, and that all Clemenceau really needed was for the Germans to establish a stable government and accept the Treaty.[56] *Revanchist* French newspapers lamented rumors that Germany would be admitted into the League within two years.[57] Lloyd George refused to support German membership. But Cecil was sure that getting Germany into the League would be critical to the success of the Treaty, and he saw opportunities in London to make his case to the British people. It was a good time to go home.

In Paris, those early June days were a "spell of comparatively slack time," as Balfour's secretary Ian Malcolm remembered it, as all enjoyed the summer weather.[58] Expecting that he was about to leave the Peace Conference for good, Cecil (like many others) engaged in a round of valedictory dinners and parties. The summer found him in a restaurant in the Bois de Boulogne, the Chalet des Iles, for a number of lunches and dinners with his nephews and nieces and various other Parisian friends. There were seasonal pleasantries such as "a blazing afternoon" afternoon on June 1 with an old friend, the president of the Board of Education Herbert Fisher, watching lawn tennis between American and Australian players, the two men relaxing in the interim between that day's contentious BED meetings.[59] He even attended the weekly Saturday-night dance at the Majestic after dinner on June 7. He hoped to tour the battlefields again before he left, but the press of business made it impossible to get away for a full day.⁶⁰

The day before he left for London, Cecil attended the Bullock-Primrose wedding. As the latter was the daughter of Britain's ambassador to France, the Earl of Derby, it was held at the British Embassy, with a small group of grandees including Balfour, Hardinge, and Philip Kerr.⁶¹ Cecil's attendance made the society pages back home. It wasn't the first time his Parisian cavorting hit the London gossip press. A few days earlier, Cecil's picture was on the photo page of the *Daily Mail*, under the perhaps sarcastic headline "Peace Conference 'Fashions,'" focusing on the hats worn by Cecil and Eric Geddes.⁶² Cecil is in a characteristic pose, tall, thin, head out, sleeves seemingly too short, watch chain across his front and kerchief jutting wildly out of his front pocket. The two men are laughing.

When Cecil left Paris on June 11, he probably did not expect to return. He had planned the trip since at least June 2, expecting to spend a few days in London before going home to Gale House for at least ten days.⁶³ Cecil aimed to prepare the move to London of the operations of both the League of Nations and the SEC.⁶⁴ House had decamped for London three days earlier to begin setting up the League, a move that had been planned since at least the start of May.⁶⁵ A week earlier it had been publicly announced that Sunderland House, leased at a nominal fee from the Duchess of Marlborough by the British Government eighteen months earlier, would shift from its designation as part of the Ministry of Blockade to become the headquarters of the League.⁶⁶

For Cecil and his staff, the futures of the League and the SEC were inseparably intertwined, and the work that they did in London flowed directly from their activities at the Peace Conference. Immediately after Cecil left Paris, Baker began sending along FO telegrams to Frank Walters who was already at work at Sunderland House, noting that they should be "seen by Lord Robert or the Secretary-General (Drummond) or both."⁶⁷ These were "I imagine, from a British point of view highly confidential" but certainly would help in the process of getting the League underway.⁶⁸

London was also important as it gave Cecil a different group of policymakers to lobby. Although the House of Commons was in recess between June 6 and June 24, Cecil hoped he might influence British policy through direct meetings with his former Cabinet colleagues. Over the previous weeks, Cecil had been persuaded by Oppenheimer that Austria (or what Oppenheimer, Chevalier, and Alberti termed "New Austria" in a report to the Finance Section of the SEC) needed significant and speedy credits to ensure food supplies. Without these, the new state would probably collapse and fall into the hands of Germany.[69] He dragged Oppenheimer back to London from Paris and set up a meeting between Oppenheimer, Chancellor of the Exchequer Austen Chamberlain, and the Treasury mandarin Sir John Bradbury. But neither Chamberlain nor Bradbury felt it possible to spend scarce funds on propping up Austria.[70]

Like many of the politicians who had been working avidly in Paris on breeding internationalism, Cecil in June 1919 began to reset his political sites on his home country. He had become the most famous British advocate of a League of Nations, and from June onward this issue sat at the core of his identity within the British political firmament. There was tremendous anticipation for the Albert Hall "demonstration" planned by the LNU on the evening of Friday, June 13 (see Figure 7.1). Cecil's speech was expected to be the main event. Two days before only a few tickets remained, and newspaper reports expected that a number of foreign ambassadors, prominent members of the War Office and Admiralty, and representatives of "practically every branch of national life" would attend. Cecil explained to reporters that he anticipated becoming very active in the LNU executive once the Peace Conference activities were over.[71] President Wilson had sent a letter to the LNU praising their efforts and expressing his regret that he could not attend the Albert Hall meeting. But as one reporter noted, Cecil as chief speaker itself made for "a very notable" gathering, as in Paris he had done "more than any other statesman to make the covenant as complete as it is."[72] Dozens of MPs, aristocrats, and other notables attended, including among others the Archbishop of Canterbury, Admiral Wemyss, Annie Besant, and Oswald Mosley.[73] Among the thousands of attendees were also a number of pro-Bolshevik women who interrupted the start of the meeting by unfurling a red banner and shouting "The League of Nations is a League of Capitalists."

After an introduction by Edward Grey, Cecil launched into his pitch for the League. Cecil's speech took up most of the program. Albert Hall was the largest in London, and before the adoption of modern microphones, Cecil had to speak with authority if he wanted to be heard by the crowd, which may have numbered near ten thousand.[74] He began by recounting the horrors of the war. No one but "a criminal or a lunatic" would want to repeat it. The League as it was created might not be perfect, but Cecil lambasted those critics who said that it would either interfere with national sovereignty, or that it would be too weak and unwieldy to make and follow through on needed policies. Cecil argued that the League Council and the Assembly would encourage open discussions that could avert war. No one, he said, preferred war to discussion. His description of how the Covenant was drawn up as a reasonably crafted and truly global compromise

THE LEAGUE OF NATIONS UNION.

ALBERT HALL DEMONSTRATION

To welcome Establishment of the League of Nations.

FRIDAY, JUNE 13th, 1919.

Programme.

7.15 to 8 p.m. Organ Recital.
  Mr. Llewelyn Bevan, L.R.A.M., A.R.C.O.

8 p.m. Address by Chairman.
  Viscount Grey of Fallodon, K.G.

  Speeches by
    The Rt. Hon. Lord Robert Cecil, M.P.
    The Rt. Hon. J. R. Clynes, M.P.
    Dr. Alexander Irvine.

10 p.m. Votes of Thanks.
  Proposed by His Grace the Archbishop of Canterbury.
  Seconded by Dr. John Clifford, M.A., D.D.

10.20 p.m. GOD SAVE THE KING.

Figure 7.1 Program for League of Nations Union Demonstration at Albert Hall, June 13, 1919. Courtesy of the Royal Albert Hall Archive Collections, RAHE/1/1919/40.

certainly overstated the role played by the various nations on the Commission and among the neutrals. But he was mostly realistic. "No one supposes that the Covenant is perfect. Miracles no longer happen." "What we do say about it is that it is a living organism. It is not, and it is not intended to be, a finished product. We hope and believe that it will grow and adapt itself to the requirements of its functions." Most people favored some degree of international cooperation, at least on issues like workers' rights, health and hygiene, "protection of native races," ending slavery and illegal drugs trades, and arms profiteering. The controversial Article 10, the guarantee of territorial integrity of League members, did not mean that national boundaries would never be changed, but rather that the process of doing so would be through "discussion and debate" rather than "by violence or war." Britain wanted the League, he claimed, not because it would benefit Britain, but simply because it wanted peace and the end of a division of nations "into separate camps." This was why, when the Allies became certain that Prussian militarism had been purged, a repentant Germany must be allowed to enter the League. Cecil anticipated that this would be soon.

Suddenly from an upper gallery, a man's voice shouted out—"Robert Cecil, you're a bloody traitor." The decorum of the meeting disintegrated, a scuffle broke out, and the resisting man was dragged from the hall. Once order was restored, Cecil lightly noted that the primary obligation of League members is that "each member will be required to live peaceably among his fellows." The crowd laughed, and Cecil completed his speech. The League was strong because the Covenant and activities of League machinery could be altered in the future if necessary. Supporting the League and the Covenant now was the best thing the public could do to support the fundamental goal of avoiding war.

It was an exciting evening. Cecil's main themes, stressing the flexibility and the universality of the League idea, shone through both to his opponents and (as seen by the heckler) to his detractors. Back in Paris, Philip Baker and James Headlam-Morley suggested that Cecil's speech might have "an extraordinarily good effect" if it was distributed in Switzerland and other neutral countries to prove that the League was not a partisan alliance.[75] According to the *Times*, Cecil's call for quick admission of Germany to the League was met with loud applause.

Cecil's Albert Hall speech brought little but praise from the press. The *Times*, for one, bought Cecil's argument completely. Their editorialists appreciated his seriousness and rejection of "fine phrases and noble sentiments" in describing simply the work that had been done in Paris. Although there might be problems, "they have planted a seed susceptible of growth" and now the League "is a living thing," that must be tended "so that when it be grown it may be trained and pruned as the needs of the nations may require."[76] The Covenant could be modified as experience required. However, many of the press reports focused more on the exciting interruptions. It was a "splendid showing under severe heckling."[77] The *Daily Mail* noted that the audience in the hall had turned angry against the man who called Cecil a traitor. The newspaper interviewed the perpetrator, "a naval officer in mufti," Lieutenant Commander Harry McLeod Fraser, who claimed that Lord Robert Cecil was responsible for the supposed laxity of the wartime blockade, and had wrecked the peace by introducing the idea of the League of Nations.[78] It was not the last time the League had trouble getting the press coverage it wanted; newspapermen liked stories, not discussions of principles.[79]

Even before the speech, there were rumors that Cecil might again be up for the US ambassadorship, after pushing aside stories about this in January and April. A *Times* correspondent asked Cecil about whether he would be appointed, and he replied that it was up to the government.[80] Cecil had been uninterested earlier, but with the possibility that the first League Council meeting would occur in Washington, the Embassy there looked more appealing than it had earlier in the spring, when the action was in Paris.

On June 25 he was in Oxford, receiving an honorary doctorate at the first real encaenia the University had in five years.[81] Cecil thoroughly enjoyed his time there the previous evening, and now "walking about in a scarlet robe" was filled with memories of his years there decades earlier.[82] Among others honored at the noontime ceremony with DCL degrees were allied leaders Marshal Joffre, General Haig, General Pershing, Admiral Beatty, and Herbert Hoover. Some called it "Allied Day" as the streets of Oxford were decorated with all the Allied flags and filled with crowds cheering the procession on the way to the Sheldonian Theatre. Cecil was a late addition to the list.[83]

The Final Return to Paris

Cecil resisted returning to Paris nearly until he left. From Oxford, on June 25, he wrote to his wife that "there is just a chance of my having to go over to Paris—but I am vigorously resisting."[84] He had other things to do. Immediately after the Oxford ceremony, Cecil went to Hitchin to make a constituency speech focusing on the need for ecumenicalism within Christianity. The need for community and unity, opposition to "bigots, uncharitableness and hatred," and avoidance of "international destruction" were all within the ability of Christians to bring about.⁸⁵ The next day, Cecil met with Fisher at his offices at the Board of Education. Fisher encouraged Cecil's suggestion that there be some pro-League teaching in the British schools.⁸⁶ Cecil appeared poised to reenter British politics.

But the next evening, on June 27, he called Oppenheimer to the War Cabinet office to discuss Austria before he returned to Paris the next morning.⁸⁷ There are no records of how he got there, but considering the tight time frame, early on June 28 Cecil must have flown to Paris. It would have been a difficult, two-hour trip in an open-cockpit airplane, and was not a journey he had made before. But he was obviously pressed for time. His urgent goal was to persuade the Big Four to allow the SEC to continue operating after the Germans and the various Allied and Associated powers signed the Treaty.

The signing was scheduled for that afternoon in the Hall of Mirrors of the Palace of Versailles, the same place where the Prussians forced France to sign the peace in 1871 that created the German Empire. It would be a momentous and perhaps solemn occasion, but it was also expected to trigger the immediate dispersal of global leaders from this unprecedented global forum that had made decisions impacting all the peoples of the world. President Wilson planned to leave from Versailles, quickly regroup in Paris, then jump on a train to Brest, where he and his entourage would board the USS *George Washington* the next day to return home to the United States. There he planned to sell his accomplishments in Paris to an increasingly skeptical Senate and public. It would be hard to imagine a more busy day on which to hold a meeting, and yet the Big Four met at 11:00 that morning.

They began with Wilson and Lloyd George signing the long promised, pivotal treaties guaranteeing assistance to France against any future "unprovoked aggression by Germany." But for most of the meeting, attention focused on Cecil and the other delegates from the SEC, including Hoover, Clémentel, and Crespi, who brought a resolution for the Four to consider: "That in some form, international consultation in economic matters should be continued until the Council of the League of Nations has had an opportunity of considering the present acute position of the international economic situation, and that it should be remitted to the Supreme Economic Council to establish the necessary machinery for the purpose."⁸⁸

The resolution had been drawn up in consultation between Salter, Wise, and Cecil over the previous week, but it was not just a British project. The day before, Hoover had submitted a note saying that the US delegation considered that signature of the peace treaty would bring an end to all binding economic arrangements, including rationing and control over German commerce, and that the existing economic bodies should not be active "except in the sheer sense of liquidation at the earliest possible moment."[89] But when this moment would come was uncertain, and Hoover notably no longer cited the Treaty signing as the moment the SEC would end. At the meeting of the Big Four on June 28, Hoover maintained an acquiescent silence. Although remaining wary that any continuation of the SEC would "give the impression to the world of an economic block of the Governments who have been aligned in war," Hoover himself had become less certain over June that dropping cooperation between the Allies and ending blockade restrictions would restart Germany or Europe. In early June, Hoover told reporters that the US government needed to do something to encourage private credits to help rebuild European trade or else "Europe will starve."[90] According to Baruch, Hoover seemed "to be inclined to flirt with the idea" of continuing the SEC if he was made chairman.[91] Perhaps Hoover had lost coherence due to overwork. "He impresses me as a man who is very tired," Baruch wrote in his diary.[92] In a meeting with Clémentel, Crespi, and E. F. Wise on June 21, Hoover declared that the SEC needed to continue dealing with the food and supply problems in Europe until the League could create an alternative.[93] Just one day before the Treaty signing, he suggested privately to Wilson that he should create a commission in the United States to raise credits for materials and food to Europe. This commission would then work in conjunction with similar bodies in European countries to facilitate the opening of national and international trade across the continent. The end goal, Hoover explained, would be to establish "some sort of economic dictatorship."[94] In effect, Hoover entered the last meeting of the Council of Four in favor of continuing, in an evolved form, the practical, "technocratic" mission of the SEC.[95]

But in front of the Big Four, Cecil was the advocate, not Hoover. He explained in dire terms what might happen if there was a "hiatus" between the demise of the SEC and the creation, under the League, of necessary institutions of international economic consultation. In what Hankey judged as a "powerful plea," Cecil asked the Big Four to mandate that the SEC establish "the necessary machinery" for bridging this gap.[96] Directly addressing President Wilson, Cecil argued that it was critical to uphold the importance of international economic relations.

Wilson knew that he was the stumbling block. He responded that the Four had already agreed that the SEC would continue to run until the peace was ratified by each government "some six weeks or two months hence," but he wished to avoid any suggestion that the Allies and Associated powers were creating some sort of permanent economic union aimed against the former Central Powers. He also suggested that he had no authority to agree to Cecil's terms on behalf of the US government. Cecil responded that even in Britain the demands for harsh action to punish Germany had waned, and that a voice of the British working people, the Trades Union Congress, had just passed a resolution demanding that the SEC continue operating as the only way to help Germany through her economic difficulties. Furthermore, Cecil pointed out that the idea that the SEC could be seen as an anti-German institution, a continuation of the wartime Alliance, was preposterous: "I remind you that it was the Supreme Economic Council which, several months ago, fed Germany, and that she couldn't have been provisioned without it." Its continual operation was in the interest of both the Allies and their former enemies.[97] Wilson conceded Cecil's point that in the "interlaced" world economy, there remained a need for consultation between states. In the end the Big Four resolved that the SEC "should be requested to suggest for the consideration of the several governments the methods of consultation which would be most serviceable for this purpose."[98]

This consultation got underway immediately. With Cecil back in the chair for the 25th meeting of the SEC on June 30, the SEC assigned its Policy Committee to consider which forms of interallied consultation would best fit the command from the Big Four.[99] Hoover issued a note describing the American views. In it, Hoover once again illustrated his belief that the primary reason for the Allied blockade was to pander to the selfishness of British traders, and reiterated his staunch opposition to the possibility that there would be any control over German trade beyond that of the Reparations Commission. But more interestingly, he also addressed the earlier French note, agreeing that the economic cooperation measures had risen and evolved as needed over the course of the war and the peace. Although Hoover reiterated that the American Government considered that all existing economic arrangements would end at the signature of the peace, and that any new organizations must be "of world character and not limited to a particular block of nations," simply describing the ways that these organizations evolved implied his acceptance of further evolution of the economic cooperation that had developed throughout the war and the Peace Conference.

Clearly many world leaders expected that economic cooperation bred during the war and the Peace Conference would continue even after the Treaty was signed. Cecil was not alone in expecting that the consultation mandated by the Big Four would be among the many ways that the peace process would continue to evolve over the coming years. Hope in this possibility was fundamental for optimistic critics of the Treaty like Cecil.

At the Hall of Mirrors

After attending the signing ceremony on June 28, British delegates described a wide variety of emotions. Frances Stevenson, Lloyd George's secretary and mistress, recognized the signing as a "great occasion," although marred in its grandiosity by the omnipresence of the Press, who "try to dominate everything" by constantly asking for interviews and photographs, and in doing so "destroying all romance, all solemnity, all majesty."[100] "I have never seen a less impressive ceremony" criticized Field-Marshal Wilson in his diary.[101]

Some of those who attended, even among the Treaty signers, were filled with desperate regret. Jan Smuts for one felt brutal. After vacillating the week before, he decided that he must sign despite his hatred of how it treated the Germans, because signing the Treaty in the name of South Africa would be seen as an international validation of the sovereignty of his country. But he always hated it and cynically assumed it would fail and that German militarism would reemerge.[102] Field-Marshal Wilson was likewise sure that the Treaty could never hold, that the "Frocks" (the politicians) "have proved their collective incompetence" by basing their hopes for peace on an impotent League of Nations.[103] Harold Nicolson famously ended his book *Peacemaking* with his diary entry for that day. After driving from Versailles back to Paris after the signing, he depressively crawled off "to bed, sick of life."[104] Along with the caustic description of the Conference by Keynes in his *Economic Consequences of the Peace*, Nicolson's widely read *Peacemaking* both reflected and helped to shape the pessimistic view of an overly cruel treaty that dominated interwar Britain.[105] Following these first-hand critics, many historians have highlighted the pessimism of British leaders throughout the post-war years due to their perception that the Versailles Treaty was too harsh. Antony Lentin argues that appeasement, a desire to revise the Treaty in favor of Germany, was already the prevailing sentiment of the British delegates at the signing in June.[106] Keynes became the apotheosis of this extremely pessimistic viewpoint, with his blockbuster book published at the end of the year focusing on the cruelty being done to Germany. The willingness and capacity of Keynes, Smuts, Nicolson, and other British delegates to publicize their opinions helped to lead to the dominance of this negative view of the Treaty in the decades thereafter. Historians since have generally agreed that the "truncated peace" of Versailles, a "peace without promise," utterly failed in the basic goal of realistically addressing Germany's place in the post-war international system.[107] For such critics, the entire peace process at Paris in 1919 can only be seen as a sad debacle.

But it is worthwhile to note that this sad desperation was not the prevailing attitude among the attendees of the signing ceremony on June 28. Some felt simply glorious. In his memoir on the Peace Conference written decades later, Maurice Hankey pointedly recognized that his feelings during the signing were the exact opposite of the pessimism that Harold Nicolson felt. Hankey's sense was that most of the men in the *galerie des Glaces*, waiting through the ponderous fifty-minute group signing of the Treaty, proudly believed that it brought peace "once more to mankind."[108] Woodrow Wilson believed they had crafted a peace of justice, righting wrongs perpetrated by Germany and creating a permanent structure for permanent peace.[109] Billy Hughes was ecstatic, certain that the Treaty would bring Australia big reparations payments and permanent control of the former German colony in New Guinea, despite the existence of the League of Nations mandate system.[110]

Lloyd George also appeared satisfied with the results, or at least unwilling to revise it. He hoped that reparations would eventually flow to Britain, while also judging that throughout the final month of negotiations he had pushed past both Wilson and Clemenceau modifications that improved the treaty's likelihood of success, with terms enabling German recovery while remaining satisfactory to those in Britain baying for German blood.[111] Lloyd George could come off as crafty and harsh toward a Germany he still feared and hated, or as intentionally unrealistic, full of "financial demagoguery" and "surrealistic" claims on Germany simply to pander to the British people.[112] But his inconsistencies during the Conference and his willingness to support fudged agreements like the reparations clauses also suggest Lloyd George's hope for real compromise both within his delegation and between the Allies, and also exposes the depth of his uncertainty about how to treat Germany and how to treat his own electorate. It took a few years after the Conference for Lloyd George to fall into the mentality of appeasement.[113] To Lloyd George, the Paris spring had culminated in a fair treaty.

There was however also a third attitude, one neither pessimistic nor satisfied. Arthur Salter, the British shipping and blockade expert, left Paris believing fully that the Allies had done all that was physically possible (given limitations on shipping and lack of available goods) to supply Europe with food over the previous few months. Salter fundamentally rejected Nicolson's nihilist assessment of the Treaty as fatally flawed.[114] "The most striking thing" about the Covenant, he wrote eighteen months after the signing of the Treaty, was that the League it envisioned was "elastic and expansive in character."[115] Salter believed that the peace would evolve over the next few years, as the new international institutions helped nurture improvement to the terms of European peace. The journalist Sidney Huddleston, who wrote for the *Westminster Gazette* and the *Contemporary Review* throughout the Conference, published a book at the same time as Keynes. Despite having some misgivings, Huddleston believed that the League of Nations would have "a golden future" if we "settle down to work again."[116] In the words of Philip Baker, the League would succeed if it became "an institution that counts in the life of the world," and it seemed on the way to becoming so. Baker bragged that they had persuaded thirty-two countries to join it, and he expected that more neutrals would soon join. He expected to get cross-party support in the House of Commons, from Conservatives, Liberals, and Labourites who all favored for one reason or another making the League "an effective organism in international life."[117] The attitude assumed that with constructive engagement and continual efforts, the League could tremendously improve an imperfect but workable peace. These cautious optimists believed that the Treaty, both in its ambiguities and in its founding of the League, created a new possibility for permanent improvement in international relations. As seen in the reaction of the *Times* to Cecil's Albert Hall speech, significant support for this evolving new internationalism existed within the mainstream of the unsettled and ripe political atmosphere of post-war Britain.

It is uncertain whether Cecil himself attended the signing ceremony. He was no longer writing a conference diary. Each delegation only received a small number of tickets to the Hall of Mirrors, but Cecil certainly would have received one of them if he wished. A few days before, Eyre Crowe had sent around a memo to the heads of each section of the British Delegation, allocating thirty-six tickets in total. As head of both the League of Nations section and the SEC, Cecil apparently had five tickets at his disposal.[118] It is hard to imagine that he missed it, considering that he had never avoided any other big events throughout the Conference.

As the Conference broke up in the hours after the Treaty was signed, delegates like Cecil were not only pleased that the long Conference was finally over, but were also pleased that the Conference poised the world for a potentially more peaceful future. Some of these optimists would lose their faith after hearing about the US Senate's rejection of the Treaty on November 19, 1919, or after the second attempt in the Senate in March of the next year, or at some other moment of disappointment over the course of international relations over the next two decades. But at the end of June 1919, many delegates were not only happy that they could finally go home, but also believed that the Conference had ushered the world toward a brighter future.

8

After Paris: July to December

Although the Peace Conference slogged on for the rest of the year in crafting treaties to present to Germany's wartime allies, Austria and Turkey, Wilson and Lloyd George returned to their capitals and these final negotiations were left to foreign secretaries and professional diplomats. A similar level of men from all the Allied countries, drawn not from the pinnacle of national politics and state service but rather from those "one level down," worked through the rest of the 1919 and the years after to create and operate the League of Nations. Many on the British delegation in Paris supported the League, not just with their best wishes but also with their post-war career decisions. Unsurprisingly, Cecil's British staff and the international acquaintances he nurtured during the months in Paris metamorphosed into the leadership ranks of the new League. At the same time, Leaguers engaged in domestic politics in their countries, trying to nurture support for the League.

Starting Up the League in London

Both during the Conference and immediately after, Cecil worked to transition to League service many who had worked for him in London during the war and in Paris during the armistice. At a Ministry of Blockade "peace luncheon," held in one of the temporary buildings still erected in the drained lake bed of St. James's Park, he reminded his former subordinates that their economic war "made the victory of the soldiers not only complete, but overwhelming. In the history of the world there had never been a blockade carried on with such complete success in circumstances of great difficulty." He believed the League would help to build international cooperation, and that the work of the wartime blockade departments was "not finished. If there was to be international cooperation, economical cooperation would be part of the work in which that organization would be essential." From this point onward, such efforts would constitute "the opening of a new chapter [and] the establishment of right and justice throughout the world."[1]

Even before this League recruitment speech to members of his wartime ministry, a number of economic warriors had already committed to working for the League. J. A. Salter was one who had learned during the war, and then in Paris, how to implement international economic controls. Salter led the British shipping authorities during the war, serving as the Chairman of the Allied Maritime Transport Executive through 1918 and early 1919, and remained critically active in shipping-related decisions in Paris in 1919. In April and May he worked in the SEC, finding ways to open Germany's economy and bring prosperity back to central Europe before it slipped across the brink of revolution. Like Cecil, Salter was certain that some interallied efforts during the war should be constructively adapted by a post-war League. On June 13, he signed on as the director of the League's Economic and Financial Section, a post he held for a dozen years. This new bureaucracy was expected to focus on compiling commercial and economic statistics for the League's leaders, information that would be necessary to the "new method of international constraint," the "economic boycott" embodied in Article 16 of the Covenant.[2]

Philip Baker was the most significant of Cecil's staffers embedded in the core of the nascent League. Particularly since the middle of March, Cecil relied on Baker. He had worked in the FO's League of Nations committee at the end of the war. As the Peace Conference wore on, Baker (or Noel-Baker, as he was often known after the war) developed into Cecil's main secretary and advisor, guiding the flow of information to and from Cecil and operating as Cecil's primary liaison to the American delegation on the League.[3] In June, when Drummond and Cecil went to London, Baker in Paris continued to funnel confidential information from the FO to both men.[4] Soon thereafter he resigned from the FO to work on the Secretary General's staff and in the League's section on Mandates for the next three years.[5] Interspersed with this work for the League, he captained the British squad at the Antwerp Olympic Games in 1920, and won a silver medal in the 1500 meter race. Over the next decades his ties to Cecil only intensified, especially in the leadership of the LNU.[6] In 1959 Noel-Baker followed in his mentor's footsteps in receiving the Nobel Peace Prize.

Frank Walters had been Cecil's secretary through much of the war, and he maintained this position during the Peace Conference. He became one of the first employees of the League, signing up as the private secretary to Drummond starting on May 15.⁷ Cecil admired Walters' charm, although speculated that his lack of initiative would not allow him to climb too high in the League.⁸ Nevertheless, Walters ended up serving in various administrative posts in the League until 1940, and after that he wrote one of the early histories of the League. Florence Margaret Dudgeon had been another of Cecil's private assistants since the start of the Peace Conference. Among her duties was to transcribe and type his diary. By June she returned to London to work for the League. Over the years she worked in various League bureaucracies in London and Geneva, including in their staff Pensions fund and the Minorities section.⁹ The Cecil connection also helped to guide the path of one of his relatives. The husband of his young niece Mima, William Ormsby-Gore, served as the first British representative on the League's Permanent Mandates Commission.¹⁰

Beyond Cecil's immediate circle, other young people who worked at the Peace Conference and bought into the Paris project declared their internationalism by taking their talents to the League. Although he had barely met Cecil during their time in Paris, the League spirit affected Nicolson, and he briefly joined the League's Political Section at the end of the war. The thirty-year old Jean Monnet attached himself to the League soon after Drummond's appointment to lead the Secretariat. A member of the French delegation advising economic minister Etienne Clémentel, Monnet had served as France's delegate to the AMTC during 1918 and had developed a close relationship with Salter which carried over into their League work over the next few years. Monnet was fluent in English and spent a lot of time with Cecil at the Conference. His wartime experiences in the AMTC nurtured his hopes that international cooperation could be successful, and in Paris 1919 this made him tremendously enthusiastic for a League.¹¹ When the revisions of the initial Covenant draft got underway, Monnet drafted reports describing possible ways to organize the League. In mid-May he left for London to work on getting the initial secretariat ready in Sunderland House, the temporary home of the League.¹² Through 1923 he worked as the deputy secretary general under Drummond. Although the misfortunes of his family brandy business caused him to quit the League, after the next world war, Monnet famously led the creation of the organizations that would become the European Union. Another Frenchman, the historian Paul Mantoux, had entered government service during the war as an assistant to Clémentel and made connections among all of the interallied economic authorities.¹³ Mantoux worked during the Conference as Clemenceau's secretary and translator and was the daily author of what became the definitive French minutes of the Council of Four. After the war, Mantoux worked until 1927 leading the Political Section of the League.¹⁴

Even among Americans, whose country eventually rejected membership in the League, the Paris experience proved vital in shaping League-focused internationalist careers, even if they ended up as abbreviated ones. Whitney Shepardson, a young American who was in Oxford on a Rhodes Scholarship when the war began, became secretary to Edward House during the Peace Conference. Shepardson spent much time shuffling around the papers of the League Commission, and by the end of the spring of 1919 had become deeply focused on the creation of new international organizations. He and other young Americans were vital in linking together with similarly second-tier but very driven British counterparts during the last days of the Conference to pair the Council on Foreign Relations of New York with the London-based Royal Institute of International Affairs. For a few months in the fall of 1919, Shepardson assisted Raymond Fosdick in setting up his office as League undersecretary.[15] Fosdick was a young protégé of Wilson who he knew from Princeton. He had worked in the War Department, and during the Peace Conference he focused on the demobilization of soldiers. Fosdick found in Paris "excitement and exhilaration," he was "ecstatic" about the future, and although he did not focus on the League, Fosdick found himself appointed on May 4, 1919 as its under secretary general.[16] As such he labored on a variety of issues in London, including organizing the first Assembly and Council meetings. But as the Treaty was being considered a second time by the Senate in early 1920, Fosdick's position "on the Secretariat was proving embarrassing" to a White House accused of jumping the gun, so he sadly resigned.[17]

It wasn't only the victorious powers whose Paris staff transitioned to League business after the signing of the Treaty. William Rappard, a Swiss professor, had worked for his government in Paris in March and April 1919 pushing for a place in the League for the wartime neutral states. After the Conference he briefly became director of the International Red Cross before he joined the League as Director of the Mandates Section.[18] Early under-secretaries and other administrative leaders came from France, Japan, Italy, the Netherlands, Norway, and the United States.[19] Countering the claims made in October by Shepardson, who wrote that the Secretariat in London was dominated by the British and (more nefariously) by the French, Raymond Fosdick wrote a report in November that he sent to various American officials, including Frank Polk, the chief US negotiator still in Paris, and Colonel House. Fosdick noted that the League was a truly international organization, its nine sections headed by two Frenchmen, "a Norwegian, a Jap, an Englishman, a Dutchman, a Belgian, an American, and an Italian," with personnel that included, "two or three Greeks, a Canadian, a Chinaman," a Swedish woman, even a Uruguayan.[20]

When exactly did League truly begin operating in London? Early inklings of League operations survive in a smattering of brief newspaper accounts. In mid-August "an important conference on international statistics" was held under "the auspices of the provisional organization of the League of Nations Secretariat." A variety of experts on international statistics in agriculture and trade gave papers, presided over by Salter, the "Director of the Economic and Finance Section of the international Secretariat of the Provisional League of Nations."[21] The Conference opened with speeches by Drummond and Cecil.[22]

More privately, certain League commissions began operating even earlier. During the summer of 1919, the commission to prepare terms of the mandates sat in London. Cecil advised Lord Milner on this commission, which included members from France, Japan, Italy, and the United States, represented by Edward House. Cecil and Milner sparred when the former suggested that Egypt should be made a League mandate.[23] This group divided the mandates into three classes, as anticipated in Article 22 of the Covenant, but it did not fully flesh out the links between the League and the mandatory powers. Uncertainty plagued Milner's commission, as US engagement in European affairs ebbed, and the committee's deliberations were also affected by the Turkish treaty being prepared at that point in Paris (the eventual Treaty of Sevres, signed on August 10, 1920). But although this mandate commission eventually was scuttled in August, it succeeded in kicking the ball further down the field, and thus helped to bridge the gap between the signing of the Treaty of Versailles and the opening of more effective League Secretariat efforts on mandates. In the Milner commission, and then in his influence on the first Mandates Section leader Philip Baker, and then at the first League Assembly in the fall of 1920, Cecil actively helped to shape the concept and reality of mandates. During the 1920s and 1930s, the mandate system epitomized what Susan Pedersen has termed the "dynamic of internationalization" that marked the League as at least a partial success.[24]

For many months, the League was headquartered in London. The final move to Geneva only took place in October 1920, when a chartered train with the staff and their families left from Victoria Station.[25] The months of 1919 were a time of much behind the scenes activity for the London League, but at least through early 1920, surprisingly little publicity. It centered at Sunderland House, Mayfair, a city palace built as a wedding gift for Consuela Vanderbilt by her father when she married the Duke of Marlborough. Sunderland House epitomized Edwardian era London high society, but during the later stages of the war, it had been turned into offices by the Ministry of Blockade. Starting in June 1919, it became the headquarters of the League of Nations.[26] By mid-September the

League sprawled into two nearby buildings, 117 and 118 Piccadilly. At that point the League employed a staff of about 100 in total, perhaps half of whom were women. Many took subordinate clerical positions such as telephone operators—by the start of October, the League employed four of these, an indication that there was a significant amount of phone traffic coming in and out of Sunderland House.[27] Most other women were secretaries—Raymond Fosdick had two US ladies who assisted him.[28] However, from the beginning a few women held more significant League roles, such as Rachel Crowdy, who began her interwar work in London as the head of (and sole member of) the League's International Health Department.[29]

The machinery of the League set up in London was "well oiled and ready for smooth operation" according to press accounts in October.[30] But it was being done with the minimum of publicity. The silence around the London League in late 1919 was intentional and tactical. European leaders still hoped to get US ratification of the Treaty, and did not yet want to make it appear that the League could succeed without US participation. Both Drummond's and Wilson's advisors knew that news about the League already building its organization could lead to howls of protest from its opponents in the US.[31] "I must not tell you much" about what we're doing, a League spokesman supposedly said to one reporter, "America might hear of it."[32] Its location in London, even temporarily, was also a potential public relations problem. As the capital of one of the Allied powers, London as headquarters could create wariness among some wartime neutrals that were considering joining the League. Having it in London also irritated the Belgians, who still believed that it should be permanently headquartered in Brussels rather than Geneva.[33] Some even generally sympathetic Frenchmen like Clémentel voiced concerns that having the League in London (especially in coordination with the SEC staff moving to London) indicated that the British were up to something.[34]

But the silence was also ironic, considering the general sense among League leaders and historians that the League's public activities both relied upon and stimulated "popular internationalism" in all nations, including Britain.[35] And in the fall of 1919, the silence surrounding the League stimulated those eager to sideline or even deride it. "No letters of fire across the front or symbolic doves with olive branches indicate that Sunderland House is really what it is," noted the *Daily Express*. The office cubicles that partitioned the grand ballroom were quiet, with the typists all sequestered in the attic.[36] League air was more stagnant than anticipatory. Sunderland House itself was easily mocked, even by those who loved the League; in Fosdick's words, it was "a garish, ornate building, splashed with gilt, and with the ceilings painted with cupids and water nymphs," "a singularly inappropriate building for a sober institution like ours," tolerable only because of its availability in office-starved London.[37]

During the summer and early fall of 1919, Drummond appointed an office in Sunderland House to Cecil, who extended copious advice to Drummond and the other leaders of the Secretariat on such things as the creation of a Permanent Military Commission, and a disarmament commission envisioned under Article 9.[38] Cecil spent so much time there during the rest of 1919 that one of the few British newspaper articles that mentioned Sunderland House did so only to give it as his address. An interview he gave to a US reporter on copartnership, definitely not a League issue, was conducted in the League offices at 117 Piccadilly Street, overlooking Green Park and Buckingham Palace.[39] Undoubtedly Cecil's sense of how the League would operate deeply affected Drummond. Cecil expected that global problems would be dealt with as they arose, that Article 19 gave the League significant flexibility, and that the balance between the League's Secretariat, Assembly, and Council would evolve as it operated.[40] Throughout his thirteen-year tenure as secretary general, Drummond similarly followed an "evolutionary approach toward the League."[41]

The cultivation of the core of the League of Nations' initial bureaucracy at the Paris Peace Conference was not surprising. Where else could it have come from? All of the world's leaders interested in creating a League were at the Conference, and all of these arrived with significant numbers of advisors and secretaries, many of whom grew more and more interested in the League as the Conference went on. Certainly some of these second- (and third-) tier delegates in Paris were actively looking for longer-term jobs, and appreciated the opportunity to sign on to a potentially well-paying and certainly interesting international diplomatic role. For others, taking one of these jobs was a hardship, forcing them away from home for longer than they had hoped. Yet the sacrifice was acceptable for believers in the League cause, who (in Fosdick's words) saw "a chance to play a part in a brave, new world."[42] These men and women understood that the creation of the Covenant had been messy, with the Commission reaching difficult and, perhaps, unhappy compromises, but overall they were inspired to serve by their Peace Conference experiences. Cecil hoped that the creation of "an international civil service" would illustrate the importance of international interests and help make war "unthinkable."[43] And indeed, these many individuals from around the world developed an "international civil society" with "its own political space" that nurtured further advancements in international cooperation over the next decades.[44] For many of the early personnel of the League of Nations, peacemaking in Paris transitioned smoothly, via London, into peacemaking in Geneva.

Economic Cooperation after Paris

It has been traditionally tempting to see 1919 as a pivot year for western economies, marked by a serious Anglo-American-led ideological abandonment of the state controls that had developed over the war years.[45] However, the actions of global leaders during the second half of 1919, both in domestic and international politics, suggest that in 1919 the future of state interventions in the economy remained an open question.[46] Even some British and American free traders questioned whether reliance on the free market was, at that moment, the path to politically stable prosperity.

An August 1 speech by Herbert Hoover exemplifies this ambivalence among the ideological free traders of the western world. At a London dinner given in Cecil's honor by the SEC, Hoover laid out a defense of government intervention that would have seemed ludicrous from him six months earlier. "Productivity in Europe today is such that Europe could not survive twelve months" without the continued operation of the SEC, which wielded authority "from Bactum to Helsingfors" and whose operations fed 200 million people.[47] At the SEC meeting earlier that day, the first to be held in London, Hoover supported a call for collective, coordinated action against profiteers. This followed on Hoover's astonishing July in Paris, where he pushed a surprisingly collectivist agenda after Wilson returned home. In discussions before the Supreme War Council on how to get food to Austria, Hoover suggested (and Balfour, Clemenceau, and the other leaders approved) that the Reparations Commission created by the Treaty of Versailles should be tasked with ensuring that Austria was provided with enough food and raw materials to allow economic rebuilding.[48] A few weeks later, Hoover supported the SEC decision to keep its own Finance Section operating at least until its duties were subsumed under either the Reparations Commission then being drawn together, or under an anticipated "International Economic Council."[49] Just days later, Hoover proposed that the various Allied governments in Europe (including Poland and Czechoslovakia) should create a new European Coal Commission to coordinate "the production, distribution and transportation of coal throughout Europe."

Hoover's support for such international action flies in the face of the dominant narrative suggesting that US leaders (and Hoover in particular) ideologically rejected government interventions and refused to cooperate in Europe's postwar economic reconstruction.[50] In July, Hoover had come to doubt his earlier stances. He now realized that the full lifting of the blockade would not prove a panacea for Europe's economic woes.

As Hoover's opinions about economic cooperation developed, confusion reigned about the US policy. When asked whether the US would have a member on the coal commission, Hoover initially noted that lack of production and tonnage in the US made it unlikely that the US could do anything to alleviate Europe's fuel shortage, but then suggested that he and Assistant Secretary of State Frank Polk, who was left in charge as the chief US delegate in Paris, would work with any European organization.[51] On Hoover's behalf, on August 11 the British FO sent a telegram to Lord Grey's mission to Washington. Hoover was waiting for a reply from Wilson with instructions, and hoped that perhaps Grey could push Wilson into a decision.[52]

With US opinion so divided at home and only lurching guidance being given to the US representatives in Paris and London, the SEC slowly disintegrated over the next few months. August 2 was the last day that US representatives attended SEC meetings. When the SEC announced the creation of a new "International Economic Council" in September, Polk refused entreaties to appoint a US representative.[53] Similarly a "Permanent Committee" of the SEC was set up and met two or three times a month until early 1920, mostly in London, but their request for a US member went unanswered.[54]

Yet some of the duties of the SEC still had to be undertaken by someone, and over the fall of 1919, various sections of the SEC rebranded themselves in order to carry on their work. Bits of its functions were picked up by the Allied Reparations Commission and international bodies like the League. Perhaps unsurprisingly, the Committee on the Organization of the Reparations Commission was tasked not just with organizing the new commission, but also in the interim with figuring out and implementing German trade policies. SEC sub-committees on Raw Materials and Provisioning were instructed by the Organization Committee to examine any purchases of goods for Germany, with a goal of ensuring that the supply interests of Europe as a whole were taken into account.[55] The British were wary of tasking the Reparations Commission with helping to feed Germany, noting that its goal should be simply to liquidate German assets. They suggested that either a new food committee, or the developing Economic Section of the League, might be entrusted with provisioning Germany.

Without instructions from Washington, the American delegates could neither support nor reject the proposal.[56] After the SEC meeting in Brussels on

September 20, its Consultative Food Committee set up subcommittees on wheat, meat, hogs, sugar, and dairy, aiming to organize purchasing orders for all the Allies. They asked for US representation, but again there was no response from the US.[57] But at the same time, Polk noted that despite their decision to leave the SEC, the US was part of the Reparations Commission.[58] Working through the Reparations Commission was a simple way to continue SEC operations. The SEC's Raw Materials section evolved into a new organization, "the Committee on Raw Materials and Statistical Information," to solve "on common lines" the problems facing the purchasing and transport of such materials. This new committee reported to both the SEC and to the Reparations Commission. Similar transformations prolonged the operations of the Finance and Food Sections of the SEC.[59]

At the November 21–23 meetings of the SEC at the Palazzo Corsini in Rome, significant discussion ensued about the future of the Council. They were advised by Arthur Salter, who although he already worked for the League, prefaced his remarks by stating that he spoke for neither the British government nor for the League, "since the League did not formally exist." To Salter, there needed to be continuity in efforts to feed Central Europe. The lapse in food organization that occurred between the armistice and the meeting in Paris must not be repeated by a lapse between the Treaty signing and the development of a functional League.[60] The SEC's Permanent Committee in London was told "to keep in close touch" with the League to figure out the best relationship between the SEC and League.[61]

One final episode, from the start of 1920, epitomizes the nature of this transition of internationalist economic activity from the Peace Conference to the post-war years. In early January, a letter went to global newspapers and to a number of governments, calling for a global economic conference. The letter suggested that the outcome of the Conference must be the creation of some sort of capital outlay from creditor countries to European countries, including Germany, that needed "working capital necessary for them to purchase the imports required for re-starting the circle of exchange." It was signed by over 100 politicians, public intellectuals, bankers, and economists in the United States, Britain, and European states, including Hoover and Cecil. According to the *New York Times*, "the precise origin of this movement has not been disclosed," but "over the last few weeks what virtually amounted to spontaneous petitions for such a conference had been received by the leading financial and commercial representatives of all the countries."[62] Like with the League, such efforts as this to maintain and create economic internationalism were bold and transformative, but they were intentionally coordinated behind the scenes. Far from spontaneous or *sui generis*, the roots of this idea of a financial conference (one eventually called together to focus on Austria at the end of 1920) were set deep within the activities of the Peace Conference.

The dominant view since 1919 is that the international bodies created during and immediately after the war were quickly, inexorably, and completely dismantled by the end of that year.[63] However looking at the proliferation and activities of the Allied economic organizations through 1919, it is apparent that despite the expressed desires of Woodrow Wilson and the US delegates to liquidate Allied economic cooperation as of June 28, these organizations never really died. Both the Reparations Commission and the Economic Section of the League of Nations traced their origins not just to the decisions of the Peace Conference, but to the personnel and activities of the SEC during the Peace Conference. Once committees were created, they tended to continue, evolving, surviving, and sometimes thriving, as the notion of regional and global political and economic interdependence became permanently embedded in regional and global institutions aiming for the common good. Ideas of cooperation in finance and development crafted during the Peace Conference eventually came to fruition in addressing the Austrian financial emergency of 1922.[64] Throughout the second half of 1919, the relationship between the SEC, the Reparations Commission, the new Allied bodies like the Consultative Food Committee, and the developing Secretariat of the League of Nations remained uncertain and yet strong.[65] The new organizations were created due to the stipulations of the Treaty, the carryover of longer-term business from before the signing of the Treaty, and to allow US internationalists to remain attached to institutions of international economic cooperation. In part, the bizarre organizational chart linking such bodies to the League of Nations allowed the US to fool itself into thinking it was living without the League.

Returning to Domestic Politics

Despite all the internationalists around him, Cecil's public face was set toward British politics for the rest of 1919. In particular, he reengaged in the House of Commons. In his memoir *A Great Experiment*, published during the next war against Germany, Cecil looked far back to his early years as a Member of Parliament before the war. His initial experiences in the House of Commons were as a gadfly debater against the Liberal government of Sir Henry Campbell

Bannerman in 1906.[66] But even after his Conservatives came to power in 1910, he often jostled and poked at those in power, particularly over the issue of Tariff Reform. He loved to speak out in the House and became known as one of its premier debaters. But "the truth is, I was never a good Party man."[67] Other than during the wartime coalition years, Cecil's greatest experiences as an MP, his preferred Parliamentary position, was in opposition.

In the House of Commons upon returning from Paris, Cecil followed form and set about attacking the government. His first blast occurred during the first week of July, when the government decided to oppose, on its third and final reading, a Women's Emancipation Bill that would make the age of voting rights the same for men and women. A number of MPs registered their disapproval about the government's stance, including some ministers, but Cecil's speech was "the most powerful speech of the debate—one of those utterances... which have the effect of turning votes."[68] Despite the government's opposition, Cecil's side won with a fifteen-vote majority. One newspaper commented that the "determined attitude" of Cecil was remarkable. His "brilliant and convincing" advocacy not only supported this bill that proclaimed women's equality, but also forcefully upheld the right of individual members to bring before the Commons bills that were not supported by the Government whip.[69] Over the next month there were few days when Parliament sat when he didn't speak.

Cecil did not always oppose the coalition. Newspapers across the world reported on his support for the Treaty during the first post–Paris Commons debate on it on July 8, and also at a number of constituent events in Hitchin a few days earlier. Cecil persuasively argued the case for the League and for the entire Treaty, primarily by describing the dire economic straits faced by a Europe that necessitated international, League-coordinated action.[70] At the second reading of the Treaty of Peace Bill, Cecil spoke extensively, arguing that the Treaty at least fulfilled the main purpose of creating peace. He appealed to the British people to support the Treaty: "If it turned out that this or that provision was not altogether the best, then we must trust to the League of Nations as the most important international experiment made in our times."[71] Lloyd George followed by expressing his appreciation for Cecil's support.

Likewise, Cecil's lengthy intervention during the July 29 debate on Russia favored Lloyd George's policy. Cecil dismissed as "fantastic nonsense" any idea that a British or Allied invasion of Russia could even be staged, let alone that it could possibly succeed. Bolshevism would fail eventually, he was sure; "let it fail of itself." The one thing the British and the Allies might do, "the League of Nations not being in existence," would be for them to "devote all our economic strength" to "compel" all the sides in the Russian conflict to stop fighting.[72] It was a characteristic suggestion, embodying his certitude that economic warfare had significant power to curtail a more damaging shooting war.

Everyone returning from Paris had a chaotic reentry into British politics, including the prime minister. By early August, rumors swirled around London that a general election was coming soon. Some Conservatives questioned the necessity of the coalition now that the war was over, and others criticized its handling of threatened coal strikes and other worker activism. The *New-York Tribune* reported that Cecil was the one man "perhaps not willing and ready, but desired by the strongest factions on both sides" to take Lloyd George's job. He had spoken "so wisely lately on the great questions of the day amid applause from both Right and Left."[73] According to another commentator, within a month of the end of the Peace Conference, Cecil "has leapt at a bound to the front rank of the men who count in Parliament. He is a force. He sways opinion. He is a formidable critic and a powerful champion, and though he has not yet attracted a party to himself, there are few men in the House who have more of the essential qualities of leadership." His ideas of adjusting the peace as needed especially hit home. "The Treaty contains within itself, in the League of Nations chapter, the machinery for its adaptation, modification, and adjustment," agreed the *Observer*'s political correspondent.[74]

Ideas swirled in London in 1919 suggesting the possibility of fundamental realignments across British party politics. New parties had been created, with the election bringing thirteen ex-Labour MPs into the House of Commons as the new National Democratic Party. The gaping fissure that had split the Liberal Party since Lloyd George nudged aside Asquith in 1916 was only exacerbated by the Lloyd George faction's uncertainty about their relationship with the Tories. A number of newspapers reported that Cecil might be interested in joining the leadership of "the new Centre Party" supposedly inaugurated in a recent dinner officiated over by Churchill.[75] However, Churchill's plans for a new party were centered on the possibility of uniting the Lloyd George Liberals with the Tories, in other words a formalization of the coalition arrangement, and possibly had the support of Lloyd George himself.[76] Cecil's ideas for a new political alignment were uncertain but unsurprisingly suggested his desire to go beyond the coalition. By the end of the month, it was well known that Cecil was reaching out to a number of "younger Unionist" MPs on his ideas of copartnership as a route to avoiding revolution.[77] At a dinner at the Criterion Restaurant, Cecil spoke on the question of "why is the Government unpopular?" A column "A Tale of Two Statesmen" compared the eloquent trickster Churchill's speech to the Centre Party meeting with Cecil's straightforward, impressive speech at Royal Albert Hall for the LNU. Cecil, it was claimed, had a mind and character "sure in the end to win the sympathy and confidence of his countrymen." His decision to resign, even his unwillingness to not give up the fight to stop Welsh Disestablishment, were proof of Cecil's "political worthiness," "political honesty and political honour."[78] The public yearned for Cecil, according to a fawning article in the *Graphic*, "a statesman discovered" who simply wanted to serve, unlike the power-hungry Lloyd George and Churchill.[79] "He is the mystery man of Parliament," explained the *Daily Mail*. "Once looked on as the type of Tory aristocrat in politics, he now seems ready to out-do the democrats in democracy ... Which way will he turn? What party will he lead? No one but himself knows. His mind plans some destiny while men are wondering."[80]

One report that circulated through US newspapers in August, written by the journalist and Irish Nationalist MP from Liverpool T.P. O'Connor, predicted that the coalition would split and the Conservatives would overthrow Bonar Law as their leader. He suggested Robert Cecil as a likely replacement in a resulting Conservative government. His brother Hugh Cecil also had leadership abilities, but Robert stood out for having more experience in the world. Not only was Hugh a bachelor while Robert was "a husband and father" (which he was not), Robert had shown impressive mettle in Paris (see Figure 8.1).[81] O'Connor might have had particular hopes for Cecil's ascendency. Unionism was always a core principle of the Cecil family's conservatism, but after the war, Cecil jettisoned any support for Edward Carson's irreconcilable Unionists and began advocating League-style self-determination for the counties of Ulster.[82] The gossip page of the *Daily Mirror* suggested that Cecil would preside over the "Anti-Carsonites" when the Unionists split into three (the third splinter would be the "business section, which is inarticulate because they have not a parliamentary speaker amongst them").[83]

His speeches on a variety of subjects were applauded by Labour benches and also by young Unionists favoring social reform, including William Ormsby-Gore, Lord Winterton, Edward Wood, Samuel Hoare, and Godfrey Locker Lampson.[84] He nurtured the feminist vote, prominently supporting Lady Astor's November 1919 by-election campaign to become the first female MP. Cecil wrote in a widely-published letter that he supported her not just because she was a friend, or because he wanted women to enter politics, but also because she favored the League.[85] Upon her victory, the *New Statesman* labeled Astor as Cecil's "protégée."[86]

Figure 8.1 Caricatures of Hugh and Robert Cecil. *The Graphic*, vol. 101 (Jan. 17, 1920), 74.

Cecil also reached out to the left. When the Labour Party leader J. M. Clynes moved that there should be a tax on capital to ensure that food and unemployment benefits continued, Cecil notably supported him in the debate.[87] In early August, Cecil pushed a question to the prime minister (and got wide publicity by giving notice of it days beforehand) asking him to do all he could to resist the revolutionary tendencies in recent railway and coal mine strikes. Cecil suggested a "positive policy" of copartnership and profit sharing in industry would woo workers away from the allures of Bolshevism.[88] Copartnership, or more simply partnership as he increasingly referred to it, remained a constant thread within his speeches through the rest of the year.[89] It made him appealing to many of the representatives of Britain's working classes. In an interview, the head of the British Trades Union Congress, Stuart Bunning, suggested that Cecil might become prime minister of a government supported by Labour and by some Liberals and Conservatives.[90]

But was Cecil looking to divide the coalition, let alone to take over a new government? His tactics made this appear doubtful. He refused to focus on creating a real unified message with a broad appeal to a possible center majority. Some of his harshest attacks on the government were on fringe topics like Welsh disestablishment. His passion over this issue, his outraged sense that the bill simply stole assets from the church to give money to the Welsh counties, led during the second reading of the new Welsh Church bill on August 6 to his bitter denunciation of Bonar Law for allowing the "undisguised robbery" of disestablishment. Bonar Law responded that his hands were tied by the coalition campaign manifesto.[91] The *Observer* noted that the issue "is regarded as (Cecil's) foible" and that his supporters were willing to allow him "considerable latitude, if not license" to push it.[92] But other admirers regarded Cecil's focus on the church issue "with the greatest misgiving."[93]

He also began to gain a reputation for histrionics. Cecil caustically attacked a government bill that aimed to end profiteering, claiming in a late night debate that the bill was a "sort of poster" to trick the country into thinking something was really being done about profiteering.[94] Not only would it lead to higher prices and more scarcity, but Cecil suggested that any future Bolshevik government in Britain might use this anti-profiteering act to turn British markets into those of Soviet Russia. The *Manchester Guardian* judged this remark "a striking illustration of the unhappy influence of all-night rhetorical dissipation."[95] Three days later, Cecil sparred again with Bonar Law, claiming that if British left to Turkey the fate of the already suffering Armenians, it might lead to the slaughter of 1.5 million more people. Bonar Law calmly noted that the United States was in a better position to deal with the Turks.[96]

Cecil again attacked the government when responding to Lloyd George's three-hour long speech to the House of Commons on August 18. Lloyd George dropped plans for post-war protectionism and rejected the Sankey Commission's proposal for nationalization of the coal mines. His bill proposed joint industrial councils, a forty-eight-hour workweek, and a wage guaranteeing a minimum standard of living for all workers. All of these were ideas Cecil agreed with, but Cecil's response was petulant. He attacked the government's attitude toward the League, suggesting "it would be better to scratch it altogether unless the Government means to work it as a reality. I am not satisfied with the attitude of some of the officials and the spirit of the bureaucracy toward it."[97]

In late August summaries of the summer session of Parliament, many agreed that despite his greatness in debate, Cecil's "increasingly critical" stances made it unlikely that he would ever rejoin the government.[98] Despite having accepted Lloyd George's "coupon" before the election and continuing to sit on the government side in the House of Commons, Cecil opposed the Lloyd George coalition over the second half of 1919. This censorious opposition attitude toward the government erected a significant hurdle for what was ostensibly Cecil primary domestic goal, to gain political support for the League of Nations. His unwillingness to prioritize probably diminished his ability to be an effective advocate for the League.

Advocating for the League

What would enable the League to work? In an opinion piece in the *Sunday Times*, Cecil explained that its effectiveness rested on two things: public opinion in favor of using the League to thwart war, and "the fear of the universal economic boycott to which the aggressive nation automatically exposes itself. So long as the memory of the Allied blockade lives in Central Europe, it is not likely that any State will wantonly incur similar sufferings."[99] At the SEC dinner in his honor at the Carlton Hotel on August 1, attended by Hoover, Clémentel, Orlando, and many other British and international grandees and widely reported in British newspapers, Cecil spoke about the seriousness of the economic situation in Europe. This crisis merited "the closest consultation" not just among the Allies but with the world beyond Europe. Global interdependence was at the core of modern civilization, he explained; "Everything that we do here, almost every casual speech, may have an effect far beyond the limits of the country." In such uncertain times, nations "should keep in the closest touch with one another." The successes of the allied efforts during the war and then during the Peace Conference suggested, Cecil argued, that the League of Nations could likewise lead such useful global consultations in the future.[100]

Through 1919, few in Britain spoke against a League of Nations. Some were skeptical about whether or how it could work, but the League "has no enemies."[101] Indeed this was true even among Conservatives, virtually all of whom assigned at least some role in world affairs to the League, even though such commitments appeared antithetical to the Conservative Party foreign policy tradition of freedom from alliances and maintenance of independence of action.[102] The remarkable cross-party consensus favoring the existence of a League was embodied in the ecumenical LNU board, and in the tactical decisions at the LNU over the next year to favor a broadly pro-League message, rather than to narrow efforts onto any specific and less universally supported League-related issues like disarmament.[103] This big-tent philosophy was supported wholeheartedly by Lord Cecil, whose Albert Hall speech in June turned out to have been the de facto beginning of his leadership of the organization. At the General Council meeting of the LNU on July 24, Cecil was elected chair of the Union. His goal was to develop full support for the League among the British people. Putting the League at the center of British policy would make the British "an example to the whole world."[104]

Lloyd George seemed unsure of what to make of the LNU. He remained uncertain about the usefulness of the League but was wary about his government's possible vulnerability to pro-League activism. Lloyd George announced that he would make a speech on October 1 at a big LNU rally planned at Mansion House, but he then backed out. The eventual LNU meeting went forward without him on October 13. Attendees including politicians, foreign ambassadors, activists, and journalists heard Asquith, Venizelos, and J. R. Clynes, the Labour spokesman, addressing the crowd, and messages from the King and from Lloyd George were read out.[105]

Cecil also spoke at that meeting. Having sent out his remarks to newspapers the day before, they were published around the world. Just a few days later the LNU announced the creation of its quarterly journal *The Covenant*, which included an article by Cecil. He then immediately launched a speaking tour, speaking to the LNU branch in Birmingham on October 20 and to the inaugural Oxford branch meeting a few days later.[106] In all of these speeches he attacked the "ignorance and indifference" of doubters.[107] Aiming to educate the public about the basics of the new organization, he regularly described the "threefold machinery of the League," the Assembly, Council, and Secretariat, and how all three would put public opinion and cooperation into action, creating an institution that repudiated "men's combative instincts." By ensuring that British people understood the League, the LNU would ensure that the Government followed pro-League policies.[108]

It was initially a triumphant speaking tour, in some ways the mirror image of Wilson's famously doomed tour through the western United States just a few weeks earlier, which culminated in the president's stroke on October 2 and his resulting incapacitation. At the Cambridge Union on October 21, Cecil's rebuttal of a caustic anti-League diatribe from the Duke of Northumberland brought the members of the Union overwhelmingly behind his appeal to the superiority of the League over any pre-war type of balance of power.[109] His side won the vote that evening, 723 to 280, and likewise a few days later at the Oxford Union he won 924 to 99. As a student at Oxford decades earlier he had been president of the Union, which probably made his victory that much sweeter.[110] The press was impressed. "Here, then, is a good sign and a healthy symptom," a columnist wrote in the *Daily Mirror* about the universities' reception of the League. "The Youth of to-day know what wat means."[111] Cecil had to postpone speeches in Liverpool and Edinburgh due to illness but within a few weeks he restarted his speaking tour in Glasgow and Leeds.

However, events in the United States soon proved decisive in the League fight in Britain. By the middle of November, after a series of very public votes and debates, it appeared possible that the Senate might ratify the Treaty with "reservations," although Wilson remained adamant in rejecting any changes. Cecil displayed a brave face in defending Wilson, explaining in the House of Commons that the Lodge reservations would gut the Covenant. He got cheers when he noted that even without US cooperation, many countries had already joined up. The League remained "the sole hope of permanent peace."[112] But despite this public support, Cecil argued in private to Clemenceau and Curzon that the British and French governments should accept virtually any reservations the Republicans might place on the Treaty.[113] In calling for changes in the territorial guarantees of Article 10, Senator Henry Cabot Lodge singled out one of the pieces of the Covenant that Cecil had always disliked.[114] Lodge's reservations aimed primarily to retain national control of deciding whether to engage in military action; he and other reservationists were less concerned about any mandate for collective economic sanctions.[115] Wilson's failure to truly understand the idea of economic sanctions decoupled from military sanctions meant that he missed opportunities for a compromise with Lodge that might have resulted in an empowered League.

After the US Senate failed to ratify the Treaty in a series of votes that culminated on November 19, British advocates of the League were left uncertain about what to do. Some considered sending Cecil on a speaking tour of the United States, but phobia of British intentions was rife in the United States and he was advised that it would only backfire.[116] This was proven only too true on the day of his long-postponed rally in Edinburgh a week after the Senate's vote. A number of US papers ran an article written by the Paris correspondent of the *New York Sun*, suggesting that some British politicians, led by Cecil, were pushing in the wake of the US rejection of the Treaty for Germany to be admitted immediately into the League.[117] Cecil's surrogates claimed that the report was nonsense, and that Germany could only be admitted by the unanimous vote of the Council, which was unlikely to meet for months.[118] The FO likewise called the report "preposterous rubbish." Similar worries undergirded charges made by Churchill that Cecil's pro-League message had already begun leading to fewer Officer Training Corps candidates volunteering at Oxford and Cambridge. Cecil's long record of calling for German entry as quickly as possible attenuated support for the League among Britons and Americans still wary of Germany.

Picking up his tour, Cecil addressed the University of Edinburgh and then a large LNU rally on November 26, then headed to Glasgow, Manchester, and Liverpool. At all stops, the message was that the League could live on even without the United States, and that it must because the people of poverty-stricken Europe needed this collaboration.[119] The League was critical for the world, and its success would be determined by "public opinion" around the world, with people engaged in desire for peace.[120] He tailored his messages for his audiences. After Cecil met in Edinburgh with a delegation of a society engaged in suppressing opium trafficking, his speech that evening explained that this was one of the League duties covered in the 23rd Article of the Covenant.[121] During a meeting with a group of Liverpool businessmen the day after his LNU rally in the city, he explained that the League Covenant was a "practical document," because adherence to the League would mean less defense spending and significant savings for British taxpayers.[122] He also jumped into internationalizing the LNU, attending a conference in Brussels of the League of Nations associations of over a dozen countries. They decided to create an organization with a secretariat in Brussels, and resolved to push the League as soon as possible to admit any state that desired membership.[123]

But Cecil's message was muddled for many members of the government, whose deeper skepticism about the role of the League was now augmented by their wariness about the intentions and loyalties of the messenger. Throughout the final session of Parliament in 1919, Cecil pressed attacks on the government's taxation and monetary policies, suggesting that incompetence in government was largely to blame for inflation in Britain.[124] On its housing policy, he hit against the Government (and gained cheers from many on the Unionist benches) with his caustic irony about the insufficiency and slowness of the government scheme.[125] His critique on the housing issue was particularly cold, based not as much on his opposition to the government's scheme but rather his charge that the government was acting spineless and inconstant in revising a policy that was only four months old.[126] "Let them for heaven's sake have definite opinions and principles, and stick to them!" he cried out.[127] His attack on the Government's Coal Industry Bill on December 11 was lacerating and in the end the bill was not brought forward for a vote.[128] He attacked the government for "a most scandalous piece of discourtesy to the House" for failing to follow procedure and print an appropriation bill before the House debated it; the Speaker declared that Cecil's indignation lacked justification.[129] His contempt for government inaction regarding starvation of Austrians was notable; simply by canceling any indemnities and Habsburg era debts, Cecil noted, the Austrian economy would significantly improve and starvation might be averted.[130] He also attacked an antidumping bill in early December.

Cecil and Lloyd George broke apart irrevocably during a wide-ranging debate on December 18 focused on foreign affairs. Sir Donald Maclean, who as the leader of the Asquith wing of the Liberals served as the leader of the opposition in Commons, led off with a rambling denunciation of the government's apparently not open diplomacy, leading into criticism of British policies toward Russia and Turkey, and culminating in his proclamation of the necessity of a League-centered foreign policy. Cecil then jumped in, repeating these complaints while adding criticism of the government's apparent cruelty toward the prostrate Austrians and its plans to spend on armaments. Cecil lamented that "when you come to acts, I see very little sign in the policy of the Government of their having accepted the real spirit of the League, and I see very little signs of it in the Estimates." "I want to ask the Government—no one would be more-pleased than I should if the Prime Minister can give me a real hearty reply—are the Government going into the League intending to make it a success? Are they really going to put their last sixpence into the League and push it forward with all the strength and power of this country?"[131]

Lloyd George's response epitomized his excellence as a leader in the House. With impressive command of the details, he described the morass of the various factions of Russia's still unresolved civil war, exposing the fallacy of Britain being able to do anything to control the situation. On Turkey he stressed the need to leave much in the hands of the United States, hoping that this might persuade the Americans to step up to what he saw as their responsibilities there. And on the League, he was caustic: "I regret that my Noble Friend the Member for Hitchin (Lord R. Cecil) has cast doubts upon the sincerity of the Government. I do not think it does any good, it I may say so quite respectfully." Cecil then interjected: "I did not desire to do that, but there is this impression abroad, and I desire to give the right hon. Gentleman an opportunity of removing it." But Lloyd George denounced Cecil's intentions: "When it is repeated, it is like every other slander—it gets more power unless it be accompanied by a very emphatic denial. I know the sincerity of the Noble Lord, but in the main people who are very sincere themselves are the last people in the world to cast suspicions on the sincerity of others, and I regret that my Noble Friend did it." Any assessment that he opposed the League were contradicted by everything he had done to build the League during the Conference, and for the "perfectly free hand" his government had given to the League "zealots" Smuts and Cecil, who had created a constitution for a League despite the doubts of other British leaders worried that constitutions unnecessarily defined what must be a living organization. He further defended the defense budget with the simple axiom "If Britain is insecure, peace is insecure; if Britain is insecure, liberty is insecure; if Britain is insecure, civilisation is insecure." Most judged Lloyd George's speech as a powerful and "unusually successful" argument in favor of the government's foreign policy.[132] The American rejection of the Treaty firmly ended Lloyd George's willingness to follow Cecil's type of internationalism. From that point forward, his relationship with Cecil took on a tremendously harsh tone, even an animus. Their wartime partnership was over.

One might argue that Cecil overextended himself starting in 1919 and would have succeeded better if he had focused just on the LNU, or on obtaining power in Parliament and in various Governments, or on creating a new centrist political party by peeling off the "young" Conservatives and others. His name was everywhere, on the masthead of a committees to do things like organizing the Institute of International Affairs in Britain, heading a campaign to have November 11 observed as "League of Nations Day," and serving as the president of the "Czech Society of Great Britain" which aimed to build relations between the two countries "in all fields."[133] Even admirers could be exacerbated by his apparent lack of focus: the *Nation* had him pegged as "a leader of men, a mind of his age, a guide out of the desert," but "*what* he is few seem able to say."[134] As the year wore on, Cecil's goals remained "inscrutable."[135]

It is worthwhile to add to this list of options the possibility that Cecil could have focused on running the SEC after August 1919, or, more broadly, on running some part of the League itself. Jean Monnet was not the only League official in the 1920s who wished for Cecil's "imagination and courage" rather than the more humdrum qualities of Drummond.[136] Perhaps as secretary general, Cecil could have transitioned more smoothly into a League of Nations role, helping to firmly embed an economic internationalism based on the wartime models that Cecil himself had helped to create and run during the war. But clearly he had decided that the life of an international bureaucrat was not for him. There is no indication that he ever considered leading the League of Nations.

The difficulty of pushing the League in the face of indefatigable domestic political opposition, despite the popularity of the League idea among the British people, also speaks to the war-weary reluctance of the British people to give any real attention, let alone primacy, to foreign policy issues in late 1919. In a column calling for November 11 to be commemorated henceforth as "League of Nations Day" to engage public opinion in favor of the League, Eustace Percy wrote in alarmist terms describing the economic and humanitarian catastrophe that plagued Europe and decried how hard it was to get anyone in Britain to notice. According to Percy, it was already regarded "as political good manners to drop all talk of foreign affairs and to devote all our attention to the cultivation of our own garden."[137] The public, and even the politicians, had grown disengaged with foreign policy in the wake of the war.[138] The League "was something of a vogue a year ago," wrote one commentator on the eve of the first League Council meeting in Paris, in January 1920. "Now it seems to have lost grip of public interest."[139] Considering this mood, it was unsurprising that the movement to label November 11 as "League of Nations Day" did not take off.

*

Cecil's unwillingness to give an inch on anything in the last half of 1919 made the League taste increasingly sour to an already skeptical Lloyd George. For Cecil's own political career, as for the fate of wartime economic collaboration, 1919 becomes a story of what if. Despite general acknowledgments of the necessity of the League and the creation of operating international institutions over the last half of 1919, it became apparent by 1920 that at least in Britain, the ideas of Cecil and other new internationalists might not be implemented as they had hoped. The last months of 1919 already indicate a divergence between the "functional internationalism" of League bureaucracies in action, and the uncertainty of League politics on the national level, a gap that would continue to mark League affairs throughout the interwar years.[140]

Conclusion

For the rest of their lives, in their memories and their memoirs, many of the Peace Conference participants looked back in awe on their six months in Paris. In Hankey's book about the Peace Conference, published forty-four years later, Paris was "the most memorable episode of my life, for had I not been the Secretary to the Cabinet of the World?"[1] According to his mistress Frances Stevenson, Lloyd George often said even decades later "that the happiest time of his life was the six months he spent in Paris during the conference."[2] "The peak of Lloyd George's career," in the judgment of his biographer Alan Sharp, for the prime minister the Conference stood out not just for his negotiations and sparring with the other world leaders, but also for his entertaining and cosmopolitan social life.[3] He was not the only one to reflect back on the Conference (either with approval, amusement, or censoriousness) as a few months of unprecedented diplomacy and comparative decadence after the end of a miserable war.

Throughout their time in Paris, all involved gathered up mementos, certain they had participated in a pivotal moment in world history. Throughout the Conference, many ordinary nondiarists were "more or less surreptitiously keeping diaries," explained Wilson's press secretary Roy Stannard Baker in his own Paris diary. "Unless he makes the record no one will know he has a part."[4] Before they left, the various world leaders exchanged autographed portraits and posed for group photos of the commissions, committees, and councils they served on, consciously creating souvenirs of the months they had worked together. They knew the time they spent was worth remembering. More than anything else, Hankey, Lloyd George, and many others experienced their months in Paris as a moment of possibility. There was some cynicism, but much of that came later, after they returned home.

The Impact of Paris on Cecil

The Peace Conference made Lord Robert Cecil a global figure, and over the interwar years he remained the "most tireless champion" of the League of Nations.[5] Five years later, in an extensive seventeen-page letter nominating Cecil to be the first recipient of the Woodrow Wilson Peace Award, Philip Noel-Baker argued that "Wilson conceived and Cecil has built. The one was the architect, the other the constructor."[6] To Noel-Baker this judgment flattered Wilson; from his experience at the Peace Conference, he knew that Cecil and other British activists had played a huge role in "conceiving" the League. But his real aim was to describe how Cecil had continually worked on the League during the half-decade since Paris. Cecil built up the LNU in Britain. He led debates in the League Assemblies, where he served as the delegate of South Africa, appointed by Smuts in 1920, 1921, and 1922, and then as British delegate as a member of Stanley Baldwin's 1923 Conservative government. Cecil also made international policy in League commissions, pushing the creation of the Draft Treaty of Mutual Assistance in 1922–3 to end aggressive warfare. Believing in the importance of galvanizing global public opinion in favor of the League, Cecil continued his Paris practice of being available to journalists from all countries as a reliable source of information about League affairs. He breathed in deeply the Geneva atmosphere, where informal diplomacy and the international dinner party circuit during the annual Assemblies mirrored that of Paris during the Peace Conference.[7] He did this even while remaining active in the House of Commons and, when invited, within the British government. In short, the dual domestic and global political role that Cecil lived in Paris 1919 was one he continued over the ensuing years.

Cecil claimed as long as a year after the Conference that he was still unsure whether he would go into "definite opposition" against the Lloyd George government.[8] But in reality he was already in opposition as soon as the Treaty was signed, developing an oddball identity as a "maverick" and "renegade," an internationalist evangelist without a political party.[9] The prominent political columnist E. T. Raymond suggested in 1920 that the war raised Cecil to the level of a true statesman, and that the only thing that could hold him back from dominating a new Conservative Party that appealed to working class voters would be if he allowed his "independence to degenerate into irresponsibility."[10] Yet over the last six months of 1919, Cecil appeared less an ambitious and crafty intriguer than simply an opposition-minded contrarian during a notably turbulent and unsettled political moment. Leaning into incessant attacks against the government after returning from Paris registers as classic Cecil self-immolation, not the expression of ambition. Frustration over the failure of the Treaty in the United States, the unwillingness of his prime minister to put the League at the core of Britain's foreign policy, and a penchant for making trouble reignited Cecil's pre-war animosity toward Lloyd George. By early 1921, his brother Hugh warned Robert that hatred of the prime minister was "becoming an obsession and unbalancing your mind."[11] But it is doubtful that becoming prime minister himself was ever Cecil's desire, in the fall of 1919 or anytime after that. The preference for not taking the reins is consistent with his infamously quixotic, and failed, attempt in 1922 to create a new party, one he hoped would be led by Lord Grey not himself.[12]

According to Noel-Baker's letter to the Wilson Foundation in 1924, "Cecil has ever been the same, a calm, reasoning, idealistic and optimistic leader."[13] Cecil's expressions of optimism during the 1920s have often been judged as political and false, inconsistent with the perception that his parliamentary and nonparliamentary activism, particularly in the LNU, was ultimately a frustrating failure. Following the understandable impulse to assign blame for the rise of the aggressive Nazi dictatorship, Cecil has been pilloried for leading the League's failed disarmament efforts throughout the 1920s and for contributing to an anti-war mentality that permeated (and, in the eyes of his critics, emasculated) British society. To historians, he has appeared increasingly monomaniacal during these years. He had set before himself a tremendous and frustrating task. His long absence from Britain during the Peace Conference probably made him more accustomed to living without Lady Cecil. He allowed his work to take control of his life, spending more and more time away from her on various League-related ventures throughout the 1920s and 1930s, perhaps to her detriment.[14] Both contemporaries and historians see him as becoming more dictatorial and unyielding in his ideas and in his dominance of the LNU as the 1920s and 1930s wore on, a "divided, enormous and ineffective" organization that mostly failed at its primary goal of persuading British governments to follow a League-centered foreign policy.[15]

However, a more forgiving analysis recognizes that Cecil found himself facing a central dilemma of all pressure-group politics, hoping to both serve in and change the minds of the Conservative government in the mid-1920s, even while using the LNU to pressure the government from the outside.[16] Into the 1930s, Cecil played a huge role in Britain and beyond in promoting the League as a new global power that unlike any other, aimed for peace. All of this activity suggests that throughout the 1930s, Cecil truly rejected as cynical all expectations about the inevitability of warfare in international affairs.

In 1919, the League was prepared to adjust in the years to come, both within its organization and in its shepherding of international peace. Looking at it from two decades later, E. H. Carr claimed that the Covenant's Article 19 allowing the possibility of future treaty revisions was merely "the gesture of an uneasy conscience" by men who doubted the fairness of their own treaty and was intended to remain "a dead letter."[17] The League was too constitutional, and the result two decades after its founding was a League marked by traditions of "frustration" and partisanship.[18] But in 1919, the difficulty of amending the Covenant was not yet known, and many hoped that any flaws in the Treaty might be revised over the years to come.[19] At the end of the year, Cecil wrote in the *Times* mocking those who asserted that the entire treaty should be torn up. "That the Treaty is imperfect and unsatisfactory in many respects, few would deny. The best feature is that in the Covenant machinery for its revision is contained."[20] Among Cecil's followers, the mantra over the next years was that the "the machinery" of the League must be utilized. The Covenant was not a dream, but rather "a real, practical scheme."[21] Even after the failure of Treaty ratification in the United States made it less possible that the League could succeed in bringing real global peace, the League did continue to evolve and sometimes succeed over the ensuing decades.

Economic Warfare for Peace after Versailles

Revulsion against the destructiveness of the Great War undergirded the unprecedented popularity of peace movement organizations like the LNU after the First World War. The resulting League of Nations, disarmament, and other peace-oriented policies have often been derided as having a "visionary quality," an "ideological" idealism fatally unattached to the real world.[22] However, Cecil and his collaborators in Paris 1919 perceived what they thought was a realistic path to uphold global peace, based on the way that the Great War was fought, particularly its "blockade." He remained certain for years thereafter that universal economic blockade remained "an enormously powerful weapon" for enforcing peace.[23] Throughout the 1920s, for League supporters like Eric Drummond and Étienne Clémentel, the possibility of implementing economic sanctions like those created by the Allies during the war remained at the core of their hopes for a powerful League. "Let the lessons of the interallied economic cooperation solidify the basis of the peace!" wrote Clémentel in 1931.[24]

Was it possible that economic warfare for peace could succeed? Just four years before the First World War began, Norman Angell famously argued that trade and mutually dependent prosperity would compel modern states to maintain peace with one another. The Great War proved Angell's assumption fundamentally incorrect, yet the idea of a blockade for peace actually took his argument a step further. If a "harmony of interests" between nations built by the international trading system made war unreasonable and unthinkable, in 1919 the threat of completely losing access to global trade and finance was considered to be a formidable sanction, one that might persuade even a great power to maintain peace rather than go to war. The logic of this reasoning helped to ensure that there was no real opposition to the economic sanctions clauses in Article 16 of the Covenant, even among critics in the United States. Notably, the "principle of automatic economic sanctions against an aggressor" was not among the "reservations" of Henry Cabot Lodge or other Senate opponents of the Treaty.[25] In Paris, all the leaders accepted that economic sanctions could indeed be created by the League not just as a necessary step before military sanctions, but as a decisive step in their own right.

However, the practicality of this vision of a peacekeeping League empowered by economic warfare was immediately called into question when the US Senate failed to ratify the Treaty of Versailles. The British Foreign Office international lawyer Cecil Hurst immediately opined that without the United States, the League would not be able to fulfill its basic duty to uphold peace: "An economic boycott with the Americans standing outside it is certain to mean that the Americans will endeavor to trade with the boycotted country."[26] When negotiations took place in 1924 for the Geneva Protocol, which would mandate binding international arbitration in all disputes, the Canadian government stayed out of the negotiations under the assumption that any economic sanctions mandated by an arbitrator would be unenforceable without the United States signing on.[27]

But despite these significant concerns, League-based economic sanctions were planned and implemented throughout the 1920s. In 1920 the League Council set up an International Blockade Committee to consider how Article 16 might be applied, and their report to the Assembly in 1921 created practical guidelines. Graduated sanctions would increase in severity as needed, would be applied by the sanctioning countries on a case-by-case basis, and would be heavily publicized so as to scare aggressive powers from even beginning a conflict in the first place.[28] Some (particularly the French delegates) saw these proposed amendments to Article 16 as a fudge, but the guidelines merely codified the expectation that economic warfare would evolve as it had during the Great War and the Paris Peace Conference. Soon, targeted sanctions actually worked to create peace on two occasions during the early 1920s, when the

League Council's threats caused Yugoslav troops to withdraw from Albania in 1921 and Greek troops to retreat from Bulgaria in 1925.[29] The potential power of economic boycott was implied in the League-sponsored "Draft Treaty of Mutual Assistance" in 1923, which then became the Geneva Protocol in 1924. In this idea of maintaining peace through collective action, sanctions would be primarily economic, with the expected benefit of enabling all nations to move toward disarmament.[30] As during the Great War, economic sanctions during the 1920s developed with flexibility and nuance, and drew support from countries beyond those initially "sending" the sanctions at a target. Belief that economic sanctions could be the enforcement mechanism for peace fed the hopes of the creators of the Kellogg-Briand Pact of 1928, which famously outlawed war.[31] The failure of Britain to ratify the Geneva Protocol should perhaps have made it apparent how skeptical even internationalist nations were about being bound to action by any treaty. Yet as suggested in the results of the iconic "Peace Ballot" of 1935, the British people agreed with the basic idea of collective security, and overwhelmingly supported the principle of economic, nonmilitary sanctions against aggressors.[32] "Quarantining the aggressors" through sanctions, argued President Franklin Roosevelt in October 1935, could limit the contagion of armed belligerency.[33]

However, during the 1930s the threat of international economic warfare against aggressive countries did not stop the slide into another world war. Threats of League-led economic boycott worked to coerce smaller states when Britain and France were in agreement, but when there was a divergence in opinion between the powers or when they faced an aggressive great power, League sanctions were unworkable. Calls for sanctions against Japan did not lead it to roll back its conquest of Manchuria.[34] Most Frenchmen and Britons were uninterested in the distant conflict between China and Japan, and in a crisis in its own region, the Pacific, the United States remained uncertain about whether to take the lead or to coordinate with Britain or the League.[35] For a variety of reasons, Article 16 of the Covenant was never invoked, and the League's failure to act in Manchuria proved to some advocates of the Geneva system that French and British leaders had never believed it could succeed.[36]

For the League, the more devastating failure came after Italy's invasion of Ethiopia in late 1935. The League Assembly declared Italy the aggressor, but the British and French dithered on devising and implementing economic punishments strong enough to change Mussolini's mind. Cecil and his LNU campaigned for the British government to press stricter League sanctions curtailing Italian oil imports.[37] However, fearing this might lead to actual military conflict with Italy, Neville Chamberlain, then the chancellor of the Exchequer, led the British Cabinet in calling for appeasement rather than confrontation.[38] Before any significant international sanctions were undertaken, the Italian conquest was a *fait accompli*, and by 1938 Chamberlain's government recognized Italy as sovereign over Ethiopia. The confrontation with Italy was a painful and very public embarrassment for the League of Nations. The Ethiopian emperor Haile Selassie gave a speech in Geneva pleading for the League to do something, even as Italian troops completed their conquest of his country. Instead of throwing their support behind Selassie, the League decided to lift its sanctions against Italy. The episode established what quickly became the paradigmatic view of economic sanctions as failures, at best a collective international scolding, rather than as a substantive step to limit aggression.

However as Greece and Yugoslavia in the 1920s suggest, some sanctions that aim "to deter the target country's martial ambitions" have actually succeeded, and undoubtedly lives have been saved.[39] Over the last century, economic sanctions have averted a number of wars, diminished the power of protagonists in other conflicts, and even deterred countries not directly targeted by sanctions from engaging in military conflict for fear they would be hit with sanctions.[40] After the Second World War, sanctions have been created to meet a broader array of goals, including regime change, reestablishment of democracy, and improving human rights within countries. Sanctions are often not effective if the goals are overly ambitious, or if they are aimed by one great power against another.[41] But the most exhaustive cumulative survey of economic sanctions over the past century has shown that sanctioners achieve their most significant goals about a third of the time.[42] Most sanctions episodes set one country (usually, the United States) against another, but the sanctions coordinated through international organizations have a significantly greater rate of success.[43] Critics of the United Nations failure to maintain world peace often focus on its inability to wield military power, yet Security Council economic sanctions (and the promise of having them rescinded) have helped end civil wars and compelled combatants to negotiating tables.[44]

The psychologist Steven Pinker, in proving that humans have become less violent over the past century, credits much of the drop in violence to the diminishing intensity of interstate warfare.[45] The development of modern economic warfare should be seen a contributing factor to why we live in a less violent world. It is notable that whereas most statesmen before 1919 saw economic warfare as integrally linked to military conflict, either as a prelude or an adjunct, it is now standard to see it as a stand-alone alternative to military conflict. The creation of different forms of warfare has enabled states, and the international community, to engage in conflict without bloodshed. Economic warfare has certainly not created world peace, but it has probably contributed to a less violent world.

Judging the Paris Peace Conference

The point of judgment for the Paris Peace Conference has always been the failure of the Treaty of Versailles to stop the next, even more horrible war only a generation later. Treaty critics complain that the Allies dictated unfair terms to the Germans. When they signed the armistice on November 11, the Germans believed the peace would follow Wilson's Fourteen Points, which promised Germany a "place of equality" with the other powers.[46] Public demands for harshness toward the Germans and trade-offs between the victorious powers led to a "settlement more draconian" than any of the individual victor states would have wanted.[47] When stewed in the misery of the Great Depression in the early 1930s, this German resentment about the Treaty fed the rise of Nazism.

However, looking at things from the perspective of the reassertion of aggressive German power after 1933 is unfair to those laboring at the Paris Conference. During the spring of 1919, it appeared to many that the threat of German and central European starvation was real and potentially politically cataclysmic, offering an opening to the spread of Bolshevism. Uncertainty reigned about not just the future, but also the present.

Critical judgments of the Paris Peace Conference also undervalue processes created at the Conference that improved the lives of Europeans both then and later. The operation of internationalist ideas at the Conference created an internationalist initiative focused on economic cooperation that, in part, lasted with the League. The Peace Conference successfully implanted new standards, mentalities, institutions, and tactics. It helped to nurture what became in the 1920s a broad belief in the necessity for multilateral cooperation between states to improve the operation of the global economy.[48] Even as the Peace Conference was still in session, some of its operations sheared off into the League Secretariat, which played some impressively independent and effective roles in international affairs through the 1920s and 1930s.[49]

This book suggests moving forward to mid-1919 the date when the League of Nations began operating. It became common after the war for historians to pinpoint the League's start at January 10, 1920, when the Treaty of Versailles came into effect, or at the January 16, 1920, first meeting of the Council of the League at the Quai d'Orsay, chaired by Leon Bourgeois.[50] However it is clear that the League was operating as early as May 1919, and that throughout that month and after a number of world leaders were already treating it as a living institution, well before the text of the Treaty of Versailles was even finalized. The creation of the Covenant has long been portrayed as embodying League advocacy during the Peace Conference. But in fact the League started coming together before the Covenant, a League whose operations could fit within the parameters of the Covenant, but which was not created entirely by that Covenant.

The context of this early League history demands a reassessment of the role of the SEC at the Peace Conference. Dismissals of the importance or effectiveness of the SEC have long been part of the critical hangover since the Conference broke up. Of the economic commissions, Reparations has always attracted the most interest as the embodiment of the Treaty's political and economic failures. However, the SEC operated with surprising effectiveness during an extremely difficult few months, linking together financial, shipping, and supply assets held by all of the Allies. It helped bridge the gaps between US pretentions of autonomy and dominance, and the British and French control of the North Atlantic, the lands of Western Europe, and most of the world's merchant shipping. In the SEC, Cecil proved himself an impressive statesmen not just as the "natural link" between the British and Americans, but also between the Anglo-Americans and the French.[51] Many of the policies the SEC pushed for were agreed to and implemented by the Big Four.

Its successes and the necessity of its operations meant that the SEC continued operating until early 1920, when many of its staff and duties shifted to the League of Nations. Long derided as a failure because it was unable to stop the Second World War, there has been a subtle but significant reappraisal of the League of Nations over the past two decades. Historians have uncovered League successes in specific global health issues, in curbing the traffic in drugs and sex, and in helping to relieve economic chaos in post-war Austria.[52] In particular the Secretariat, the international bureaucracy of experts, proved its value during the 1920s and 1930s.[53] Considering the continuity of personnel and ethos, it is not a stretch to see the successes of the SEC in 1919 as the earliest example of one of these League successes: a focused effort, truly international in scope, to coordinate the feeding of destitute Germans.

Following in the footsteps of Keynes, both contemporaries and historians have suggested that President Wilson's temperament, awkward interpersonal skills, and increasing frailty left him vulnerable to the crafty Lloyd George and Clemenceau who created an unviable, harsh Treaty of Versailles. In his creation of a League of Nations and his often combative and ultimately failed attempt to push it through the Senate, Wilson hoped to create a new internationalist order. Paradoxically, he instead presided over a reassertion of American isolationism. The history of attempts to revive the European economy in early 1919 suggest that Wilson's greater failure at Paris was his unwillingness to figure out a way to either finance significant US loans to Europe, or to arrange a cancellation of some or all interallied war debts. A variety of such schemes were suggested and supported by Keynes, Cecil, Clémentel, and even by Wilson's own economic advisors between March and June. Such support would have entailed significant political risk for Wilson in the United States, but he was already risking much by championing a League. Adequate US financial assistance could have fundamentally changed the dynamic over reparations and war guilt, creating a better treaty while kick-starting trade within and between Europe and the rest of the world.[54] Instead, wagering all his political capital on the Treaty itself, and in particular on the League, Wilson refused to confront the "financial isolationism" of Congress and the American people. In February 1920 the US government ended all government loans to any foreign country, including destitute Germany.[55] As long as the Allies needed to pay off their loans to the United States, reparations would remain an uncertain but worrisome burden on Germany. The Europeans were left to their own devices on how to revive their economies.

Herbert Hoover later defended Wilson's efforts on European reconstruction, but this book suggests that Wilson left much undone.[56] Atop Sally Marks' list of critical problems the Big Four failed to even address, one should place their inadequate attention to the financial and economic settlement.[57] Over the ensuing years, continual concerns about government finances magnified the importance of reparations in French politics.[58] Wilson's unwillingness to tackle the financial and debt issue set the standard later followed by the Harding and Coolidge Administrations through the 1920s.[59] This problem of financial uncertainty remained untackled for five years, and even then the Dawes Plan did not fully stabilize European finances.[60] Instead it gave US investors an overblown sense of German stability, unleashing a pent-up burst of private lending from the United States to Germany and creating new financial imbalances.[61]

Historians have increasingly contested the borders between internationalism and isolationism in interwar US politics. Wilson has long been castigated for demanding an internationalism in Paris that went beyond that acceptable by the American public or the Congress. Yet Benjamin Coates has described how many of the President's opponents were not isolationists, but simply advocates of a different, more "legalist" internationalism than that held by Wilson.[62] Attacking the "Wilson as embattled internationalist" paradigm from a different angle, Robert Boyce suggests that Wilson's view of a League of laws, and his rebuffing of French calls for a League army, actually reflected his own long-standing isolationism, one well rooted in American tradition.[63] This judgment understates the radical anti-isolationism inherent in Wilson's League project, but it suggests the depth of reluctance of any policymakers in the United States, including Wilson, to commit any resources to any foreign state. The political impossibility of a government-led economic internationalism in 1919 would seem to have been proven by the way that Wilson's successors, the Harding and Coolidge administrations, "backed and prodded by Congress, took a very special and limited view of America's contribution to the reconstruction of Europe."[64] For America in the 1920s, investment in Europe was overwhelmingly privatized and profit-driven, with reconstruction following a volunteerist ethos that Hoover then embodied as president at the end of the decade.[65] Americans considered that repaying debts and free market probity signified their own righteousness in contrast to European profligacy.

But it is worthwhile to point out that this vision of economic morality really hardened in the United States over the course of the 1920s. In Paris during 1919, the fluid viewpoints of Wilson's supposedly dogmatic economic advisors, and their tentative but real steps away from doctrinaire laissez-faire, suggest that a bold attempt to reset the European economy might have gained political support among Americans more broadly. A real new economic internationalism was actually developing and operating throughout the Peace Conference, with the possibility that it might become the norm in the years to come, despite the opposition of that supposed internationalist, Woodrow Wilson. At the end of his long lament on the failures of the United States leaders between 1916 and 1931, Adam Tooze suggests that the lesson of the entire era was one that was never applied, namely that "international coalition and cooperation was the only appropriate response to the experience of uneven and combined development."[66] Wilson's failure at Paris was rooted in the limited nature of his internationalism, one focused entirely on diplomacy and politics, and insufficiently attuned to the practical demands of the global economy.

This book refocuses the story of the creation of the League away from Wilson, who (again, according to Hoover) was supposedly the only real champion for the League of Nations in Paris, where he faced down Europeans whose hearts had been frozen by the war.[67] Undoubtedly the president's support for a League was critical to placing it at the top of the agenda at the peace talks, a decision long seen as at least a tactical mistake by Wilson with negative repercussions for his future dealings both with the European powers and his own Senate. But it was quite possible in 1919 that even without wholehearted championing by the US president, a League would have been created. Clemenceau has ordinarily been portrayed as exemplifying the complete cynicism of the French, supporting plans for a League simply "to retain Wilson's goodwill, for strategic reasons."[68] Yet the historian Peter Jackson has argued that Clemenceau was truly open-minded to the possibilities of internationalism throughout the Peace Conference.[69] Similarly the always-flexible Lloyd George was willing to follow overwhelming public demand in Britain, and was certain that his government "had to support *some* kind of post-war international organization of states to promote peace."[70] In the United States, Wilson faced increasingly deft and telling opposition from Republicans as 1919 progressed. But even many of his supposedly isolationist opponents in the Senate would have been pleased to end the year with the formation of some sort of a League, and in the presidential race the next year, the Republican candidate Warren Harding agreed that the United States should participate in a League.[71] One could easily imagine that the significant support in Britain, France, and the United States for a League, indeed the general expectation that a League must be created, could have resulted in the creation during the Paris Peace Conference of a League unshackled from the Treaty of Versailles, and thus less tainted by that Treaty's other failings. It was a terrible burden for the League of Nations to be so tightly connected both to the Treaty of Versailles, and also to Wilson, the increasingly impractical, inflexible, and failed president.

Lord Robert Cecil has often since been linked with Wilson as deserving ridicule for taking unrealistic, morally superior stands. Yet in 1919, his hopes were rooted in his expectation that the League would evolve and transform over the years to come. Cecil was pragmatic, not dogmatic, and expected that the League would be as well. His vision of a future world organization appears quite similar to the reality of the primary global body, the United Nations, a century later: a modest-sized organization focused on practical-minded humanitarian relief, global health and welfare, peacemaking, and peacekeeping, one that embodied the aspirations of those who believed peace preferable to war, but an organization whose most significant decisions would rest on the consensus of the great powers. Cecil's belief in the coercive power of the universal economic blockade remains embodied in the repeated use of "economic sanctions" imposed by the United Nations, the European Union, and other international organizations.

It has been easy, and sometimes politically savvy, to denigrate collective security as a "myth," with its believers only proving the hollowness of twentieth-century liberal internationalism.[72] Yet by manipulating access to trade, finance, and communications, the very sinews of modern globalization, sanction-wielders have often successfully transformed various behaviors of targeted countries.[73] Targeted economic sanctions have become "enforcement mechanisms for international norms."[74] Like their Allied counterparts during the First World War, economic warriors in the twenty-first century have at times have cleaved broad strokes through a targeted economy, and in other places have narrowed their scope to attack specific industries, companies, or even individuals.

Economic sanctions do not always live up to their goals, but then again, neither do military campaigns. Political theorists have tended to agree that the economic "outcasting" of global aggressors is a morally preferable alternative to violent war.[75] In the words of Edward Carr, "generally speaking, there is a sense in which dollars are humaner than bullets even if the end pursued be the same."[76] But there are certainly some downsides to economic war. All efforts at economic warfare tend to reinforce smuggling and criminality.[77] Sanctioning regimes routinely fail at the task of planning for how they might be unwound after reaching a settlement.[78]

The most important charge against economic sanctions is that they hurt ordinary people, even while leaving unscathed the ruling elites whose policies the sanctions aim to change. This problem has been illustrated by the international sanctions regimes placed upon Iraq and Iran over the past three decades, which caused significant suffering.[79] However, since the earliest days of international economic warfare during and after the First World War, those waging economic campaigns have recognized the destructiveness of their blockades to the lives of ordinary enemy citizens. During the next World War, the United Nations Relief and Rehabilitation Administration developed as the first United Nations organization to begin operations, in that case not just during the peacemaking but before the war even ended.[80] In working to remedy German and Austrian starvation and restart their economies even before the Treaty was signed in June 1919, the blockaders of the Great War set new norms for the humanitarian response that could be expected after military and economic sanctions led a foe to accept defeat.

Historians of the League of Nations have long overlooked the importance of the ideas and the reality of economic warfare in its creation. During their six months in Paris, a small group of statesmen transformed the wartime Allied blockade system, crafted a League of Nations that looked to use economic warfare to maintain peace, and served in organizations of economic cooperation rooted both in the war and in the peacemaking process which then became permanent post-war institutions. The creation of modern ideas about economic war, with international consultation in developing and applying sanctions, remains a significant legacy of the Paris Peace Conference.

Notes

Introduction

1 Zara Steiner, *The Lights That Failed: European International History 1919–1933* (Oxford: Oxford University Press, 2005), 606.
2 Patrick Cohrs, *The Unfinished Peace after World War I: America, Britain and the Stabilisation of Europe, 1919–1932* (Cambridge: Cambridge University Press, 2006), 17.
3 The frustration comes through in Sally Marks's extended review essay, "Mistakes and Myths: The Allies, Germany, and the Versailles Treaty, 1918–1921," *The Journal of Modern History* 85, no. 3 (2013): 632–4.
4 This is a central argument of Cohrs, *The Unfinished Peace*. Also, see Eric Goldstein, *The First World War Peace Settlements, 1919–1925* (London: Longman, 2002), 91.
5 Akira Iriye, *Global Community: The Role of International Organizations in the Making of the Contemporary World* (Berkeley: University of California Press, 2002), 30–5.
6 Matthew S. Seligmann, "Failing to Prepare for the Great War? The Absence of Grand Strategy in British War Planning before 1914," *War in History* 24, no. 4 (2017): 414–37; on Admiralty hopes for the power of blockade, see Nicholas Lambert, *Planning Armageddon: British Economic Warfare and the First World War* (Cambridge, MA: Harvard University Press, 2012); Stephen Cobb, *Preparing for Blockade 1885–1914: Naval Contingency for Economic Warfare* (Farnham, UK: Ashgate, 2013); and John Ferris, "Pragmatic Hegemony and British Economic Warfare, 1900–1918: Preparations and Practice," in *Britain's War at Sea, 1914–1918: The War They Thought and the War They Fought*, ed. Greg Kennedy (London: Routledge, 2016).
7 For the overall experience of Britain's economic war, see Eric Osborne, *Britain's Economic Blockade of Germany, 1914–1919* (London and New York: Frank Cass, 2004). For one example of the way the "Logic of the Economic Blockade" mandated constant expansion of contraband and rationing measures, see T. G. Otte, "'Allah Is Great and the NOT Is His Prophet': Sea Power, Diplomacy and Economic Warfare. The Case of the Netherlands, 1900–1918," in *Britain's War at Sea*, ed. Greg Kennedy (London: Routledge, 2016), 55. On how the steadily expanding Allied control of vital resources impacted Germans, see Alan Kramer, "Blockade and economic warfare," in *The Cambridge History of the First World War, Volume II: The State*, ed. Jay Winter (Cambridge: Cambridge University Press, 2014), 460–89; Avner Offer,

The First World War: An Agrarian Interpretation (Oxford: Oxford University Press, 1989), ch. 25; and Michael B. Miller, *Europe and the Maritime World: A Twentieth-Century History* (Cambridge: Cambridge University Press, 2012), ch. 6. On British economic warfare in neutral countries beyond Europe, see Phillip Dehne, *On the Far Western Front: Britain's First World War in South America* (Manchester and New York: Manchester University Press, 2009).

8   Isabel V. Hull, *A Scrap of Paper: Breaking and Making International Law during the Great War* (Ithaca, NY, and London: Cornell University Press, 2014), 324. For more on the arguments about the international legality of the various stages of the "blockade," see Stephen C. Neff, "Disrupting a Delicate Balance: The Allied Blockade Policy and the Law of Maritime Neutrality during the Great War," *European Journal of International Law* 29, no. 2 (2018): 459–75.

9   Osborne, *Britain's Economic Blockade*, 194.

10 John Maynard Keynes, *The Economic Consequences of the Peace* (New York: Harcourt, Brace, and Howe, 1920). Many historians have written about the impact of Keynes's book, including Antony Lentin, *Lloyd George and the Lost Peace: From Versailles to Hitler, 1919–1940* (Basingstoke: Palgrave, 2001), 67–70; and Niall Ferguson, *The Pity of War* (New York: Basic Books, 1999), 399–417.

11 Cecil of Chelwood, Viscount (Lord Robert), *A Great Experiment: An Autobiography* (New York: Oxford University Press, 1941); and *All the Way* (London: Hodder and Stoughton, 1949).

12 Glenda Sluga and Patricia Clavin, "Rethinking the History of Internationalism," in *Internationalisms: A Twentieth-Century History*, ed. Glenda Sluga and Patricia Clavin (Cambridge: Cambridge University Press, 2017), 7–8. On Cecil as ambitious for power, see Peter Yearwood, *Guarantee of Peace: The League of Nations in British Policy, 1914–1925* (Oxford: Oxford University Press, 2009). For a vociferous defense of Cecil's actions in the 1930s, see J. Kenneth Brody, *The Avoidable War, Volume 1: Lord Cecil and the Policy of Principle, 1933–1935* (New Brunswick and London: Transaction Publishers, 1999), 331–41.

13 Corelli Barnett, *The Collapse of British Power* (Phoenix Mill: Sutton, 1984), 419–23; and Edward H. Carr, *The Twenty Years' Crisis, 1919–1939: An Introduction to the Study of International Relations*, 2nd ed. (London: Macmillan, 1962), 34–8.

14 Brody, *The Avoidable War, Volume 1*, 334.

15 Stephen Roskill, "Lord Cecil and the Historians," *Historical Journal* 25, no. 4 (1982): 954.

16 Daniel Gorman, *International Cooperation in the Early Twentieth Century* (London: Bloomsbury, 2017), 154.

17 Those who have described Cecil's time in Paris as focused entirely on the creation of the League include Gaynor Johnson, *Lord Robert Cecil: Politician and Internationalist* (Farnham, UK: Ashgate, 2013); George W. Egerton, *Great Britain*

and the Creation of the League of Nations: Strategy, Politics, and International Organization, 1914–1919 (Chapel Hill: University of North Carolina Press, 1978); Yearwood, *Guarantee of Peace*; and Lord Cecil himself in *A Great Experiment: An Autobiography* (New York: Oxford University Press, 1941).

18 Margaret MacMillan, *Paris 1919: Six Months That Changed the World* (New York: Random House, 2003), ch. 7.
19 John Milton Cooper, *Breaking the Heart of the World: Woodrow Wilson and the Fight for the League of Nations* (Cambridge: Cambridge University Press, 2001); Richard Striner, *Woodrow Wilson and World War I: A Burden Too Great to Bear* (Lanham, MD: Rowman & Littlefield, 2014), ch. 6; and David A. Andelman, *A Shattered Peace: Versailles 1919 and the Price We Pay Today* (Hoboken, NJ: John Wiley & Sons, 2008), 288–9.
20 Cecil, *A Great Experiment*, 100.
21 Professor Herron's description to Headlam-Morley, Jan. 25, 1919, in Sir James Headlam-Morley, *A Memoir of the Paris Peace Conference 1919* (London: Methuen, 1972), 16.
22 David Hunter Miller, *The Drafting of the Covenant*, vol. I (New York and London: G.P. Putnam's Sons, 1928), 555. Cecil was elevated to the peerage as Viscount Cecil of Chelwood in 1923.
23 H. W. V. Temperley, ed., *A History of the Peace Conference of Paris*, vol. VI (London: Henry Frowde and Hodder & Stoughton, 1920), 485.
24 Johnson, *Lord Robert Cecil*, ch. 3.
25 Yearwood, *Guarantee of Peace*, 112.
26 Marks, *The Illusion of Peace*, 15.
27 Yearwood, *Guarantee of Peace*, 24–33; Carr, *Twenty Years' Crisis*, 36–7.
28 Robert Boyce, *The Great Interwar Crisis and the Collapse of Globalization* (Basingstoke: Palgrave Macmillan, 2009), 47–8.
29 Anthony D'Agostino, *The Rise of Global Powers: International Politics in the Era of the World Wars* (Cambridge: Cambridge University Press, 2012), 114.
30 Hugh Cecil, "The Development of Lord Robert Cecil's Views on the Securing of a Lasting Peace 1915–1919" (D.Phil thesis, Oxford University, Oxford, 1971), 406.
31 For example, see F. S. Northedge, *The League of Nations: Its Life and Times, 1920–1946* (New York: Holmes & Meier, 1986).
32 Susan Pedersen, *The Guardians: The League of Nations and the Crisis of Empire* (New York: Oxford University Press, 2015), 5; Patricia Clavin, *Securing the World Economy: The Reinvention of the League of Nations, 1920–1946* (Oxford: Oxford University Press, 2013); and Daniel Gorman, *The Emergence of Internationalist Society in the 1920s* (Cambridge: Cambridge University Press, 2012), 108.
33 MacMillan, *Paris 1919*, 92.

34 For the overwhelming centrality of military force to US judgments about the effectiveness and necessity of the League and the United Nations, see Edward C. Luck, *Mixed Messages: American Politics and International Organization 1919-1999* (Washington, DC: Brookings Institution Press, 1999), ch. 7.
35 Text of League of Nations Covenant at http://avalon.law.yale.edu/20th_century/leagcov.asp (accessed Oct. 1, 2018).
36 Text of undated speech by Lord Robert Cecil, in "Press" folder, NBKR 4X/31-2.
37 Hugh Cecil, "The Development of Lord Robert Cecil's Views," 403.
38 Gary Clyde Hufbauer, Jeffrey J. Schott, Kimberly Ann Elliott, and Barbara Oegg, *Economic Sanctions Reconsidered*, 3rd ed. (Washington, DC: Peterson Institute for International Economics, 2007); and Alan P. Dobson, *US Economic Statecraft for Survival 1933-1991: Of Sanctions, Embargoes and Economic Warfare* (London and New York: Routledge, 2002), 287.
39 Oona A. Hathaway and Scott J. Shapiro, *The Internationalists: How a Radical Plan to Outlaw War Remade the World* (New York: Simon and Schuster, 2017), ch. 7.
40 Dobson, *US Economic Statecraft*, 35.
41 William Mulligan, *The Great War for Peace* (New Haven, CT and London: Yale University Press, 2014), 272-3; and Bruno Cabanes, *The Great War and the Origins of Humanitarianism, 1918-1924* (Cambridge: Cambridge University Press, 2014).
42 In *Guarantee of Peace*, Peter Yearwood stresses that the League sat at the core of British foreign policy during and immediately after the war, but he does not explain the central place of economic sanctions to those who hoped the League might wield some real authority.
43 Adam Tooze, *The Deluge: The Great War, America and the Remaking of the Global Order, 1916-1931* (New York: Viking, 2014), 517-18. This phrase "higher realism" was applied by the historian Arthur Link to Wilson's hopes for the League; see Stephen A. Schuker, "The Rhineland Question: West European Security at the Paris Peace Conference of 1919," in *The Treaty of Versailles: A Reassessment after 75 Years*, ed. Manfred F. Boemeke, Gerald D. Feldman, and Elisabeth Glaser (Washington, DC: German Historical Institute, and Cambridge: Cambridge University Press, 1998).
44 For example, the chapter on the Peace Conference in Gaynor Johnson's biography of Cecil does not mention anything he did in Paris other than work on the League. Also, see Alan Sharp, *The Versailles Settlement: Peacemaking after the First World War, 1919-1923*, 2nd ed. (Basingstoke: Palgrave Macmillan, 2008), 61. Similarly, Egerton only notes Cecil's League Covenant negotiations. The exception is Hugh Cecil, "The Development of Lord Robert Cecil's Views," which covers Cecil's work with the SEC, even while disparaging the SEC as "not powerful."
45 Offer, *The First World War*, 78.

46 C. Paul Vincent, *The Politics of Hunger: The Allied Blockade of Germany, 1915–1919* (Athens and London: Ohio University Press, 1985), 158–60.

47 Mary Elizabeth Cox, "Hunger Games: Or How the Allied Blockade in the First World War Deprived German Children of Nutrition, and Allied Food Aid Subsequently Saved Them," *Economic History Review* 68, no. 2 (2015): 615–16.

48 Marks, "Mistakes and Myths," 651.

49 For a prime example of the SEC being overlooked, MacMillan mentions it only once in *Paris 1919*.

50 Antony Lentin, *General Smuts: South Africa* (London: Haus, 2010), 75.

51 Frank M. Surface and Raymond L. Bland, eds., *American Food in the World War and Reconstruction Period: Operations of the Organizations under the Direction of Herbert Hoover 1914–1924* (Stanford, CA: Stanford University Press, 1931); Cox, "Hunger Games," 624; Cabanes, *The Great War and the Origins of Humanitarianism*, 212; Klaus Schwabe, *Woodrow Wilson, Revolutionary Germany, and Peacemaking, 1918–1919: Missionary Diplomacy and the Realities of Power* (Chapel Hill: University of North Carolina Press, 1985), 191–210; Elisabeth Glaser, "The Making of the Economic Peace," in *The Treaty of Versailles*, ed. Manfred F. Boemeke, Gerald D. Feldman, and Elisabeth Glaser (Cambridge: Cambridge University Press, 2013), 390–1; and Julia Irwin, "Taming Total War: Great War-Era American Humanitarianism and Its Legacies," in *Beyond 1917: The United States and the Global Legacies of the Great War*, ed. Thomas W. Zeiler, David K. Ekbladh, and Benjamin C. Montoya (New York: Oxford University Press, 2017), 123.

52 On the "new internationalists," see Frank Trentmann, "Coping with Shortage: The Problem of Food Security and Global Visions of Coordination, c. 1890s–1950," in *Food and Conflict in Europe in the Age of the Two World Wars*, ed. Frank Trentmann and Flemming Just (London: Palgrave Macmillan, 2006), 27–33. Gorman details the wide variety of movements and ideas in *The Emergence of Internationalist Society in the 1920s*.

53 Sluga and Clavin, "Rethinking the History," 11. For one history that focuses on the importance of war experiences in nurturing internationalism but then skips over the peacemaking months, see Frank Trentmann, "After the Nation State: Citizenship, Empire and Global Coordination in the New Internationalism, 1914–1930," in *Beyond Sovereignty: Britain, Empire, and Transnationalism, c. 1880–1950*, ed. Kevin Grant, Philippa Levine, and Frank Trentmann (Houndmills, Basingstoke and New York: Palgrave Macmillan, 2007), 38–40.

54 The year 1920 is the starting point for a number of recent histories of internationalism, such as Gorman's *The Emergence of International Society*; and Clavin, *Securing the World Economy*.

55 For the broadly internationalist paradigm of French post-war international relations, see Peter Jackson, *Beyond the Balance of Power: France and the Politics*

of *National Security in the Era of the First Word War* (Cambridge: Cambridge University Press, 2013), 6–7. On the transition from war to peace, the *sortie de guerre*, as a "humanitarian moment," see Cabanes, *The Great War*, introduction.

56 Among the many serious academic histories of the Paris Conference that focus entirely on the Big Four, a good recent example is Cohrs, *The Unfinished Peace*, chs. 2–3. There are also many somewhat less academic books that, focusing on personality clashes, even go so far as to fabricate conversations Thucydides-style; for example, see David Sinclair, *Hall of Mirrors* (London: Century, 2001).

57 Quote from Steiner, *The Lights That Failed*, 17. Steiner argues that an extremely small circle of advisors influenced the triumvirate of Clemenceau, Lloyd George, and Wilson. Sally Marks suggests that the only two British delegates who mattered were Lloyd George and Foreign Secretary Arthur Balfour.

58 The "Makers of the Modern World" series, published by Haus and edited by Alan Sharp, includes biographies of many of the Conference notables, including Lloyd George, Wilson, and Clemenceau, but much of the list focuses on marginal conference attendees like Ion Bratianu of Romania and the Maharajah of Bikaner.

59 On the importance of historians examining the details of the negotiations, rather than using a "broad brush" approach, see Marc Trachtenberg, "Reparation at the Paris Peace Conference, and Political Economy versus National Sovereignty: Reply," *Journal of Modern History* 51, no. 1 (1979): 85.

60 Eustace Percy, *Some Memories* (London: Eyre & Spottiswoode, 1958), 60–1.

61 On this sense of hope and expectation during the 1920s, see Gorman, *The Emergence of International Society*, 18; and Steiner, *The Lights That Failed*, 630–2.

1 Bringing Baggage to Paris

1 For the global ubiquity of revolutionary feeling, and the reasons for its successes across eastern Europe, see Richard Bessel, "Revolution," in *The Cambridge History of the First World War, Volume II*, ed. Jay Winter (Cambridge: Cambridge University Press, 2014), 126–44.

2 Erez Manela, *The Wilsonian Moment: Self-Determination and the International Origins of Anticolonial Nationalism* (New York and Oxford: Oxford University Press, 2006); and Jay Winter, *Dreams of Peace and Freedom* (New Haven, CT, and London: Yale University Press, 2006), ch. 2.

3 Henri Barbusse, *Under Fire* (New York: Penguin Classics, 2004), 305.

4 Alan Sharp, *The Versailles Settlement: Peacemaking after the First World War, 1919–1923*, 2nd ed. (Basingstoke: Palgrave Macmillan, 2008), 158–60.

5 Smuts wrote a letter on Dec. 3, 1918, congratulating Cecil on being named by Lloyd George and Balfour as head of the League of Nations Section at the Peace

Conference. Add. Ms. 51076. Inga Floto suggests that Cecil's appointment occurred later in the month at the instigation of Woodrow Wilson, but the prime minister had made this decision, and Cecil accepted, far before Wilson arrived in London; Inga Floto, *Colonel House in Paris: A Study of American Policy at the Paris Peace Conference 1919* (Princeton, NJ: Princeton University Press, 1980), 85–90.

6 Lord Robert Cecil to Lady Eleanor Cecil, Jan. 7, 1919, CHE 6/6, NRA 10632 Gascoyne-Cecil Papers, Hatfield House Library and Archive.

7 On the excitement the world felt for Wilson, see Manela, *The Wilsonian Moment*, 19–21; and Mark Mazower, *Governing the World: The History of an Idea* (New York: The Penguin Press, 2012), 118.

8 "Conference and the Press, Arrival of Delegates," *The Times*, Jan. 8, 1919, p. 7.

9 Frederick Douglas How, *The Marquis of Salisbury* (London: Isbister, 1902), 265; Cecil of Chelwood, *All the Way* (London: Hodder and Stoughton, 1949), 18–19; and Kenneth Rose, *The Later Cecils* (London: Weidenfeld and Nicolson, 1975), 38.

10 British Red Cross Society, *Reports by the Joint War Committee and the Joint War Finance Committee of the British Red Cross Society and the Order of St. John of Jerusalem in England on Voluntary Aid rendered to the Sick and Wounded at Home and Abroad and to British Prisoners of War, 1914–1919* (London: HMSO, 1921), 359; Cecil, *All the Way*, 126–9.

11 Cecil to Lady Cecil, Jan. 7, 1919, CHE 6/6. On the Crowe-Cecil relationship at the Ministry of Blockade, see Phillip Dehne, "The Ministry of Blockade and the Fate of Free Trade during the First World War," *Twentieth Century British History* 27, no. 3 (2016).

12 Sir Valentine Chirol, *Fifty Years in a Changing World* (London: Jonathan Cape, 1927), 332.

13 Cecil to Lady Cecil, Jan. 8, 1919, CHE 6/7.

14 For example, to alleviate a lack of staff from the Treasury, in mid-February John Maynard Keynes drew into his orbit McKinnon Wood of the FO and J. R. M. Butler, a Fellow of Trinity College, Cambridge, who "arrived here for some temporary work." John Maynard Keynes, *Collected Writings of John Maynard Keynes, Volume XVI: Activities 1914- 1919: The Treasury and Versailles* (London: Macmillan, 1971), 404–5. In one of his memoirs, Cecil stated that Butler was one of his own secretaries, in *A Great Experiment: An Autobiography* (New York: Oxford University Press, 1941), 66.

15 Jan. 13, 1919 Headlam-Morley to Koppel at FO, in Sir James Headlam-Morley, *A Memoir of the Paris Peace Conference 1919* (London: Methuen, 1972), 1–2.

16 "The British Delegation Offices," *Irish Times*, Jan. 14, 1919.

17 On British attempts and difficulties organizing accommodations, communications, and security in Paris in December 1918 and January 1919, see Sally Marks, "Behind the Scenes at the Paris Peace Conference of 1919," *Journal of British Studies* 9, no. 2

(1970): 154–80. Many of the US delegates had been in Paris for weeks by this time. House had settled into the Crillon by Dec. 9, 1918; David Hunter Miller, *My Diary at the Peace Conference of Paris, with Documents* (New York: Printed for the author by the Appeal printing company, 1924).

18 Cecil to Lady Cecil, Jan. 7, 1919, CHE 6/6.
19 Note on the diary of Sir James Headlam-Morley by Miss Hughes, his secretary at the Peace Conference; in Headlam-Morley, *Memoir*, xli–xlii.
20 B. C. Busch, *Hardinge of Penshurst: A Study in the Old Diplomacy* (Hamden, CT: Archon Books, 1980), 274–7.
21 Sir Francis Oppenheimer, *Stranger within: Autobiographical Pages* (London: Faber and Faber, 1960), 348–54.
22 Johnson, *Lord Robert Cecil*, 70.
23 Sibyl Crowe and Edward Corp, *Our Ablest Public Servant: Sir Eyre Crowe 1864–1925* (Braunton Devon: Merlin Books, 1993), 330.
24 Doc. 13: Hardinge to Balfour, Oct. 10, 1918; and Doc. 15, W.T.I.D. "Diagram to Illustrate the Foreign Office Memorandum of October 10, 1918, Respecting Peace Negotiations," Oct. 28, 1918, in *British Documents on Foreign Affairs—Reports and Papers from the Foreign Office Confidential Print. Part II, From the First to the Second World War. Series I, the Paris Peace Conference of 1919*, vol. 1, ed. M. L. Dockrill, Kenneth Bourne and Donald Cameron Watt (Frederick, MD: University Publications of America, 1989) (hereafter *BDFA*, vol. 1).
25 Erik Goldstein, *Winning the Peace: British Diplomatic Strategy, Peace Planning, and the Paris Peace Conference, 1916–1920* (Oxford: Clarendon Press, 1991), 79–85.
26 Crowe and Corp, *Our Ablest Public Servant*, 328–31.
27 Cecil diary, Jan. 10, 1919, Add. Ms. 51131, Cecil of Chelwood Papers, British Library, London.
28 Quoted in Alan Sharp, *David Lloyd George: Great Britain* (London: Haus, 2008), 62–3.
29 On the disarray and lack of planning among the US delegation, largely due to the enigmatic views of Woodrow Wilson, see F. S. Marston, *The Peace Conference of 1919: Organization and Procedure* (London: Oxford University Press, 1944); for an example of the complete refusal of Wilson to prepare for the Conference, see experience of George Beer on the trip to Europe with Wilson, see Susan Pedersen, *The Guardians: The League of Nations and the Crisis of Empire* (New York: Oxford University Press, 2015), 17–19.
30 David French, *Strategy of the Lloyd George Coalition* (Oxford: Clarendon Press, 1995); and David Stevenson, *With Our Backs to the Wall: Victory and Defeat in 1918* (Cambridge, MA: Belknap Press of Harvard University Press, 2011), 112.
31 On the administrative and ministerial innovations of the war, see Kathleen Burk, ed., *War and the State: The Transformation of British Government,*

1914–1919 (London: George Allen & Unwin, 1982). On Cecil's efforts to bridge gaps between ministries related to the blockade see Phillip Dehne, *On the Far Western Front: Britain's First World War in South America* (Manchester and New York: Manchester University Press, 2009), chs. 3 and 5.

32 Described in FO minute from Headlam-Morley to Sir William Tyrrell, Jan. 16, 1919, in Headlam-Morley, *Memoir*, 3–4.
33 Busch, *Hardinge of Penshurst*, 290.
34 Cecil's height at age fifty, according to his British Empire Army Certificate of Identity for Civilians Wearing the Red Cross Brassard, of April 13, 1918, folio 8, CHE 30.
35 John Grigg, *Lloyd George: War Leader, 1916–1918* (London: Allen Lane, 2002), 148.
36 Cecil diary, Jan. 13, 1919, Add. Ms. 51131.
37 Peter Yearwood, *Guarantee of Peace: The League of Nations in British Policy, 1914–1925* (Oxford: Oxford University Press, 2009), 33.
38 "The dead parliament: Its personalities and history," *Manchester Guardian*, Nov. 22, 1918, 4.
39 Letter from Thomas Jones to his wife on evening of Nov. 28, 1916, in Thomas Jones, *Whitehall Diary*, vol. 1 (London: Oxford University Press, 1969), 3.
40 Quoted in Yearwood, *Guarantee of Peace*, 32.
41 Stevenson diary, Dec. 2, 1916, in A. J. P. Taylor, ed., *Lloyd George: A Diary by Frances Stevenson* (London: Hutchinson, 1971), 130–1.
42 See Cecil's discussion with his niece's husband Eddy Hartington, the future 9th Duke of Devonshire; Cecil diary, Feb. 2, 1919, Add. Ms. 51131.
43 Letter from Cecil to Lady Cecil, Apr. 27, 1916, CHE 5/149.
44 John Turner, *Lloyd George's Secretariat* (Cambridge: Cambridge University Press, 2009).
45 For glimpses into these new ministries, see Burk, *War and the State*; and Dehne, "The Ministry of Blockade."
46 Seth Tillman, *Anglo-American Relations at the Paris Peace Conference of 1919* (Princeton, NJ: Princeton University Press, 1961), 28–32; and William Mulligan, *The Great War for Peace* (New Haven, CT, and London: Yale University Press, 2014), 229–30.
47 Cecil to Curzon, with copy to Lloyd George. Oct. 4, 1918, Add. Ms. 51076.
48 Cecil to Lloyd George, Sept. 7, 1918, Add. Ms. 51076.
49 Lord Riddell recounting in his diary a conversation he had at dinner in London with Lloyd George on Feb. 23, 1919, in Lord George Allardice Riddell, *Lord Riddell's Intimate Diary of the Peace Conference and after, 1918–1923* (London: Victor Gollancz, 1933), 24–5.
50 Peter Yearwood, "'On the Safe and Right Lines': The Lloyd George Government and the Origins of the League of Nations, 1916–1918," *Historical Journal* 32, no. 1 (1989): 150.

51 See Philip Williamso, ed., *The Modernisation of Conservative Politics: The Diaries and Letters of William Bridgeman 1904–1935* (London: The Historians' Press, 1988); and Lord Robert Cecil and the Rev. H. J. Clayton, *Our National Church* (London: Frederick Warne, 1913).

52 F. Russell Bryant, ed., *The Coalition Diaries and Letters of H.A.L. Fisher, 1916–1922: The Historian in Lloyd George's Cabinet* (Lewiston and New York: The Edwin Mellen Press, 2006), 333–4.

53 Yearwood, *Guarantee of Peace*, 105–6.

54 Hugh Cecil, "The Development of Lord Robert Cecil's Views on the Securing of a Lasting Peace 1915–1919" (D.Phil thesis, Oxford University, Oxford, 1971), 35–6.

55 Cecil to Balfour, May 5, 1918, Add. Ms. 49738, Balfour Papers, British Library, London.

56 Cecil to Lloyd George, June 7, 1918, and Lloyd George's reply of same day, Add. Ms. 51076.

57 Cecil to Lloyd George, June 21 and 23, 1918, Add. Ms. 51076.

58 The phrase Cecil had used when deciding to stay in the government, Cecil to Lloyd George, June 23, 1918. Add. Ms. 51076. Copies of correspondence between Cecil and Lloyd George of Nov. 10, 1918 and Nov. 21, 1918 can be found in the National Archives, FO 800/207.

59 "Lord Robert Cecil Resigns; Disagreed with Lloyd George," *New York Times*, Nov. 23, 1918.

60 P. M. H. Bell, *Disestablishment in Ireland and Wales* (London: SPCK, 1969), 244–5.

61 Taylor, *Lloyd George*, 38–41; Bell, *Disestablishment*, 300–1.

62 Bell, *Disestablishment*, 241–2, 266–7.

63 *The Scotsman*, Nov. 23, 1918, 7.

64 Cecil diary, Jan. 13, 1919, Add. Ms. 51131.

65 Copy of Cecil's letter of resignation to Lloyd George, Nov. 21, 1918, in Cecil to Balfour, Nov. 22, 1918. FO 800/207.

66 G. H. Bennett, *British Foreign Policy during the Curzon Period, 1919–24* (New York: St. Martin's Press, 1995), 1.

67 Major-General Sir C. E. Callwell, *Field-Marshall Sir Henry Wilson: His Life and Diaries*, vol. II (London: Cassell, 1927), 162. On the continued use of Cecil in the Cabinet and as the leader of the FO on the final day of 1918, see David Lloyd George, *The Truth about the Peace Treaties* (London: Victor Gollancz, 1938), 204–8.

68 Harold Begbie ("A Gentleman with a Duster"), *The Mirrors of Downing Street: Some Political Reflections* (New York and London: G.P. Putnam's Sons, 1921), 88.

69 F. M. L. Thompson, *English Landed Society in the Nineteenth Century* (London: Routledge and Kegan Paul, 1963), esp. chs. X–XI.

70 David Cannadine, *The Decline and Fall of the British Aristocracy* (New York: Vintage, 1999), 250.

71 Much to the chagrin of Joseph Chamberlain, who during this campaign was largely successful in rooting out free traders from the Conservative benches in the House of Commons; see Peter T. Marsh, *Joseph Chamberlain: Entrepreneur in Politics* (New Haven, CT, and London: Yale University Press, 1994), 626–7.

72 On the longer term rivalry between Lord Salisbury and Joseph Chamberlain over control of the Conservative Party in the 1890s and early 1900s, see Peter T. Marsh, *The Discipline of Popular Government: Lord Salisbury's Domestic Statecraft, 1881–1902* (Sussex: The Harvester Press, 1978).

73 Cannadine, *Decline and Fall*, 220–2; Frank Trentmann, *Free Trade Nation: Commerce, Consumption, and Civil Society in Modern Britain* (Oxford and New York: Oxford University Press, 2008), 167.

74 Cecil to the electors of North Herts, Nov. 26, 1918, Add. Ms. 51162.

75 On Cecil's surprise in being appointed to the Paris delegation, see letter from Cecil to Hugh Cecil, Jan. 14, 1921, Add. Ms. 51157.

76 Floto, *Colonel House*, 85–90.

77 George N. Barnes, *From Workshop to War Cabinet* (London: Herbert Jenkins, 1924), 222.

78 Hugh Cecil, "Lord Robert Cecil and the League of Nations during the First World War," in *Home Fires and Foreign Fields: British Social and Military Experience in the First World War*, ed. Peter Liddle (London: Brassey's Defence Publishers, 1985), 70–1; and Hugh Cecil, "Lord Robert Cecil: Nineteenth-Century Upbringing," *History Today* 25 (1975): 118–27.

79 Cecil, "The Development of Lord Robert Cecil's Views," 101–4.

80 George W. Egerton, *Great Britain and the Creation of the League of Nations: Strategy, Politics, and International Organization, 1914–1919* (Chapel Hill: University of North Carolina Press, 1978), ch. 2.

81 Mazower, *Governing the World*, 129. Hugh Cecil doubts that Lord Robert Cecil read any of the books on ideas of a League, by Woolf, Angell, or Lowes Dickinson; see "The Development of Lord Robert Cecil's Views," 103.

82 Maurice Cowling, *The Impact of Labour 1920–1924: The Beginning of Modern British Politics* (Cambridge: Cambridge University Press, 1971), 60–6.

83 Peter Raffo, "The Anglo-American Preliminary Negotiations for a League of Nations," *Journal of Contemporary History* 9, no. 4 (1974): 154; and Margaret MacMillan, *Paris 1919: Six Months That Changed the World* (New York: Random House, 2003), 90.

84 Martin Ceadel, *Semi-Detached Idealists: The British Peace Movement and International Relations, 1854–1945* (Oxford: Oxford University Press, 2000), chs. 8–9.

85 Robert Lansing, *The Peace Negotiations: A Personal Narrative* (Boston, MA, and New York: Houghton Mifflin, 1921), 88.

86 On the "accidental" nature of his immersion in the blockade see Cecil's memoir *All the Way*, 124–30.
87 Lord Grey to Cecil, Oct. 24, 1916, CHE 93/148.
88 Dehne, "The Ministry of Blockade."
89 Cecil, "The Development of Lord Robert Cecil's Views," 39–44.
90 See Cecil to Lord Bertie in Paris about blacklisting, Aug. 1, 1916, FO 800/195. Also, Cecil letters to and from Coudert, Jan. 1916, FO 800/196.
91 On the importance of international legality to the British blockaders, see Isabel V. Hull, *A Scrap of Paper: Breaking and Making International Law during the Great War* (Ithaca, NY, and London: Cornell University Press, 2014), 322–5.
92 George Scott, *The Rise and Fall of the League of Nations* (London: Hutchinson, 1973), 17.
93 Cecil, *A Great Experiment*, 47.
94 Cecil's "Memorandum on Proposals for Diminishing the Occasion of Future Wars," in *A Great Experiment*, Appendix I.
95 Cecil to Trevelyan, Sept. 18, 1935, Add. Ms. 51193.
96 Memo by Cecil, "President Wilson's reply to the Pope's Peace Proposal and the Economic Policy of the Allies Declared at the Paris Conference (1916)," Aug. 31, 1917, FO 800/197.
97 Although some within the FO disagreed with some of Phillimore's premises, such as the leading League expert in the FO's Intelligence Department, Lord Eustace Percy, who noted that sometimes a cooling-off period might actually see tempers rise and that peace must rest on a continued alliance between Britain and the United States; see Percy's report, copy in NBKR 4X/28, the Papers of Baron Noel-Baker, Churchill Archives Centre, Cambridge.
98 Cecil to Lady Cecil, Aug. 14, 1918, CHE 6/4.
99 Cecil diary, Jan. 12, 1919, Add. Ms. 51131.
100 Copies of letters between Spens and Adam Block, sent to Cecil on June 7, 1918. Add. Ms. 51093.
101 Editorial in *The Scotsman*, Nov. 14, 1918, 4.
102 Copy of Memorandum of Oct. 5, 1918 by Cecil to War Cabinet on the League of Nations, marked "Very Secret, P. 29." Add. Ms. 51102.
103 Cecil's outline of his speech at Birmingham on Nov. 12, 1918. Add. Ms. 51195.
104 Copy of a League of Nations Draft Convention; uncertain date, with Sept. 1916, May 1917, and "aft. Dec. 17 1918" written on it. Add. Ms. 51102.
105 Undated report "Can a League of Nations Armed with the Weapon of Economic Isolation Safeguard the World's Peace?," in NBKR 4X/34.
106 Copy of Cockerill report entitled "Can a League of Nations Armed with the Weapon of Economic Isolation Safeguard the World's Peace?" Add. Ms. 51162.

2 Getting Down to Business: January

1. George H. Nash, *The Life of Herbert Hoover: Master of Emergencies, 1917–1918* (New York and London: W.W. Norton, 1996), 480. Letter from Hoover to Wilson from London, Nov. 11, 1918, on need for US control of post-war wheat rather than the interallied pool favored by Britain; in *The Blockade of Germany After the Armistice 1918–1919: Selected Documents of the Supreme Economic Council, Superior Blockade Council, American Relief Administration, and Other Wartime Organizations*, ed. S. L. Bane and R. H. Lutz (Stanford, CA: Stanford University Press, 1942). Much later, Hoover claimed falsely that in December 1918 Cecil had agreed to the abolition of the wartime interallied councils; in Herbert Hoover, *The Ordeal of Woodrow Wilson* (New York: McGraw-Hill, 1958), 86.
2. Herbert Hoover, *Memoirs*, vol. 1 (New York: Macmillan, 1951–2), ch. 33.
3. Cecil diary, Jan. 7, 1919. Robert H. Van Meter Jr., "Herbert Hoover and the Economic Reconstruction of Europe, 1918–21," in *Herbert Hoover: The Great War and its aftermath*, ed. Lawrence Gelfand (Iowa City: University of Iowa Press, 1979), 158–61.
4. Letter from Hoover to Wilson, Jan. 8, 1919, in Herbert Hoover, *Two Peacemakers in Paris: The Hoover-Wilson Post-Armistice Letters* (College Station: Texas A&M University Press, 1978).
5. Lord Salter, *Memoirs of a Public Servant* (London: Faber and Faber, 1961), 133.
6. "Our London Correspondence," *Manchester Guardian*, Nov. 15, 1918, 4.
7. George W. Egerton, *Great Britain and the Creation of the League of Nations: Strategy, Politics, and International Organization, 1914–1919* (Chapel Hill: University of North Carolina Press, 1978), 83.
8. Cecil diary, Jan. 7, 1919, Add. Ms. 51131.
9. H. J. Elcock, *Portrait of a Decision: The Council of Four and the Treaty of Versailles* (London: Eyre Methuen, 1972), 61.
10. Cecil diary, Jan. 8, 1919, Add. Ms. 51131.
11. Cecil diary, Jan. 11, 1919, Add. Ms. 51131.
12. For example, see "French Plans for League Complete," *Christian Science Monitor*, Jan.17, 1919, p. 2.
13. Cecil diary, Jan. 9, 1919, Add. Ms. 51131.
14. Description of Bourgeois by Stephen Bonsal, *Unfinished Business* (New York: Doubleday, Doran, 1944), 17–21.
15. Cecil diary, Jan. 25, 1919, Add. Ms. 51131.
16. Cecil diary, Jan. 16, 1919, Add. Ms. 51131.
17. Cecil diary, Jan. 22, 1919, Add. Ms. 51131.
18. Cecil diary, Jan. 29, 1919. Add. Ms. 51131.

19 See description of interview in a number of newspapers, including "Lord Cecil says League should be taken up first," *St. Louis Post-Dispatch*, Jan. 10, 1919; "Cecil says League is necessary first step toward peace," *New-York Tribune*, Jan. 10, 1919; "Cecil would form peace league first," *New York Times*, Jan. 10, 1919.

20 *The Atlanta Constitution*, Dec. 28, 1919, p. A5.

21 "Cecil Gives British View upon League," *Chicago Daily Tribune*, Jan. 15, 1919, p. 1; and "Cecil Opposes World Police to Keep Peace," *New-York Tribune*, Jan. 15, 1919, p. 1.

22 "At the Conference," *Irish Times*, Jan. 24, 1919, p. 3.

23 Cecil diary, Jan. 21, 1919, Add. Ms. 51131.

24 Cecil diary, Jan. 19, 1919, Add. Ms. 51131.

25 Cecil diary, Feb. 3, 1919, Add. Ms. 51131.

26 Cecil diary, Jan. 19, 1919, Add. Ms. 51131.

27 Cecil diary, Feb. 6, 1919, Add. Ms. 51131.

28 Cecil diary, Jan. 22, 1919, Add. Ms. 51131.

29 On meetings between Lansing, House, and Cecil on Jan. 8, see House diary in *The Papers of Woodrow Wilson*, ed. S. L. Bane and R. H. Lutz, vol. 53 (Princeton, NJ: Princeton University Press, 1966–4), 693. On House's importance to Wilson, see Inga Floto, *Colonel House in Paris: A Study of American Policy at the Paris Peace Conference 1919* (Princeton, NJ: Princeton University Press, 1980), 99.

30 House diary, Jan. 30, 1919, in Link, *The Papers of Woodrow Wilson*, v. 54, 386.

31 Cecil diary, Jan. 25, 1919, Add. Ms. 51131; David Hunter Miller, *The Drafting of the Covenant*, vol. I (New York and London: G.P. Putnam's Sons, 1928), 54.

32 Cecil diary, Jan. 21, 1919, Add. Ms. 51131.

33 This idea that Miller had no instructions suggests not just Wilson's inattentiveness, but also his mistrust of lawyers in general. Miller was chosen as Wilson's primary legal advisor in Paris precisely because he was not an eminent international lawyer before the war; Benjamin Allen Coates, *Legalist Empire: International Law and American Foreign Relations in the Early Twentieth Century* (Oxford: Oxford University Press, 2016), 153.

34 Miller, *The Drafting*, 51–3.

35 Cecil diary, Jan. 27, 1919, Add. Ms. 51131. Also see note from Cecil, League of Nations Commission folder, NBKR 4X/27.

36 See criticism in Sibyl Crowe and Edward Corp, *Our Ablest Public Servant: Sir Eyre Crowe 1864–1925* (Braunton Devon: Merlin Books, 1993), 305: "Cecil's views … like those of some wind-battered weathercock, changed constantly."

37 Cecil to War Cabinet, Dec. 17, 1918, annexed in Draft Minutes of IWC meeting 46 of Dec. 24, 1918. NBKR 4X/27.

38 See Hull, *A Scrap of Paper*, chs. 5–6.

39 Cecil diary, Jan. 13, 1919; Jan. 20, 1919; Feb. 1, 1919, Add. Ms. 51131. In December, Percy suggested that the scholar Alfred Zimmern, assigned as a temporary clerk to

the FO in May 1918, should obviously be one of the FO's staffers for Cecil on the League, but that he had been turned to down go to Paris for "the obvious (reason) of parentage." Zimmern's parents were German Jews, and he had been born in Germany. See Percy memo to Cecil, Dec. 17, 1918, in Labour folder, NBKR 4X/28.

40 L. F. Fitzhardinge, "W.M. Hughes and the Treaty of Versailles, 1919," *Journal of Commonwealth Political Studies* 5, no. 2 (1967): 133.

41 Minutes of Jan. 1, 1919 meeting at FO, Cecil chairing. In League of Nations Commission folder, NBKR 4X/27.

42 James Watson, *William F. Massey: New Zealand* (London: Haus, 2010), 65–71; and David Reynolds, *The Long Shadow: The Legacies of the Great War in the Twentieth Century* (New York: W.W. Norton, 2014), 107–8.

43 W. M. Hughes, *Splendid Adventure; A Review of Empire Relations within and without the Commonwealth of Britannic Nations* (London: E. Benn, 1929), 7–12.

44 R. C. Snelling, "Peacemaking, 1919: Australia, New Zealand and the British Empire Delegation at Versailles," *Journal of Imperial and Commonwealth History* 4, no. 1 (1975): 16.

45 George W. Egerton, "Great Britain and the League of Nations: Collective Security as Myth and History," in *The League of Nations in Retrospect: Proceedings of the Symposium* (Berlin and New York: Walter de Gruyter, 1983), 76.

46 W. M. Hughes, "Foreword," in *The 38th Battalion A.I.F. The Story and Official History*, ed. Eric Fairey (Bendigo, Australia: Bendigo Advertiser and the Cambridge Press, 1920).

47 W. M. Hughes, *Crusts and Crusades; Tales of Bygone Days* (Sydney: Angus and Robertson, 1947), 228–32.

48 William Roger Louis, *Great Britain and Germany's Lost Colonies, 1914–1919* (Oxford: Clarendon Press, 1967), 155.

49 Cecil diary, Jan. 8, 1919, Add. Ms. 51131.

50 On the "Wilsonian Moment," see Manela. Cecil diary, Jan. 22, 1919, Add. Ms. 51131.

51 Cecil diary, Jan. 25, 1919, Add. Ms. 51131.

52 Cecil diary, Jan. 27, 1919, Add. Ms. 51131.

53 Cecil diary, Jan. 26, 1919, Add. Ms. 51131.

54 Elcock, *Portrait*, 73–9.

55 Cecil diary, Jan. 28, 1919, Add. Ms. 51131.

56 BED Meeting #5, Jan. 28, 1919, 3:00 p.m., in *British Documents On Foreign Affairs—Reports and Papers from the Foreign Office Confidential Print. Part II, From the First to the Second World War. Series I, the Paris Peace Conference of 1919*, vol. 3, ed. M. L. Dockrill, Kenneth Bourne, and Donald Cameron Watt (Frederick, MD: University Publications of America, 1989).

57 Louis, *Great Britain and Germany's Lost Colonies*, 134–5.

58 Cecil diary, Jan. 28 and 29, 1919, Add. Ms. 51131. On the creation of the three level mandate system, see Pederson, *The Guardians*.

59 Cecil diary, Feb. 3, 1919, Add. Ms. 51131.
60 P. G. Edwards, *Prime Ministers and Diplomats: The Making of Australian Foreign Policy 1901–1949* (Melbourne: Oxford University Press, 1983), 43.
61 Lady Cecil at Lambton Castle to Lord Cecil in Paris, Jan. 29, 1919. CHE 18/11.
62 For example, Canadian Prime Minister Robert Borden believed that Wilson in his Plenary Session speech on the League on Feb. 14 "should have expressed appreciation of General Smuts' work upon which the proposals reported were largely based," Borden, Robert Laird, *Robert Laird Borden: His Memoirs* (New York: Macmillan, 1938), 912.
63 Cecil diary, Jan. 24, 1919, Add. Ms. 51131.
64 For example, Mark Mazower significantly overstates the importance of Smuts to the creation of the League Covenant, in *No Enchanted Palace: The End of Empire and the Ideological Origins of the United Nations* (Princeton, NJ, and Oxford: Princeton University Press, 2009), 40–5. Quote from David Lloyd George, *The Truth about the Peace Treaties* (London: Victor Gollancz, 1938), 616.
65 Cecil diary, Jan. 13, 1919, Add. Ms. 51131.
66 Cecil diary, Jan. 31, 1919, Add. Ms. 51131.
67 Cecil diary, Jan. 28, 1919, Add. Ms. 51131.
68 Cecil diary, Jan. 17, 1919. Add. Mss. 51131.
69 Lord Hankey, *The Supreme Command 1914–1918*, vol. 2 (London: George Allen and Unwin, 1961), 721.
70 Cecil diary, Jan. 13, 1919, Add. Ms. 51131.
71 Cecil diary, Jan. 20, 1919, Add. Ms. 51131.
72 Cecil diary, Jan. 23, 1919, Add. Ms. 51131.
73 Keith Nielson, "Managing the War: Britain, Russia and *Ad Hoc* Government," in *Strategy and Intelligence: British Policy during the First World War*, ed. Michael Dockrill and David French (London: Hambledon Press, 1996), 118.
74 On the disagreements about Russia policy, see letters between Cecil and Lloyd George on June 7, 1918 and from Cecil to Lloyd George on June 21 and 23, 1918; in Cecil of Chelwood papers, Add. Ms. 51076.
75 Egerton, *Great Britain and the Creation of the League of Nations*, 57, 69.
76 David P. Billington Jr., *Lothian: Philip Kerr and the Quest for World Order* (Westport, CT, and London: Praeger Security International, 2006), 56–7.
77 Cecil diary, Jan. 31, 1919, Add. Ms. 51131.
78 Miller, *Diary*, Jan. 24, 1919.
79 Yearwood agrees that Cecil was right in deciding to continue with his cooperation with the Americans along the lines he had been doing; in *Guarantee of Peace: The League of Nations in British Policy, 1914–1925* (Oxford: Oxford University Press, 2009), 111. Egerton suggests otherwise, saying that in reading Kerr's plan aloud to Cecil and Smuts, Lloyd George was implicitly commanding them on the

negotiating stance they should take with Wilson, and that Cecil willfully ignored this directive in his ensuing negotiations over the next few weeks; in *Great Britain and the Creation of the League of Nations,* 119-29.

80 Cecil diary, Jan. 11, 1919, Add. Ms. 51131.
81 Cecil diary, Jan. 16, 1919, Add. Ms. 51131.
82 Cecil diary, Jan. 15, 1919, Add. Ms. 51131.
83 Cecil diary, Jan. 13, 1919, Add. Ms. 51131.
84 Quote from Cecil to Fisher, Nov. 11, 1918, in F. Russell Bryant, ed., *The Coalition Diaries and Letters of H.A.L. Fisher, 1916-1922: The Historian in Lloyd George's Cabinet* (Lewiston, NY: The Edwin Mellen Press, 2006), 318.
85 Cecil diary, Jan. 7, 1919, Add. Ms. 51131. For the tenor and intensity of Derby's social life while Ambassador in Paris, see David Dutton, ed., *Paris 1918: The War Diary of the British Ambassador, the 17th Earl of Derby* (Liverpool: Liverpool University Press, 2001).
86 On a previous talkative luncheon between Cecil and Lawrence in October 1918, see Bryant, *Coalition Diaries,* 312-14; also Lawrence James, *The Golden Warrior: The Life and Legend of Lawrence of Arabia* (New York: Skyhorse, 2008), 238-9.
87 On Cecil meeting Feisul on Dec. 30, 1918, see "Court Circular," *The Times,* Wed., Jan. 1, 1919, p. 11. Cecil letter to Lloyd George in February 1919, in Elcock, *Portrait,* 112.
88 Cecil diary, Jan. 11, 1919. David Hunter Miller was astonished at this dinner that the League of Nations was not addressed by any of the eight people present, who included Cecil, Lionel Curtis, and Cecil's secretary Major Walters; see his diary, Saturday, Jan. 11, 1919.
89 Cecil diary, Jan. 16, 1919.
90 Cecil to Balfour, Jan., 30 1919, FO 800/215.
91 Cecil diary, Jan. 31, 1919.
92 Cecil to Lloyd George, Feb. 4, 1919, copied in Balfour papers, FO 800/215.
93 Cecil diary, Feb. 4 and 5, 1919.
94 Georgina Howell, *Daughter of the Desert: The Remarkable Life of Gertrude Bell* (Basingstoke: Macmillan, 2006), ch. 10.
95 Cecil to Lady Cecil, Jan. 22, 1919, CHE 6/13. Others enjoyed the food at the Majestic, seeing it as a relief from war-rationed Britain; for instance, see Hankey, *Supreme Command,* 74.
96 Cecil diary, Jan. 22 1919; Jan. 31, 1919. Cecil to Lady Cecil, Jan. 22. 1919, CHE 6/13.
97 Cecil diary, Feb. 4, 1919.
98 Lady Cecil to Lord Cecil, Jan. 26, 1919, CHE 18/10.
99 Cecil diary, Jan. 15, 1919.

100 Cecil diary, Jan. 28, 1919.
101 Hugh Cecil and Mirabel Cecil, *Imperial Marriage: An Edwardian War and Peace* (London: John Murray, 2002), 5–10.
102 Cecil diary, Feb. 2, 1919.
103 Cecil diary, Jan. 17, 1919.
104 Cecil diary, Feb. 2, 1919.
105 Miller, *Diary*, Jan. 26, 1919.
106 Cecil to Lady Cecil, Feb. 1, 1919, CHE 6/16.
107 Cecil diary, Jan. 15, 1919.
108 Cecil diary, Jan. 21, 1919
109 Hoover, *Memoirs*, vol. 1, 480–2.
110 Hoover, *Two Peacemakers in Paris*, xliv.
111 There is very little historical writing about the importance of dinner parties in early 20th century British politics, but it is worthwhile to note that Winston Churchill, another notable dinner companion, similarly had a penchant for dinner companions sometimes chosen for political and diplomatic purposes, but also often chosen simply to "satisfy his wide-ranging curiosity" about non-political topics; see Cita Stelzer, *Dinner with Churchill: Policy-Making at the Dinner Table* (London: Short Books, 2011), ch. 1 and p. 224.
112 Giovanni Dell'Orto, *American Journalism and International Relations: Foreign Correspondence from the Early Republic to the Digital Era* (Cambridge: Cambridge University Press, 2013), 106.
113 John Maxwell Hamilton, *Journalism's Roving Eye: A History of American Foreign Reporting* (Baton Rouge: Louisiana State University Press, 2009), 168–9.
114 Jonathan Silberstein-Loeb, *The International Distribution of News: The Associated Press, Press Association, and Reuters, 1848–1947* (Cambridge: Cambridge University Press, 2014).
115 "The Peace Conference: Meeting Next Saturday," *Times of India*, Jan. 18, 1919, p. 9.
116 Hamilton, *Journalism's Roving Eye*, 151.
117 Joseph R. Hayden, *Negotiating in the Press: American Journalism and Diplomacy, 1918–1919* (Baton Rouge: Louisiana State University Press, 2010), 94.
118 William Allen White, *The Autobiography of William Allen White* (New York: Macmillan, 1946), 549, 560.
119 Hayden, *Negotiating in the Press*, 89.
120 Hamilton, *Journalism's Roving Eye*, 142–3.
121 Harold Nicolson, *Peacemaking 1919* (New York: Grosset & Dunlap, 1965), 241.
122 Cecil diary, Jan. 14, 1919.
123 For an example of such off-the-record discussions, see his meeting with Jean Herbette, the foreign editor of *Le Temps* in Paris, from Cecil diary, Jan. 9, 1919, who the next day published what to Cecil's mind was "a very accurate account

of our conversation, though not expressly attributed to me, so that he has done exactly what I asked him to do." Cecil diary, Jan. 11, 1919.
124 Cecil diary, Jan. 8, 1919.

3 Fashioning the Covenant: February 1–14

1 David Hunter Miller, *The Drafting of the Covenant*, vol. I (New York and London: G.P. Putnam's Sons, 1928), prefatory note.
2 Erez Manela, *The Wilsonian Moment: Self-Determination and the International Origins of Anticolonial Nationalism* (New York and Oxford: Oxford University Press, 2006), 71, 74, 104, 108.
3 Peter Jackson, *Beyond the Balance of Power: France and the Politics of National Security in the Era of the First World War* (Cambridge: Cambridge University Press, 2013), chs. 7–8.
4 Cecil diary, Feb. 1, 1919.
5 Cecil diary, Feb. 1, 1919.
6 Cecil diary, Feb. 3, 1919.
7 Cecil diary, Feb. 3, 1919.
8 Cecil diary, Feb. 3, 1919.
9 Cecil to Lady Cecil, Feb. 3, 1919, CHE 6/47.
10 House diary, in Arthur S. Link, ed., *The Papers of Woodrow Wilson*, vol. 54 (Princeton, NJ: Princeton University Press, 1966–1994), 459–60.
11 Cecil diary, Feb. 3, 1919.
12 Miller, *Drafting*, 130–6.
13 Cecil diary, Feb. 3, 1919.
14 Miller, *Drafting*, 123.
15 Miller, *Drafting*, ch. X.
16 David Hunter Miller, "The Making of the League of Nations," in *What Really Happened at Paris: The Story of the Peace Conference, 1918–1919. By American Delegates*, ed. Edward M. House and Charles Seymour (New York: Charles Scribner's Sons, 1921).
17 Cecil diary, Jan. 31, 1919.
18 Headlam-Morley to John Bailey, Feb. 15, 1919, in Sir James Headlam-Morley, *A Memoir of the Paris Peace Conference 1919* (London: Methuen, 1972); and Miller, "The Making of the League of Nations," 408.
19 W. K. Hancock, *Smuts: The Sanguine Years, 1870–1919* (Cambridge: Cambridge University Press, 1962), 507; and Antony Lentin, *General Smuts: South Africa* (London: Haus, 2010), 58–9.
20 Headlam-Morley to John Bailey, Feb. 15, 1919.

21 Hugh Cecil and Mirabel Cecil, *Imperial Marriage: An Edwardian War and Peace* (London John Murray, 2002), 97.
22 Miller, *Drafting*, 126.
23 Miller, *Drafting*, 123–6.
24 Cecil diary, Feb. 4, 1919.
25 Stephen Bonsal, *Unfinished Business* (New York: Doubleday, Doran, 1944), 26.
26 Cecil diary, Feb. 4, 1919; and Miller, *The Drafting*, 156.
27 Cecil diary, Jan. 13, 1919.
28 David Hunter Miller, *My Diary at the Peace Conference of Paris, with Documents* (New York: Printed for the author by the Appeal printing company, 1924), Jan. 21, 1919.
29 Cecil diary, Jan. 31, 1919.
30 Cecil diary, Feb. 4, 1919.
31 Cecil diary, Feb. 5, 1919.
32 Cecil diary, Feb. 5, 1919.
33 Another description of the Cecil-centrism of this selection process is in James Barros, "The Role of Sir Eric Drummond," in *The League of Nations in Retrospect: Proceedings of the Symposium* (Berlin and New York: Walter de Gruyter, 1983), 31–4.
34 Cecil diary, Feb. 6, 1919; Andrew Dalby, *Eleftherios Venizelos: Greece* (London: Haus, 2010), 95, 101; and James Barros, *Office without Power: Secretary-General Sir Eric Drummond, 1919-1933* (Oxford: Clarendon Press, 1979), 3–4.
35 See Hankey's report of IWC meeting where on the League there was "Satisfactory Discussion, Tending in the Direction I Have Always Advocated." Hankey diary, Dec. 24, 1918, HNKY 1/5.
36 That is, Barros, *Office without Power*, 2.
37 Avner Offer, *The First World War: An Agrarian Interpretation* (Oxford: Oxford University Press, 1989), Part 3.
38 Hankey to Lord Esher, Feb. 16, 1919, HNKY 4/11.
39 Cecil diary, Feb. 6, 1919.
40 Miller, *Drafting*, 168–74.
41 Bonsal, *Unfinished Business*, 29.
42 Memo on "Art. V of the Covenant. President Wilson and Arbitration," with many notes by Cecil. Court and Arbitration Folder, NBKR 4X/28.
43 Miller, *Drafting*, 168–74.
44 E. J. Dillon, *The Inside Story of the Peace Conference* (New York and London: Harper & Brothers, 1920), 493.
45 Geoffrey Sherington, *Australia's Immigrants 1788-1978* (Sydney: George Allen & Unwin, 1980), 91. Hughes to House, May 5, 1919, quoted in Carl Bridge, *William Hughes: Australia* (London: Haus, 2011), 83.

46 Bridge, *William Hughes*, 69.
47 Kristofer Allerfeldt, "Wilsonian Pragmatism? Woodrow Wilson, Japanese Immigration, and the Paris Peace Conference," *Diplomacy and Statecraft* 15 (2004): 559–64.
48 Paul Birdsall, *Versailles Twenty Years after* (London: George Allen & Unwin, 1941), 94–5.
49 Cecil diary, Feb. 6, 1919.
50 Miller, *Drafting*, 243–59.
51 Bonsal, *Unfinished Business*, 30.
52 Miller, *Drafting*, 212–17.
53 Cecil diary, Feb. 9, 1919.
54 Cecil diary, Feb. 13, 1919.
55 See meeting between Cecil and Bourgeois, Cecil diary, Feb. 17, 1919.
56 Miller, *Drafting*, 260–2.
57 Cecil diary, Feb. 12, 1919.
58 Cecil diary, Feb. 14, 1919.
59 Cecil diary, Feb. 14, 1919.
60 Georges-Henri Soutou, *L'or et le sang: Les buts de guerre économique de la Premiere Guerre Mondiale* (Paris: Fayard, 1989), 484–6.
61 Cecil diary, Feb. 15, 1919.
62 Bonsal, *Unfinished Business*, 52–6.
63 Miller, *Drafting*, 268–9.
64 *New York Times*, May 29, 1921, 24.
65 Cecil diary, Feb. 12, 1919.
66 Miller, *Drafting*, 122.
67 Cecil diary, Feb. 13, 1919.
68 Cecil to Lady Cecil, Feb. 1, 1919, CHE 6/16.
69 Cecil diary, Feb. 7, 1919 (but Cecil's diary is inaccurate here, the meeting actually took place on Feb. 8).
70 Cecil diary, Feb. 8, 1919.
71 Feb. 10, 1919 (3:00), SWC 13th session, 3rd meeting. *British Documents on Foreign Affairs—Reports and Papers from the Foreign Office Confidential Print. Part II, From the First to the Second World War. Series I, the Paris Peace Conference of 1919*, vol. 2, ed. M. L. Dockrill, Kenneth Bourne, and Donald Cameron Watt (Frederick, MD: University Publications of America, 1989) (hereafter *BDFA*).
72 Cecil to Lady Cecil, Jan. 28, 1919, CHE 6/17; and Cecil to Lady Cecil, Feb. 7, 1919, CHE 6/18.
73 Cecil diary, Feb. 10, 1919.
74 Cecil diary, Feb. 11, 1919.
75 Cecil diary, Feb. 14, 1919.

76 Pity the poor translator: Bonsal complained about "having to translate his (Bourgeois's) interminable speeches, while Cecil and the rest of the great men can let their thoughts wander off to more agreeable pastures." *Unfinished Business*, 30.
77 Cecil to Lady Cecil, Feb. 14, 1919. CHE 6/21.
78 Miller, *Diary*, Feb. 14, 1919.
79 Gaynor Johnson, *Lord Robert Cecil: Politician and Internationalist* (Farnham, UK: Ashgate, 2013), 106; George W. Egerton, *Great Britain and the Creation of the League of Nations: Strategy, Politics, and International Organization, 1914–1919* (Chapel Hill: University of North Carolina Press, 1978), 139–40; and Seth Tillman, *Anglo-American Relations at the Paris Peace Conference of 1919* (Princeton, NJ: Princeton University Press, 1961), 132–3.
80 Major-General Sir C. E. Callwell, *Field-Marshall Sir Henry Wilson: His Life and Diaries*, vol. II (London: Cassell, 1927), 169.
81 Egerton, *Great Britain and the Creation of the League of Nations*, 119–29; and Inga Floto, *Colonel House in Paris: A Study of American Policy at the Paris Peace Conference 1919* (Princeton, NJ: Princeton University Press, 1980), 90.
82 Cecil diary, Feb. 4, 1919.

4 Feeding Germany: Mid-February through March

1 Sir Ian Malcolm, *Lord Balfour: A Memory* (London: Macmillan, 1930), 103.
2 Herbert Hoover, *Memoirs* (New York: Macmillan, 1951–2), 341–52.
3 Robert Gerwarth, *The Vanquished: Why the First World War Failed to End* (New York: Farrar, Straus and Giroux, 2016), 248.
4 C. Paul Vincent, *The Politics of Hunger: The Allied Blockade of Germany, 1915–1919* (Athens and London: Ohio University Press, 1985), 50.
5 Phillip Dehne, "The Ministry of Blockade and the Fate of Free Trade during the First World War," *Twentieth Century British History* 27, no. 3 (2016).
6 On the French prioritization of employment, see Marc Trachtenberg, "'A New Economic Order': Etienne Clementel and French Economic Diplomacy during the First World War," *French Historical Studies* 10, no. 2 (1977): 333.
7 In his *Memoirs,* Hoover describes himself and his fellow American delegates as being completely incapable of understanding why British or French leaders might favor not favor immediately reinstating free trade.
8 For example, Vincent, *The Politics of Hunger*, ch. 5. On opposition in Britain to continuing the blockade during the armistice period, see Martin Ceadel, *Semi-Detached Idealists: The British Peace Movement and International Relations, 1854–1945* (Oxford: Oxford University Press, 2000), 239–41; and Bruno Cabanes, *The Great War and the Origins of Humanitarianism, 1918–1924* (Cambridge: Cambridge University Press, 2014), 274–80.

9   For example, Lord Hankey, *The Supreme Command 1914–1918*, vol. 2 (London: George Allen and Unwin, 1961), ch. 82.
10 Letter from Hoover to Colonel House, Feb. 13, 1917, printed in Herbert Hoover, *The Ordeal of Woodrow Wilson* (New York: McGraw-Hill, 1958), 5–6.
11 "Lords and Labour Claims," *The Times*, Feb. 20, 1919, p. 9.
12 "Liberty in Industry, an Analogy from Politics." Letter from Cecil to *The Times* on Feb. 22, 1919, printed on Mon., Feb. 24, p. 12.
13 International Labour Office, "Profit-Sharing and Labour Co-Partnership in Great Britain," *International Labour Review* 4 (1921): 114–26.
14 Larry G. Gerber, "Corporatism in Comparative Perspective: The Impact of the First World War on American and British Labour Relations," *The Business History Review* 62, no. 1 (1988): 106–8, 125; Charles Maier, *Recasting Bourgeois Europe: Stabilization in France, Germany, and Italy in the Decade after World War I* (Princeton, NJ: Princeton University Press, 1975), 138–50; and Niall Ferguson, *The Pity of War* (New York: Basic Books, 1999), 396.
15 "League of Nations. Lord Robert Cecil on Its Practical Effect." *Sunday Times*, Feb. 23, 1919, p. 7.
16 "League not panacea, But Best Plan Offered to Prevent War, Cecil Says." *Baltimore Sun*, Feb. 23, 1919, p. 22.
17 Riddell diary of Feb. 23, 1919, in Lord George Allardice Riddell, *Lord Riddell's Intimate Diary of the Peace Conference and after, 1918–1923* (London: Victor Gollancz, 1933), 24–5.
18 George Goldberg, *The Peace to End Peace: The Paris Peace Conference of 1919* (New York: Harcourt, Brace & World, 1969), 188–9.
19 Cecil to Lady Cecil, Mar. 1, 1919. CHE 6/24.
20 Dehne, "The Ministry of Blockade."
21 Eustace Percy, *Some Memories* (London: Eyre & Spottiswoode, 1958), 72.
22 Feb. 25, 1919 (3:00 p.m.), 2nd meeting, Cecil chairing. *British Documents on Foreign Affairs—Reports and Papers from the Foreign Office Confidential Print. Part II, From the First to the Second World War. Series I, the Paris Peace Conference of 1919*, vol. 12, ed. M. L. Dockrill, Kenneth Bourne, and Donald Cameron Watt (Frederick, MD: University Publications of America, 1989).
23 Cecil diary, Mar. 21, 1919. Add. Ms. 51131.
24 Kendrick A. Clements, *The Life of Herbert Hoover: Imperfect Visionary 1918–1928* (New York: Palgrave Macmillan, 2010), 3–5.
25 Clements, *The Life of Herbert Hoover*, 10.
26 Letter from House to Wilson, Nov. 27, 1918, in Hoover, *The Ordeal of Woodrow Wilson*, 95.
27 Clements, *The Life of Herbert Hoover*, 12.
28 McCormick diary, Nov. 19, 1917, in Michael Barton, ed., *Citizen Extraordinaire: The Diplomatic Diaries of Vance McCormick in London and Paris, 1917–1919*,

with *Other Documents from a High-Minded American Life* (Mechanicsburg, PA: Stackpole Books, 2004).

29 For example, Austen Chamberlain immediately informed Cecil when appointing Keynes as the Treasury representative to the SEC on Feb. 24; see John Maynard Keynes, *Collected Writings of John Maynard Keynes, Volume XVI: Activities 1914–1919: The Treasury and Versailles* (London: Macmillan, 1971), 415.
30 Keynes, *Collected Writings*, 415.
31 Cecil diary, Feb. 27, 1919.
32 Cecil's characterization of Hughes in David Hunter Miller, *My Diary at the Peace Conference of Paris, with Documents* (New York: Printed for the author by the Appeal printing company, 1924), Mar. 18.
33 Kristofer Allerfeldt, "Wilsonian Pragmatism? Woodrow Wilson, Japanese Immigration, and the Paris Peace Conference," *Diplomacy and Statecraft* 15 (2004): 555.
34 Feb. 27 (5:00 p.m.), 10th BED meeting, BDFA, Part II, Series I: The Paris Peace Conference of 1919. Vol. 3.
35 Tammy M. Proctor, "An American enterprise? British Participation in US Food Relief Programmes (1914–1923)," *First World War Studies* 5, no. 1 (2014): 35–7.
36 Hoover, *Memoirs*, vol. 1, 297.
37 On the important successes of the AMTC in 1918, see Elizabeth Greenhalgh, *Victory through Coalition: Britain and France during the First World War* (Cambridge: Cambridge University Press, 2005), ch. 10.
38 Hoover to Wilson on Jan. 1, 1919, and Wilson's approval of Hoover's plan on Jan. 13, 1919, in Herbert Hoover, *Two Peacemakers in Paris: The Hoover-Wilson Post-Armistice Letters* (College Station: Texas A&M University Press, 1978), 38–40.
39 Gary Dean Best, "Food Relief as Price Support: Hoover and American Pork, January-March 1919," *Agricultural History* 45, 2 (1971): 79–84.
40 Letter of Jan. 14, 1919, quoted in Keynes, *Collected Writings*, 391–4.
41 Hoover, *Memoirs*, 329.
42 H. W. V. Temperley, ed., *A History of the Peace Conference of Paris*, vol. I (London: Henry Frowde and Hodder & Stoughton, 1920), 311.
43 Klaus Schwabe, *Woodrow Wilson, Revolutionary Germany, and Peacemaking, 1918–1919: Missionary Diplomacy and the Realities of Power* (Chapel Hill: University of North Carolina Press, 1985), 192–3.
44 Harry R. Rudin, *Armistice 1918* (New Haven, CT: Yale University Press, 1944), 381.
45 BED, Secret W.C.P. 187. "The Economic Situation in Europe." Memorandum by Lord Robert Cecil, Mar. 2, 1919, CHE 31/27.
46 Copy of Keynes report of Mar. 7, 1919, in NBKR 4X/34.
47 Cecil to Lady Cecil, Mar. 5, 1919. CHE 6/28.
48 Cecil to Lady Cecil, Mar. 6, 1919. CHE 6/29.

49 Mar. 7, 1919 (12:00), 6th SEC meeting, Cecil chair. BDFA, Part II, Series I: The Paris Peace Conference of 1919. Vol. 12.
50 McCormick diary, Mar. 10, 1919, in Barton,*Citizen Extraordinaire*; Baruch diary, May 20, 1919, Peace Negotiations Memoranda, Comments and Notes in Diary Form; April 12–June 27, 1919; Bernard M. Baruch Papers, vol. 656; and Public Policy Papers, Department of Rare Books and Special Collections, Princeton University Library.
51 Hoover, *Memoirs*, vol. 1, 341.
52 In his often egomaniacal *Memoirs*, Hoover claims that in front of the Big Four, "Cecil read my proposed agreement and endorsed it." 341–52.
53 Robert Skidelsky, *John Maynard Keynes: A Biography. Vol. 1. Hopes Betrayed, 1883–1920* (London: Macmillan, 1983), 360–2.
54 Mar. 8, 1919 meeting of the SWC, *BDFA* vol. 2.
55 Skidelsky, *John Maynard Keynes, Vol. I*, 362.
56 Cecil diary, Mar. 8, 1919.
57 Schwabe, *Woodrow Wilson*, 205. Herbert Hoover later claimed, apparently incorrectly, that the plan passed by the SWC (Council of Ten) on March 8 was one that he had created with the help of Cecil; see Hoover, *The Ordeal of Woodrow Wilson*, 163–5. Thomas Lamont also claimed to have authored the compromise, saying that when he returned from Spa, he and a few others were sent into a room by Clemenceau, Lloyd George, and House, where "they locked us in and we worked out a formula by which a certain amount of gold was to be sent with the (German) ships," a decision then ratified by the three leaders of the SWC; see Thomas Lamont, "Reparations: Questions Answered," in *What Really Happened at Paris: The Story of the Peace Conference, 1918-1919. By American Delegates*, ed. Edward M. House and Charles Seymour (New York: Charles Scribner's Sons, 1921), 485.
58 Donald Markwell, *John Maynard Keynes and International Relations* (Oxford: Oxford University Press, 2006), 60–3.
59 Cecil diary, Mar. 1919; Markwell, *John Maynard Keynes*, 60–3.
60 McCormick (incorrectly) saw the SWC's decision as sending back to Germany the same proposal that Germany demanded at Spa; McCormick diary, Mar. 8, 1919.
61 Among those suggesting that the Brussels agreement followed an Anglo-American plan, see Arno Mayer, *Politics and Diplomacy of Peacemaking: Containment and Counterrevolution at Versailles, 1918-1919* (New York: Alfred A. Knopf, 1967), 509–13. For a view of the Brussels agreement as a victory for Hoover, see Schwabe, *Woodrow Wilson*, 208–9.
62 Cecil to Lady Cecil, Mar. 9, 1919. CHE 6/30.
63 Mar. 17, 1919 (10:00 a.m.), 8th SEC meeting, Clementel chair, *BDFA* vol. 12. Also Keynes, *Collected Writings XVI*, 415.

64 24 Mar. 1919 (10:00 a.m.), 10th meeting, Cecil chair. *BDFA* vol. 12.
65 Barton, *Citizen Extraordinaire*, 135 (diary entry for Mar. 28, 1919).
66 McCormick believed, as the US delegates tended to do, that the British were wary of releasing the blockade due to their desires "to protect British trade." Barton, *Citizen Extraordinaire*, 133 (diary entry for Mar. 24, 1919).
67 Report of Cecil to BED, Mar. 2, 1919, CHE 31/27.
68 Cecil diary, Feb. 13, 1919.
69 Clements, *The Life of Herbert Hoover*, 4.
70 For Clémentel's hopes for permanent post-war allied economic cooperation and control of natural resources, see Trachtenberg, "A New Economic Order."
71 Mar. 1 (11:30 a.m.), 11th BED meeting, *BDFA* vol. 3.
72 Cecil diary, Mar. 9, 1919.
73 "Lord R. Cecil on the League," *The Times*, Mar. 10, 1919, p. 11.
74 Memos of Mar. 5-7, 1919 between J.M. Butler and Cecil, in "Folder: Discussion re neutral powers, especially Switzerland," NBKR 4X/28.
75 Cecil diary, Mar. 10, 1919.
76 "Neutrals and the League," *The Times*, Feb. 26, 1919, p. 10.
77 Cecil diary, Mar. 11, 1919.
78 John Milton Cooper, *Breaking the Heart of the World: Woodrow Wilson and the Fight for the League of Nations* (Cambridge: Cambridge University Press, 2001), 55-7.
79 Miller, *Diary*, Mar. 11, 1919.
80 Inga Floto, *Colonel House in Paris: A Study of American Policy at the Paris Peace Conference 1919* (Princeton, NJ: Princeton University Press, 1980), 149-63.
81 Antony Lentin, *General Smuts: South Africa* (London: Haus, 2010), 64.
82 Cecil to Percy, 13/3/1919, NBKR 4X/26.
83 "Lord R. Cecil on the Covenant," *The Times*, Wed., Mar. 19, 1919, p. 11.
84 Floto, *Colonel House in Paris*, 178-85.
85 Cecil diary, Mar. 16, 1919; House diary, in Arthur Link, ed., *The Papers of Woodrow Wilson*, vol. 55 (Princeton, NJ: Princeton University Press, 1966-94), 538-9.
86 Miller, *Diary*, Mar. 18, 1919.
87 Floto, *Colonel House in Paris*, 173.
88 Miller, *Diary*, Mar. 18, 1919.
89 Hughes's 'Notes on the Draft Covenant', 21/3/1919, in NBKR 4X/31-2; L.F. Fitzhardinge, "W.M. Hughes and the Treaty of Versailles, 1919," *Journal of Commonwealth Political Studies* 5, no. 2 (1967): 138-9.
90 Cecil diary, Mar. 14, 1919.
91 Cecil diary, Mar. 22, 1919.
92 Miller, *Drafting*, ch. XXV; Cecil diary, Feb. 28, 1919; Letter from Cecil to House on Mar. 8 explaining Clemenceau's interest was in security, not in creating an army, in Paul Birdsall, *Versailles Twenty Years after* (London: George Allen & Unwin, 1941), 131-2.

93 Cecil to Lady Cecil, Mar. 28, 1919, CHE 6/35.
94 Bonsal, *Unfinished Business*, 160.
95 House diary, Mar. 27, 1919, in *The Papers of Woodrow Wilson*, vol. 56, 335.
96 Miller, *Diary*, Mar. 20–22, 1919.
97 Cecil diary, Mar. 24, 1919.
98 Lady Cecil to Lord Cecil, Mar. 12, 1919, CHE 18/36.
99 Cecil diary, Mar. 9, 1919.
100 Mar. 27, 1919 (11:30 a.m.), Council of Foreign Ministers meeting, *BDFA* vol. 3.
101 According to an *Art and Archaeology* review (vol. 9, 1920, p. 288), a display of twenty-three of these busts went on display at the Reinhardt Galleries in New York, and would be traveling to the Chicago Art Institute and a half-dozen other places around the United States.
102 "Peace Conferees Shown in Bronze," *New York Times*, June 19, 1919, p. 9.
103 Lady Cecil to Lord Cecil, Mar. 22, 1919, CHE 18/39.
104 Philip Baker looked into getting Cranborne as an assistant for Cecil in what was obviously an attempt to make some work for his not particularly serious 26-year-old nephew. On Feb. 26, Baker explained to Cecil that he had spoken to Theodore Russell back at the FO, and that Cranborne "was to come to the Foreign Office this morning and give his final decision, but at 12:50 p.m. had not turned up." NBKR 4X/28.
105 Cecil to Lady Cecil, Apr. 4, 1919. CHE 6/37.
106 W. M. Hughes, *Crusts and Crusades; Tales of Bygone Days* (Sydney: Angus and Robertson, 1947), 232–4. On British women in Paris in 1919, see Helen McCarthy, *Women of the World: The Rise of the Female Diplomat* (London: Bloomsbury, 2014), 81–5.
107 Cecil diary, Mar. 26, 1919.
108 Cecil to Lady Cecil, Mar. 13, 1919, CHE 6/31.
109 Cecil to Lady Cecil, Mar. 19, 1919, CHE 6/32.
110 Lady Cecil to Cecil, Mar. 22, 1919, CHE 18/39.
111 Grayson diary, Mar. 18, 1919, in *The Papers of Woodrow Wilson*, vol. 56, 62.
112 Hoover, *Memoirs*, 480–2.
113 Hankey diary, July 2, 1919, HNKY 1/5.
114 Cecil, *Imperial Marriage*, 98.
115 Hoover, *Memoirs*, vol. 1, 297–8.
116 Clement, *The Life of Herbert Hoover*, 5.
117 Hoover, *Memoirs*, vol. 1, 352.
118 Hoover, *Two Peacemakers in Paris*, xxxi.
119 Hoover, *Memoirs*, vol. 1, 298–300. For Hoover's take on how European mentalities made a lasting peace impossible, see his *The Ordeal of Woodrow Wilson*.
120 Barton, *Citizen Extraordinaire*, 119 (diary entry of Mar. 1, 1919).
121 Cecil diary, Mar. 28, 1919.

122 Mar. 28, 1919 (11:00 a.m.), Council of Foreign Ministers, *BDFA* vol. 1.
123 Vincent, *Politics of Hunger*, 115–23.

5 Impending Catastrophe: April

1 Shari Benstock, *Women of the Left Bank: Paris 1900–1940* (Austin: University of Texas Press, 1986), 40–2; and Hermione Lee, *Edith Wharton* (New York: Alfred A. Knopf, 2007), 290.
2 Quoted in R. J. Q. Adams, *Balfour: The Last Grandee* (London: John Murray, 2007), 110; Sir Ian Malcolm, *Lord Balfour: A Memory* (London: Macmillan, 1930), 103.
3 Cecil diary, Apr. 2, 1919.
4 Antony Lentin, *General Smuts: South Africa* (London: Haus, 2010), ch. 4.
5 John Maynard Keynes, *Collected Writings of John Maynard Keynes, Volume XVI: Activities 1914–1919: The Treasury and Versailles* (London: Macmillan, 1971), 417–29.
6 "Paralysis of Europe. A Task Too Great for Tired Men," *Manchester Guardian,* Apr. 2, 1919.
7 Cecil diary, Apr. 3 and 4, 1919.
8 Cecil's suggestion to Lloyd George that it was the French who had the most extreme demands was probably wrong, perhaps even intentionally so. On the moderate level of French demands compared to those of the British commissioners, and Clemenceau's hopes for a fixed sum in the Treaty, see Marc Trachtenberg, "Reparation at the Paris Peace Conference," *Journal of Modern History* 51, no. 1 (1979): 24–55.
9 Apr. 4, 1919 from Cecil to Lloyd George, Add. Ms. 51076.
10 Marc Trachtenberg, "'A New Economic Order': Etienne Clementel and French Economic Diplomacy during the First World War," *French Historical Studies* 10, no. 2. (1977).
11 See Cecil's support for the Foreign Office Political Intelligence department report on post-war economic policy as a threat against Germany during the war; 1/8/1918, copy in Economic Commission, League of Nations 1919/1920 folder, NBKR 4X/34.
12 On the transformation of Cecil's Free Trade ideas during the war, see Phillip Dehne, "The Ministry of Blockade and the Fate of Free Trade during the First World War," *Twentieth Century British History* 27, no. 3 (2016): 354–5.
13 SEC address can be seen in subcommittee memos attached to SEC minutes of Apr. 15; also, J. A. Salter, *Allied Shipping Control: An Experiment in International Administration* (Oxford: Clarendon Press, 1921), 229.
14 Cecil diary, Mar. 26, 1919.

15 Cecil diary, Mar. 26, 1919.
16 Cecil diary, Mar. 29, 1919.
17 Donald Markwell, *John Maynard Keynes and International Relations* (Oxford: Oxford University Press, 2006), 65-7.
18 Seth Tillman, *Anglo-American Relations at the Paris Peace Conference of 1919* (Princeton, NJ: Princeton University Press, 1961), 268-9.
19 Étienne Clémentel, *La France et la Politique Économique Interalliée* (New Haven, CT: Yale University Press, 1931), 317.
20 Minutes of meeting of Raw Material Section, Apr. 4, 1919, Baruch Papers, Box/Volume 391; Jean Monnet, *Mémoires* (Paris: Fayard, 1976), 86.
21 Baruch Papers, Box/Volume 390.
22 Finance Section memo, Apr. 9, 1919, Baruch Papers, Box/Volume 391.
23 Michael Barton, ed., *Citizen Extraordinaire: The Diplomatic Diaries of Vance McCormick in London and Paris, 1917-1919, with Other Documents from a High-Minded American life* (Mechanicsburg, PA: Stackpole Books, 2004), 145 (diary entry for Apr. 8, 1919).
24 Barton, *Citizen Extraordinaire*, 142 (diary entry for Apr. 4, 1919); "British Deny Trade Cables Leak Secrets," *New York Tribune*, Apr. 6, 1919.
25 "Note Submitted by the British Delegates on the General Economic Position in Europe," appendix to meeting of Apr. 7, 1919 (10:00 a.m.), 11th SEC meeting, Cecil chair, *British Documents on Foreign Affairs—Reports and Papers from the Foreign Office Confidential Print. Part II, From the First to the Second World War. Series I, the Paris Peace Conference of 1919*, vol. 12, ed. M. L. Dockrill, Kenneth Bourne, and Donald Cameron Watt (Frederick, MD: University Publications of America, 1989).
26 Apr. 7 and 9, 1919, 11th SEC meeting, Cecil chair. *BDFA* vol. 12.
27 Cecil diary, Apr. 9, 1919.
28 Fred B. Pitney, "What Language Does Peace Speak?" *New York Tribune*, Apr. 6, 1919.
29 In a very impressionistic bit of evidence, the number of times that the word "Paris" was mentioned in the *San Francisco Chronicle* went from a peak of 320 in March to only 203 in June, the month that the Treaty was signed. In the *Washington Post*, the decline was from 223 in March to 144 in June.
30 William Allen White, *The Autobiography of William Allen White* (New York: Macmillan, 1946), 566.
31 Chester M. Wright, "The Peace Show," *New York Tribune*, Mar. 20, 1919, p. 12.
32 White, *Autobiography*, 566.
33 Hugh Cecil, "The Development of Lord Robert Cecil's Views on the Securing of a Lasting Peace 1915-1919" (D.Phil thesis, Oxford University, Oxford, 1971), 232.
34 George W. Egerton, *Great Britain and the Creation of the League of Nations: Strategy, Politics, and International Organization, 1914-1919* (Chapel Hill: University of North Carolina Press, 1978), 156-62.

35 David Hunter Miller, *The Drafting of the Covenant*, vol. I (New York and London: G.P. Putnam's Sons, 1928), 339–50.
36 Miller, *Drafting*, 350–3.
37 Miller, *Diary*, Mar. 26, 1919.
38 Cecil diary, Apr. 3, 1919.
39 Miller, *Drafting*, ch. XXIX.
40 Apr. 4, 1919 from Cecil to Lloyd George, Add. Ms. 51076.
41 Cecil to Balfour, Apr. 5, 1919, Add. Ms. 51071A.
42 Balfour to "My dear Bob," Apr. 7, 1919, Add. Ms. 51071A.
43 Cecil diary, Mar. 28, 1919.
44 Cecil diary, Mar. 29, 1919.
45 Cecil diary, Apr. 8, 1919.
46 Confidential letter from Cecil to House on Apr. 8, 1919, reprinted in Miller, *Drafting*, 419–21, and also in Arthur Link, ed., *The Papers of Woodrow Wilson*, vol. 57 (Princeton, NJ: Princeton University Press, 1966–94), 143–4; and Add. Ms. 51094.
47 Cecil diary, Apr. 8, 1919 but includes account of the ensuing two days.
48 Tillman, *Anglo-American Relations*, 291–4.
49 Jerry W. Jones, "The Naval Battle of Paris," *Naval War College Review* 62, no. 2 (2009): 84–5.
50 "Dramatic Discussion over Monroe Doctrine," *Boston Daily Globe*, Apr. 12, 1919; and "Britain Wins Day for U.S. on Monroe Issue," *New York Tribune*, Apr. 12, 1919.
51 14th League Commission meeting of Apr. 10, 1919, NBKR 4X/26.
52 15th League Commission meeting of Apr. 11, 1919, in *The Papers of Woodrow Wilson*, vol. 57, 256–7.
53 Miller, *Drafting*, vol. I, ch. XXVIII.
54 BED Minutes, Apr. 8, 1919 (11:30 a.m.), 18th meeting, *BDFA* vol. 4. On the anti-Bolshevik goals of the ILO, see Sandrine Kott, "Cold War Internationalism," in Internationalisms, ed. Glenda Sluga and Patricia Clavin, 342–7.
55 Cecil diary, Apr. 8, 1919.
56 Cecil diary, Mar. 29, 1919.
57 Cecil diary, Mar. 31, 1919.
58 David Hunter Miller, *My Diary at the Peace Conference of Paris, with Documents* (New York: Printed for the author by the Appeal printing company, 1924), Apr. 11, 1919.
59 Cecil diary, Apr. 11, 1919.
60 Paul Birdsall, *Versailles Twenty Years after* (London: George Allen & Unwin, 1941), 97–9.
61 David Hunter Miller, "The Making of the League of Nations," in *What Really Happened at Paris: The Story of the Peace Conference, 1918–1919. By American*

Delegates, ed. Edward M. House and Charles Seymour (New York: Charles Scribner's Sons, 1921), 415; and Miller, *Drafting*, 461.
62 Jay Winter, *Dreams of Peace and Freedom* (New Haven, CT and London: Yale University Press, 2006), 70.
63 L. F. Fitzhardinge, "W.M. Hughes and the Treaty of Versailles, 1919," *Journal of Commonwealth Political Studies* 5, no. 2 (1967): 139.
64 Kristofer Allerfeldt, "Wilsonian Pragmatism? Woodrow Wilson, Japanese Immigration, and the Paris Peace Conference," *Diplomacy and Statecraft*, 15 (2004): 559–64.
65 Cecil diary, Apr. 26, 1919.
66 Cecil to Lady Cecil, Mar. 30, 1919, CHE 6/36.
67 Cecil to Lady Cecil, Mar. 28, 1919, CHE 6/35.
68 Apr. 10, 1919, Cecil to Lloyd George, Add. Ms. 51076.
69 Barton, *Citizen Extraordinaire*, 146 (diary entry for Apr. 9, 1919).
70 Cecil diary, Apr. 11, 1919.
71 Cecil diary, Apr. 5, 1919.
72 House diary, Apr. 6, 1919, in *The Papers of Woodrow Wilson*, vols. 57, 53; and Cecil diary, Apr. 5, 1919.
73 "Cecil Sees Grave Economic Situation," *Wall Street Journal*, Apr. 17, 1919, p. 2.
74 "Lord R. Cecil on the League," *The Times*, Wed., Apr. 16, 1919, p. 11. "The League in Being This Summer. An Interview with Lord R. Cecil," *Manchester Guardian*, Apr. 16, 1919. Other clippings of 16/4/1919 in NBKR 4X/31–2.
75 Cecil diary, Apr. 12–19, 1919.
76 "Paris Debate To-Day," *The Times*, Wed., Apr. 16, 1919, p. 12.
77 A. J. P. Taylor, ed., *Lloyd George: A Diary by Frances Stevenson* (London: Hutchinson, 1971), 179, n. 3; and David Lloyd George, *The Truth about the Peace Treaties*, vol. 1 (London: Victor Gollancz, 1938), 562–3.
78 "Lord R. Cecil's High Reputation," *Manchester Guardian*, Apr. 14, 1919.
79 Lloyd George, Speech to the House of Commons, Apr. 16, 1919, *Parliamentary Debates*, Commons, 5th ser., vol. 114, cols. 2955–6. http://api.parliament.uk/historic-hansard/commons/1919/apr/16/world-going-to-pieces (accessed Dec. 18, 2018).
80 Inbal Rose, *Conservatism and Foreign Policy during the Lloyd George Coalition 1918–1922* (London: Frank Cass, 1999), 35–7.
81 "British Concern at Economic Outlook," *The Christian Science Monitor*, Apr. 18, 1919, p. 1; and *The Scotsman*, Apr. 17, 1919.
82 Taylor, *Lloyd George: A Diary*, 180–1.
83 "From Private Correspondence," *The Scotsman*, Apr. 17, 1919, p. 5.
84 "Peace Policy. Mr. Ll. George's Apologia," *The Times*, Thurs., Apr. 17, 1919, pp. 13–14.

85 Lord Robert Cecil, Speech to the House of Commons, Apr. 16, 1919, *Parliamentary Debates*, Commons, 5th ser., vol. 114, cols. 2961–71. http://api.parliament.uk/historic-hansard/commons/1919/apr/16/world-going-to-pieces (accessed Dec. 18, 2018).
86 "The economic position of Europe," *Manchester Guardian*, Apr. 19, 1919, p. 6.
87 *The Scotsman*, Apr. 17, 1919, p. 5.
88 Easter Recess (Adjournment), Apr. 16, 1919, *Parliamentary Debates*, Commons, 5th ser., vol. 114, cols. 3000-22. http://api.parliament.uk/historic-hansard/commons/1919/apr/16/easter-recess-adjournment-1 (accessed Dec. 18, 2018).
89 "British Concern at Economic Outlook," *Christian Science Monitor*, Apr. 18, 1919.
90 David Stevenson, "Britain, France and the Origins of German Disarmament, 1916–19," *Journal of Strategic Studies* 29, no. 2 (2006): 201.
91 Egerton, *Great Britain and the Creation of the League of Nations*, 57–62.
92 Cecil diary, Apr. 22, 1919.
93 Barton, *Citizen Extraordinaire*, 151 (diary entry of Apr. 17, 1919).
94 Cecil to Lady Cecil, undated but likely Apr. 6, 1919. CHE 6/23.
95 Cecil diary, Apr. 20, 1919.
96 Cecil diary, Apr. 20, 1919.
97 Paul Mantoux, *The Deliberations of the Council of Four*, Trans. and ed. Arthur Link and Manfred F. Boemeke (Princeton, NJ: Princeton University Press, 1992).
98 Cecil diary, Apr. 21, 1919.
99 Herbert Hoover, *America's First Crusade* (New York: Charles Scribner's Sons, 1942), 42–50.
100 Cecil diary, Apr. 22, 1919.
101 Tillman, *Anglo-American Relations*, 269.
102 Adam Tooze, *The Deluge: The Great War, America and the Remaking of the Global Order, 1916–1931* (New York: Viking, 2014), 300–1.
103 Keynes, *Collected Writings XVI*, 429–36.
104 Herbert Hoover, *The Ordeal of Woodrow Wilson* (New York: McGraw-Hill, 1958), 148–9.
105 Hankey's February 1919 correspondence with Esher and Lord Curzon in HNKY 4/11.
106 Copies of this report exist in various places, including NBKR 4X/38; and *BDFA* vol. 4.
107 Hankey to Adeline Hankey, Apr. 12, 1919, HNKY 3/25.
108 Hankey diary, Apr. 15, 1919, HNKY 1/5.
109 Stephen Roskill, *Hankey: Man of Secrets, Volume II 1919–1931* (London: Collins, 1972), 66–7.
110 Lord Hankey, *The Supreme Control at the Paris Peace Conference 1919* (London: George Allen & Unwin, 1963), 103–6.

111 Eustace Percy, *Some Memories* (London: Eyre & Spottiswoode, 1958), 69.
112 BED minutes, Apr. 21, 1919, 11:00 a.m. and 5:30 p.m., 25th and 26th meetings, *BDFA* vol. 4.
113 Miller, *Drafting*, 481.
114 Egerton, *Great Britain and the Creation of the League of Nations*, 203.
115 Sir Clement Jones, "W.M. Hughes at the Paris Peace Conference," HNKY 24/2.
116 Barton, *Citizen Extraordinaire*, 153 (diary entry of Apr. 21, 1919).
117 Cecil diary, Apr. 23, 1919.
118 Apr. 23, 1919 (10:00 a.m.), 14th SEC meeting, Cecil chair. *BDFA* vol. 12.
119 Cecil diary, Apr. 25, 1919. Hugh Cecil suggests that Robert Cecil had an important and bitter feud with the British Blockade and Admiralty authorities in London who resisted ending the blockade, but certainly the main resistance to ending the blockade was in Paris; see Cecil, "The Development of Lord Robert Cecil's Views," 336–42.
120 Cecil to Lloyd George and Balfour, Apr. 28, 1919, Add. Ms. 51076.
121 Cecil diary, Apr. 28, 1919; and Apr. 28 1919 (10:00 a.m.), 15th SEC meeting, Cecil chair, *BDFA* vol. 12.
122 Major-General Sir C. E. Callwell, *Field-Marshall Sir Henry Wilson: His Life and Diaries*, vol. II (London: Cassell and Company, 1927), 184.
123 Apr. 28, 1919 (10:00 a.m.), 15th SEC meeting, Cecil chair, *BDFA* vol. 12.
124 Cecil diary, Apr. 27, 1919.
125 Cecil diary, Apr. 30, 1919.
126 Walters to Shepardson, Apr. 29, 1919, quoted in Sami Sare, *The League of Nations and the Debate on Disarmament (1918–1919)* (Rome: Edizioni Nuova Cultura, 2013), 232.
127 For examples, see NBKR 4X/34.
128 Cecil diary, Apr. 28, 1919.
129 Cecil diary, May 4, 1919.
130 Cecil to Lady Cecil, Apr. 28, 1919, CHE 6/38.
131 Miller, *Diary*, Feb. 23 and 24.
132 Cecil diary, Apr. 27, 1919.
133 Virginia Woolf diary, Thurs., Aug. 19, 1920, in Anne Oliver Bell (ed.), *The Diary of Virginia Woolf, Volume Two: 1920–1924* (New York and London: Harcourt Brace Jovanovich, 1978), 59–60.
134 Wilson to Cecil, May 2, 1919, Add. Ms. 51094.
135 "English Press Comments on the Covenant on April 29th and 30th," NBKR 4X/31–2.
136 Press accounts of this decision to meet in October in the *New York Tribune*, the *Boston Daily Globe*, the *New York Times*, and elsewhere on Apr. 30, 1919.

6 Ending the Economic War: May

1. Tyler Stovall, *Paris and the Spirit of 1919: Consumer Struggles, Transnationalism and Revolution* (Cambridge: Cambridge University Press, 2012), ch. 4.
2. Peter Jackson, *Beyond the Balance of Power: France and the Politics of National Security in the Era of the First Word War* (Cambridge: Cambridge University Press, 2013), 329.
3. Characterization by a French minister to Cecil, Cecil diary, May 1, 1919.
4. May 1, 1919 (11:00 a.m.), Wilson, LG, Clemenceau and Pichon, and Hankey and Mantoux, Papers Relating to the Foreign Relations of the United States, 1919: The Paris Peace Conference, vol. V (Washington, DC: US Government Printing Office, 1919).
5. Antony Lentin, *Lloyd George and the Lost Peace: From Versailles to Hitler, 1919–1940* (Basingstoke: Palgrave, 2001), ch. 1.
6. Cecil diary, Apr. 23, 1919.
7. Superior Blockade Council memo, May 13, 1919, Bernard M. Baruch Papers, Box 387, Public Policy Papers, Department of Rare Books and Special Collections, Princeton University Library.
8. Cecil diary, Apr. 23, 1919.
9. May 5, 1919 (10:00 a.m.), 16th meeting, Cecil chair, *British Documents on Foreign Affairs—Reports and Papers from the Foreign Office Confidential Print. Part II, From the First to the Second World War. Series I, the Paris Peace Conference of 1919*, vol. 12, ed. M. L. Dockrill, Kenneth Bourne, and Donald Cameron Watt (Frederick, MD: University Publications of America, 1989).
10. Cecil diary, May 5, 1919.
11. "Conference Sanctions Terms of Peace," *Boston Globe*, May 7, 1919; and "To Keep Screws on Huns," *Baltimore Sun*, May 7, 1919.
12. Cecil diary, May 8, 1919.
13. Paul Mantoux, *The Deliberations of the Council of Four*, trans. and ed. Arthur Link and Manfred F. Boemeke, vol. II (Princeton, NJ: Princeton University Press, 1992), May 9, 1919, 9–11.
14. Council of Four meeting with SEC leaders, May 9, 1919 (10:30 a.m.), *FRUS* vol. 5.
15. Donald Markwell, *John Maynard Keynes and International Relations: Economic Paths to War and Peace* (Oxford: Oxford University Press, 2006), 65–7.
16. Baruch diary, Apr. 21, 1919 and May 9, 1919, Baruch Papers, Box 656.
17. George Goldberg, *The Peace to End Peace: The Paris Peace Conference of 1919* (New York: Harcourt, Brace & World, 1969), 189.
18. Cecil diary, Apr. 29 and May 8, 1919.
19. Baruch to Cecil, May 27, 1919, Baruch Papers, MC006, Box 381.
20. Baruch diary, May 2 and 3, 1919, Baruch Papers, Box 656.

21 Baruch to Wilson, May 7, 1919, Baruch Papers, Box 45.
22 Markwell, *John Maynard Keynes,* 65–7.
23 Lentin, *Lloyd George and the Lost Peace,* ch. 2.
24 William Morris Hughes, *Crusts and Crusades; Tales of Bygone Days* (Sydney: Angus and Robertson, 1947), 228–32.
25 On the failure of the European Economic Committee due to French rejections of reparation proposals, see Keynes to Bradbury, May 22, 1919, in John Maynard Keynes, *Collected Writings of John Maynard Keynes, Volume XVI: Activities 1914–1919: The Treasury and Versailles* (London: Macmillan, 1971), 447. On how Melchior's apocalyptic vision of Europe's economic future influenced Keynes during the Peace Conference, see Niall Ferguson, *Paper and Iron: Hamburg Business and German Politics in the Era of Inflation, 1897–1927* (Cambridge: Cambridge University Press, 1995), 226–8.
26 Keynes to Philip Kerr, May 10, 1919. Keynes, *Collected Writings XVI,* 441–3.
27 Sir Francis Oppenheimer, *Stranger Within: Autobiographical Pages* (London: Faber and Faber, 1960), 354–61.
28 T. G. Otte, "Between Hammer and Anvil: Sir Francis Oppenheimer, the Netherlands Overseas Trust and Allied Economic Warfare, 1914–1918," in *Diplomats at War: British and Commonwealth Diplomacy in Wartime,* ed. Christopher Baxter and Andrew Stewart (Leiden and Boston, MA: Martinus Nijhoff, 2008), 85–108.
29 Oppenheimer, *Stranger within,* chs. 17, 20, and 22.
30 Oppenheimer, *Stranger within,* 366.
31 Cecil diary, May 13, 1919.
32 Baruch diary, May 10, 1919, Baruch Papers, Box 656.
33 Cecil diary, May 13, 1919.
34 Keynes, *Collected Writings XVI,* 458.
35 Keynes, *Collected Writings XVI,* 459.
36 Cecil diary, May 24, 1919.
37 Baruch diary, May 27, 1919, Baruch Papers, Box 656.
38 "The Present Position with Regard to the Blockade of Germany," appendix to meeting of May 13, 1919 (12:00 noon), 18th SEC meeting, Cecil chair, *BDFA* vol. 12.
39 Cecil diary, May 14, 1919.
40 Mantoux, The Deliberations of the Council of Four, vol. II, May 14, 1919, 64–5.
41 May 14, 1919 (11:45 a.m.), Council of Four meeting, *FRUS* vol. 5.
42 "Providing for German Refusal; Close Blockade Plans," *Manchester Guardian,* May 15, 1919.
43 Margaret MacMillan, *Paris 1919: Six Months That Changed the World* (New York: Random House, 2003), 224–5.

44 Cecil diary, May 12, 1919.
45 Mantoux, The Deliberations of the Council of Four, vol, II, May 14, 1919, 66.
46 May 14, 1919 (11:45 a.m.), Council of Four meeting, *FRUS* vol. 5.
47 May 19, 1919 (10:00 a.m.), 19th SEC meeting, Cecil chair, *BDFA* vol. 12.
48 H. W. V. Temperley, ed., *A History of the Peace Conference of Paris*, vol. I (London: H. Frowde, Hodder & Stoughton, 1920–24), 337.
49 Macmillan, *Paris 1919*, 228; and Robert Gerwarth, *The Vanquished: Why the First World War Failed to End* (New York: Farrar, Straus and Giroux, 2016), 193–4.
50 Report of Enemy Tonnage Sub-Committee, 20th meeting of SEC, May 26, 1919, *BDFA* vol. 12.
51 Herbert Hoover, *The Ordeal of Woodrow Wilson* (New York: McGraw-Hill, 1958), 102–4.
52 Hoover to Wilson on May 14, 1919, in Herbert Hoover, *Two Peacemakers in Paris: The Hoover-Wilson Post-Armistice Letters* (College Station: Texas A&M University Press, 1978).
53 Patricia Clavin, "The Austrian Hunger Crisis and International Organization after the First World War," *International Affairs* 90, no. 2 (2014): 271.
54 Hoover to Wilson on Apr. 25, 1919, in Hoover, *Two Peacemakers in Paris*.
55 May 12, 1919, 17th SEC meeting, Cecil chair, *BDFA* vol. 12.
56 May 19, 1919, appendix of DGR Hoover's report of May 15, 19th SEC meeting, Cecil chair, *BDFA* vol. 12.
57 C. Paul Vincent, *The Politics of Hunger: The Allied Blockade of Germany, 1915–1919* (Athens and London: Ohio University Press, 1985), ch. 4.
58 Herbert Hoover, *America's First Crusade* (New York: Charles Scribner's Sons, 1942), 72.
59 Photo of May 5, 1919, of a map in Hoover's office in the Crillon, 2T 94, MC 202, Gilbert F. Close Papers, Series 4: Paris Peace Conference Photographs, Box 2, Department of Rare Books and Special Collections, Princeton University Library.
60 Surface, *American Food*, 42–3. Stephen Porter notes that the creators of the United Nations Relief and Rehabilitation Administration after World War II believed that Hoover's scheme in 1919 unfairly charged suffering nations; in "Humanitarian Diplomacy after World War II: The United Nations Relief and Rehabilitation Administration," in Robert Hutchings and Jeremi Suri, eds., *Foreign Policy Breakthroughs: Cases in Successful Diplomacy* (New York: Oxford University Press, 2015), 28–9.
61 Herbert Hoover, "The Economic Administration," in *What Really Happened at Paris: The Story of the Peace Conference, 1918–1919. By American Delegates*, ed. Edward M. House and Charles Seymour (New York: Charles Scribner's Sons, 1921), 338–9.

62 Superior Blockade Council memo, May 13, 1919, Baruch Papers, Box 387.
63 Final meeting was on May 15, 1919, with neither Cecil nor Loucheur attending; see Baruch Papers, Box 391.
64 Report for Raw Materials Committee of the SEC on "Coal situation in Europe," Apr. 17, 1919, Baruch Papers, Box 391.
65 Minutes of Committee on Coal, Apr. 25, 1919, Baruch Papers, Box 391.
66 Hoover, "The Economic Administration," 346.
67 Clifford R. Lovin, *A School for Diplomats: The Paris Peace Conference of 1919* (Lanham, MD: University Press of America, 1997), 29.
68 James Grant, *Bernard Baruch: The Adventures of a Wall Street Legend* (New York: Simon & Schuster, 1983), 184.
69 Temperley, A History of the Peace Conference of Paris, vol. I, 296–9.
70 Julia Irwin, "Taming Total War: Great War-Era American Humanitarianism and its Legacies," in *Beyond 1917: The United States and the Global Legacies of the Great War*, ed. Thomas W. Zeiler, David K. Ekbladh, and Benjamin C. Montoya (New York: Oxford University Press, 2017), 134–5.
71 "Make Plans to Launch League of Nations," *New York Times*, May 1, 1919.
72 "The League & the Monroe Doctrine: Statement by Lord R. Cecil," *Manchester Guardian*, May 2, 1919.
73 "Germany's Admission to the League," *Manchester Guardian*, May 2, 1919.
74 "Lord Robert Cecil on the League," *The Scotsman*, May 3, 1919.
75 "Plans to Organize League of Nations," *Atlanta Constitution*, May 7, 1919.
76 Correspondence in League of Nations Health Commission 1919/1920 folder, NBKR 4X/34.
77 Education Commission, League of Nations 1919/1920 folder, NBKR 4X/34; F. Russell Bryant, ed., *The Coalition Diaries and Letters of H.A.L. Fisher, 1916–1922: The Historian in Lloyd George's Cabinet* (Lewiston, NY: The Edwin Mellen Press, 2006), 404.
78 Treaties with Poland folder, NBKR 4X/35.
79 Cecil to Hankey, May 28, 1919, NBKR 4X/31-2.
80 Baker to Cecil, May 27, 1919, NBKR 4X/31-2.
81 Baker to Cecil, Apr. 9, 1919, NBKR 4X/38.
82 Note by Drummond on organization, 9/5/1919; and Drummond memo on 31/5/1919, in NBKR 4X/38.
83 James Barros, *Office without Power: Secretary-General Sir Eric Drummond, 1919–1933* (Oxford: Clarendon Press, 1979), 75.
84 Walters to Lord C. Stuart, 14/5/1919, NBKR 4X/38.
85 Notes for upcoming "Organization Committee" meeting, 9/6/1919, NBKR 4X/38.
86 Correspondence of May 1919, Air Commission 1919 folder, NBKR 4X/35.

87 Baker to Drummond, May 1919, Folder: Military Commission, League of Nations 1919/1920, NBKR 4X/34.
88 May 21, 1919 (11:00 a.m.), Wilson, LG, and Clemenceau present, *FRUS* vol. V.
89 Nansen's letter to the Big Four, and their response, was published widely, including in *The Times*, Apr. 19, 1919, p. 10. On Nansen's ensuing work with Russian refugees, see Bruno Cabanes, *The Great War and the Origins of Humanitarianism, 1918–1924* (Cambridge: Cambridge University Press, 2014), ch. 3.
90 "A New Project for Russia," *The Times*, Apr. 19, 1919, p. 11.
91 Memo of May 16, 1919, presented in letter from Cecil to Hankey of May 16, in May 20, 1919 (11:00 a.m.), Big Four meeting, *FRUS* vol. V.
92 June 17, 1919 (4:00 p.m.), Big Four meeting, *FRUS* vol. V.
93 May 29, 1919 (11:00 a.m.), *FRUS* vol. VI.
94 Cecil diary, May 31, June 3, and June 5, 1919. Quotation from Edmonds, who attributed the plan to the ideas of P. B. Noyes, a US industrialist and friend of Wilson, but Noyes was not at the Commission; J. E. Edmonds, *The Occupation of the Rhineland 1918–1929* (London, HMSO, 1987, originally 1944), 186–7.
95 Cecil diary, May 6, 1919.
96 Richard Davenport-Hines, *Ettie: The Intimate Life and Dauntless Spirit of Lady Desborough* (London: Weidenfeld & Nicolson, 2008), 231.
97 Cecil diary, May 10, 1919.
98 HughCecil and Mirabel Cecil, *Imperial Marriage: An Edwardian War and Peace* (London: John Murray, 2002), 97–9.
99 See Cecil to Lady Cecil, Jan. 22, 1919, CHE 6/13; and Mar. 6, 1919, CHE 6/29.
100 Lady Cecil to Lord Cecil, May 16, 1919, CHE 18/44.
101 Cecil to Lady Cecil, Apr. 28, 1919, CHE 6/38.
102 "The Church and Welsh Disestablishment," *The Scotsman*, May 16, 1919.
103 Cecil diary, May 21, 1919.
104 "Our London Correspondence," *Manchester Guardian*, May 21, 1919.
105 "Peace Terms and the League of Nations," *Manchester Guardian*, May 22, 1919.
106 "A Healthy Infant: Lord Robert Cecil on a League of Nations," *The Scotsman*, May 22, 1919.
107 Cecil diary, May 22, 1919.
108 Cecil diary, May 22, 1919.
109 "Lord R. Cecil and Mr. Clynes on Labour Co-Partnership," *The Scotsman*, May 23, 1919.
110 Stuart Ball, "The Conservative Party, the Role of the State and the Politics of Protection, c. 1918–1932," *History: Journal of the Historical Association* 96 (2011): 289.
111 Maurice Cowling, *The Impact of Labour 1920–1924: The Beginning of Modern British Politics* (Cambridge: Cambridge University Press, 1971), ch. III.

7 The Mentality of Appeasement? June

1. F. Russell Bryant, ed., *The Coalition Diaries and Letters of H.A.L. Fisher, 1916–1922: The Historian in Lloyd George's Cabinet*, vol. II (Lewiston, NY: The Edwin Mellen Press, 2006), 424.
2. Sir James Headlam-Morley, *A Memoir of the Paris Peace Conference 1919* (London: Methuen, 1972), 105.
3. See US reparations delegation memo of June 3, 1919, in Bernard Baruch, *The Making of the Reparation and Economic Sections of the Treaty* (New York: Harper & Bros., 1920), 67–9.
4. W. K. Hancock, *Smuts: The Sanguine Years, 1870–1919* (Cambridge: Cambridge University Press, 1962), 527.
5. Antony Lentin, *General Smuts: South Africa* (London: Haus, 2010), 96–104.
6. Carl Bridge, *William Hughes: Australia* (London: Haus, 2011), ix.
7. Bridge, *William Hughes*, 102.
8. Antony Lentin, *Lloyd George and the Lost Peace: From Versailles to Hitler, 1919–1940* (Basingstoke: Palgrave, 2001), 32–5.
9. Major-General Sir C. E. Callwell, *Field-Marshall Sir Henry Wilson: His Life and Diaries*, vol. II (London: Cassell, 1927), 200.
10. David P. Billington, Jr., *Lothian: Philip Kerr and the Quest for World Order* (Westport, CT and London: Praeger Security International, 2006), 62; and Clifford R. Lovin, *A School for Diplomats: The Paris Peace Conference of 1919* (Lanham, MD: University Press of America, 1997), 18–22.
11. Cecil diary, May 31, 1919.
12. Lentin, *Lloyd George and the Lost Peace*, 13–9; Antony Lentin, *Lloyd George, Woodrow Wilson, and the Guilt of Germany: An Essay in the Pre-History of Appeasement* (Leicester: Leicester University Press, 1984), 112; Bruce Kent, *The Spoils of War: The Politics, Economics and Diplomacy of Reparations, 1918–1932* (Oxford: Clarendon Press, 1989), 93–4; and Stella Rudman, *Lloyd George and the Appeasement of Germany, 1919–1945* (Newcastle upon Tyne: Cambridge Scholars, 2011), 21–2.
13. David Lloyd George, *The Truth about the Peace Treaties*, vol. 1 (London: Victor Gollancz, 1938), 731.
14. Cecil diary, May 3, 1919.
15. Cecil diary, May 26, 1919.
16. Cecil to Lloyd George, May 27, 1919, Add. Ms. 51076.
17. Cecil diary, June 1, 1919.
18. Notes by Lord Cecil of Dec. 1933 on Lord George Allardice Riddell, *Lord Riddell's Intimate Diary of the Peace Conference and after, 1918–1923* (London: Victor Gollancz, 1933), CHE 28/6.

19 On Smuts defense of reparations at this meeting, see Marc Trachtenberg, "Reparation at the Paris Peace Conference," *Journal of Modern History* 51, no. 1 (1979): 47–8.
20 Cecil to Lady Cecil, June 2, 1919, CHE 6/40.
21 Sir Francis Oppenheimer, *Stranger Within: Autobiographical Pages* (London: Faber and Faber, 1960), 374–5.
22 Lentin, *Lloyd George and the Lost Peace*, 67–70; Lovin, *A School for Diplomats*, 73–4; and Harold Nicolson, *Peacemaking 1919* (New York: Grosset & Dunlap, 1965), 210.
23 Lovin, *A School for Diplomats*, 73; and Whitney H. Shepardson, *Early History of the Council on Foreign Relations* (Stamford, CT: The Overbrook Press, 1960), 2.
24 Minutes of the meeting including a list of participants on 30/5/1919, NBKR 4X/29.
25 Michael L. Dockrill, "The Foreign Office and the 'Proposed Institute of International Affairs 1919," *International Affairs* 56, no. 4 (1980): 669–70.
26 Shephardson, *Early History*, 2–3.
27 Cecil diary, May 30, 1919.
28 Cecil diary, June 7, 1919.
29 Cecil diary, May 20 and 25, 1919.
30 Nicolson, *Peacemaking*, 371.
31 "America's Record in War Commended," *Christian Science Monitor*, June 3, 1919; "Says League Rejection Would Mar U.S. Record," *New York Tribune*, June 3, 1919.
32 "America's Part in War and Peace, Lord R. Cecil's Tribute," *The Times*, June 2, 1919, p. 11.
33 "Treaty 'Leak' Turmoil Grows," *Detroit Free Press*, June 6, 1919. "Republicans Appear to be Testing League as a Party Issue by Senate Debate," *St. Louis Post-Dispatch*, June 7, 1919.
34 "The Senate and Britain," *The Times*, June 11, 1919, p. 13.
35 House to Cecil, Dec. 13, 1920, Add. Ms. 51095.
36 June 10, 1919 (3:30 p.m.), 22nd SEC meeting, *British Documents on Foreign Affairs—Reports and Papers from the Foreign Office Confidential Print. Part II, From the First to the Second World War. Series I, the Paris Peace Conference of 1919*, vol. 13, ed. M. L. Dockrill, Kenneth Bourne, and Donald Cameron Watt (Frederick, MD: University Publications of America, 1989).
37 Memorandum from Mr. McCormick regarding blockade of Hungary and Bolshevik Russia, Appendix to June 2, 1919 (10:00 a.m.), 21st SEC meeting, *BDFA* vol. 13.
38 Memorandum from British Delegates regarding future work of the Supreme Economic Council as regards Russia, June 10, 1919 (3:30 p.m.), 22nd SEC meeting, *BDFA* vol. 13.
39 Note from American Delegates on proposition in British memorandum on Allied Economic Policy in Russia, June 10, 1919 (3:30 p.m.), 22nd SEC meeting, *BDFA* vol. 13.

40   Reports from Food Section of June 14, Communication Section of June 19, and Finance Section of June 24, 1919, in Folder: Economic Commission, League of Nations 1919/1920, NBKR 4X/34.
41   Allied Economic Policy in Russia: Report from the Food Section, June 14, 1919, in 23rd SEC meeting, June 16, 1919, *BDFA* vol. 13.
42   "Memorandum on Railway Transportation Situation in Bolshevik Russia: From Communication Section," June 19, 1919, in 24th SEC meeting, June 23, 1919, *BDFA* vol. 13.
43   Letter from Hankey to SEC, June 17, 1919, 24th SEC meeting, June 23, 1919, *BDFA* vol. 13.
44   Undated telegram from Cecil to Wise, probably on June 20, 1919, in NBKR 4X/34.
45   "Memorandum by British Delegation on the Future of the Supreme Economic Council," June 20, 1919, in 24th SEC meeting, June 23, 1919, *BDFA* vol. 13.
46   "Memorandum from the French Delegation on Inter-Allied Co-operation after Peace," June 20, 1919, Appendix in minutes of 24th SEC meeting, June 23, 1919, *BDFA* vol. 13.
47   Robert Laird Borden, *Robert Laird Borden: His Memoirs*, vol. II (New York: Macmillan, 1938), 965.
48   Juliet Nicolson, *The Great Silence, 1918–1920: Living in the Shadow of the Great War* (London: John Murray, 2009), 116–21.
49   John Maynard Keynes, *Collected Writings of John Maynard Keynes, Volume XVI: Activities 1914–1919: The Treasury and Versailles* (London: Macmillan, 1971), 467–9.
50   June 6, 1919, Council of Four meeting 4:00, Papers Relating to the Foreign Relations of the United States, 1919: The Paris Peace Conference, vol. VI (Washington, DC: US Government Printing Office, 1919).
51   Cecil diary, June 8, 1919; also in NBKR 4X-33.
52   Oppenheimer, *Stranger Within*, 388.
53   Cecil diary, June 9, 1919.
54   "London Letter," *Daily Mail*, 4 June 1919, p. 4
55   Charles T. Thompson, *The Peace Conference Day by Day: A Presidential Pilgrimage Leading to the Discovery of Europe* (New York: Brentano's, 1920), 391–2.
56   Peter Yearwood, *Guarantee of Peace: The League of Nations in British Policy, 1914–1925* (Oxford: Oxford University Press, 2009), 131. For examples of reports on Clemenceau supposedly favoring this Cecil-House plan for German entry, see "What Germany Must Do before She Can Enter League of Nations," *Courier and Argus* (Dundee), June 10, 1919, p. 5; and "Allies Agree on Answer to German Pleas," *Chicago Daily Tribune*, June 13, 1919, p. 2.
57   "Huns Guaranteed Admission to League," *Nottingham Evening Post*, June 10, 1919, p. 1; and "Causes of Paris Delays," *The Times*, June 11, 1919, p. 12.

58 Sir Ian Malcolm, *Lord Balfour: A Memory* (London: Macmillan, 1930), 74.
59 Bryant, *The Coalition Diaries*, 425.
60 Cecil to Lady Cecil, June 7, 1919, CHE 6/42.
61 "Marriage of Lord Derby's Daughter," *Manchester Guardian*, June 11, 1919, p. 6.
62 *Daily Mail*, June 7, 1919.
63 Cecil to Lady Cecil, June 2, 1919, CHE 6/40.
64 Keynes to Bradbury of Treasury, June 6, 1919, *Collected Writings XVI*, 473.
65 Thompson, *The Peace Conference Day by Day*, 392; Baker to George Newman, 6/5/1919, NBKR 4X/34.
66 "Sunderland House," *Daily Mail*, June 3, 1919, p. 5.
67 Baker to Walters, June 12, 1919, NBKR 4X/31–2.
68 Baker to Colum Stuart, June 26, 1919, NBKR 4X/31–2.
69 Memorandum by Sir Francis Oppenheimer relative to the situation in Austria, June 3, 1919; and Report of the Finance Section of the SEC, 9 June, 1919, *Documents on British Foreign Policy, 1919–1939, Series 1, Vol. 6: Central Europe, June 1919-January 1920*, ed. E .L. Woodward and Rohan Butler (London: H.M. Stationery Office, 1946), 40–56.
70 Oppenheimer, *Stranger Within*, 395.
71 "League of Nations: British Campaign in Its Support," *Daily Mail*, June 11, 1919, p. 6.
72 "London Letter," *Western Daily Press* (Yeovil), June 13, 1919, p. 5.
73 This section comes from the transcript and account of the meeting in *The Times*, June 14, 1919, p. 16.
74 My sincere thanks to Suzanne Keyte, the Archivist of the Royal Albert Hall, for this information.
75 Baker to Colum Stuart, 20/6/1919, NBKR 4X/31–2 and NBKR 4X/28.
76 "A Living Thing," *The Times*, June 14, 1919, p. 13.
77 "Lord Robert Cecil May Be Sent Here," *Washington Post*, June 22, 1919, p. 10.
78 "Lord R. Cecil Interrupted," *Daily Mail*, June 14, 1919, p. 1. Interestingly, Fraser was successfully sued for libel by Sir Alfred Mond, the First Commissioner of Works, for a large public poster he had put up in March calling Mond a "traitor" for his supposedly favorable actions toward German shareholders; see "Sir A. Mond's Libel Action," *The Times*, Dec. 6, 1919, p. 4.
79 Helen McCarthy, *The British People and the League of Nations; Democracy, Citizenship and Internationalism c. 1918–45* (Manchester: Manchester University Press, 2011), 215.
80 "Lord Robert Cecil May Be Sent Here," *Washington Post*, June 22, 1919, p. 10.
81 "Oxford Encaenia. D.C.L. for War Leaders," *The Times*, June 26, 1919, p. 10.
82 Cecil to Lady Cecil, June 25, 1919, CHE 6/43.
83 "D.C.L. For the Prince," *The Times*, June 19, 1919, p. 14.

84 Cecil to Lady Cecil, June 25, 1919, CHE 6/43.
85 "A New Period," *Daily Mail*, June 26, 1919, p. 7.
86 Fisher diary of June 26, 1919, in Bryant, *The Coalition Diaries*, vol. II, 436.
87 Oppenheimer, *Stranger Within*, 396.
88 Copy of resolution of June 28, 1919 in Folder: Economic Commission, League of Nations 1919/1920, NBKR 4X/34. Also, June 28, 1919 (11:00 a.m.), *FRUS* vol. VI.
89 "American Note on Suggestions of Various Allies as to Economic Co-operation after Peace," June 27, 1919, Appendix in minutes of June 30, 1919 (10:00 a.m.), 25th SEC meeting, Cecil in chair, *BDFA* vol. 13.
90 Hoover to Wilson, June 7, 1919, in Herbert Hoover, *Two Peacemakers in Paris: The Hoover-Wilson Post-Armistice Letters* (College Station: Texas A&M University Press, 1978).
91 Baruch diary, June 13, 1919, Baruch Papers, Box 656.
92 Baruch diary, June 14, 1919, Baruch Papers, Box 656.
93 Wise to Hankey, June 21, 1919, NBKR 4X/34.
94 Hoover to Wilson, June 27, 1919, in Hoover, *Two Peacemakers in Paris*.
95 Clavin, "The Austrian Hunger Crisis," 274–5.
96 Lord Hankey, *The Supreme Control at the Paris Peace Conference 1919* (London: George Allen & Unwin, 1963), 186–9.
97 Paul Mantoux, *The Deliberations of the Council of Four*, trans. and ed. Arthur Link and Manfred F. Boemeke, vol. II (Princeton, NJ: Princeton University Press, 1992), June 25, 1919.
98 June 28 (11:00 a.m.), Council of Four, *FRUS* vol. VI.
99 June 30, 1919 (10:00 a.m.), 25th SEC meeting, Cecil in chair, *BDFA* vol. 13.
100 Frances Lloyd George, *The Years That Are Past* (London: Hutchinson, 1967), 164–5; and A. J. P. Taylor, ed., *Lloyd George: A Diary by Frances Stevenson* (London: Hutchinson, 1971), 187.
101 Callwell, *Field-Marshall Sir Henry Wilson*, vol. II, 201.
102 Lentin, *General Smuts*, 105–22.
103 Callwell, *Field-Marshall Sir Henry Wilson*, vol. II, 202.
104 Nicolson, *Peacemaking*, 371.
105 Patrick Cohrs, *The Unfinished Peace after World War I: America, Britain and the Stabilisation of Europe, 1919–1932* (Cambridge: Cambridge University Press, 2006), 70–1.
106 Lentin, *General Smuts*, 96.
107 Cohrs, *The Unfinished Peace*, 17; and Michael L. Dockrill and J. Douglas Goold, *Peace without Promise: Britain and the Peace Conferences 1919–23* (Hamden, CT: Archon Books, 1980).
108 Hankey, *Supreme Control*, 189.

109 Seth Tillman, *Anglo-American Relations at the Paris Peace Conference of 1919* (Princeton, NJ: Princeton University Press, 1961), 363–4.
110 Peter Spartalis, *The Diplomatic Battles of Billy Hughes* (Sydney: Hale & Iremonger, 1983).
111 See the final chapter of volume I of his *The Truth about the Peace Treaties*.
112 For a punitive Lloyd George, see Marc Trachtenberg, *Reparation in World Politics: France and European Economic Diplomacy, 1916–1923* (New York: Columbia University Press, 1980), 48–9; Robert E. Bunselmeyer, *The Cost of the War, 1914–1919: British Economic War Aims and the Origins of Reparation* (Hamden, CT: Archon Books, 1975); and Kent, *The Spoils of War*, 33, 56.
113 Lentin, *Lloyd George and the Lost Peace*, 13–18; Rudman, *Lloyd George*, 269.
114 Lord Salter, *Memoirs of a Public Servant* (London: Faber and Faber, 1961), 148–52.
115 J. Arthur Salter, *Allied Shipping Control: An Experiment in International Administration* (Oxford: Clarendon Press, 1921), 266–7.
116 Sisley Huddleston, *Peace-Making at Paris* (London: T. Fisher Unwin, 1919), 236, 240.
117 Baker to Cecil, July 15, 1919, NBKR 4X-33.
118 Memo by Crowe, June 24, 1919, NBKR 4X/31–2.

8 After Paris: July to December

1 "An Honest Peace: Lord R. Cecil's Belief in the League," *The Times*, July 17, 1919, 9.
2 World Peace Foundation, The League of Nations, vol. III, no. 1–2 (Boston, MA: World Peace Foundation, 1920), 16.
3 See Baker's interaction with David Hunter Miller, a lead US negotiator on the League, during April and May 1919; in David Hunter Miller, *My Diary at the Peace Conference of Paris, with Documents*, vol. I (New York: Printed for the author by the Appeal printing company, 1924).
4 26/6/1919 from Baker to Colum Stuart, in NBKR 4X/31–32.
5 SusanPedersen, *The Guardians: The League of Nations and the Crisis of Empire* (New York: Oxford University Press, 2015), 48–52; and http://www.lonsea.de/pub/person/4914.
6 Donald S. Birn, *The League of Nations Union 1918–1945* (Oxford: Clarendon Press, 1981), 73–80; and D.J. Whittaker, *Fighter for Peace: Philip Noel-Baker 1889–1982* (York: William Sessions, 1989), ch. 2.
7 http://www.lonsea.de/pub/person/4880.
8 Cecil to Lady Cecil, June 6, 1919, CHE 6/41.
9 http://www.lonsea.de/pub/person/9970.

10 Pedersen, *The Guardians*, 62.
11 Frederic J. Fransen, *The Supranational Politics of Jean Monnet: Ideas and Origins of the European Community* (Westport, CT: Greenwood Press, 2001), 29; and François Duchêne, *Jean Monnet: The First Statesman of Interdependence* (New York: W.W. Norton, 1994), 40–1.
12 14/5/1919, Frank Walters to Lord Colum Stuart; and 9/6/1919 notes; in Folder: Organisation of the League of Nations, NBKR 4X/38.
13 Jean Monnet, Mémoires (Paris, Fayard, 1976), 78.
14 http://www.lonsea.de/pub/person/5090.
15 R.B. Fosdick in London to Frank Polk in Paris, Aug. 12, 1919, in Raymond B. Fosdick, *Letters on the League of Nations* (Princeton, NJ: Princeton University Press, 1966), 18–19.
16 Raymond B. Fosdick, *Chronicle of a Generation: An Autobiography* (New York: Harper & Brothers, 1958), 187. Cable from House to Fosdick, May 4, 1919, Fosdick Papers, Box 9: Correspondence L, Folder 1; Public Policy Papers, Department of Rare Books and Special Collections, Princeton University Library.
17 Fosdick to Hoover, Jan. 28, 1920. Fosdick Papers, Box 7: Correspondence H-J, Folder 1.
18 http://www.lonsea.de/pub/person/5423.
19 "Allies Are Ready to Launch League without America," *St. Louis Post-Dispatch*, Oct. 1919, A1.
20 Fosdick confidential to Polk Nov. 5, 1919, Fosdick Papers, Box 09, Folder 1: League of Nations.
21 "World Statistics," *The Times*, Aug. 15, 1919, 13.
22 "International Statistics," *Manchester Guardian*, Aug. 19, 1919, 11.
23 Pedersen, *The Guardians*, 33–5.
24 Pedersen, *The Guardians*, 405.
25 Pedersen, *The Guardians*, 7.
26 NBKR 4X/31–2.
27 "Is it true?" *Chevrons*, Oct. 1919, 3.
28 "Women's Place in the League of Nations," *New-York Tribune*, Oct. 12, 1919, H5.
29 DanielGorman, *The Emergence of International Society in the 1920s* (Cambridge: Cambridge University Press, 2012), 60–5.
30 "Allies Are Ready to Launch League without America," *St. Louis Post-Dispatch*, Oct. 12, 1919, A1.
31 James Barros, *Office without Power: Secretary-General Sir Eric Drummond, 1919–1933* (Oxford: Clarendon Press, 1979), 75.
32 "Peace Comes to Mayfair," *Daily Express*, Aug. 27, 1919.
33 Barros, *Office without Power*, 80–1.
34 Baruch diary, June 14, 1919, Baruch Papers 656.

35 Susan Pedersen, "Empires, States and the League of Nations," in *Internationalisms: A Twentieth-Century History*, ed. Glenda Sluga and Patricia Clavin (Cambridge: Cambridge University Press, 2017), 116.
36 "Peace Comes to Mayfair," *Daily Express*, Aug. 27, 1919.
37 Raymond B. Fosdick, *Chronicle of a Generation: An Autobiography* (New York: Harper & Brothers, 1958), 189.
38 Sami Sare, *The League of Nations and the Debate on Disarmament (1918-1919)* (Rome: Edizioni Nuova Cultura, 2013), 240–58; and Fosdick, *Chronicle of a Generation*, 195.
39 "Cecil – Coming Political Ace among Britons," *Chicago Daily Tribune*, Oct. 13, 1919, 7.
40 Fosdick in London to Frank Polk, Aug. 12, 1919, in Fosdick, *Letters on the League*, 22–3; and also, Fosdick, *Chronicle of a Generation*, 195.
41 Barros, *Office without Power*, 37–8.
42 Fosdick, *Chronicle of a Generation*, 188–9.
43 Text of undated speech by Cecil, in "Press" folder, NBKR 4X/31-2.
44 Daniel Gorman, *International Cooperation in the Early Twentieth Century* (London: Bloomsbury, 2017), 209–10.
45 Barry Supple, "War Economies," in *The Cambridge History of the First World War, Vol. II*, ed. Jay Winter; and Georges-Henri Soutou, "Diplomacy," in *The Cambridge History of the First World War, Vol. II*, ed. Jay Winter, 323, 534–5.
46 Tyler Stovall, *Paris and the Spirit of 1919: Consumer Struggles, Transnationalism and Revolution* (Cambridge: Cambridge University Press, 2012), 23; Frank Trentmann, *Free Trade Nation: Commerce, Consumption, and Civil Society in Modern Britain* (Oxford and New York: Oxford University Press, 2008); and Frank Trentmann, "Coping with Shortage: The Problem of Food Security and Global Visions of Coordination, c. 1890s–1950," in *Food and Conflict in Europe in the Age of the Two World Wars*, ed. Frank Trentmann and Flemming Just (London: Palgrave Macmillan, 2006), 27.
47 "Productivity Low, Says Herbert Hoover," *Atlanta Constitution*, Aug. 2, 1919.
48 Notes of a meeting of the Heads of Delegations of the Five Great Powers held in M. Pichon's Room at the Quai d'Orsay, Paris, on July 17, 1919, 3:30, Documents on British Foreign Policy, 1919-1939, Series 1, vol. 1, ed. E.L. Woodward and Rohan Butler (London: H.M. Stationery Office, 1946), 121–6.
49 July 26, 1919 (6:00 p.m.), 28th SEC meeting, Clémentel in chair, *British Documents on Foreign Affairs—Reports and Papers from the Foreign Office Confidential Print. Part II, From the First to the Second World War. Series I, the Paris Peace Conference of 1919*, vol. 13, ed. M. L. Dockrill, Kenneth Bourne, and Donald Cameron Watt (Frederick, MD: University Publications of America, 1989).

50 Kendrick A. Clements, *The Life of Herbert Hoover: Imperfect Visionary 1918–1928* (New York: Palgrave Macmillan, 2010), 22.
51 Notes of a meeting of the Heads of Delegations of the Five Great Powers held in M. Pichon's Room at the Quai d'Orsay, Paris, on Tues., Aug. 5, 1919, at 3:30 p.m. *DBFP* vol. 1, 308–18.
52 Telegram No. 563 from Curzon to Lindsay, Aug. 11, 1919, *DBFP* vol. 5.
53 Donald Markwell, *John Maynard Keynes and International Relations* (Oxford: Oxford University Press, 2006), 89; and Seth Tillman, *Anglo-American Relations at the Paris Peace Conference of 1919* (Princeton, NJ: Princeton University Press, 1961), 273–4.
54 Sept. 20, 1919, 30th SEC meeting (in Brussels), *BDFA* vol. 15.
55 SEC Note for the Supreme Council on procedure for the supply of foodstuffs and raw materials to Germany and Austria, *DBFP* vol. 1.
56 Record of a meeting in Paris on Sept. 25, 1919, of the Committee on Organization of the Reparation Commission, *DBFP* vol. 5.
57 Sept. 20, 1919, 30th SEC meeting (in Brussels), *BDFA*, vol. 15; Report of the proceedings of the Consultative Food Committee, Nov. 4, 1919, *DBFP* vol. 5, 839–41.
58 Notes of a meeting of the Heads of Delegations of the Five Great Powers held in M. Pichon's Room at the Quai d'Orsay, Paris, on Tuesday, Sept. 30, 1919 (10.30 a.m.), *DBFP*, vol. 1.
59 Functions of the Raw Materials Committee: Note by the Permanent Committee, Nov. 12, 1919, *DBFP* vol. 5, 845–6.
60 Résumé of Mr. Salter's remarks on the relations of the SEC with the League of Nations and the Reparation Commission, *DBFP* vol. 5.
61 31st meeting of the SEC, Nov. 21–23, 1919, *DBFP* vol. 5, 829–39.
62 "Powers to Confer on World Finance to Save Europe," *New York Times*, Jan. 15, 1920, 1.
63 For example, Monnet, *Mémoires*, 87–9.
64 Patricia Clavin, "Men and Markets: Global Capital and the International Economy," in Internationalisms, ed. Glenda Sluga and Patricia Clavin, 98–9.
65 Relations between the SEC and the League of Nations: Questionnaire of the French Delegation, Nov. 15, 1919, *DBFP* vol. 5, 848.
66 Cecil of Chelwood, Viscount (Lord Robert), *A Great Experiment: An Autobiography* (New York: Oxford University Press, 1941), 30–1.
67 Cecil, *A Great Experiment*, 189.
68 F. Russell Bryant (ed.), *The Coalition Diaries and Letters of H.A.L. Fisher, 1916–1922: The Historian in Lloyd George's Cabinet*, vol. II (Lewiston, NY: The Edwin Mellen Press, 2006), 437–8; and "A Government Defeat in Commons," *Manchester Guardian*, July 5, 1919, 9.

69. "The Awakening of Parliament," *Christian Science Monitor*, July 9, 1919, 20. This bill was eventually defeated in the House of Lords.
70. "Lord R. Cecil on the Peace," *The Observer*, July 6, 1919, 12; "Europe Bordering on Financial Ruin Says Lord Robert Cecil," *Atlanta Constitution*, July 9, 1919, 7; and E. H. Carr, *Britain: A Study of Foreign Policy from the Versailles Treaty to the Outbreak of War* (London: Longmans, Green, 1939), 101.
71. "The Debate on the Treaty Bill," *Manchester Guardian*, July 22, 1919, 8.
72. "The Debate on Russian Withdrawal," *Manchester Guardian*, July 30, 1919, 9; and Hansard, July 28, 1919.
73. "Lord Robert Cecil urged to succeed Lloyd George," *New-York Tribune*, Aug. 4, 1919, 6.
74. "Scenes at St. Stephen's," *The Observer*, July 27, 1919, 8.
75. "British Focus Interest on New Centre Party," *New-York Tribune*, July 17, 1919, 2.
76. Richard Toye, *Lloyd George & Churchill: Rivals for Greatness* (London: Macmillan, 2007), 213–4.
77. "Our London Correspondence," *Manchester Guardian*, Aug. 1, 1919, 6; "Lord Robert Cecil on Social Unrest," *The Scotsman*, Aug. 1, 1919, 4; and "Labour Unrest: Is the Government Unpopular?" *The Scotsman*, Aug. 8, 1919, 6.
78. "A Tale of Two Statesmen," *The Spectator*, Aug. 2, 1919, 136.
79. "A Statesman Discovered: The Rise of Lord Robert Cecil," *The Graphic*, Aug. 30, 1919, 280.
80. "Men of the Session," *Daily Mail*, Aug. 20, 1919, 4.
81. T. P. O'Connor, "Bonar Law or Lord Cecil may succeed Lloyd George," *Minneapolis Morning Tribune*, Aug. 11, 1919, 6.
82. "Ireland," *Manchester Guardian*, Oct. 10, 1919, 6; and "Urges Referendum on Irish Dominion, Lord Robert Cecil Takes Limelight in England," *Boston Globe*, Nov. 5, 1919, 13.
83. "To-Day's Gossip," *Daily Mirror*, July 16, 1919, 11.
84. "Scenes at St. Stephen's: Politics and Persons, Reputations of the Session," *The Observer*, Dec. 21, 1919, 8.
85. "Lord R. Cecil's Letter to Lady Astor," *Manchester Guardian*, Nov. 6, 1919, 7.
86. "Observations," *New Statesman*, Dec. 6, 1919, 271.
87. "Lord R. Cecil Supports Mr. Clynes' Call for Capital Levy Inquiry," *Daily Mirror*, Oct. 31, 1919.
88. "Lord R. Cecil & Labour Policy," *Manchester Guardian*, Aug. 5, 1919, 6.
89. "Classes in Britain Must Cooperate: Lord Robert Cecil, though Not Prepared to Acquit Them of Self-Seeking, Says Workmen Should Be Treated as Partners," *Christian Science Monitor*, Dec. 20, 1919, 7.
90. "Three 'Advanced' Parties Plan Drive Against Lloyd George," *Baltimore Sun*, Sept. 18, 1919, 5.

91 "Welsh Church Bill," *Manchester Guardian*, Aug. 7, 1919, 8.
92 "Scenes at St. Stephen's," *The Observer*, Aug. 10, 1919, 5.
93 "Lord Robert Cecil," *The Nation*, Sept. 6, 1919, 670.
94 "Profiteering & Trusts: New Bill in the Autumn," *Manchester Guardian*, Aug. 15, 1919, 7.
95 "The Plan to Check Profiteering," *Manchester Guardian*, Aug. 14, 1919. 7; "Profiteering Bill, All-Night Debate," *Manchester Guardian*, Aug. 14, 1919, 12; and "Editorial," *The Scotsman*, Aug. 15, 1919, 4.
96 "Labour and the Mine Proposals," *Manchester Guardian*, Aug. 19, 1919, 9.
97 "Britain to Drop High Protection," *Boston Daily Globe*, Aug. 19, 1919, 1.
98 "Scenes at St. Stephen's," *The Observer*, Aug. 24, 1919, 11.
99 Lord Robert Cecil, "League of Nations: Hopeful Outlook," *Sunday Times*, July 6, 1919, 10.
100 "The Supreme Economic Council: Lord R. Cecil to Resign," *Manchester Guardian*, Aug. 2, 1919, 7. "Of Vital Importance: Lord R Cecil and the Council's Work," *The Scotsman*, Aug. 2, 1919, 7.
101 *The Scotsman*, Nov. 27, 1919, 8.
102 Inbal Rose, *Conservatism and Foreign Policy during the Lloyd George Coalition 1918–1922* (London: Frank Cass, 1999), xxvi, 29, 63.
103 Birn, *The League of Nations Union*.
104 "League of Nations Union: Lord R. Cecil Chairman," *Manchester Guardian*, July 25, 1919, 4.
105 "To-Day's Gossip," *Daily Mirror*, Oct. 11, 1919, 11
106 Advertisement, *The Scotsman*, Oct. 17, 1919, 1; and "The Universities," *The Observer*, Oct. 19, 1919, 15.
107 "League of Nations: Lord Robert Cecil's Campaign," *Manchester Guardian*, Oct. 21, 1919, 8.
108 "League of Nations, Lord Robert Cecil's Campaign," *Manchester Guardian*, Oct. 23, 1919, 7.
109 "Lord R. Cecil and Duke of Northumberland Debate on the League," *Manchester Guardian*, Oct. 22, 1919, 7.
110 "Lord Robert Cecil's Campaign: Oxford for League of Nations," *Manchester Guardian*, Oct. 24, 1919, 8.
111 "To-Day's Gossip," *Daily Mirror*, Oct. 27, 1919, 5.
112 "Cecil says Treaty Almost Repudiated," *New York Times*, Nov. 18, 1919, 1.
113 Drummond to Fosdick in Washington, Dec. 15, 1919, in Fosdick, *Letters on the League*, 83.
114 See Chapter 3; and David Hunter Miller, "The Making of the League of Nations," in *What Really Happened at Paris: The Story of the Peace Conference, 1918–1919. By American Delegates*, ed. Edward M. House and Charles Seymour (New York: Charles Scribner's Sons, 1921), 403–4.

115 John Milton Cooper, *Breaking the Heart of the World: Woodrow Wilson and the Fight for the League of Nations* (Cambridge: Cambridge University Press, 2001), 221–2.
116 Fosdick to Huntington Gilchrist, Jan. 28, 1920, in Fosdick, *Letters on the League*, 115.
117 "Offer Germany League Place? Senate's Action Starts a Teutonic Overture," *Los Angeles Times*, Nov. 26, 1919, I5.
118 "Cecil's Friends Deny," *New York Times*, Nov. 26, 1919, 2.
119 "The League and O.T.C. Recruiting," *Manchester Guardian*, Nov. 27, 1916, 6.
120 *The Scotsman*, Nov. 27, 1919, 8.
121 *The Scotsman*, Nov. 27, 1919, 8.
122 "Lord Robert Cecil and the Covenant: No Possible Alternative," *Manchester Guardian*, Dec. 8, 1919, 12; and "Commerce and the League of Nations," *The Scotsman*, Dec. 8, 1919, 5.
123 "A Code To Prevent War," *The Times*, Dec. 5, 1919, 13.
124 "Inflated Currency Causes Much of High Living Cost, Says Lord Robert Cecil," *Washington Post*, Dec. 23, 1919, 6.
125 "A Subsidy for Housing," *Manchester Guardian*, Nov. 22, 1919, 9.
126 "Ministers and Their Housing Policy: The Manchester Apologia, Lord R. Cecil's Criticisms," *Manchester Guardian*, Dec. 9, 1919, 9.
127 "Not Machiavellian: Lord Robert Cecil and the Housing Policy," Dec. 9, 1919, 7.
128 "The Government and the Coal Tangle," *Manchester Guardian*, Dec. 12, 1919, 9.
129 "The Only Remedy," *Irish Times*, Dec. 18, 1919, 7.
130 "The Crime Against Europe," *The Nation*, Dec. 27, 1919, 442–3.
131 Hansard, Dec. 18, 1919, 734.
132 "British Premier Speaks on League," *Christian Science Monitor*, Dec. 22, 1919, 1.
133 "Institute of International Affairs," *The Scotsman*, Aug. 21, 1919, 3; "Armistice Anniversary as League Day," *Manchester Guardian*, Sept. 12, 1919, 3; and "At Home," *Manchester Guardian*, Dec. 15, 1919, 14.
134 "A London Diary," *The Nation*, Aug. 23, 1919, 609–10. A similar sentiment in article on "Lord Robert Cecil," *The Nation*, Sept. 6, 1919.
135 "Scenes at St. Stephen's: Politics and Persons, Reputations of the Session," *The Observer*, Dec. 21, 1919, 8.
136 Monnet, *Mémoires*, 100.
137 Eustace Percy, "A Lesson of Armistice Day," *The Spectator*, Nov. 8, 1919, 607.
138 It is notable that many histories describing the incredible political turmoil in Britain during and after the war, the machinations of Lloyd George, and the disintegration of the Liberal Party and rise of Labour basically ignore foreign affairs; for example, see Trevor Wilson, *The Downfall of the Liberal Party 1914–1935* (London: Collins, 1966).
139 H. H. Harris, "Brilliant Brothers: Lords Robert & Hugh Cecil," *The Graphic*, Jan. 17, 1920, 74.

140 Phrase used by Gorman, *The Emergence of International Society*, 12; also on the dichotomy during the 1920s between successful "technical" work and the expanding political challenges faced by the League, see Patricia Clavin, *Securing the World Economy: The Reinvention of the League of Nations, 1920–1946* (Oxford: Oxford University Press, 2013), ch. 1.

Conclusion

1 Lord Hankey, *The Supreme Control at the Paris Peace Conference 1919* (London: George Allen & Unwin, 1963), 193.
2 Frances Lloyd George, *The Years That Are Past* (London: Hutchinson, 1967), 165.
3 Alan Sharp, *David Lloyd George: Great Britain* (London: Haus, 2008), 57.
4 R. S. Baker Paris diary, Apr. 28, 1919, *The Papers of Woodrow Wilson Project Records*, MC 178 1761–1992, Series 2: Audio-Visual Materials, Box 452, Public Policy Papers, Department of Rare Books and Special Collections, Princeton University Library.
5 Zara Steiner, *The Lights that Failed: European International History 1919–1933* (Oxford: Oxford University Press, 2005), 349.
6 Letter from Baker to Secretary of Woodrow Wilson Foundation in New York, 1924, NBKR 4X/25.
7 Sally Marks, *The Illusion of Peace: International Relations in Europe 1918–1933* (New York: St. Martin's Press, 1976), 36.
8 Cecil to Clynes, June 11, 1920, Add Ms. 51162.
9 Richard S. Grayson, *Liberals, International Relations and Appeasement: The Liberal Party, 1919–1939* (London: Frank Cass, 2001), 60, 65
10 E. T. Raymond, *All and Sundry* (New York: Henry Holt, 1920), 270.
11 Hugh Cecil to Robert Cecil, Jan. 12, 1921, Add. Ms. 51157.
12 Maurice Cowling, *The Impact of Labour 1920–1924: The Beginning of Modern British Politics*. (Cambridge: Cambridge University Press, 1971), 60–5.
13 Letter from Baker to Secretary of Woodrow Wilson Foundation in New York, 1924, NBKR 4X/25.
14 There are a number of examples of Lady Cecil's increasing isolation during this post-war period. From the moment of his return from Paris, Lord Cecil's social calendar became increasingly busy. For example, in November Cecil attended a banquet at Buckingham Palace for France's Poincaré, while Lady Cecil was one of the few invited who sent their regrets. "Court Circular," *The Times*, Nov. 11, 1919, 17. After Lady Cecil told her in August 1920 that Lord Cecil would be away for a month, busy plotting on the LNU with Oswald Mosley, Virginia Woolf couldn't help but pity her awkward, deaf old friend Nelly: "One guesses at isolation

unspeakable; never was there such a look of solitude on any human face as on hers; as if always away from life, alone, forced to bear it, & be grateful for any help. Her body incredibly little & shrunk, eyes slightly fading, cheeks sunk in –," in Anne Oliver Bell, ed., *The Diary of Virginia Woolf, Volume Two: 1920–1924* (New York and London: Harcourt Brace Jovanovich, 1978), 60.

15 Martin Ceadel, *Semi-Detached Idealists: The British Peace Movement and International Relations, 1854–1945* (Oxford: Oxford University Press, 2000), 426; Donald S. Birn, *The League of Nations Union 1918–1945* (Oxford: Clarendon Press, 1981); Susan Pedersen, *Eleanor Rathbone and the Politics of Conscience* (New Haven, CT, and London: Yale University Press, 2004), 279; and Richard Overy, *The Twilight Years: The Paradox of Britain between the Wars* (New York: Penguin, 2009), 258–9.

16 Helen McCarthy, *The British People and the League of Nations; Democracy, Citizenship and Internationalism c. 1918–45* (Manchester: Manchester University Press, 2011), 59–60.

17 E. H. Carr, *Britain: A Study of Foreign Policy from the Versailles Treaty to the Outbreak of War* (London: Longmans, Green, 1939), 99.

18 E. H. Carr, *Conditions of Peace* (New York: Macmillan, 1942), 168.

19 Ruth Henig, *The League of Nations* (London: Haus, 2010), 62.

20 Cecil, "The League of Nations, an Integral Part of Settlement," *The Times*, Dec. 20, 1919, 8. He addressed this letter from "League of Nations, 117 Picadilly."

21 Cecil speech in Edinburgh, "Practical Idealism: Lord Robert Cecil on League of Nations," *The Scotsman*, Nov. 27, 1919, 9.

22 Ceadel, *Semi-Detached Idealists*, 1–5.

23 Cecil to Churchill, July 24, 1924, Add. Ms. 51073.

24 James Barros, *Office without Power: Secretary-General Sir Eric Drummond, 1919–1933* (Oxford: Clarendon Press, 1979), 47–9; and Étienne Clémentel, *La France et la Politique économique interalliée* (New Haven, CT: Yale University Press, 1931), 321 (my translation).

25 Peter Yearwood, *Guarantee of Peace: The League of Nations in British Policy, 1914–1925* (Oxford: Oxford University Press, 2009), 141.

26 Henig, *The League of Nations*, 60.

27 Daniel Gorman, *The Emergence of International Society in the 1920s* (Cambridge: Cambridge University Press, 2012), 45.

28 Henig, *The League of Nations*, 86–7; and Yearwood, *Guarantee of Peace*, 165–7.

29 Henig, *The League of Nations*, 88–9.

30 Steiner, *The Lights That Failed*, 379–83.

31 Oona A. Hathaway and Scott J. Shapiro, *The Internationalists: How a Radical Plan to Outlaw War Remade the World* (New York: Simon and Schuster, 2017), xvii, 165.

32 Ceadel, *Semi-Detached Idealists*, 325.

33 David Reynolds, *The Long Shadow: The Legacies of the Great War in the Twentieth Century* (New York: W.W. Norton, 2014), 216–33.
34 Alan P. Dobson, *US Economic Statecraft for Survival 1933–1991: Of Sanctions, Embargoes and Economic Warfare* (London and New York: Routledge, 2002), 43.
35 On the importance of proximity to a nation's reaction to international problems, see E. H. Carr, *The Twenty Years' Crisis, 1919–1939: An Introduction to the Study of International Relations* (London: Macmillan, 1962), 103–5.
36 Steiner, *The Lights That Failed*, 750.
37 Cecelia Lynch, *Beyond Appeasement: Interpreting Interwar Peace Movements in World Politics* (Ithaca, NY, and London: Cornell University Press, 1999), 116–17.
38 Cecil of Chelwood, Viscount (Lord Robert), *All the Way* (London: Hodder and Stoughton, 1949), 207–8.
39 Gary Clyde Hufbauer, Jeffrey J. Schott, Kimberly Ann Elliott, and Barbara Oegg, *Economic Sanctions Reconsidered* (Washington, DC: Peterson Institute for International Economics, 2007), 70–1.
40 Hufbauer et al., *Economic Sanctions Reconsidered*, 157.
41 Eduardo Porter, "Want to Punish Putin? Economic Sanctions Probably Won't Cut It." *New York Times*, July 26, 2017, B3.
42 Hufbauer et al., *Economic Sanctions Reconsidered*, 158.
43 Hufbauer et al., *Economic Sanctions Reconsidered*, 175.
44 Luck, *Mixed Messages*, 151–2.
45 Steven Pinker, *The Better Angels of Our Nature: Why Violence Has Declined* (New York: Penguin, 2012).
46 E. H. Carr, *International Relations between the Two World Wars* (London: Macmillan, 1948), 4–6.
47 Quote referring to the ultimate Treaty stipulations on German disarmament, in David Stevenson, "Britain, France and the Origins of German Disarmament, 1916–19," *Journal of Strategic Studies* 29, no. 2 (2006): 204; and also Adam Tooze, *The Deluge: The Great War, America and the Remaking of the Global Order, 1916–1931* (New York: Viking, 2014), 295.
48 Patricia Clavin, *Securing the World Economy: The Reinvention of the League of Nations, 1920–1946* (Oxford: Oxford University Press, 2013), 16–25.
49 Pedersen, Susan. *The Guardians: The League of Nations and the Crisis of Empire* (New York: Oxford University Press, 2015), 11; and Mark Mazower, *Governing the World: The History of an Idea* (New York: The Penguin Press, 2012), 143.
50 For example, F. S. Northedge, *The League of Nations: Its Life and Times, 1920–1946* (New York: Holmes & Meier, 1986), 70; and World Peace Foundation, *The League of Nations*, vol. III, nos. 1–2 (Boston, MA: World Peace Foundation, 1920), 1–2.
51 Seth Tillman, *Anglo-American Relations at the Paris Peace Conference of 1919* (Princeton, NJ: Princeton University Press, 1961), 406.

52 Pedersen, *The Guardians*, 9; and Patricia Clavin, "The Austrian Hunger Crisis and International Organization after the First World War," *International Affairs* 90, no. 2 (2014).
53 Mazower, *Governing the World*, 143.
54 Marc Trachtenburg explains the link between US refusal to help European reconstruction and the resulting British and French demands for reparations to enable their reconstruction, in Marc Trachtenberg, "Reparation at the Paris Peace Conference," *The Journal of Modern History* 51, no. 1 (1979): 51–2. Also, Klaus Schwabe, *Woodrow Wilson, Revolutionary Germany, and Peacemaking, 1918–1919: Missionary Diplomacy and the Realities of Power* (Chapel Hill: University of North Carolina Press, 1985), ch. 6.
55 Carl P. Parrini, *Heir to Empire: United States Economic Diplomacy, 1916–1923* (Pittsburgh, PA, University of Pittsburgh Press, 1969), chapter III.
56 Herbert Hoover, *The Ordeal of Woodrow Wilson* (New York: McGraw-Hill, 1958), 87. Edward House intriguingly noted the failed opportunity to link loan forgiveness and reparations to support European reconstruction, in "The Versailles Peace in Retrospect," in Edward Mandell House and Charles Seymour, eds., *What Really Happened at Paris: The Story of the Peace Conference, 1918–1919. By American Delegates* (New York: Charles Scribner's Sons, 1921), 427–9.
57 Sally Marks, "Mistakes and Myths: The Allies, Germany, and the Versailles Treaty, 1918–1921," *Journal of Modern History* 85, no. 3 (2013): 638–9.
58 Steiner, *The Lights That Failed*, 184–5.
59 Steiner, *The Lights That Failed*, 189.
60 Bruce Kent, *The Spoils of War: The Politics, Economics and Diplomacy of Reparations, 1918–1932* (Oxford: Clarendon Press, 1989), 66–8, 77–8; and William Mulligan, *The Great War for Peace* (New Haven, CT, and London: Yale University Press, 2014), 363–4.
61 Steiner, *The Lights That Failed*, 249–50, 431–2.
62 Coates, *Legalist Empire*, 162–8.
63 Robert Boyce, *The Great Interwar Crisis and the Collapse of Globalization* (Basingstoke: Palgrave Macmillan, 2009), 47–8, 70.
64 Steiner, *The Lights That Failed*, 620.
65 David Ekbladh, *The Great American Mission: Modernization and the Construction of an American World Order* (Princeton, NJ: Princeton University Press, 2010), 23–5.
66 Tooze, *The Deluge*, 517–18.
67 Hoover, *The Ordeal of Woodrow Wilson*, 300.
68 Boyce, *The Great Interwar Crisis*, 44.
69 Peter Jackson, *Beyond the Balance of Power: France and the Politics of National Security in the Era of the First Word War* (Cambridge: Cambridge University Press, 2013).

70 Jeanne Morefield, *Covenants without Swords: Idealist Imperialism and the Spirit of Empire* (Princeton, NJ: Princeton University Press, 2005), 16.
71 John Milton Cooper, *Breaking the Heart of the World: Woodrow Wilson and the Fight for the League of Nations* (Cambridge: Cambridge University Press, 2001), 424–6; and Yearwood, *Guarantee of Peace*, 144–5.
72 George W. Egerton, "Great Britain and the League of Nations: Collective Security as Myth and History," in *The League of Nations in Retrospect: Proceedings of the Symposium* (Berlin and New York: Walter de Gruyter, 1983).
73 Jessica T. Mathews, "Nuclear Diplomacy: From Iran to North Korea?" *New York Review of Books*, Aug. 17, 2017, 21; and Lee Jones, *Societies under Siege: Exploring How International Economic Sanctions (Do Not) Work* (Oxford: Oxford University Press, 2015), 2–5.
74 Francesco Giumelli, *The Success of Sanctions: Lessons Learned from the EU Experience* (Farnham, Surrey: Ashgate, 2013), 184.
75 Hathaway and Shapiro, *The Internationalists*, 394–5.
76 Carr, *The Twenty Years' Crisis*, 131.
77 R. T. Naylor, *Economic Warfare: Sanctions, Embargo Busting, and Their Human Cost* (Boston, MA: Northeastern University Press, 1999).
78 Hufbauer et al., *Economic Sanctions Reconsidered*, x.
79 Joy Gordon, "The Human Costs of the Iran Sanctions," *Foreign Policy*, October 18, 2013, https://foreignpolicy.com/2013/10/18/the-human-costs- of-the-iran-sanctions/.
80 Stephen Porter, "Humanitarian Diplomacy after World War II: The United Nations Relief and Rehabilitation Administration," in *Foreign Policy Breakthroughs: Cases in Successful Diplomacy*, ed. Robert Hutchings and Jeremi Suri (New York: Oxford University Press, 2015).

Bibliography

Published Document Collections

BDFA volumes 1–15.
British Documents on Foreign Affairs—Reports and Papers from the Foreign Office Confidential Print. Part II, From the First to the Second World War. Series I, the Paris Peace Conference of 1919, edited by M. L. Dockrill, Kenneth Bourne, and Donald Cameron Watt. Frederick, MD: University Publications of America, 1989.
DBFP volumes 1–27.
Documents on British Foreign Policy, 1919–1939, Series 1, Volumes 1–27, edited by E. L. Woodward and Rohan Butler. London: H.M. Stationery Office, 1946.
FRUS volumes V and VI.
Papers Relating to the Foreign Relations of the United States, 1919: The Paris Peace Conference. Washington, DC: US Government Printing Office, 1919.

Archival Sources

Balfour Papers, British Library, London. Add. Ms. 49738.
Cecil of Chelwood Papers. British Library, London. Add. Ms. 51071–51204.
Gilbert Close Papers
National Archives, Kew. FO 800/195, 196, 197, 207, 215
Papers of Robert Edgar Algernon Gascoyne-Cecil, Viscount Cecil of Chelwood. Hatfield House Library and Archives. CHE 1–118.
Princeton, Mudd Manuscript Library, Bernard M. Baruch Papers.
Ray Stannard Baker Papers
Raymond B. Fosdick Papers
The Archives of Lord Hankey of the Chart (Maurice Hankey), Churchill Archives Centre, Cambridge. HNKY.
The Papers of Baron Noel-Baker, Churchill Archives Centre, Cambridge. NBKR.

British Newspapers Cited

The Courier and Argus
Daily Express
Daily Mail
The Graphic
The Irish Times
The Manchester Guardian
The Nation
The New Statesman
The Nottingham Evening Post
The Observer
The Scotsman
The Spectator
The Times (London)

United States Newspapers Cited

The Atlanta Constitution
The Baltimore Sun
Boston Daily Globe
Chicago Daily Tribune
The Christian Science Monitor
The Los Angeles Times
The New York Times
New-York Tribune
St. Louis Post-Dispatch
The Wall Street Journal

Memoirs, Diaries, and Other Primary Sources

Bane, Suda Lorena, and Ralph Haswell Lutz, eds. *The Blockade of Germany after the Armistice 1918–1919: Selected Documents of the Supreme Economic Council, Superior Blockade Council, American Relief Administration, and Other Wartime Organizations*. Stanford, CA: Stanford University Press, 1942.

Barbusse, Henri. *Under Fire*. New York: Penguin Classics, 2004.

Barnes, George N. *From Workshop to War Cabinet*. London: Herbert Jenkins, 1924.
Barton, Michael, ed. *Citizen Extraordinaire: The Diplomatic Diaries of Vance McCormick in London and Paris, 1917–1919, with Other Documents from a High-Minded American Life*. Mechanicsburg, PA: Stackpole Books, 2004.
Baruch, Bernard M. *The Making of the Reparation and Economic Sections of the Treaty*. New York: Harper & Brothers, 1920.
Begbie, Harold ("A Gentleman with a Duster"). *The Mirrors of Downing Street: Some Political Reflections*. New York and London: G.P. Putnam's Sons, 1921.
Bell, Anne Oliver, ed. *The Diary of Virginia Woolf, Volume Two: 1920–1924*. New York and London: Harcourt Brace Jovanovich, 1978.
Bonsal, Stephen. *Unfinished Business*. New York: Doubleday, Doran, 1944.
Borden, Robert Laird. *Robert Laird Borden: His Memoirs*. New York: Macmillan, 1938.
British Red Cross Society. *Reports by the Joint War Committee and the Joint War Finance Committee of the British Red Cross Society and the Order of St. John of Jerusalem in England on Voluntary Aid rendered to the Sick and Wounded at Home and Abroad and to British Prisoners of War, 1914–1919*. London: His Majesty's Stationery Office, 1921.
Bryant, F. Russell, ed. *The Coalition Diaries and Letters of H.A.L. Fisher, 1916–1922: The Historian in Lloyd George's Cabinet*. 4 vols. Lewiston, NY: The Edwin Mellen Press, 2006.
Callwell, C. E., Major-General Sir. *Field-Marshall Sir Henry Wilson: His Life and Diaries*. Vol. II. London: Cassell, 1927.
Cecil, Lord Robert, and the Rev. H. J. Clayton. *Our National Church*. London: Frederick Warne, 1913.
Cecil of Chelwood, Viscount (Lord Robert). *All the Way*. London: Hodder and Stoughton, 1949.
Cecil of Chelwood, Viscount (Lord Robert). *A Great Experiment: An Autobiography*. New York: Oxford University Press, 1941.
Chirol, Sir Valentine. *Fifty Years in a Changing World*. London: Jonathan Cape, 1927.
Clémentel, Étienne. *La France et la Politique économique interalliée*. New Haven, CT: Yale University Press, 1931.
Dillon, Emile Joseph. *The Inside Story of the Peace Conference*. New York and London: Harper & Brothers, 1920.
Dutton, David, ed. *Paris 1918: The War Diary of the British Ambassador, the 17th Earl of Derby*. Liverpool: Liverpool University Press, 2001.
Fosdick, Raymond B. *Chronicle of a Generation: An Autobiography*. New York: Harper & Brothers, 1958.
Fosdick, Raymond B. *Letters on the League of Nations*. Princeton, NJ: Princeton University Press, 1966.
Hankey, Lord. *The Supreme Command 1914–1918*. Vol. 2. London: George Allen and Unwin, 1961.

Hankey, Lord. *The Supreme Control at the Paris Peace Conference 1919*. London: George Allen & Unwin, 1963.

Headlam-Morley, Sir James. *A Memoir of the Paris Peace Conference 1919*. London: Methuen, 1972.

Hoover, Herbert. *America's First Crusade*. New York: Charles Scribner's Sons, 1942.

Hoover, Herbert. "The Economic Administration." In *What Really Happened at Paris: The Story of the Peace Conference, 1918–1919. By American Delegates*, edited by Edward M. House and Charles Seymour. New York: Charles Scribner's Sons, 1921.

Hoover, Herbert. *Memoirs*. New York: Macmillan, 1951–2.

Hoover, Herbert. *The Ordeal of Woodrow Wilson*. New York: McGraw-Hill, 1958.

Hoover, Herbert. *Two Peacemakers in Paris: The Hoover-Wilson Post-Armistice Letters*. College Station: Texas A&M University Press, 1978.

House, Edward Mandell, and Charles Seymour, eds. *What Really Happened at Paris: The Story of the Peace Conference, 1918–1919. By American Delegates*. New York: Charles Scribner's Sons, 1921.

How, Frederick Douglas. *The Marquis of Salisbury*. London: Isbister, 1902.

Huddleston, Sisley. *Peace-Making at Paris*. London: T.F. Unwin, 1919.

Hughes, William Morris. *Crusts and Crusades; Tales of Bygone Days*. Sydney: Angus and Robertson, 1947.

Hughes, William Morris. "Foreword." In *The 38th Battalion A.I.F. The Story and Official History*, edited by Eric Fairey. Bendigo, Australia: Bendigo Advertiser and the Cambridge Press, 1920.

Hughes, William Morris. *Splendid Adventure; A Review of Empire Relations Within and without the Commonwealth of Britannic Nations*. London: E. Benn, 1929.

International Labour Office, "Profit-Sharing and Labour Co-Partnership in Great Britain," *International Labour Review* 4 (1921).

Jones, Thomas. *Whitehall Diary*. London, New York: Oxford University Press, 1969.

Keynes, John Maynard. *Collected Writings of John Maynard Keynes, Volume XVI: Activities 1914–1919: The Treasury and Versailles*. London: Macmillan, 1971.

Keynes, John Maynard. *The Economic Consequences of the Peace*. New York: Harcourt, Brace and Howe, 1920.

Lamont, Thomas. "Reparations: Questions Answered." In *What Really Happened at Paris: The Story of the Peace Conference, 1918–1919. By American Delegates*, edited by Edward M. House and Charles Seymour. New York: Charles Scribner's Sons, 1921.

Lansing, Robert. *The Peace Negotiations: A Personal Narrative*. Boston, MA, and New York: Houghton Mifflin, 1921.

Link, Arthur, ed. *The Papers of Woodrow Wilson*. Vols. 53–63. Princeton, NJ: Princeton University Press, 1966–94.

Lloyd George, David. *The Truth about the Peace Treaties*. London: Victor Gollancz, 1938.
Lloyd George, Frances. *The Years That Are Past*. London: Hutchinson, 1967.
Malcolm, Sir Ian. *Lord Balfour: A Memory*. London: Macmillan, 1930.
Mantoux, Paul. *The Deliberations of the Council of Four*. Translated and edited by Arthur Link and Manfred F. Boemeke. Princeton, NJ: Princeton University Press, 1992.
Miller, David Hunter. *The Drafting of the Covenant, Volume 1*. New York and London: G.P. Putnam's Sons, 1928.
Miller, David Hunter. "The Making of the League of Nations." In *What Really Happened at Paris: The Story of the Peace Conference, 1918-1919. By American Delegates*, edited by Edward M. House and Charles Seymour. New York: Charles Scribner's Sons, 1921.
Miller, David Hunter. *My Diary at the Peace Conference of Paris, with Documents*. New York: Printed for the author by the Appeal printing company, 1924.
Monnet, Jean. *Mémoires*. Paris, Fayard, 1976.
Nicolson, Harold. *Peacemaking 1919*. New York: Grosset & Dunlap, 1965.
Oppenheimer, Sir Francis. *Stranger Within: Autobiographical Pages*. London: Faber and Faber, 1960.
Percy, Lord Eustace. *Some Memories*. London: Eyre & Spottiswoode, 1958.
Raymond, E. T. *All and Sundry*. New York: Henry Holt, 1920.
Riddell, Lord George Allardice. *Lord Riddell's Intimate Diary of the Peace Conference and after, 1918-1923*. London: Victor Gollancz, 1933.
Salter, J. Arthur. *Allied Shipping Control: An Experiment in International Administration*. Oxford: Clarendon Press, 1921.
Salter, Lord. *Memoirs of a Public Servant*. London: Faber and Faber, 1961.
Shepardson, Whitney. *Early History of the Council on Foreign Relations*. Stamford, CT: Overbrook Press, 1960.
Surface, Frank M., and Raymond L. Bland, eds. *American Food in the World War and Reconstruction Period: Operations of the Organizations under the Direction of Herbert Hoover 1914-1924*. Stanford, CA: Stanford University Press, 1931.
Taylor, A. J. P., ed. *Lloyd George: A Diary by Frances Stevenson*. London: Hutchinson, 1971.
Thompson, Charles T. *The Peace Conference Day by Day: A Presidential Pilgrimage Leading to the Discovery of Europe*. New York: Brentano's, 1920.
White, William Allen. *The Autobiography of William Allen White*. New York: Macmillan, 1946.
Williamson, Philip, ed. *The Modernisation of Conservative Politics: The Diaries and Letters of William Bridgeman 1904-1935*. London: The Historians' Press, 1988.
World Peace Foundation. *The League of Nations*. Vol. III, nos. 1-2. Boston, MA: World Peace Foundation, 1920.

Secondary Sources—Monographs, Articles

Adams, R. J. Q. *Balfour: The Last Grandee*. London: John Murray, 2007.
Allerfeldt, Kristofer. "Wilsonian Pragmatism? Woodrow Wilson, Japanese Immigration, and the Paris Peace Conference." *Diplomacy and Statecraft* 15 (2004): 545–72.
Andelman, David. *A Shattered Peace: Versailles 1919 and the Price We Pay Today*. Hoboken, NJ: John Wiley and Sons, 2008.
Ball, Stuart. "The Conservative Party, the Role of the State and the Politics of Protection, c. 1918–1932." *History: Journal of the Historical Association* 96 (2011).
Barnett, Correlli. *The Collapse of British Power*. Phoenix Mill: Sutton, 1984 (first edition 1972).
Barros, James. *Office without Power: Secretary-General Sir Eric Drummond, 1919–1933*. Oxford: Clarendon Press, 1979.
Barros, James. "The Role of Sir Eric Drummond." In *The League of Nations in Retrospect: Proceedings of the Symposium*, edited by United Nations Library (Geneva, Switzerland). Berlin and New York: Walter de Gruyter, 1983.
Bell, P. M. H. *Disestablishment in Ireland and Wales*. London: SPCK, 1969.
Bennett, G. H. *British Foreign Policy during the Curzon Period, 1919–24*. New York: St. Martin's Press, 1995.
Benstock, Shari. *Women of the Left Bank: Paris 1900–1940*. Austin: University of Texas Press, 1986.
Bessel, Richard "Revolution." In *The Cambridge History of the First World War, Volume II: The State*, edited by Jay Winter. Cambridge: Cambridge University Press, 2014.
Best, Gary Dean. "Food Relief as Price Support: Hoover and American Pork, January–March 1919." *Agricultural History* 45, no. 2 (1971): 79–84.
Billington, David P. Jr. *Lothian: Philip Kerr and the Quest for World Order*. Westport, CT, and London: Praeger Security International, 2006.
Birdsall, Paul. *Versailles Twenty Years after*. London: George Allen & Unwin, 1941.
Birn, Donald S. *The League of Nations Union 1918–1945*. Oxford: Clarendon Press, 1981.
Boyce, Robert. *The Great Interwar Crisis and the Collapse of Globalization*. Basingstoke: Palgrave Macmillan, 2009.
Bridge, Carl. *William Hughes: Australia*. London: Haus, 2011.
Brody, J. Kenneth. *The Avoidable War, Volume 1: Lord Cecil and the Policy of Principle, 1933–1935*. New Brunswick and London: Transaction Publishers, 1999.
Bunselmeyer, Robert E. *The Cost of the War, 1914–1919: British Economic War Aims and the Origins of Reparation*. Hamden, CT: Archon Books, 1975.
Burk, Kathleen, ed. *War and the State: The Transformation of British Government, 1914–1919*. London: George Allen & Unwin, 1982.
Busch, Briton Cooper. *Hardinge of Penshurst: A Study in the Old Diplomacy*. Hamden, CT: Archon Books, 1980.

Cabanes, Bruno. *The Great War and the Origins of Humanitarianism, 1918–1924.* Cambridge: Cambridge University Press, 2014.
Cannadine, David. *The Decline and Fall of the British Aristocracy.* New York: Vintage, 1999.
Carr, E. H. *Britain: A Study of Foreign Policy from the Versailles Treaty to the Outbreak of War.* London: Longmans, Green, 1939.
Carr, E. H. *Conditions of Peace.* New York: Macmillan, 1942.
Carr, E. H. *International Relations between the Two World Wars.* London: Macmillan, 1948.
Carr, E. H. *The Twenty Years' Crisis, 1919–1939: An Introduction to the Study of International Relations.* London: Macmillan, 1962.
Ceadel, Martin. *Semi-Detached Idealists: The British Peace Movement and International Relations, 1854–1945.* Oxford: Oxford University Press, 2000.
Cecil, Hugh P. "The Development of Lord Robert Cecil's Views on the Securing of a Lasting Peace 1915–1919." D.Phil thesis, Oxford University, Oxford, 1971.
Cecil, Hugh P. "Lord Robert Cecil and the League of Nations during the First World War." In *Home Fires and Foreign Fields: British Social and Military Experience in the First World War*, edited by Peter Liddle. London: Brassey's Defence Publishers, 1985.
Cecil, Hugh P. "Lord Robert Cecil: Nineteenth-Century Upbringing." *History Today* 25 (1975): 118–27.
Cecil, Hugh, and Mirabel Cecil. *Imperial Marriage: An Edwardian War and Peace.* London: John Murray, 2002.
Clavin, Patricia. "The Austrian Hunger Crisis and International Organization after the First World War." *International Affairs* 90, no. 2 (2014): 265–78.
Clavin, Patricia. "Men and Markets: Global Capital and the International Economy." In *Internationalisms: A Twentieth-Century History*, edited by Glenda Sluga and Patricia Clavin. Cambridge: Cambridge University Press, 2017.
Clavin, Patricia. *Securing the World Economy: The Reinvention of the League of Nations, 1920–1946.* Oxford: Oxford University Press, 2013.
Clements, Kendrick A. *The Life of Herbert Hoover: Imperfect Visionary 1918–1928.* New York: Palgrave Macmillan, 2010.
Coates, Benjamin Allen. *Legalist Empire: International Law and American Foreign Relations in the Early Twentieth Century.* Oxford: Oxford University Press, 2016.
Cobb, Stephen. *Preparing for Blockade 1885–1914: Naval Contingency for Economic Warfare.* Farnham, UK: Ashgate, 2013.
Cohrs, Patrick. *The Unfinished Peace after World War I: America, Britain and the Stabilisation of Europe, 1919–1932.* Cambridge: Cambridge University Press, 2006.
Cooper, John Milton. *Breaking the Heart of the World: Woodrow Wilson and the Fight for the League of Nations.* Cambridge: Cambridge University Press, 2001.
Cowling, Maurice. *The Impact of Labour 1920–1924: The Beginning of Modern British Politics.* Cambridge: Cambridge University Press, 1971.

Cox, Mary Elisabeth. "Hunger Games: Or How the Allied Blockade in the First World War Deprived German Children of Nutrition, and Allied Food Aid Subsequently Saved Them." *Economic History Review* 68, no. 2 (2015): 600–31.

Crowe, Sibyl, and Edward Corp. *Our Ablest Public Servant: Sir Eyre Crowe 1864–1925*. Braunton Devon: Merlin Books, 1993.

D'Agostino, Anthony. *The Rise of Global Powers: International Politics in the Era of the World Wars*. Cambridge: Cambridge University Press, 2012.

Dalby, Andrew. *Eleftherios Venizelos: Greece*. London: Haus, 2010.

Davenport-Hines, Richard. *Ettie: The Intimate Life and Dauntless Spirit of Lady Desborough*. London: Weidenfeld & Nicolson, 2008.

Dehne, Phillip. "The Ministry of Blockade and the Fate of Free Trade during the First World War." *Twentieth Century British History* 27, no. 3 (2016): 333–56.

Dehne, Phillip. *On the Far Western Front: Britain's First World War in South America*. Manchester: Manchester University Press, 2009.

Dell'Orto, Giovanni. *American Journalism and International Relations: Foreign Correspondence from the Early Republic to the Digital Era*. Cambridge: Cambridge University Press, 2013.

Dobson, Alan P. *US Economic Statecraft for Survival 1933–1991: Of Sanctions, Embargoes and Economic Warfare*. London and New York: Routledge, 2002.

Dockrill, Michael L. "The Foreign Office and the Proposed Institute of International Affairs 1919." *International Affairs* 56, no. 4 (1980): 665–72.

Dockrill, Michael L., and J. Douglas Goold. *Peace without Promise: Britain and the Peace Conferences 1919–23*. Hamden, CT: Archon Books, 1980.

Duchêne, François. *Jean Monnet: The First Statesman of Interdependence*. New York: W.W. Norton, 1994.

Edmonds, J. E. *The Occupation of the Rhineland 1918–1929*. London: HMSO, 1987. Originally 1944.

Edwards, P. G. *Prime Ministers and Diplomats: The Making of Australian Foreign Policy 1901–1949*. Melbourne: Oxford University Press, 1983.

Egerton, George W. *Great Britain and the Creation of the League of Nations: Strategy, Politics, and International Organization, 1914–1919*. Chapel Hill: University of North Carolina Press, 1978.

Egerton, George W. "Great Britain and the League of Nations: Collective Security as Myth and History." In *The League of Nations in Retrospect: Proceedings of the Symposium*, edited by United Nations Library (Geneva, Switzerland). Berlin and New York: Walter de Gruyter, 1983.

Ekbladh, David. *The Great American Mission: Modernization and the Construction of an American World Order*. Princeton, NJ: Princeton University Press, 2010.

Elcock, H. J. *Portrait of a Decision: The Council of Four and the Treaty of Versailles*. London: Eyre Methuen, 1972.

Ferguson, Niall. *Paper and Iron: Hamburg Business and German Politics in the Era of Inflation, 1897–1927*. Cambridge: Cambridge University Press, 1995.

Ferguson, Niall. *The Pity of War*. New York: Basic Books, 1999.
Ferris, John "Pragmatic Hegemony and British Economic Warfare, 1900–1918: Preparations and Practice." In *Britain's War at Sea, 1914–1918: The War They Thought and the War They Fought*, edited by Greg Kennedy. London: Routledge, 2016.
Fitzhardinge, L. F. "W.M. Hughes and the Treaty of Versailles, 1919." *Journal of Commonwealth Political Studies* 5, no. 2 (1967): 130–42.
Floto, Inga. *Colonel House in Paris: A Study of American Policy at the Paris Peace Conference 1919*. Princeton, NJ: Princeton University Press, 1980.
Fransen, Frederic J. *The Supranational Politics of Jean Monnet: Ideas and Origins of the European Community*. Westport, CT: Greenwood Press, 2001.
French, David. *The Strategy of the Lloyd George Coalition, 1916–1918*. Oxford: Clarendon Press, 1995.
Gerber, Larry G. "Corporatism in Comparative Perspective: The Impact of the First World War on American and British Labour Relations." *The Business History Review* 62, no. 1 (1988): 93–127.
Gerwarth, Robert. *The Vanquished: Why the First World War Failed to End*. New York: Farrar, Straus and Giroux, 2016.
Giumelli, Francesco. *The Success of Sanctions: Lessons Learned from the EU Experience*. Farnham, Surrey: Ashgate, 2013.
Glaser, Elisabeth. "The Making of the Economic Peace." In *The Treaty of Versailles: A Reassessment after 75 Years*, edited by Manfred F. Boemeke, Gerald D. Feldman, and Elisabeth Glaser. Washington, DC: German Historical Institute, and Cambridge: Cambridge University Press, 1998.
Goldberg, George. *The Peace to End Peace: The Paris Peace Conference of 1919*. New York: Harcourt, Brace & World, 1969.
Goldstein, Erik. *The First World War Peace Settlements, 1919–1925*. London: Longman, 2002.
Goldstein, Erik. *Winning the Peace: British Diplomatic Strategy, Peace Planning, and the Paris Peace Conference, 1916–1920*. Oxford: Clarendon Press, 1991.
Gorman, Daniel. *The Emergence of International Society in the 1920s*. Cambridge: Cambridge University Press, 2012.
Gorman, Daniel. *International Cooperation in the Early Twentieth Century*. London: Bloomsbury, 2017.
Grant, James. *Bernard Baruch: The Adventures of a Wall Street Legend*. New York: Simon & Schuster, 1983.
Grayson, Richard S. *Liberals, International Relations and Appeasement: The Liberal Party, 1919–1939*. London: Frank Cass, 2001.
Greenhalgh, Elizabeth. *Victory through Coalition: Britain and France during the First World War*. Cambridge: Cambridge University Press, 2005.
Grigg, John. *Lloyd George: War Leader, 1916–1918*. London: Allen Lane, 2002.
Hamilton, John Maxwell. *Journalism's Roving Eye: A History of American Foreign Reporting*. Baton Rouge: Louisiana State University Press, 2009.

Hancock, W. K. *Smuts: The Sanguine Years, 1870–1919*. Cambridge: Cambridge University Press, 1962.

Hathaway, Oona A., and Scott J. Shapiro. *The Internationalists: How a Radical Plan to Outlaw War Remade the World*. New York: Simon and Schuster, 2017.

Hayden, Joseph R. *Negotiating in the Press: American Journalism and Diplomacy, 1918–1919*. Baton Rouge: Louisiana State University Press, 2010.

Henig, Ruth. *The League of Nations*. London: Haus, 2010.

Howell, Georgina. *Daughter of the Desert: The Remarkable Life of Gertrude Bell*. Basingstoke: Macmillan, 2006.

Hufbauer, Gary Clyde, Jeffrey J. Schott, Kimberly Ann Elliott, and Barbara Oegg. *Economic Sanctions Reconsidered*. 3rd ed. Washington, DC: Peterson Institute for International Economics, 2007.

Hull, Isabel V. *A Scrap of Paper: Breaking and Making International Law during the Great War*. Ithaca, NY, and London: Cornell University Press, 2014.

Iriye, Akira. *Global Community: The Role of International Organizations in the Making of the Contemporary World*. Berkeley: University of California Press, 2002.

Irwin, Julia. "Taming Total War: Great War-Era American Humanitarianism and Its Legacies." In *Beyond 1917: The United States and the Global Legacies of the Great War*, edited by Thomas W. Zeiler, David K. Ekbladh, and Benjamin C. Montoya. New York: Oxford University Press, 2017.

Jackson, Peter. *Beyond the Balance of Power: France and the Politics of National Security in the Era of the First World War*. Cambridge: Cambridge University Press, 2013.

James, Lawrence. *The Golden Warrior: The Life and Legend of Lawrence of Arabia*. New York: Skyhorse, 2008.

Johnson, Gaynor. *Lord Robert Cecil: Politician and Internationalist*. Farnham, UK: Ashgate, 2013.

Jones, Jerry W. "The Naval Battle of Paris." *Naval War College Review* 62, no. 2 (2009): 77–89.

Jones, Lee. *Societies under Siege: Exploring How International Economic Sanctions (Do Not) Work*. Oxford: Oxford University Press, 2015.

Kent, Bruce. *The Spoils of War: The Politics, Economics and Diplomacy of Reparations, 1918–1932*. Oxford: Clarendon Press, 1989.

Kott, Sandrine. "Cold War Internationalism." In *Internationalisms: A Twentieth-Century History*, edited by Glenda Sluga and Patricia Clavin. Cambridge: Cambridge University Press, 2017.

Kramer, Alan. "Blockade and Economic Warfare." In *The Cambridge History of the First World War, Volume II: The State*, edited by Jay Winter, 460–89. Cambridge: Cambridge University Press, 2014.

Lambert, Nicholas. *Planning Armageddon: British Economic Warfare and the First World War*. Cambridge, MA: Harvard University Press, 2012.

Lee, Hermione. *Edith Wharton*. New York: Alfred A. Knopf, 2007.

Lentin, Antony. *General Smuts: South Africa*. London: Haus, 2010.

Lentin, Antony. *Lloyd George and the Lost Peace: From Versailles to Hitler, 1919–1940.* Basingstoke: Palgrave, 2001.

Lentin, Antony. *Lloyd George, Woodrow Wilson, and the Guilt of Germany: An Essay in the Pre-History of Appeasement.* Leicester: Leicester University Press, 1984.

Louis, William Roger. *Great Britain and Germany's Lost Colonies, 1914–1919.* Oxford: Clarendon Press, 1967.

Lovin, Clifford R. *A School for Diplomats: The Paris Peace Conference of 1919.* Lanham, MD: University Press of America, 1997.

Luck, Edward C. *Mixed Messages: American Politics and International Organization 1919–1999.* Washington, DC: Brookings Institution Press, 1999.

Lynch, Cecelia. *Beyond Appeasement: Interpreting Interwar Peace Movements in World Politics.* Ithaca, NY, and London: Cornell University Press, 1999.

MacMillan, Margaret. *Paris 1919: Six Months That Changed the World.* New York: Random House, 2003.

Maier, Charles. *Recasting Bourgeois Europe: Stabilization in France, Germany, and Italy in the Decade after World War I.* Princeton, NJ: Princeton University Press, 1975.

Manela, Erez. *The Wilsonian Moment: Self-Determination and the International Origins of Anticolonial Nationalism.* New York and Oxford: Oxford University Press, 2006.

Marks, Sally. "Behind the Scenes at the Paris Peace Conference of 1919." *Journal of British Studies* 9, no. 2 (1970): 154–80.

Marks, Sally. *The Illusion of Peace: International Relations in Europe 1918–1933.* New York: St. Martin's Press, 1976.

Marks, Sally. "Mistakes and Myths: The Allies, Germany, and the Versailles Treaty, 1918–1921." *Journal of Modern History* 85, no. 3 (2013): 632–59.

Markwell, Donald. *John Maynard Keynes and International Relations: Economic Paths to War and Peace.* Oxford: Oxford University Press, 2006.

Marsh, Peter T. *The Discipline of Popular Government: Lord Salisbury's Domestic Statecraft, 1881–1902.* Sussex: The Harvester Press, 1978.

Marsh, Peter T. *Joseph Chamberlain: Entrepreneur in Politics.* New Haven, CT, and London: Yale University Press, 1994.

Marston, F. S. *The Peace Conference of 1919: Organization and Procedure.* London: Oxford University Press, 1944.

Mayer, Arno. *Politics and Diplomacy of Peacemaking: Containment and Counterrevolution at Versailles, 1918–1919.* New York: Alfred A. Knopf, 1967.

Mazower, Mark. *Governing the World: The History of an Idea.* New York: The Penguin Press, 2012.

Mazower, Mark. *No Enchanted Palace: The End of Empire and the Ideological Origins of the United Nations.* Princeton, NJ, and Oxford: Princeton University Press, 2009.

McCarthy, Helen. *The British People and the League of Nations; Democracy, Citizenship and Internationalism c. 1918–45.* Manchester: Manchester University Press, 2011.

McCarthy, Helen. *Women of the World: The Rise of the Female Diplomat.* London: Bloomsbury, 2014.

Miller, Michael B. *Europe and the Maritime World: A Twentieth-Century History*. Cambridge: Cambridge University Press, 2012.

Morefield, Jeanne. *Covenants without Swords: Idealist Imperialism and the Spirit of Empire*. Princeton, NJ: Princeton University Press, 2005.

Mulligan, William. *The Great War for Peace*. New Haven, CT, and London: Yale University Press, 2014.

Nash, George H. *The Life of Herbert Hoover: Master of Emergencies, 1917-1918*. New York and London: W.W. Norton, 1996.

Naylor, R. T. *Economic Warfare: Sanctions, Embargo Busting, and Their Human Cost*. Boston, MA: Northeastern University Press, 1999.

Neff, Stephen C. "Disrupting a Delicate Balance: The Allied Blockade Policy and the Law of Maritime Neutrality during the Great War." *European Journal of International Law* 29, no. 2 (2018): 459-75.

Nicolson, Juliet. *The Great Silence, 1918-1920: Living in the Shadow of the Great War*. London: John Murray, 2009.

Nielson, Keith. "Managing the War: Britain, Russia and *Ad Hoc* Government." In *Strategy and Intelligence: British Policy during the First World War*, edited by Michael Dockrill and David French. London: Hambledon Press, 1996.

Northedge, F. S. *The League of Nations: Its Life and Times, 1920-1946*. New York: Holmes & Meier, 1986.

Offer, Avner. *The First World War: An Agrarian Interpretation*. Oxford: Oxford University Press, 1989.

Osborne, Eric W. *Britain's Economic Blockiade of Germany, 1914-1919*. London and New York: Frank Cass, 2004.

Otte, T. G. "Between Hammer and Anvil: Sir Francis Oppenheimer, the Netherlands Overseas Trust and Allied Economic Warfare, 1914-1918." In *Diplomats at War: British and Commonwealth Diplomacy in Wartime*, edited by Christopher Baxter and Andrew Stewart. Leiden and Boston, MA: Martinus Nijhoff, 2008.

Otte, T. G. "'Allah Is Great and the NOT Is His Prophet': Sea Power, Diplomacy and Economic Warfare. The Case of the Netherlands, 1900-1918." In *Britain's War at Sea, 1914-1918: The War They Thought and the War They Fought*, edited by Greg Kennedy. London: Routledge, 2016.

Parrini, Carl P. *Heir to Empire: United States Economic Diplomacy, 1916-1923*. Pittsburgh, PA: University of Pittsburgh Press, 1969.

Pedersen, Susan. *Eleanor Rathbone and the Politics of Conscience*. New Haven, CT, and London: Yale University Press, 2004.

Pedersen, Susan. "Empires, States and the League of Nations." In *Internationalisms: A Twentieth-Century History*, edited by Glenda Sluga and Patricia Clavin. Cambridge: Cambridge University Press, 2017.

Pedersen, Susan. *The Guardians: The League of Nations and the Crisis of Empire*. New York: Oxford University Press, 2015.

Porter, Stephen. "Humanitarian Diplomacy after World War II: The United Nations Relief and Rehabilitation Administration." In *Foreign Policy Breakthroughs: Cases in Successful Diplomacy*, edited by Robert Hutchings and Jeremi Suri. New York: Oxford University Press, 2015.

Proctor, Tammy M. "An American Enterprise? British Participation in US Food Relief Programmes (1914–1923)." *First World War Studies* 5, no. 1 (2014): 29–42.

Raffo, Peter. "The Anglo-American Preliminary Negotiations for a League of Nations." *Journal of Contemporary History* 9, no. 4 (1974): 153–76.

Reynolds, David. *The Long Shadow: The Legacies of the Great War in the Twentieth Century*. New York: W.W. Norton, 2014.

Rose, Inbal. *Conservatism and Foreign Policy during the Lloyd George Coalition 1918–1922*. London: Frank Cass, 1999.

Rose, Kenneth. *The Later Cecils*. London: Weidenfeld and Nicolson, 1975.

Roskill, Stephen. *Hankey: Man of Secrets, Volume II 1919–1931*. London: Collins, 1972.

Roskill, Stephen. "Lord Cecil and the Historians." *The Historical Journal* 25, no. 4 (1982): 953–4.

Rudin, Harry R. *Armistice 1918*. New Haven, CT: Yale University Press, 1944.

Rudman, Stella. *Lloyd George and the Appeasement of Germany, 1919–1945*. Cambridge: Cambridge Scholars, 2011.

Sare, Sami. *The League of Nations and the Debate on Disarmament (1918–1919)*. Rome: Edizioni Nuova Cultura, 2013.

Schuker, Stephen A. "The Rhineland Question: West European Security at the Paris Peace Conference of 1919." In *The Treaty of Versailles: A Reassessment after 75 Years*, edited by Manfred F. Boemeke, Gerald D. Feldman, and Elisabeth Glaser. Washington, DC: German Historical Institute, and Cambridge: Cambridge University Press, 1998.

Schwabe, Klaus. *Woodrow Wilson, Revolutionary Germany, and Peacemaking, 1918–1919: Missionary Diplomacy and the Realities of Power*. Chapel Hill: University of North Carolina Press, 1985.

Scott, George. *The Rise and Fall of the League of Nations*. London: Hutchinson, 1973.

Seligmann, Matthew S. "Failing to Prepare for the Great War? The Absence of Grand Strategy in British War Planning before 1914." *War in History* 24, no. 4 (2017): 414–37.

Sharp, Alan. *David Lloyd George: Great Britain*. London: Haus, 2008.

Sharp, Alan. *The Versailles Settlement: Peacemaking after the First World War, 1919–1923*, 2nd ed. Basingstoke: Palgrave Macmillan, 2008.

Sherington, Geoffrey. *Australia's Immigrants 1788–1978*. Sydney: George Allen & Unwin, 1980.

Silberstein-Loeb, Jonathan. *The International Distribution of News: The Associated Press, Press Association, and Reuters, 1848–1947*. Cambridge: Cambridge University Press, 2014.

Sinclair, David. *Hall of Mirrors*. London: Century, 2001.

Skidelsky, Robert. *John Maynard Keynes: A Biography. Vol. 1. Hopes Betrayed, 1883–1920*. London: Macmillan, 1983.

Sluga, Glenda, and Patricia Clavin, eds. *Internationalisms: A Twentieth-Century History*. Cambridge: Cambridge University Press, 2017.

Snelling, R. C. "Peacemaking, 1919: Australia, New Zealand and the British Empire Delegation at Versailles." *Journal of Imperial and Commonwealth History* 4, no. 1 (1975): 15–28.

Soutou, Georges-Henri, "Diplomacy." In *The Cambridge History of the First World War, Volume II: The State*, edited by Jay Winter. Cambridge: Cambridge University Press, 2014.

Soutou, Georges-Henri. *L'or et le sang: Les buts de guerre économique de la Premiere Guerre Mondiale*. Paris: Fayard, 1989.

Spartalis, Peter. *The Diplomatic Battles of Billy Hughes*. Sydney: Hale & Iremonger, 1983.

Steiner, Zara. *The Lights That Failed: European International History 1919–1933*. Oxford: Oxford University Press, 2005.

Stelzer, Cita. *Dinner with Churchill: Policy-Making at the Dinner Table*. London: Short Books, 2011.

Stevenson, David. "Britain, France and the Origins of German Disarmament, 1916–19." *Journal of Strategic Studies* 29, no. 2 (2006): 195–224.

Stevenson, David. *With Our Backs to the Wall: Victory and Defeat in 1918*. Cambridge, MA: Belknap Press of Harvard University Press, 2011.

Stovall, Tyler. *Paris and the Spirit of 1919: Consumer Struggles, Transnationalism and Revolution*. Cambridge: Cambridge University Press, 2012.

Striner, Richard. *Woodrow Wilson and World War I: A Burden Too Great to Bear*. Lanham, MD: Rowman & Littlefield, 2014.

Supple, Barry. "War Economies." In *The Cambridge History of the First World War, Volume II: The State*, edited by Jay Winter. Cambridge: Cambridge University Press, 2014.

Temperley, H. W. V., ed. *A History of the Peace Conference of Paris*. Vols. 1–6. London: H. Frowde, Hodder & Stoughton, 1920–4.

Thompson, F. M. L. *English Landed Society in the Nineteenth Century*. London: Routledge and Kegan Paul, 1963.

Tillman, Seth. *Anglo-American Relations at the Paris Peace Conference of 1919*. Princeton, NJ: Princeton University Press, 1961.

Tooze, Adam. *The Deluge: The Great War, America and the Remaking of the Global Order, 1916–1931*. New York: Viking, 2014.

Toye, Richard. *Lloyd George & Churchill: Rivals for Greatness*. London: Macmillan, 2007.

Trachtenberg, Marc. "'A New Economic Order': Étienne Clémentel and French Economic Diplomacy during the First World War." *French Historical Studies* 10, no. 2. (1977): 315–41.

Trachtenberg, Marc. "Reparation at the Paris Peace Conference." *Journal of Modern History* 51, no. 1 (1979): 24–55.

Trachtenberg, Marc. "Reparation at the Paris Peace Conference, and Political Economy versus National Sovereignty: Reply." *Journal of Modern History* 51, no. 1 (1979): 24–55.

Trachtenberg, Marc. *Reparation in World Politics: France and European Economic Diplomacy, 1916–1923*. New York: Columbia University Press, 1980.

Trentmann, Frank. "After the Nation State: Citizenship, Empire and Global Coordination in the New Internationalism, 1914–1930." In *Beyond Sovereignty: Britain, Empire, and Transnationalism, c. 1880–1950*, edited by Kevin Grant, Philippa Levine, and Frank Trentmann. Houndmills, Basingstoke and New York: Palgrave Macmillan, 2007.

Trentmann, Frank. "Coping with Shortage: The Problem of Food Security and Global Visions of Coordination, c. 1890s–1950." In *Food and Conflict in Europe in the Age of the Two World Wars*, edited by Frank Trentmann and Flemming Just. London: Palgrave Macmillan, 2006.

Trentmann, Frank. *Free Trade Nation: Commerce, Consumption, and Civil Society in Modern Britain*. Oxford and New York: Oxford University Press, 2008.

Turner, John. *Lloyd George's Secretariat*. Cambridge: Cambridge University Press, 2009.

Van Meter, Robert H. Jr. "Herbert Hoover and the Economic Reconstruction of Europe, 1918–21." In *Herbert Hoover: The Great War and Its Aftermath*, edited by Lawrence Gelfand. Iowa City: University of Iowa Press, 1979.

Vincent, C. Paul. *The Politics of Hunger: The Allied Blockade of Germany, 1915–1919*. Athens and London: Ohio University Press, 1985.

Watson, James. *W.F. Massey: New Zealand*. London: Haus, 2010.

Whittaker, D. J. *Fighter for Peace: Philip Noel-Baker 1889–1982*. York: William Sessions, 1989.

Wilson, Trevor. *The Downfall of the Liberal Party 1914–1935*. London: Collins, 1966.

Winter, Jay, ed. *The Cambridge History of the First World War, Volume II: The State* Cambridge: Cambridge University Press, 2014.

Winter, Jay. *Dreams of Peace and Freedom*. New Haven, CT, and London: Yale University Press, 2006.

Yearwood, Peter. *Guarantee of Peace: The League of Nations in British Policy, 1914–1925*. Oxford: Oxford University Press, 2009.

Zeiler, Thomas W., David K. Ekbladh, and Benjamin C. Montoya. *Beyond 1917: The United States and the Global Legacies of the Great War*. New York: Oxford University Press, 2017.

Index

Adamson, William 122
Admiralty (Royal Navy) 2, 45, 77, 116, 134, 169
Albania 208
Alberti, Adriano 168
Allied Maritime Transport Council (AMTC) 24, 39–40, 74, 83, 90, 95, 180–1
American Relief Administration (ARA) 85, 104, 144–6, 165
Amery, Leo 34
Angell, Norman 58, 206–7
Anglo-Jewish Association 148
Archbishop of Canterbury 73, 154, 169
Archbishop of York 154
Argentina 87, 144
Armenia 194–5
armistice 8, 13, 22, 25, 35, 39, 46, 75, 77, 86, 88, 104, 145, 157, 179, 210
  renewal talks 89–92, 108
Asquith, Cynthia 107
Asquith, Herbert 21, 23, 30–3, 37, 119, 129, 155, 191, 196, 199
Asquith, Margot 55
Astor, Lady Nancy 192
Astoria, Hotel viii, 17–18, 114
Attolico, Bernardo 95, 150
Auchincloss, Gordon 84, 130
Australia 45–9, 62, 69, 87, 117–18, 127, 129, 158, 167, 177
Austria 52, 83, 93–4, 105, 123, 140, 144, 160–1, 168–9, 173, 179, 186, 189, 199, 211, 215

Baker, Philip (Noel-) ix, 16–17, 44–5, 108, 129, 147–8, 168, 171, 178, 180, 183, 204–5
Baker, Roy Stannard ix, 203
Baldwin, Stanley 204
Balfour, Arthur 11, 17–19, 22, 25–7, 41–2, 48, 54, 75–6, 77, 97, 100, 103, 107–8, 115, 118, 129, 152–3, 157, 159, 167–8, 186
Banat 142
Barbusse, Henri 13
Barnes, George 30, 117–18
Baruch, Bernard viii–ix, 56, 84–5, 90, 104, 108, 110–11, 138–9, 141, 143, 146, 174
Bavaria 100, 123
Beatty, Admiral David 172
Beaverbrook, Lord Max Aitken 23
Beer, George Louis 162
Belgium 62, 65, 76, 83, 163, 165, 182, 184
  humanitarian relief in 39, 80, 84–5, 145
Bell, Gertrude 54–5
Benes, Edvard 52
Besant, Annie 169
Big Four (also Council of Four) 10, 63, 83, 86, 103–5, 112–13, 115, 118, 125–9, 131, 134–9, 141–2, 149–52, 155, 158, 161, 164–7, 173–5, 181, 211–12
blockade 2–3, 116–17, 163, 177, 215–16
  as peacekeeping measure 6–8, 33–3, 72, 195, 206–7
  during the Peace Conference 8–9, 39, 74, 77–80, 87–95, 104–5, 111–12, 118, 123, 126–9, 134–8, 141–2, 144–6, 164, 174–5, 187
  during the war 2–3, 6–7, 18, 24, 31–2, 36–7, 83, 172, 179
Blockade, Ministry of 16–17, 20, 23–4, 31–2, 45–6, 83, 134, 162, 168, 179–80, 183
Bolshevism 26, 35, 39, 51, 88, 111, 121, 133, 142, 150, 154, 164, 190, 210
  in Britain 169, 194
  possible spread to Germany 80, 91, 100, 114, 117–18
Board of Education (British) 147, 167, 173
Bonar Law, Andrew 21–3, 25–6, 81, 192, 194–5

Borah, William 163
Borden, Robert 75, 127, 165–6
Bourgeois, Léon 41–2, 61–4, 70, 75, 98–9, 117, 130, 147, 211
Bourget, Paul 107
Bradbury, Sir John 169
Brand, Robert 108, 110
Braun, Friedrich von 90
British Empire Delegation (BED) 45–50, 88, 94–5, 117–18, 127–8, 157, 160, 162, 167
  opposition to Japanese racial amendment in 69, 117–18
British Empire Economic Committee 86
British League committee in Paris 43, 62, 65, 67, 178, 180
British Red Cross Society 31
  Wounded and Missing Enquiry Department 16, 31, 55
Brussels 187–8, 198
  armistice negotiations in 91–2, 108
  as possible League headquarters 184
Brussels agreement 92–3, 100, 129
Bulgaria 208
Bunning, Stuart 194

Cabinet (British) 23, 26, 31–2, 34, 50, 52–3, 73–4, 85, 157, 160–1, 168, 209
Cabinet Office (British) 19, 34, 66, 73, 126–8
Cambon, Jules 19
Campbell Bannerman, Sir Henry 189
Canada 45, 62, 75, 127, 165, 182, 207
Carson, Edward 192
Cecil, Lady Beatrice Edith Mildred Gascoyne- (Mima) 55–6, 102, 181
Cecil, Lady Mary Alice Gascoyne- (Moucher) 56, 102, 153
Cecil, Lord Edward 28, 153
Cecil, Lord Hugh viii, 26, 28–9, 192–3, 205
Cecil, Lord Robert 3–1, 15–37, 39–59, 95–9, 112–14, 137–43, 150–2, 201
  connecting economic warfare and the League 6–8, 32–7, 88–9, 141–3, 207–9, 214–15
  in the Conservative Party 21–2, 24–5, 28–9, 34–7, 154–5, 196, 200, 204–5
  and the Dominions 45–51, 86, 117–19, 127–8, 160
  feelings about Wilson 43, 62–3, 69–70, 97–8
  golf and tennis 11, 55, 57, 100, 103, 167
  in the House of Commons 81, 120–4, 185–95, 199–200
  ideas about Free Trade and Tariff Reform 28–9, 95, 109, 190
  ideas about industrial copartnership 81–2, 154, 194
  ideas about revising the Treaty 95, 159–62, 206
  ideas about the French 41–2, 44, 70–1, 79, 84, 98–9
  ideas about Welsh Church 21, 25–6, 30, 70, 154, 194
  lack of understanding of the US 162–3
  in the League Commission 9, 40, 48, 61–73, 75–6, 114
  in the LNU 154, 169–71, 195–8, 204–5, 208
  as Minister of Blockade 17, 20, 23–4, 29, 31–2, 46, 83
  nurturing Drummond as League leader 127, 129, 148–9, 185, 201
  nurturing the London League 146–7, 168, 179–86, 201
  penchant for resigning 25–8, 51, 115
  position in the British government after resigning 27–9, 157, 160–1, 178
  praise in the press 108, 113, 121, 171–2, 178, 191
  and the press 42, 57–9, 82, 112–13, 147
  relationship with Lloyd George 20–4, 50–2, 113–16, 134–5, 160, 166–7, 190–5, 199–202, 204–5
  religious views of 172–3
  in the SEC 8–9, 73–4, 80, 82–6, 89–91, 93–5, 104–5, 111–12, 128–9, 135–7, 141–3, 163–6, 211–12
  social life in Paris 11, 52–7, 100–4, 107, 125, 152–4, 167–8
  support for international economic cooperation 94–5, 108–11, 125–6, 131, 166, 172–5, 179–80, 186–8, 212–14
  support for Germany entering League 166–7, 171, 198

support for women's rights 23, 99, 190, 192
Cecil, Lady Eleanor (Nelly) 15, 17, 28, 49, 55, 72–3, 75–6, 80, 100, 102–3, 205
   move to Paris 119–20, 125, 129–30, 153–4
Cecil, Violet (later Lady Milner) 64, 153
Chamberlain, Austen 24, 108, 141, 157, 169
Chamberlain, Joseph 29
Chamberlain, Neville 209
China 4, 62, 117, 182, 208
Churchill, Winston 100, 121, 157, 191–2, 198
Clemenceau, Georges 1, 6, 10, 14, 22, 34, 40–3, 54, 58, 74–6, 79, 91–2, 96, 100, 105, 117, 128, 130, 134, 137–8, 151–2, 158, 160, 177, 181, 186, 197, 212
   beliefs about the League 61, 98–9, 167, 214
Clémentel, Etienne 41, 71, 90–1, 93–4, 98–9, 105, 109–11, 128, 143, 150, 173–4, 181, 184, 195, 206, 212
Clive, General Sir Sidney 99
Close, Gilbert ix, 136, 145
Clynes, J. R. 123–4, 194, 196
Cockerill, General George 37
Colban, Erik 149
Committee of Imperial Defence 20, 66
Congress of Vienna 11, 48
Conservative Party (Britain) 14, 17, 21–3, 25–6, 28–9, 34, 36–7, 50, 53, 81, 123, 155, 178, 190–2, 194, 196, 200, 204–5
Consultative Food Committee 188–9
Coolidge, Calvin 212–13
copartnership 81–2, 154, 185, 191, 194
Council of Four. *See* "Big Four"
Council on Foreign Relations 161–2, 182
Cranborne, Lady Betty 102, 119–20, 125, 153
Cranborne, Lord Robert "Bobbety" 28, 102, 119–20, 125, 153
Crespi, Silvio 83, 143, 173–4
Crillon, Hotel 40–1, 57, 63, 133
Crowdy, Rachel 184
Crowe, Eyre 17, 31, 34, 45, 161, 178
Cunliffe, Lord 140–1, 158–9, 166
Curtis, Lionel 17, 45, 48, 50, 161–2
Curzon, Lord George 22, 27, 54, 197

Czechoslovakia 15, 51–2, 123, 161, 186, 200

Davidson, Jo 100–1
Davis, Norman 84–5, 138, 140–1, 143
Dawes Plan 212
Denikin, General Anton 151
Derby, Lord Edward Stanley 53, 125, 168
Desborough, Ettie 152–3
disarmament 4, 31, 34–5, 116, 185, 196, 205–6, 208
Disraeli, Benjamin 29
Dmowski, Roman 118
Doherty, Charles 45
Dominions 44–9, 67, 69, 83, 86, 117–19, 127–8
Drummond, Eric 127, 129, 146–9, 168, 180–1, 183–6, 201, 206
Dudgeon, Florence Margaret 102, 148, 181
Durham, Bishop of 73
Durham, Earl of 28

economic sanctions 3–4, 7–8, 11, 34, 72, 82, 142–3, 197–8, 206–10, 215–16
Edward, Prince of Wales 121
Edwards, Clement 122
Esher, Lord 126
Estonia 93, 105
Erzberger, Mattias 88
Ethiopia 4, 6, 208–9
European Coal Commission 186
European Economic Committee 138, 140–1

Faisal, Prince 53–4, 166
Fisher, Colonel 154
Fisher, Herbert A. L. 25, 147, 157, 167, 173
Fitzjames, Duchess Rosa de 107–8, 153
Foch, Marshal Ferdinand viii, 41, 70, 74–5, 79, 84, 96, 100–1, 151–2
Fontainebleau conference 113–14, 159
Foreign Office (FO) 16–19, 22, 24–5, 27, 31, 33, 40, 44–5, 49, 51, 53, 102, 127, 129, 140, 148, 168, 180, 187, 198, 207
Fosdick, Raymond ix, 148–9, 182, 184–5
Fourteen Points 14, 24, 157, 210
France 10, 13–15, 19, 36, 44, 52–4, 50, 63, 65–6, 76, 80, 83–4, 87, 93, 96, 100, 120, 130, 134, 145, 148, 162, 167–8, 173, 181–3, 208, 214

arguing with Americans 70, 94, 98, 104, 111, 126
  Bolshevik threat in 133
  desires for control of Rhineland 150-2
  favoring punishment of Germany 90-1
  leverage over the blockade 87-9
  support for a League 40-2, 61
Fraser, Harry McLeod 172

Gale House 168
Gama, Domicio da 15
Geddes, Eric 168
Geneva 45, 126-7, 130, 147-8, 181, 183-4, 186, 204, 208-9
Geneva Protocol 207-8
George V, King 73, 196
Germany 1, 6, 13-14, 47-8, 51-2, 61, 65, 70, 84, 163, 169, 173, 177, 189, 210-12, 215
  Allied fear of Bolshevik revolution in 80, 88-9, 111-12, 114
  appeasement of 3, 113-14, 157-9, 175-6
  delegation in Versailles 157
  economic blockade of 2-3, 8-9, 16, 18, 31-2, 34-7, 77-80, 87, 126-9, 134-5, 140, 142, 164, 174
  efforts to resupply with food 74-5, 88-94, 100, 104-5, 108, 135-46, 155, 165, 180, 187-8
  possible entry into the League 42, 96, 99, 147, 154, 166-7, 171, 198
  reparations and 108-9, 139, 158-9
  response to creation of League 149-50, 166
  and the Rhineland 150-2
Gladstone, William 29
Greece 34, 66, 76, 182, 208-9
Grey, Lord Edward 25, 30-3, 103, 129, 169, 187, 205
guarantee of peace 5, 8

Haig, General Douglas 172
Hankey, Maurice ix, 3, 34, 80, 177, 203
  ideas about a League 50-1, 66
  as potential head of the League 66-7, 73, 95-6, 126-7, 129
  as secretary to Big Four 103, 126-7, 174
  taking control of British delegation, 19-20

Harding, Warren 212-14
Hardinge, Lord Charles 17-20, 168
Hatfield House 16
Headlam-Morley, James 17, 148, 157, 171
Hitler, Adolf 158
Hoare, Samuel 123, 192
Hoover, Herbert 3, 9, 39-40, 52, 74, 77, 80, 84-8, 90-4, 104-5, 125, 137, 142-6, 150, 164, 172-5, 195, 212-14
  becoming more internationalist 137, 174, 186-8
  and Belgian relief 39, 80, 145
  beliefs about US righteousness 85-7, 144-6
  demeanor of 57, 84, 103
  as Director of Relief and Rehabilitation 87, 143-4
  as head of ARA 85-7
  in SEC 84-8, 90-4, 104-5, 128, 135, 142-4, 172-5
House, Colonel Edward 3, 29-30, 41, 43-4, 48, 63-4, 68-70, 84-5, 97-8, 100, 103, 111, 114, 116, 119, 124-7, 130, 137-8, 163, 166-7, 182-3
  creating the London League office 146-7, 168
  support for a League 33-4, 44, 58
House of Commons 14, 21, 24, 26, 28-9, 81, 119-24, 140, 168, 178, 189-95, 197, 199-200, 204
  new political parties in 122, 155, 191
Huddleston, Sidney 178
Hughes, William (Billy) 45-50, 69, 98, 102, 108, 117-19, 127-9, 139, 158-60, 162, 177
  disliked by others 75-6, 86, 117-18, 160
Hungary 108, 118, 142, 164
Hurst, Cecil 44-5, 62, 99, 127, 207
Hurst-Miller draft Covenant 62, 65
Hymans, Paul 62, 65

Imperial War Cabinet (IWC) 27, 45-6, 66, 126
India 18, 27, 45, 57
Influenza 74, 111
Institute of International Affairs 161-2, 182, 200
Inter-Allied Aerial Commission 149
Inter-Allied Council on Food Supplies 39

International Labour Convention 117–18, 122
International Labour Organization 117
International Red Cross 31, 182
Iran 215
Iraq 215
Italy 4, 6, 10, 36, 40, 63, 66, 83, 88, 93–4, 111, 138, 142–5, 165, 182–3, 208–9

Japan 4, 6, 26, 36, 40, 46, 49, 63, 69, 96, 98, 117–19, 147, 158, 182–3, 208
Joffre, Marshal Joseph 172
Johnstone, Sir Alan and Lady Antoinette 56–7
Jones, Clement 127–8

Kellogg-Briand Pact 208
Kerr, Philip 24, 51–2, 66, 157, 159, 168
Keynes, John Maynard 3, 74–5, 82–3, 85–9, 92, 137–41, 158, 161–2, 166, 212
  Economic Consequences of the Peace 10, 176–8, 212
  plans for European financial relief 108, 125–6, 137, 140, 166
Klotz, Louis-Lucien 91
Kolchak, Admiral Alexander 151, 164
Koo, Wellington 62

Labour Co-partnership Society 81, 154
Labour, Ministry of 45
Labour Party 21, 30, 81, 117, 121–4, 154–5, 178, 191–2, 194, 196
Lamont, Thomas 84, 108, 143, 241
Lansing, Robert 3, 22, 31, 44, 58, 112
Larnaude, Ferdinand 64, 70, 72, 114, 117
Lawrence, T.E. 53–4, 152, 166
League of Nations viii, 3–9, 15, 17, 19, 29–36, 40–3, 52–3, 55–7, 60, 86, 100, 103, 120, 136, 155, 163, 190–2, 199–202, 204–14
  American views on 80, 96, 127, 163, 189, 212–14
  Assembly 49, 169, 182–3, 196, 204, 208
  British views on 22–3, 29–37, 45–6, 50–2, 64, 76, 113–17, 121–4, 127–8, 154, 163, 169–72, 176–8, 195–202, 205
  connection to the Treaty 4, 98, 157–8, 162, 177

  connections to existing international organizations 147–8
  connections to the SEC 104, 134, 142–3, 164–5, 167–71, 174–5, 187–9, 211
  Council 65–6, 72, 97, 117, 147, 151, 165, 169, 173, 182, 196, 207, 211
  discussions about admitting Germany 147, 166–7
  Dominion views on 46–50, 117–19, 127–30
  Draft Treaty of Mutual Assistance 204
  Economic and Financial Section 180, 183, 187–9
  and economic warfare 3–8, 311–37, 44, 59, 72, 89, 142–3, 151, 155, 190–1, 207–9, 215
  Education Commission 147–8
  finding a chancellor of 66–7, 73, 95–6, 126–7, 129, 201
  French views on 40–2, 61, 70–1, 84, 98–9, 167, 212, 214
  Geneva Protocol 207–8
  German views on 149–50
  International Blockade Committee 207–8
  International Health Department 184, 211
  and mandates 147, 177, 183
  Mandates Section 180, 182–3
  minorities and racial provisions 68–70, 118–19
  Minorities Section 181
  neutrals in the League 62, 96, 171
  operating in London 9–10, 146–9, 168, 179–89, 210–11
  Organization Committee 136, 147–9, 152
  Permanent Mandates Commission 181
  Permanent Military Commission 185
  placing headquarters in Geneva 45, 95–6, 126–7, 147, 204
  plans to launch in Washington 130, 147
  Political Intelligence branch 148
  Political Section 181
  and the press 42, 58, 82, 97, 113, 184–5, 188–9
  reaction to invasions of Ethiopia and Manchuria 6, 208–9
  Secretariat 7, 126, 148–9, 180–3, 185, 189, 196, 210–12

support by Conference plenary 75-6, 80
League of Nations Commission 9,
    40-2, 55, 59, 61-76, 80, 97-100, 104,
    114-15, 117, 121-2, 128-30, 149-50,
    161-2, 167, 171, 182, 185
    debate over racial equality amendment
        118-19, 147, 158
    drafting committee 99, 114-15
    meetings of 63-76, 98-9
League of Nations Covenant 4-8, 32,
    40, 43-4, 47, 50, 61-73, 80, 82, 89,
    96-9, 117-18, 127-31, 147, 149-66,
    169-72, 177, 185, 197-8, 211
    Article 1 (membership) 127
    Article 8 (arms sales) 68
    Article 9 (disarmament commission)
        149, 185
    Article 10 (territorial guarantee) 67,
        127, 171, 197
    Article 12 (waiting period before war)
        72
    Article 13 (arbitration) 68
    Article 16 (sanctions) 7, 72, 127, 142,
        180, 207-8
    Article 19 (treaty amendments) 67, 114,
        127, 162, 185, 206
    Article 21 (Monroe Doctrine) 98, 114-
        17, 127, 147
    Article 22 (mandates) 147, 183
    approval by the Peace Conference 75-6,
        80, 96, 129-30
League of Nations Organization
    Committee (or "executive
    committee") 129, 136, 147-8, 152
League of Nations Union (LNU) 99, 154,
    180, 196-8, 200, 204-6, 267
    Albert Hall demonstration 169-71, 192,
        196
    The Covenant (journal) 196
    Peace Ballot of 1935 208
Lenin, Vladimir 51, 151
Lloyd George, David 1, 3, 5-6, 10, 14-15,
    20-30, 32-4, 37, 53, 73, 82, 105,
    107-10, 119-20, 125-31, 134-5, 137,
    151-2, 157, 160-1, 166-7, 173, 176,
    179, 190-2, 195, 203-5, 212, 214
    attitude toward Germany 79, 134-5,
        141-2, 167
    and Coalition government 14, 21, 25,
        154-5

and the Dominions 44-50, 117
forcing France into compromise 91-2
in the House of Commons 120-4,
    199-200
Marconi scandal 21
policies toward Russia 151
relationship with Clemenceau 41-3, 54
satisfaction with the Treaty 158-9, 177
views on the League 15, 51-2, 61, 76,
    113-16, 127, 196-7, 198-202
war aims speech January 1918 24, 124
Lloyd, William 45
Locker Lampson, Godfrey 192
Lodge, Henry Cabot 96-7, 197-8, 207
London x, 9, 16, 18, 20, 22, 28, 45, 53-4,
    73, 82, 85, 87, 97, 103, 111, 120, 127,
    129, 147, 149, 152, 154-5, 157, 160,
    162-3, 165-9
    League in 179-86
Long, Walter 116
Loucheur, Louis 91, 110, 152
Loudon, John 62, 99

Maclay, Sir Joseph 92
Maclean, Sir Donald 199
Majestic, Hotel viii, 16-17, 39-41, 52-6,
    97, 102, 107, 115, 119, 130, 133, 140,
    153, 161-2, 167
Makino, Baron 69, 118
Malcolm, Ian 77, 107, 167
mandates 47-9, 147, 177, 183
Mantoux, Paul 148-9, 181
Marie, Queen of Roumania 102-3
Marlborough, Duchess of 149, 168, 183
Massey, William "Farmer Bill" 46-50
McCormick, Vance 84-5, 87, 90, 93, 103,
    105, 111, 119, 128, 145, 164
Melchior, Carl 91, 140, 251
Métro 55, 133
Miller, David Hunter 5, 44, 57, 61-2, 64,
    68, 98-9, 114, 118, 127, 130, 146, 163
Millet, Philippe 54
Milner, Lord 153, 167, 183
Mitchell-Thomson, Sir William 85, 93, 129
Monnet, Jean 95, 108, 110, 148-9, 181, 201
Monroe Doctrine 58, 96-8, 114-17, 120,
    147
Morgenthau, Henry (Jr.) 125
Mosley, Oswald 169, 267
Munitions, Ministry of 108

Murat, Princesses Lucien and Marie 55
Mussolini, Benito 208–9

Nansen, Fridtjof 150
National Democratic Party 122, 155, 191
Nazis 1, 143, 205, 210
Newman, George 147
New Zealand 45–6, 75
Netherlands 62, 140, 182
Nicolson, Harold 3, 58, 161, 176–7, 181
Nobel Peace Prize 4, 180
Northcliffe, Lord 121
Northumberland, Duke of 50, 197
Norway 99, 150, 182

O'Connor, T. P. 192
Office International d'Hygiene 147
Olympics 16, 180
Oppenheimer, Francis 140, 160–1, 168–9, 173
Orlando, Vittorio 10, 62–4, 75, 99, 143, 195
Ormsby-Gore, William (Billy) 55–6, 181, 192
Ottoman Empire 14, 66, 166

Palace Murat 43
Paris Economic Conference of 1916 109
Peace Ballot 4, 208
Peel, Sir Sidney and Lady Delia 56
Penson, Henry 20
Percy, Lord Eustace 17, 45, 50, 97, 201, 228, 230–1
Permanent Court of Arbitration 41, 67
Permanent Court of International Justice 148–9
Pershing, General John J. 172
Pessoa, Epitácio 15
Phillimore Committee 33, 43, 46, 228
Pichon, Stephen 74, 94, 98, 100, 112, 130, 147
Pilsudski, General 143
Place de la Concorde viii, 77–8, 134
Poland 15, 22, 52, 93, 105, 118, 123, 137, 142–3, 148, 186
Polignac, Marquise de 103
Polk, Frank 182, 187–8
Portugal 61–2, 72
Primrose, Victoria 125, 168

racial equality amendment 98, 117–19, 147, 158
Rappard, William 99, 182
Raymond, E. T. 204
Reading, Lord 52
Reparations Commission 47, 85, 108–9, 139, 158–9, 186–9
reparations 76, 79, 87, 91, 94, 108–10, 114, 125–6, 137, 139–41, 145, 149, 158–60, 166, 177, 211–12
Reuters 57, 82
Rhineland 41, 91, 99, 149–52, 165
Riddell, Lord 82
Robinson, Henry 84, 95
Romania (or Roumania) 75, 129, 142, 222
Roosevelt, Franklin 125, 208
Rothschild, Germaine Alice de 55, 102
Rotterdam 90, 92
Round Table 45, 51, 161–2
Royal Albert Hall viii, 154, 169–71, 178, 192, 196
Royal Navy. *See* Admiralty
Russia 13–14, 19, 26, 65, 111, 144, 199–200
    Allied intervention in 26, 51–2, 100, 121–3, 151, 164, 190–1
    humanitarian intervention in 144, 150–1, 164–5
    threatened spread of Bolshevism from 39, 80, 82, 88, 117–18, 121–2, 150, 154, 164, 194
    the "Whites" in 107, 122, 151

Sackville-West, General Charles 149
Salisbury, First Earl of 16
Salisbury, Lord Robert Gascoyne-Cecil, 3rd Marquess of 22–3, 28–30, 55
Salisbury, Lord James Gascoyne-Cecil 4th Marquess of (Jem) 27–9, 102, 153
Salter, Arthur 40, 86, 95, 99, 143, 149, 173, 177–8, 180–1, 183, 188
Samuel, Herbert 54
Sazonov, Sergey 107
Selassie, Haile 209
Senate (US) 4, 13–14, 67, 96–8, 127, 163, 173, 178, 182, 197–8, 207, 212–14
Serbia 72, 76, 142–3
Shepardson, Whitney 84, 182
Sinha, Baron 45
Smillie, Robert 81

Smith, Llewellyn 85
Smuts, Jan 34, 43, 45, 47–50, 54, 68, 97, 104, 107–8, 166, 204
  in the League Commission 49–50, 64, 97, 99, 118–19, 200
  opposition to the Treaty 157–62, 166, 176
South Africa 9, 34, 45, 47–9, 64, 160, 176, 204
Statutory Lists 31, 34
Stevenson, Frances 122, 176, 203
Sumner, Lord John Hamilton 108, 135, 140–1, 166
Sunderland House 149, 168, 181, 183–5
Superior Blockade Council 83, 141
Supreme Command at Versailles 26, 149, 151–2
Supreme Council of Supply and Relief 83
Supreme Economic Council (SEC) viii, 8–9, 73–4, 80, 82–95, 103–5, 115, 119, 121, 128–9, 135–8, 143, 152, 162, 178, 180, 184, 186, 195–6, 211–12
  and the blockade 86–9, 92–5, 104–5, 128–9, 142–3
  Blockade Section of 89, 93, 135–6, 145
  Coal Committee 145
  continuing the SEC in the League 9, 150, 162–5, 168, 173–5, 186–9, 211–12
  and economic reconstruction of Europe 9, 86–92, 104, 111–13, 143–6, 151, 155, 166, 175, 186, 211–12
  efforts in Russia 164–5
  Enemy Tonnage Committee 144
  Finance Section 89, 93, 168, 186, 188
  Food Section 89, 93, 187–8
  headquarters and staff of 109–10, 143
  move to London 163, 168, 184, 186–8, 195, 201
  Permanent Committee 187–8
  Policy Committee 175
  Raw Materials Section of 85, 110–11, 135, 145, 187–8
  Shipping Section 89, 93, 95
  threat to restart blockade of Germany 135–6, 142, 144
  use of the press 112–13, 136
Supreme War Council (SWC) 20, 51, 66, 73–6, 83, 91–3, 100, 135, 186
Sweden 182
Sykes-Picot agreement 54

Taylor, Alonso 52
Temperley, Harold 146
Thwaites, General William 75, 96. 151
Trades Union Congress 24, 124, 175, 194
Treasury (British) 75, 86, 137, 140–1, 148, 169, 223, 240
Treasury (US) 125, 137–8, 141
Treaty of Sevres 183
Treaty of Versailles 4, 8–11, 97–9, 109, 117, 123, 135–6, 147, 149–50, 154–5, 157–67, 173–5, 186, 188–91, 197–8, 200, 204–7, 210–15
  British criticism of 157–62, 165–7, 176–8
  perception as a failure 102 11, 176, 210–16
  US failure to ratify 4, 67, 97, 127, 182–4, 197–8, 205, 207, 212–14
Trier, Agreement of 88
Troubridge, Admiral Ernest 138
Turkey 24, 53, 179, 183, 194–5, 199–200

United Nations 6–7, 209, 214–15, 220, 252
United States (US) 1, 4–7, 9–10, 13–14, 18–20, 26, 29, 31, 34, 36, 39–40, 42–5, 48–9, 50, 52, 57–9, 62, 65–70, 76, 79–80, 82–8, 90–8, 104, 112–17, 124–9, 134–9, 141, 144–6, 160–6, 172–5, 182–9, 192, 195, 197–200, 205–9, 211–14
  support for free trade in 39, 93–5, 109–10, 164
Uruguay 144, 182
USS George Washington 20, 57, 80, 173
USS Orizaba 57

Vanderbilt, Consuela. See Marlborough, Duchess of
van Hamel, Joost Adriaan 149
Venizelos, Eleftherios 34, 66–7, 72, 99, 114, 130, 196
Versailles, Palace of 173, 178
Vesnitch, Milenko 72, 99

Walters, Francis 16, 55, 102, 129, 148–9, 168, 180–1
War Cabinet 20, 23–4, 35, 44, 47, 51, 66, 173
War Office 37
War Trade Advisory Committee 83

War Trade Board 85
War Trade Corporation 141
War Trade Intelligence Department (WTID) 20, 111
Ward, Joseph 75
Weizmann, Chaim 54
Welsh Church, disestablishment of 21, 25–7, 30, 70, 154, 192, 194
Wemyss, First Sea Lord Admiral Rosslyn E. 92, 169
Weygand, General Maxime 41
Wharton, Edith 107
White House 130, 182
White, William Allen 58, 112
Whitley Councils 81
Wilson, Sir Henry, General 27, 76, 129, 152, 157, 159, 176
Wilson, Woodrow 1, 3–6, 10, 14–15, 22, 29–30, 34, 39–40, 47–8, 56–9, 74–6, 80, 85–7, 100, 108, 113–19, 124, 134, 137–8, 141–2, 144–5, 149, 151, 157, 160, 169, 173–5, 179, 182, 184, 186–7, 188, 197, 203, 210, 212–14
   absence from Paris in March 80, 92, 96–7
   belief in the Treaty 4, 177
   in the League Commission 49, 59, 61–70, 76, 114–15, 117
   isolation from other delegates 43, 57–8, 103, 212
   lack of comprehension of French 19, 64
   planning for the Conference 14, 19–20, 42–4, 51
   praise for Cecil 5, 130
   rejection of European financial relief 125–6, 137–42, 174–5, 189, 212–13
   relationship with the Senate 4, 96–8, 127, 163, 173, 197–8
Wise, E. F. 173–4
Wiseman, William 97, 116, 146
Wolf, Lucien 148
Wood, Edward 192
Woodrow Wilson Peace Award 204–5
Woolf, Leonard 30
Woolf, Virginia 30, 267–8
Wright, Chester 113

Yugoslavia 208–9

www.ingramcontent.com/pod-product-compliance
Lightning Source LLC
Chambersburg PA
CBHW050323020526
44117CB00031B/1617